The Romance of
Stamp Collecting

The Romance of Stamp Collecting

Notes from the

World of Stamps, Stamp Collecting

and Stamp Collectors

REVISED EDITION

BY

Ernest A. Kehr

Thomas Y. Crowell Company · *New York*

Invitation to Experience

Some folks collect stamps simply to satisfy the acquisitiveness which is part of every man's nature; some pursue this wonderful avocation as a limitless source of relaxation and pleasure; still others accumulate new issues for their monetary worth or inherent attractiveness.

But whatever the reason for its pursuit, philately offers you rich dividends in an entirely unexpected direction, a bonus that increases in proportion to the enthusiasm and seriousness with which you collect. The collection of postage stamps automatically enrolls you in a universal fraternity based on a mutual interest in a common hobby —one which knows no barriers of race, color, creed, or nationality; one which forms a common denominator of men, women, and youngsters in every walk of life, in every social stratum.

As a professional journalist-lecturer, I have had numerous occasions to experience personally this usefully important fact; many times doors were opened solely because world figures who had vital information to give also were stamp collectors.

While in Alaska in 1950, I was anxious to get details of the United States Air Force's Weather Reconnaissance (VLR) operations to and over the North Pole. By chance, the Commanding Officer, General Dale V. Gaffney, happened to be an old stamp-collector friend. After having been turned down by several subordinates, I mentioned my desire to my fellow philatelist and immediately obtained permission to participate in one of the "Ptarmigan" operations. This enabled me to become one of the first to describe these vital flights across the top of the world.

A few years later, my Madrid-Congo plane was grounded in Lisbon, and I was compelled to tarry at Estoril. Early the following morning I received a telephone call. "A mutual friend told me you were here. Would it be convenient to come over and talk stamps?" It was ex-King Carol of Romania, whose comfortable villa, Mar y Sol, was only a short distance from my hotel.

We discussed not only stamps, but conditions in Romania under the Communist regime. I was thus given tremendously informative facts that put me at a strong advantage over my journalistic colleagues.

While in Argentina I was given an extraordinary opportunity to enjoy a flying tour to get firsthand information and photographs in every corner of the vast country, solely because President Juan D. Perón had an amateur's interest in stamps and wished to lavish his government's hospitality upon a fellow philatelist.

Entrees to world leaders are sometimes made possible even though they themselves are not stamp collectors. His Eminence, Francis Cardinal Spellman, once arranged a private audience with His Holiness, Pope Pius XII, a rare privilege which never would have been my good fortune if the cardinal were not so enthusiastic a collector.

A high government official, and president of the Philatelic Society of Egypt, made it possible for me to interview both President Mohammed Naguib and Gamal Nasser in Egypt at a time when the world was waiting for factual reports about the aims and ambitions of the revolutionary government that had successfully ousted Farouk.

I obtained similar exclusive interviews with President Ramon Magsaysay, in the Philippines; General Francisco Franco, in Spain; Dr. Ali Sastroamidjojo, Prime Minister of Indonesia; Prime Minister Mohammed Ali, of Pakistan; ex-King Humberto, of Italy; Prince Bernhard, of the Netherlands; President Theodor Heuss, of the Federal Republic of Germany; and a number of others; all because mutual friends—developed through stamp collecting—provided the necessary introductions.

You may never find yourself in a position where such advantages will make the difference between success and failure in professional work. But whether you do or not, it's wonderful to know that when you collect stamps you immediately join the ranks of a vast army of celebrities and ordinary folks who enjoy it with you.

As a stamp collector you share your avocation with bankers and bakers; diplomats and dressmakers; presidents and physicians; editors and engineers; Hollywood stars and Haitian historians; tycoons and teachers. To meet and talk or correspond with them you need neither social register listing nor formal presentation. The simple, "I'm a stamp collector, too," is quite sufficient as an adequate, effective introduction and a ramp to close, lasting friendship.

Contents

Part V—Glossary

List of Illustrations

Part I
History of the Stamp

[1] The Beginnings of Postal Service

Postage stamps are amazingly remarkable things. Because of them, common citizens have defied royalty, nations have made fortunes, dictators have subjugated neighboring lands, and countless millions of individuals on all six continents and the islands between have enjoyed more fun than they ever believed was possible.

There isn't a town in the world where postage stamps aren't known and used every day in the week. Postage stamps are so much a part of all our lives that we may not realize that they are relatively new. Robert Fulton sailed his steamboat up the Hudson River a generation before postage stamps were even thought of. Joseph Michel Montgolfier, inventor of the balloon, made his first flight fifty-seven long years before the first adhesive postage stamp was put on sale in England.

Until May 6, 1840, postage stamps were as unheard of, as jet aircraft, and even then, the British populace refused to think that they were anything more than a temporary, fleeting novelty.

Chronicles that record the history of man from the earliest days of civilization are packed with reports of methods that would accelerate the speed with which messages could be transmitted. In many books of the Bible, the ancients spoke of "post" services. Seven centuries before Christ preached in Galilee, Tiberias, and Bethany, "King Hezekiah and the princes throughout Israel and Judah . . . sent letters . . . which passed from city to city through the country of Ephraim and Manasseh even unto Zebulum."

At about the same time, according to the writings of Confucius, Chinese rulers on the other side of the globe maintained a "royal post" to carry communications across the vast expanses of the Asiatic mainland by primitive wagon or mounted courier.

The Persians had a letter-carrier system so efficient that it is still the symbol of sure mail service today. Herodotus, the historian, described the service of Cyrus so vividly that his phrases remind you of a Hollywood thriller script. "Now there is no mortal thing faster than these messengers. Men and horses were stationed at intervals along the roads that linked the settlements of the empire . . . one man and one horse for each day's journey for as long as the route required. And neither snow nor rain nor heat nor gloom of night stays these couriers from the swift accomplishment of their appointed rounds. He who sets off first passes the message on to the second and the second to the third and so on from the next to the next just like a torch which the Greeks transport in honor of Poseidon. The Persians call this course of riders, 'post riding.' "

Later, as the Roman Empire expanded its domain across the ancient map, and effective rule depended upon the speed with which Rome could keep in touch with its far-flung outposts, Caesar Augustus developed an imperial mail service. He built postal stations along the military roads at which mounted couriers might change horses, snatch a bit of food, and be on their way to distant colonial destinations. The Romans inaugurated the first sea post to transport mail to foreign territories. They gave us the Latin root word, *posita*, from which we have derived "postoffice" and "postage stamp."

On this side of the Atlantic, the Incas and the Aztecs had similar systems maintained by long distance runners who carried messages microscopically inscribed on lima beans. These, incidentally, were the only ones of the earlier services available to the public. All the others were intended solely for royal or official mail. In many cases, couriers who accepted private messages to be carried along with a ruler's dispatches, were immediately slain for violating their trust.

Like many other elements of history during the so-called Dark Ages, little is known about postal service until the thirteenth century. The Catholic Church hierarchy and Charlemagne both had systems patterned along the lines of the earlier Roman service. Neither actual letters, postal markings, nor documentary evidence, however, is extant to prove it. Charlemagne built stations for his court messengers and laid a postal system for the Holy Roman Empire in much the same manner as did Augustus a number of centuries before him. Royal courier service in England is first mentioned during the reign of the notorious Henry VIII. Edward IV established one that operated from York to Edinburgh, but after the war with Scotland it was abandoned.

In the days of the early posts, we must remember that in those days soldiers and a small handful of traders were the only persons who journeyed more than a few miles from home. There was little public need for the transportation of written messages to friends and relatives abroad. Only a small number of educated men—chiefly clergymen—were able to write. This art increased during the Middle Ages, and the need for postal service increased accordingly.

In those days the Church, courts of governments, merchants and advocates, all maintained their own independent services to assure speed and surety. The Fugger family of Germany, for instance, great international bankers, maintained a private courier service that covered almost the entire European continent.

In parts of Europe postal services of varying efficiency were available to persons who could afford the high rates charged for the carriage of messages. The University of Paris offered a student-family courier service in the twelfth and thirteenth centuries. In Spain and in towns of the Hanseatic League (in what now is Germany) there were mail facilities during the 1300's.

Marco Polo, the fabulous Venetian whose extraordinary travels and accomplishments were commemorated in 1954, by a set of Italian postage stamps, describes in great detail the systems of Kublai Khan which remained unsurpassed for more than six hundred years. That great Mongol leader used the service mentioned by Confucius and the improvements introduced by his grandfather, Genghis Khan, upon which to found his system. An idea of its vastness may be imagined when one realizes that about ten thousand postal stations were dotted throughout his empire and were webbed together by maintenanced roads. The service was headquartered in Khanbaliq, the capital, and extended in every direction—to populous centers and through the vast deserts and mountain regions. In each town post offices were built where the post riders might obtain fresh mounts and rest accommodations and where clerks were assigned to keep records of dispatches, accept communications destined for citizens of the town, or deliver to the couriers letters intended for other places. And when towns were more than twenty to thirty miles apart, extra stations were set up between them.

Each station had from fifty to as many as several hundred Mongolian steeds, which were furnished by the nearest town or village. The riders might easily be compared to our own pony-express horsemen of the last century. In the normal course of affairs a carrier would ride from 75 to 90 miles a day, but in times of grave emergency

—when carrying news of a rebellion or natural disaster—he might be required to cover 250 miles in the saddle. By means of relays, letters of great importance were carried as far as 320 miles in a single day. Kublai Khan's service maintained boats to cross rivers and lakes and camels to carry letters of less importance.

Nothing but the most exacting service was tolerated from both riders and clerks, and at least once a month an imperial inspector made his rounds to see that this service was up to par. Books and equipment were examined, and heavy penalties were imposed when evidence of negligence was found. The failure promptly to deliver a message or to lose one en route was tantamount to crime, and punishment was severe. Neither weather, illness, nor accident served to excuse them in their failure.

The swifter service was used almost exclusively for royal and military messages and always went by steed. Secondary "mail" consisted primarily of nonofficial parcels and correspondence, official baggage and war material. This service was available to merchants, bankers, landlords, and private citizens who could write.

Records do not say how long this extraordinary service lasted, but it is a safe guess that it did not long outlast its creator. An imperial service was maintained through the next several centuries and down to the revolution of 1911, but it was a feeble substitute, costly and inefficient, compared with the mighty organization reported by Marco Polo.

Contemporary with the imperial post were local services called *hongs*, which were similar to the private enterprises operated in the United States between 1835 and 1855. These hongs carried messages and express for businessmen who needed a service to cover areas not covered by the imperial post. In fact, the imperial post often availed itself of this supplementary service with the result that the operators prospered. They were not outlawed until the modern postal reforms of 1878 and 1912.

Different, yet no less remarkable and certainly more profitable, was the vast postal monopoly of the house of Thurn and Taxis, which was established in central Europe during the fifteenth and sixteenth centuries. For four centuries this stateless family collected tribute in the form of postal revenues from some of the most powerful kingdoms, dukedoms, and principalities on the continent of Europe. Their forebears, the Della Torres, ruled Milan from 1259 to 1313. Driven out by a political feud, they found refuge near Bergamo, in the shadow of Mount Tasso, whose name they added to their own as a sort of token of appreciation. It consequently became the house of Torres and Tasso, a name which was Teutonized to Thurn and Taxis when the family swore allegiance to the German emperor in Vienna.

In 1450 Roger of Thurn and Taxis pledged himself to the Holy Roman Empire, was knighted by Frederick III in Vienna, and a decade later was granted the right to establish a horse post linking Tyrol and the Italian states. Forty years later his son, Franz, was made postmaster general of Austria, the Low Countries, Spain, Burgundy, and Italy.

In 1516, at the request of Emperor Maximilian, Franz established a service that went from Vienna to Brussels, knitting together the more distant points of the empire. Through the sixteenth century additions were made to this service by both Franz and his brother, Leonhard. Some routes—such as that from Vienna to Nuremberg— were short lived; some proved highly profitable and were retained and expanded. In approximately 1595 Count Leonhard was appointed postmaster general of the Holy Roman Empire, and in 1615 Lamoral von Taxis was designated hereditary postmaster general of the realm. Under him that monopoly provided the family with a highly lucrative income.

Under terms of the monopoly, the family was permitted to keep all the profits, as the court was interested in only a swift and dependable service through which its messages could be transported. Accordingly such service as was offered to the populace was available on a "what the traffic will bear" policy. Toward the end of the sixteenth century disturbances in the Netherlands and political, social, and religious quarrels in other parts of the realm resulted in the withdrawal of royal patronage, and profits collapsed to drive Leonhard into debt.

Some years later Emperor Rudolf II restored this valuable patronage, and once again the monopoly became a paying proposition. In 1616 Emperor Matthias, brother and successor to Rudolf, granted the Thurn and Taxis household a hereditary and permanent right to carry the mails, and from then on dividends were frequent and substantial. The service was expanded until Thurn and Taxis was synonymous with European mail. They served Austria, Bavaria, Baden, Brunswick, Prussia, Hannover, Luxemburg, Oldenburg, Saxony, Holstein, Lauenburg, Nassau, Mecklenburg-Schwerin, Saxe-Coburg, Saxe-Meiningen, Saxe-Weimar, Bremen, Schwarzburg,

Frankfurt am Main, Hamburg, and Lubeck. Thurn and Taxis' monopolistic prosperity continued uninterrupted for two hundred years until the Napoleonic Wars, which upset the balance of power. Yet, although this service began its decline then, it actually continued well into the nineteenth century and in fact served Germany until Bismarck began his unification of the various states and introduced a government postal administration in 1867.

The history of postage stamps, however, is the climax of postal service in England, a service which dates back to the early seventeenth century. Before this time no public mail service was available in the British Isles. Until then only the court had the advantages of couriers, who were known as the "king's messengers." Some of the documents which had been carried by this service still are extant and a few of them have reached the philatelic market and have been sold for fabulous sums to postal history students.

In 1533 Henry VIII established the service from which modern English postal systems stem and appointed one Bryan Tuke as a court officer to put "posts in all places most expedient." Regular routes, with stations to serve them, were established for scheduled trips. By 1567 the posts were a going enterprise available to members of the government, and Queen Elizabeth gave the title of chief post master to Thomas Randolf, introducing a term which was the forerunner of our modern "postmaster general." Even then, the posts were primarily intended for government dispatches; however, private citizens might prevail upon the couriers to convey letters or small parcels when their bags were not too full of official documents and reports.

A law of 1591 stipulated that messages addressed to points outside the realm could be sent only by the royal posts, for Queen Elizabeth realized that if such an edict were in force her officers could control —censor, if you will—the contents and thereby police intelligence between members of the court and officials of those nations on the continent with which England's queen was so constantly quarreling. It also provided her with a means of detecting treasonable plots against her. In 1603 James I extended the royal monopoly to include domestic correspondence, again with no intention of serving the public but with the avowed object rather of discovering conspiracies and other matters of peculiar interest to the royal house. The great postal monopolies of the day thus sprang from no hankering for socialism, but had their origin in the desire of these English monarchs to protect themselves against treason and plot.

By about this time, and shortly thereafter, quite a number of enterprising individuals established private posts in direct competition with the governments' service, both in England and in other countries. Their establishment was provoked by a number of causes: the royal post always gave precedence to royal documents; rates were high; private correspondence was censored.

In England the inefficiency of the royal posts, as far as the public was concerned, provoked Mathewe deQuester and his son to establish a private service in direct competition with the king's, which was under the supervision of John Lord Stanhope, master of the posts from 1607. By offering a service which was dependable, which carried mail on a first-come-first-dispatched basis, and which was not subject to censorship, deQuester built up a business that was welcomed and extensively used by merchants, refugees from religious persecution on the continent, and others who had business with France, the Low Countries, Hamburg, and beyond. His cheaper rates, too, were an advantage that soon resulted in a thriving, lucrative enterprise. As was to be expected, Lord Stanhope (who had been making quite a sizable income for himself as master of the posts) felt the financial pinch of this competition. He went to King James, argued that this enterprise was unlawful, and urged the monarch to issue an edict prohibiting its continuance. But instead of backing Lord Stanhope, King James legalized the merchant's company and even appointed deQuester to handle all foreign mail, giving him the title "Postmaster of England for Foreign Parts out of the King's Dominions."

DeQuester remained in office until 1632, when he lost his son and assigned his patents to William Frizell and Thomas Witherings, two of his associates. The latter continued the service and eventually became the first of England's outstanding postal reformers. By 1635 Witherings had accumulated sufficient authority to institute upon his own initiative a number of revolutionary changes. He opened a letter office in London, the first regular post office in England. He revived some of the older royal posts, which had fallen into decay, and laid out new trunk routes connecting London with the principal towns of the kingdom, and with Scotland and Ireland.

To put the new system on a self-paying basis—the old one had cost the court approximately £3,400 a year—he drew up a schedule of rates covering the cost of transporting letters and parcels, the individual charges being determined by the *distance* they were carried. Until then there had been no set rate for anything—the fees depended upon who was sending a message. It was said that some officials even used the posts to carry personal effects from one of their homes to another without charge. This was the introduction of postage, or "portage," as it was then known. Until then "postage" had been applied only to the hiring or use of horses. Not until the act of 1764 was "postage" used in the sense of a charge upon a letter.

Witherings realized that his estimated expenses would never be met unless the mails could be used more widely than they had been. He decided to throw them open to the public, to everyone without qualification or exception. Thus, under Witherings the once royal posts at last became a public institution. The act of 1657 confirmed the Witherings reform and created "The Post Office of England" under the jurisdiction of an officer who was to be called "Postmaster-General and Comptroller." The pattern then laid down has been substantially preserved to this day.

Commerce was everywhere increased in consequence of these reforms, the postal income rose, and it appeared that the Witherings' system was more than paying for itself. He still had to buck private carriers who were doing business in many towns, but they offered no serious competition. By then the official rates were as cheap as those of the private posts, and under Witherings the system was as efficient and more dependable.

The reforms endured, but Witherings soon became the target of a series of vicious attacks, as profit-seeking politicians soon realized that the system might be turned into a source for what today would be called graft. A long dispute followed, and eventually a member of Parliament, Edmund Prideaux, manipulated himself into the post-mastership. His deal consisted of footing all the costs of running the post office and paying a royalty of £5,000. In return he was permitted to keep all the revenues and whatever profit he could drag out of the enterprise. This was in 1644. Nine years later he was worked out of office because of his failure to play ball with the Cromwell and Royalist factions alike. The monopoly was thereupon turned over to one Captain John Manley at £10,000, and thereafter each succeeding official to whom the patents were granted had to pay an increased fee, reflecting the increased business which the post office yielded.

During all this time, and until William and Mary decided to put the postal system on a nonpartisan basis by appointing one man from each party to head it, this office of postmaster general was a highly political football, giving the man who held office not only a lucrative source of income but also an opportunity of keeping track of his enemies through the prerogative of censorship. Indeed, Crutchley states that individuals "such as Prideau, Thurloe, Arlington and Rochester all were politicians whose object was to be in a position to control the circulation of news for their own and their party's ends."

Following the move by William and Mary other reforms were instituted, an important one being that of shortening the distance a letter might have to travel—and thereby cutting the rates which citizens were compelled to pay. Under Ralph Allen, the need for routing all letters through the main London offices was eliminated. Allen's system made it possible for a person in one town to send a letter directly to another town laterally across a postal route instead of over a longer, vertical pair of routes via the capital. For instance, a letter from Norwich could be sent directly to Warwick via Northampton. He also devised a more accurate bookkeeping scheme which all but eliminated the terrific graft that long had been enjoyed by country postmasters and others, thereby increasing postal revenues. Some years later John Palmer introduced the mail coach, which increased the speed of the mails over the time consumed by footmen and mounted riders.

But with all these improvements, the mails still were far from the efficiency, convenience, and economy levels that would have encouraged popular patronage and satisfaction. The rates were high and beyond the budget of all but business people and the wealthy gentry. From the Post Office's point of view, the rates had to be, for they were reckoned on a basis of paying for the service. Since a great portion of the mail carried was from government officials who enjoyed the privilege of franking, whatever little nonofficial mail was transported had to pay for the expense of the whole venture. A cartoon published early in the nineteenth century and reproduced on the cover of *The Philatelist*,[1] one of England's foremost philatelic publications, showed a coach laden with everything from an official document to a sack of laundry, with a frank on each one, and, just beside the driver, a small pouch containing letters for which postage had been paid.

The cry for cheaper postage was heard everywhere. Dreamers wrote prose and poetry requesting it; politicians used it as platform

[1] Published monthly by Robson Lowe, Ltd., 50 Pall Mall, London.

timber for campaigns. And on occasions reductions were introduced, but each time they lasted a short time and then returned to their former levels. Finally in 1837 one Rowland Hill, who was termed by a critic to have been "an impecunious Birmingham school teacher of radical opinions," published a pamphlet under the title, "Post Office Reform: It's Importance and Practicability."

Hill had a background that included a measure of proficiency in such varied fields as bookkeeping, invention of mechanical devices, drawing, sciences, and teaching. He chanced to be born in an era of English history during which political, social, and economic reform was rife. And while Hill was said to have advocated reforms in other fields, he worked hardest at the postal system. He studied its faults and failings and eventually developed a plan whereby revenues might be increased by the sensible reduction of rates. Today as we read his pamphlet we appreciate its simple practicability; yet when it was published during the year of Victoria's ascension to the throne, it met with little but scorn, attack, and opposition.

Hill argued that not only should rates come down, but the whole postal system should be overhauled and streamlined. For about a year he made surveys and sought facts. Officials, fearing what he might discover, denied him the right to examine records. But with the aid of his brother, Matthew D. Hill, a member of Commons from Hull, and Robert Wallace, a member of Commons from Greenock (who had himself long agitated for cheaper postage), he was enabled to get at some of the pertinent data upon which to base his researches.

Hill insisted that the idea of charging postage according to the *distance* a letter had to travel was foolish. He showed that the only variable cost in the handling of the mails was that of conveyance, and that the differences in this cost were so insignificant that they were inconsequential. He demonstrated that the postal system had to maintain a certain number of clerks, offices, coaches and other "tools" of the business whether a thousand letters were carried or ten, and that the overhead cost of transporting a letter between two offices in the London area was about the same as the cost of sending one between London and Edinburgh, although the postal rate between the latter cities was about forty times higher. He suggested that rates be reckoned on the basis of weight, with a uniform rate prevailing throughout the entire kingdom. As a basic rate Hill proposed one penny for a half-ounce letter regardless of the distance it was to be sent or the number of pages or enclosures it contained. Rates up to this time were reckoned on the number of sheets a letter contained, irrespective of weight. Hill was proposing a drastic cut, for at that time the average letter cost slightly less than a shilling. In effect he was asking that the government slash its rates by about 95 per cent. But he argued that increased patronage would result in an eventual increased revenue. More letters would, he said, be carried at one penny than at the then-current rates, and thereby income would rise.

As we look at the picture now—we, who are familiar with the principles of mass production and nationwide sales programs—Hill's plan was almost a century ahead of its time. Contemporaries ridiculed it because, for several decades before him, postmasters general had tried to solve decreasing revenues by jacking up the cost of postage. But besides advocating penny postage from a purely business point of view, Hill argued that the empire would be fortified; for, the closer its citizens might be to one another, the firmer would their loyalties be. He had yet another reason. Under the rate system the amount of bookkeeping and accounting required to figure the postage revenues was little short of staggering. The chances of a dishonest clerk's altering the books for personal, illicit profit were likewise tremendous. A uniform rate would eliminate the complicated bookkeeping, and accounts might be more easily audited.

But Hill also had figured out a way whereby the operation of the penny-post scheme would be simplified once it was introduced. To appreciate it we must remember postal customs of that era. It was usual to send a letter either prepaid or collect—"paid" or "due" they called it then. If the sender cared to prepay the high rates he might do so, but it was more usual to dispatch the letter and allow the recipient to pay the fees when it was delivered. This was well and good when letters were sent in good faith, but many times a person would pay six pence or a shilling—or more—only to find that the communication was from a nuisance. Sir Walter Scott mentioned that he often received manuscripts from aspiring writers (and persons who might have used their time to better advantage) and had to pay exorbitant fees until he once determined to refuse all mail addressed to him. Naturally, the Post Office had transported the letters, and then to be left without payment for this service represented a loss.

"Modify this unbusinesslike procedure and you're eliminating unnecessary work and costs," Hill argued. To modify it he suggested the introduction of "little paper bags" which people could buy and in which a letter could be enclosed. He intended that these bags—or envelopes, as we know them today—be imprinted with a device that could not easily be counterfeited and that would show that the one-penny fee had been paid by the person using it.

Hill's envelopes served a double purpose. They would be a convenience for the public inasmuch as quantities of them might be bought whenever a person was near a post office and used when needed. No longer would it be necessary to stand in line at an office and wait until a busy or preoccupied clerk was ready to accept a letter, determine the rate, and accept payment. They would improve the efficiency of the clerks and do away with complicated records. A clerk would be consigned a definite quantity of them and, when he needed more, he would have to pay for those he had sold. That was all there was to it. But this idea was ridiculed, as was his plan for penny postage.

But although Hill got nowhere with the government even after he had been granted an interview with the chancellor of the exchequer, he continued his struggle and printed additional copies of his brochure for distribution to businessmen and the public. Response from that quarter was instantaneous. Merchants and public-spirited citizens sent petitions to Parliament to have it adopted. The press of the day rallied behind the plan and supported it editorially, with the London *Thunderer* (now the London *Times*) spearheading the cause by saying, "it might well be termed the cause of the whole people of the United Kingdom" against the politicians of the Post Office. The more important merchants organized themselves to foster the Hill plan in what must have been a tremendous publicity campaign, if we are to judge it by samples of the posters, handbills, placards, and other advertising media which still are extant.[2] By the end of 1837 Parliament was compelled by public opinion to consider the matter of sufficient importance to designate a committee to study its practicability further.

This committee convened from February 7 to July 3, 1838, and during its convocation it was literally deluged with petitions and

[2] While many are in museums and libraries both here and in England, one of the best collections of Hill documents in existence was formed by Dr. Thaddeus Hyatt, formerly of the Metropolitan Life Insurance Company. When they were exhibited at the International Stamp Exhibition at the New York World's Fair, 1940, of which the writer was director, these documents attracted the foremost philatelic and postal history students in the country. They had never been publicly displayed before, nor have they been since.

letters advocating the adoption of the plan. The four-score witnesses who were asked to offer testimony so unanimously denounced the contemporary postal abuses and pleaded for the reforms that the committee inclined to recommend it. However, Lord Lichfield, the postmaster general, denounced the plan as "the most extravagant of all the wild and visionary schemes" of which he had ever heard. One Paul Measor, a postal official of Exeter, said it was "entirely repugnant to reason." Other officials, evidently trying to defend their positions, were equally vehement in their objections. They used such terms as "utterly fallacious," "preposterous," and "utterly unsupported by fact." The committee itself was split.

The committee recommended the plan upon the single vote of Robert Wallace, which swung the decision; but even then the committee refused to reduce the rate below twopence. That satisfied apparently no one outside of a few officials and the dissenting members of the committee, and finally a large delegation of Parliament members, spurred to action by petitions from their constituency, called upon the Cabinet and demanded that Hill's plan be adopted in total. But even that failed. The whole matter then became a political pawn. The Melbourne government was in difficulties over the Jamaica Bill, which was proposed to suspend that colony's constitution for five years. The radical members of Parliament agreed to support that bill only in return for the government's support of the Hill plan. Eventually postal reform was passed to become what was called "one of the greatest social reforms ever introduced—a bribe by a tottering government to secure political support."

The House of Commons passed the measure by a vote of nearly two to one, after which it was sent to the upper chamber. The House of Lords, however, was firmly opposed to the reform and it took a substantial amount of lobbying to convince the Duke of Wellington, leader of that group, to fall into line and muster support when it came to a vote. After more than two years of bitter struggle on the part of Rowland Hill and his colleagues, the measure finally was passed by the House of Lords and Queen Victoria gave it her blessing on August 27, 1839. In an address from the throne, she voiced hope that it would yield an increase in trade and "be productive of much social advantage and improvement."

The statute thus enacted brought about a literally new postal law by repealing ninety-nine other acts or parts of acts of Parliament, adopted the Hill plan exactly as its creator had framed it, eliminated the much abused franking privilege, and set the stage for the introduction of postage stamps and a world-wide revolution in postal history.

Rowland Hill was given an office with the Treasury Department from which he might supervise the transitional work. By January 10, 1840, the Post Office was ready to introduce uniform one-penny postage rates and on that date they went into effect, although the little paper bags were not ready for distribution.

Between the time Hill first suggested envelopes and the passing of the statute, the idea of adhesive postage stamps was conceived in England. Philatelic students are divided in their opinions as to whether the "inventor" was really Rowland Hill or Patrick Chalmers. Even as this is being written yet another claim for the credit of having invented the postage stamp idea was accidentally discovered by Alfred Eccles, a New Zealand philatelist while he was hunting for other information at the Auckland Public Library. The claim is in the form of a pamphlet published in 1877 and addressed to Queen Victoria by one Francis Worrell Stevens. In it he states that the reduced rate and postage stamp ideas were his and that Rowland Hill had "stolen" them in 1833 or 1834, when Hill was in his employ and persuaded him to reveal his details, which Hill later proposed as his own.

Hill, however, is universally regarded as the father of the postage stamp. At any rate, the Treasury Department posted rules of a contest to which every citizen, artist, inventor, and designer was publicly invited. The contest was a tremendous success, with nearly three thousand designs and ideas submitted. Although the original award was £100, four of the entries were thought so worthy of consideration that each was given a similar prize.

None of these ideas, however, pleased Rowland Hill, who had his own conception. He felt that the cost of manufacture had to be the least possible without sacrificing security from faking. The designs submitted were simple enough to allow mass production at a negligible cost; but, by this very reason, they might be counterfeited by dishonest persons. Accordingly Hill discarded the entire lot of submitted ideas, including the winners, and himself drew a sketch of what he felt should be a postage stamp. That crude sketch—as rough as any layout idea—still is preserved in the collection built by His late Majesty, King George V, and is at present in Buckingham Palace. This sketch, together with scores of pages containing essays leading to the Penny Black, was displayed as one of the highlights in the Court of Honor at the Centenary International Philatelic Exhibition in New York, May 17 to 25, 1947.

It consisted of a profile of Queen Victoria, the words, "Postage" at the top, and "One Penny" at the bottom. When it was submitted to the chancellor of the exchequer, he approved it immediately and it went into production. Hill omitted the name of the country on this label for he felt that the face of the monarch was sufficient to identify it as a British document, and to this day not one of the several hundred stamps issued in England has had the issuing country's name included in the design.

Henry Corbould, a London artist, was assigned to the job of creating a finished drawing from Hill's rough sketch. He selected the City Medal (executed by William Wyon and struck to commemorate the Queen's visit to Guildhall in 1837) from which to reproduce the Victoria portrait, and this one was used on all British stamps issued under her long reign.

The next problem was that of finding a printing process by which huge quantities of the stamps could be produced and yet be kept so exactly alike that counterfeits might easily be detected.

Perkins, Bacon and Company of London had the answer to that question. Just before the beginning of the nineteenth century, Jacob Perkins, an American of English ancestry, had obtained a patent in the United States for a process whereby soft steel engravings might be hardened and transferred to soft steel plates, which in turn could be used as a printing surface. Perkins formed a partnership with Gideon Fairman in Philadelphia and later migrated to England where he hoped to obtain a contract to engrave and print English currency. This dream failed at first because certain persons felt that a "foreigner" was not to be trusted with so important an assignment. Perkins subsequently formed a partnership with Charles Heath and, through the latter's financial and social standing, Perkins eventually got the desired work. When the stamp-making problem arose, Perkins was ready to offer a solution. On December 3, 1839, he signed a contract to produce stamps at a cost not to exceed eightpence per thousand, including all manufacturing expenses except that of the paper, which was to be supplied by the Stamp Office. This was to be a specially made paper so watermarked that a device in the form of a small crown would appear on the back of each of the 240 stamps on the sheet. The watermarking was intended as additional security against counterfeiting. The paper contract was given to the Rush Mills, of Northampton.

The Corbould drawing was turned over to the firm and Charles Heath translated it into a fine steel engraving. (Here again the element of controversy faces the philatelic student, for there is some evidence that much, if not all, of the engraving was accomplished by Frederick Heath, Charles' son.)

From here on the manufacture of the world's first adhesive postage stamp was a matter of intricate mechanical work. The soft steel die, on which the design was engraved, was hardened by the secret Perkins process. Subsequently a soft steel roll was passed over it under the tremendous leverage pressure of a transfer machine until every graven line was duplicated in reverse on the roll. This roll was in turn hardened by the same process.

The hardened "transfer roll," as it is technically known, then became not unlike a rubber stamp and was rolled onto another soft steel plate 240 times, giving that many replicas of the original die. From this large plate one sheet of 240 stamps could be printed at one time. As a final counterfeiting preventive, each stamp carried two letters to indicate its position in the sheet. For each horizontal row the letter was engraved in the lower left-hand corner of each stamp: *A* for the first row, *B* for the second, and so on. For each vertical row the letter was engraved in the lower right-hand corner, *A* for the first row on the left, *B* for the second row, and so on. Today a collector can pick up any one of these stamps and, by looking at the letters in the corners, determine from what position on the sheet the stamp came. *B-C*, for instance, would be the third stamp in the second horizontal row; *T-L*, the very last one in the lower right corner.

The same design was used for a twopenny stamp, which was simultaneously issued but printed in blue instead of black, with "Two Pence" inscribed at the bottom. This stamp was intended for use either to prepay postage on a double-weight letter or to pay the postage-due charges on a single-weight one that was sent collect instead of prepaid. By charging twice as much for a letter that was dispatched collect, a practice which the Hill plan hoped to eliminate, the Post Office hoped that patrons would adopt the new system of their own accord. In the main, the assumption was correct, but eventually the prepayment of all mail charges was compelled by law. In the United States this procedure was enacted in 1855.

Meanwhile a supply of the envelopes suggested by Hill also was being produced. None of the contest suggestions was satisfactory, and William Mulready, a member of the Royal Academy, was commissioned to execute an envelope. His work was truly a masterpiece of allegoric art; its symbolism covered the entire face of the envelope except a small portion in which the address might be inscribed.

The stamps and the Mulready wrappers were placed on sale in England on May 1, 1840, for initial use on the sixth. On that first-day sale of the world's first adhesive stamps more than 60,000 of them were purchased by an eager public. Many persons wanted to obtain a sample of this adhesive, which "most certainly is doomed to extinction," as a souvenir to be handed down to posterity. Others bought them out of pure curiosity; a few purchased them with sincere intentions of using them on letters.

Before the day was over speeches had been made and editorials printed in contemporary newspapers denouncing or criticizing the innovation. The stamps were accused of "insulting" Her Majesty because the portrait was "such an ugly representation." (Collectors the world over, and art experts, too, today laud this stamp as the most beautiful ever produced, and Queen Victoria herself was so pleased with the portrait that throughout her entire reign she insisted that it be retained on all stamps that were issued.) The stamps were attacked on every conceivable score, not the least ridiculous of which was that put forward by "experts" who predicted the entire destruction of the English populace. The gum on the back of the stamps, they said, would be infected by germs of the plague, thus causing mass disease and death "within a year." We know now that these predictions were foolish, yet at the time many of them were believed and the fire of protest against the introduction of the stamps was kept alive for some time.

The real ridicule, however, was aimed at the Mulready wrappers. The masterpiece of this artist was lambasted by word and caricature. Even before they went into use on May 6, lampooners and satirists made gag-facsimiles of them for sale at stationery stores in various parts of the country. This series of attacks was so successful that the original Mulready wrappers were almost immediately removed from sale at the post offices. So many of them were left unsold that special furnaces had to be built to burn them after it was decided to authorize their destruction. Collectors today are interested in both the originals and the caricatures; and, although the former are not common, some of the copies bring substantially more in the market when they are offered.

The Post Office had forearmed itself against counterfeiting—by steel engraving, uniformity, the control letters, and the watermarks —but it did not think of the practice of persons' removing the postmark and using the cleaned stamp over again.

The Post Office learned to its regret, however, that dishonest persons had begun stamp laundries, and often an otherwise honest person removed cancellations just for the satisfaction of beating the Post Office. The black postmarks on a black stamp were a set-up for a bit of one-penny chiseling, and only the perpetrators and the Almighty can know how many of these stamps did duty on two, three, or more letters before the Queen's face itself was washed away. At first the Post Office tried to remedy the situation by using red postmarking ink; but that cost too much, and so in 1841 the one-penny stamps were printed in red ink. That solved the problem for the time being and, in spite of the various obstacles and handicaps, adhesive stamps proved their worth and were here to stay.

They were here to stay not only because they were successful in England but because their efficiency was recognized by progressive persons throughout the world. Within less than a year stamps were adopted by Alexander Greig, who operated a private mail-delivery service in New York City. Unlike the privateers in England, mentioned earlier, Greig and a number of others in New York and elsewhere in the United States did not compete with the Post Office Department. The Post Office undertook the conveyance of letters only between its offices, so a person wishing to dispatch a communication had to walk from his home or place of business to the nearest post office, which might be miles away. If he expected a letter, he would have to make a trip a day until he received it.

Needless to say this was an unnecessary inconvenience and it did not take long before some common-sense thinkers thought themselves into business. For a specified fee—usually a cent—they would carry a letter in either direction between a home, shop, or office to the nearest postal station. Greig's was one of the more progressive of these services. In addition to supplying carriers who called for letters, he built mail boxes in various strategic points throughout the city into which persons might drop letters between the times when the carriers toured their routes.

When the boxes were emptied, records were kept of those senders who had deposited letters, and on the next trip, or at the end of the month, if clients had regular accounts, the usual fee was collected. The stamp idea was a natural for Greig and he lost no time in having some of his own engraved and printed as soon as he heard about them from England. There was only one difference between England's and Greig's. In England a person had to pay face value regardless of how many or how few stamps he purchased. Greig offered a discount if a person bought a hundred or more at a time.

In March, 1843, Zurich, Switzerland, introduced stamps to the continent, when four- and six-rappen stamps made their appearance, to prepay postal rates on letters for delivery within the city and within the canton, respectively. Geneva followed in October.

Brazil was the first government in the Western Hemisphere to copy the idea when, in July, 1843, three black stamps were issued there. These, because they consisted of an oval of intricate engraved curlicues enclosing the numeral of value, were called bull's eyes by contemporaries. That name has stuck, and people who wish to feel that they are more than novice collectors still refer to them by that name.

In 1845 the canton of Basel, Switzerland, issued its first postage stamp; but, not content with the idea of just a plain design printed in black (as had been Great Britain's, Zurich's, and Brazil's first), this tiny government introduced a novelty in the form of a stamp printed in two colors with the vignette—a small dove with a letter in its beak—embossed to make what still is referred to as a gem in philatelic circles.

During the same year, in the United States, the postmasters of Baltimore, New York, and St. Louis decided that postage stamps might increase the efficiency of their work and accordingly issued their own stamps for use within the area over which they had jurisdiction. Robert H. Morris, of New York, went even further. He visualized the national use of such convenient adhesives and made attempts to distribute them to other cities' postal officials. Today these attractive black stamps, portraying George Washington, are known to have been used in Albany, Boston, Charleston, Jersey City, New Hamburg, Philadelphia, Sing Sing, and Washington, D.C. Later the same year two stamps were issued by the remote British colony of Mauritius in the Indian Ocean. The story of the Mauritius stamps is a romance all of its own and will be reported in a subsequent chapter.

In 1848 Bermuda joined the adhesive parade and in 1849 Belgium, Bavaria, and France followed. By 1850 about sixty different postage stamps had been issued in Europe, America, and Africa. It is amazing to think that if one of those persons who had purchased a copy of the Penny Black on May 1, 1840, "as a souvenir," had obtained a single copy of each stamp that was subsequently issued by other nations during that first decade of their use he would have had to spend less than about $5. And then, if he had put those few stamps aside in a place where some lucky descendant could find them today, they would have a list value of nearly $150,000!

By 1850 it was fairly well proved that the postage stamp was a good thing and a great help in postal affairs, and governments all over the world climbed aboard the band wagon. By the end of that decade we find stamps used not only throughout Europe, Brazil, Mauritius, and the United States but in Australia as well, for by then their use already had extended to the provinces of New South Wales and Victoria.

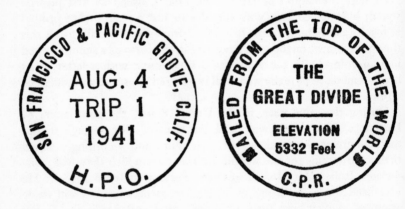

Collectors are interested in postmarks, too. At left is one used by a mobile post office in California. At right is one applied to souvenir mail sent from Canadian Pacific Railway trains as they cross the Great Divide at the Alberta–British Columbia border.

[2] Postage Stamps in the United States

The initial efforts toward establishing a postal system in what now is known as the United States were introduced by Massachusetts Colony in 1676, and by Pennsylvania Colony in 1683, when chief post offices were opened in Boston and Philadelphia, respectively. These systems were designed solely for the convenience of these colonies, rather than for the benefit of the North American colonial settlement in general.

In the annual report of the Postmaster General of the United States, published on November 29, 1851, we find the following historical notes:

As early as 1677, upon the petition of several merchants of Boston, Mr. John Hayward, scrivener, was appointed by the court, "to take in and convey letters according to their direction."

This was probably the first post office and mail service authorized in America. Local and imperfect arrangements for the conveyance of mails were afterwards made, at different periods, in several colonies, until 1710, when the British Parliament passed an act authorizing the Postmaster General "to keep one chief letter office in New York, and other chief letter offices in each of Her Majesty's[1] provinces or colonies in America." Deputy Postmasters General for North America were subsequently and from time to time appointed by the Postmaster General in England, and Doctor Benjamin Franklin was so appointed in 1755. He was removed in 1774.

On the 26th of July, 1775, the Continental Congress determined "that a Postmaster General be appointed for the United Colonies," and to allow him "a salary of one thousand dollars per annum for himself and three hundred dollars per annum for a secretary and comptroller." An election was held and Benjamin Franklin was unanimously chosen for this position.

[1] Queen Anne, 1702–1714.

From that time on post offices and post roads were developed as the nation itself grew and expanded its frontiers. Service increased and more or less standard rates were established for letters sent between any two points within the territory. Our service simulated that in Europe, whereby mail might be sent without the prepayment of charges which were calculated on the distance a letter had to travel and the number of sheets it comprised.

There were no envelopes in those days, and the sender usually folded the letter itself in such a manner that its page or pages became at one time both message and wrapper. If such a letter was prepaid, it was either indorsed in manuscript or by handstamping, "Paid." If the charges were to be collected from the recipient, it was marked "Due," or some kindred expression. The name and date-stamp of the dispatching post office, and sometimes the transit and receiving office, too, were applied. These are known today as "stampless covers," and although most of them antedate letters to which adhesives were affixed, only relatively few rarer types are worth more than the price of a cigar.

The United States Post Office Department undertook to carry mail only between post offices: there was no regular carrier service as we know it today.

The lack of this door-to-door service inspired any number of private individuals to set up what we now know as "local posts." The operators of these messenger services undertook either to deliver letters which they collected at the post office to homes or business offices of citizens, or to bring to the post office such mail as clients wished to post.

Among the first of these was the City Despatch Post, organized and owned by Alexander M. Greig and Henry Thomas Windsor, with offices at 46 William Street, in New York City.

Greig was born in Scotland in 1803 and, after adventures in many parts of the world, came to the United States and settled down at 14 Tomkins Place, Brooklyn. Windsor was an English merchant, whose firm had a branch office at 45 Broad Street, New York. While on a business trip to this country Windsor met Greig and the two became close friends. Windsor had left England soon after the Penny Post of Rowland Hill had been introduced (January 10, 1840) and, having witnessed its immediate success, discussed with Greig the possibilities of introducing a similar system in New York.

A partnership was arranged, plans for the business were prepared, and the services of the new firm were advertised through a printed circular which stated:

The necessity of a medium of communication by letter from one part of the city to another being universally admitted, and the Penny Post, lately existing, having been relinquished, the opportunity has been embraced to reorganize it under an entirely new propriety and management, and upon a much more comprehensive basis, by which DESPATCH, PUNCTUALITY, and SECURITY —those essential elements of success—may at once be attained, and the inconvenience now experienced be entirely removed.

The Penny Post to which the circular refers was in operation during 1841, and while names and details of its ownership and services are shrouded in oblivion, Henry C. Needham, in his *United States Local Stamps*, speculates that Greig, the "father of American postage stamps," had some interest in that business.

The circular continued, "Letter boxes will be placed throughout every part of the city in conspicuous places; and all letters deposited therein, not exceeding one ounce in weight, will be punctually delivered three times a day at three cents each. . . ."

All letters might be forwarded either prepaid or collect. To prepay the charges, Greig—probably at the suggestion of Windsor, who had become familiar with the Penny Black—arranged to have engraved and printed labels which he might sell in advance to customers at three cents apiece or at $2.50 a hundred in large lots.

Greig placed his order for these adhesives with Rawdon, Wright & Hatch, engravers and printers of 48 Merchants Exchange. The stamp measures 18½ by 22 millimeters, slightly smaller than the regular current stamps of the United States, and features a reverse likeness of John Trumbull's Washington portrait. Around this is an oval frame inscribed "City Despatch Post—Three Cents," and flutings are in each of the corners. Although the Perkins method of transferring the original die design to the printing plate was employed, these stamps were rocked into the printing plate sideways and not lengthwise as now is the usual practice. The original plate consisted of forty-two designs, comprising seven vertical rows of six stamps each.

Although this adhesive was purely private in nature, it was the first postage stamp ever issued in America, and the second in the entire world, the Swiss and Brazilian government stamps having been introduced more than a year later.

In addition to his simple post, Greig initiated also registered mail and special delivery service. To register a letter the sender was required to affix an additional three-cent stamp. The other service was described as follows: "A special despatch will be expedited with any letter or packet, not exceeding one pound in weight (to an address within the city limits) at one shilling a mile. . . ."

Various students have offered dates on which the stamps were supposed to have been issued: Henry C. Needham says, February 12, 1842; Both John A. Klemann and John N. Luff say, February 15. Recently, however, Elliott Perry, one of the most thorough students of early United States stamps alive today, declared that he had come across a clipping which advertised the City Despatch Post in which the proprietors state: ". . . deliveries commence this day, Monday, 7th February . . . at the Principal Office, 46 William Stret, where free stamps may be purchased." Mr. Perry does not dispel the possibility that the printing plant might have been delinquent in delivering the stamps on the promised date, but he does insist that the aforementioned dates cannot be correct.

The success of the Greig-Windsor enterprise was so startling that S. R. Hobbie, First Assistant Postmaster General, wrote a letter to John Lorimer Graham, postmaster of New York, on August 1, 1842, authorizing the latter to purchase the City Despatch Post and to "obtain the necessary fixtures, pouches, boxes, labels, stamps, etc., at not exceeding $1,200 for the whole, and to appoint a clerk to superintend said establishment at not exceeding $1,000 per annum."

Within seven months of its inception, then, the private City Despatch Post was absorbed by the New York Post Office, and on August 13, 1842, Mr. Greig placed an advertisement in the local newspapers, in which he thanked his customers for the support they had given him. He also explained that his business had been fully acquired by Postmaster Graham and that the latter would offer the same dependable service. Mr. Greig was appointed to superintend the service for the government, but a little more than two years later, tendered his resignation, received the commendation and praise of his colleagues, and then moved to Cuba. The climate and business conditions, however, were poor and he returned to the United States. He died in Astoria, Long Island, on November 18, 1862.

When the New York Post Office took over the City Despatch Post, business was carried on much as usual, for they had purchased the business, lock, stock and postage stamps. During the interim—between the time of the purchase—which is stated by Elliott Perry to have been August 12, 1842, and the time new stamps with the correct inscription could be produced, the Greig-Windsor adhesives were employed. Almost immediately, the same firm, Rawdon, Wright, and Hatch, was asked to prepare distinctive stamps for what now was known as the United States City Despatch Post, and according to researches the plate consisted of from 96 to 120 subjects. John Luff states that there were 100 subjects in the full plate, but later students are reluctant to take this figure as absolutely accurate and prefer to leave it as an assumption until such time as more multiple pieces can be found with which to complete their study and plating.[2]

While the City Despatch Post and such other private carriers as the American Letter Mail Company of Boston, Philadelphia, and way points; D. O. Blood and Company, of Philadelphia; Boyd's City Express, of New York; Hale and Company, of New York City and various New England communities; the Hartford, Connecticut, Mail Route; Hoyt's Letter Express, of Rochester, New York; the Letter Express, in Western New York; Pomeroy's Letter Express, also in Western New York; and W. Wyman, of Boston, all had similar services and used distinctive adhesive stamps of varying graphic and artistic qualities before the first of the Postmasters' Provisionals were introduced in 1845.

On May 21, 1845, Robert H. Morris was appointed postmaster at New York, and evidently this civic leader appreciated the advantages and convenience of adhesive stamps used on regular mail just as his predecessor had for locally delivered mail. We have no record to prove the exact date on which he decided to issue his own postage stamps, but we do know that on July 12, 1845, he received the first supply of the now famous five-cent "New York" stamp from Rawdon, Wright, and Hatch. Considering the quality of the engraving and the time necessary to produce a die of this character, it is reasonable to assume that the ordering of it must have been one of Mr. Morris's first official acts upon his appointment.

The stamp consists of a portrait of George Washington, surrounded by the inscription, "New York Post Office, Five Cents." Until 1921, collectors believed these had been printed in sheets of one hundred

[2] See "Plating," on pages 166 to 169.

subjects. In 1890, Hiram E. Deats, one of the early American students of stamps, who still lives in Flemington, New Jersey, began doubting that the sheets were so large and started his own plating studies. He was joined in this work by O. S. Hart and John Luff, and their deductions led them to believe that the sheet only consisted of fifty subjects. Actual proof that the sheet consisted of forty subjects arranged in eight horizontal rows of five stamps each was presented by A. Hatfield, Jr., who had obtained a sufficient number of multiple pieces to prove unquestionably his plating work.

The bill submitted to Postmaster Morris shows that the engraving of the steel plate for the stamps cost $40; 1,000 impressions cost $10, and the paper and gumming cost $5.01.

On July 12, 1845, when the stamps were delivered, Mr. Morris wrote to the postmasters at Boston, Philadelphia, Albany, and Washington (the cities within the 300-mile radius to which the five-cent rate applied) as follows:

> I have adopted a stamp which I sell at 5 cents each. The accompanying is one. I prefer losing the cost of making them to having it insinuated that I am speculating out of the public. Your office of course will not officially notice my stamp, but will be governed only by the post office stamp of prepayment. Should there by any accident be deposited in your office a letter directed to the City of New York with one of my stamps upon it, you will mark the letter unpaid the same as though no stamp was upon it, though when it reaches my office I shall deliver it as a paid letter. In this manner the account of the offices will be kept, as now, there can be no confusion, and as each office is the judge of its own stamps there will be no danger from counterfeits.

This letter indicates that Mr. Morris was issuing the stamp on his own initiative and had no intentions of giving any other postmaster the impression that his was an officially recognized franking adhesive. However, there are, according to John Luff, letters in the files of the Post Office Department, in Washington, through which local postmasters inquired as to the authenticity of the Morris postage stamp, and in each case the answer was in the affirmative.

Apparently the Postmaster General was apprised of the tremendous success of the New York stamp during the first year of its use, and asked that Mr. Morris send supplies of it to such other cities as Albany,

Boston, Philadelphia, Charleston, South Carolina, and Washington, where it might be used as a test of the practicability of adopting postage stamps for universal use.

Meanwhile a few other postmasters decided to experiment with adhesive stamps and issued designs of their own for local use. In 1845 the postmasters of Baltimore, New Haven, Connecticut, and St. Louis issued their well-known "James M. Buchanan," "Paid" and "Bear" stamps; the following year Daniel Bryan, of Alexandria, Virginia, Martin F. Revell, of Annapolis, Maryland, Frederick N. Palmer, of Brattleboro, Vermont, H. W. Scovell, of Lockport, New York, Worcester Webster, of Boscawen, New Hampshire, Asa H. Waters, of Millbury, Massachusetts, and Welcome B. Sayles, of Providence, Rhode Island, joined the parade and issued the remainder of the classic prefederal stamps of this country.

The few existing Postmasters' Provisionals are all wrapped in dramatic stories, both concerning their production and use and the circumstances under which they were discovered among dusty papers in attics and cellars and then sold for fabulous fortunes. But none of the stories is more unusual than that which surrounds the unique Boscawen provisional.

This bit of crinkly yellowish paper is simply inscribed, "Paid-5-Cents," and affixed to a letter which is addressed to "Miss Achsah P. French, Care of Theodore French, Esq., Concord, N.H." It was discovered and recorded for philately by Hiram Deats, who received it from a Mr. H. H. Lowrie, of Plainfield, New Jersey, in February, 1894, with a letter which stated, in part:

> The old and very curious envelope I have owned for the past 29 years and came into possession of it at the general post-office in Washington, D.C. through William M. Ireland, who was then chief clerk and Third Asst. P. M. General. As you will see, the mailing office, Boscawen, was written on the corner, as was the custom of the P.M.'s in those days, when no cancellation stamp was used. It performed duty as a postal envelope and I do not doubt but it is as genuine as any provisional issues of the period before stamps were issued.

Mr. Deats purchased the item and later sold it through an agent of the Scott Stamp and Coin Company, to Ferrary, in whose collection it remained until it was auctioned in Paris in 1922.

Meanwhile, philatelic investigations failed to disclose any evidence that such a stamp ever was officially issued, so even today it still is a mystery stamp.

When the Ferrary material was sold Arthur Hind purchased it for approximately $11,000 and brought it back to this country. It remained in the Hind collection until 1933, when, with the rest of his stamps, it was offered at public auction.

The first of the Hind sales was held at the Waldorf Astoria Hotel, New York, on Monday, November 20, 1933. Collectors, dealers, and their agents came from far and wide to participate in this event. Hind had had a great collection for which he paid substantial sums at times when prices were high. The sale came in the middle of the depression and great speculation as to how stamp prices would hold up while the Hind Estate took a bad beating through the sale of stocks, bonds, and other securities.

About 200 to 250 people, many among them philatelic celebrities, some just spectators, and a generous representation from the press attended. Walter S. Scott mounted the podium and opened the sale by offering one of the Alexandria postmaster provisionals. Starting bids were about one third of the catalogue prices, but much to everyone's surprise bidding was active, and when they were knocked down the lots began bringing relatively high prices.

By the time the first seven or eight lots were offered and sold, it seemed that prices for these rare old stamps were truly holding their own. The eleventh lot consisted of the Boscawen stamp. Mr. Scott described it and asked for a bid. In the meantime, the late Frank Marquis, who was a small dealer in the Nassau Street area, had been noticing that the reporters in the room were carefully making notes, not only of the buyers, but also of the persons who offered first bids on these stamps.

Apparently thinking that he would get a bit of publicity, he announced, in a strong voice, "five thousand dollars," when a floor bid was called for on the Boscawen. (This was just one third of the then-list price). Mr. Scott called for more bids, but all he got was a hush of silence. Not another person in the room raised the bidding, and while reporters were getting Mr. Marquis' name and address, Mr. Scott announced, "Sold to Frank Marquis, at $5,000."

Such a development staggered even the buyer, for he paled and stumbled from the room, beads of perspiration pouring from his forehead. Mr. Marquis got his name in the paper, but within the next few days he had to sell or mortgage nearly all of his stock to raise the amount he had paid for the questionable rarity.

For four years Mr. Marquis vainly sought a buyer for this stamp, and finally, to pay all the accumulated interest on the loans he had been compelled to float, he offered the stamp at another public auction through Hugh C. Barr, early in February, 1937.

When it came up for sale, Mr. Barr anounced that he had received three mail bids, and was opening it at $4,700, fifty dollars above the second highest offer.

Eugene Klein, Philadelphia dealer, through an agent, raised the bidding to $5,050. Mr. Barr obtained it for $5,100 in behalf of a "client whose identity he had sworn to keep secret, other than that he lived in the Midwest."

Unless it was sold quietly since then, the Boscawen provisional still is owned by that man.

The use of the Postmasters' stamps, especially those of New York, had proved the value of adhesive franking indices, and on March 3, 1847, the United States passed an act "that to facilitate the transportation of letters by mail, the Postmaster General be authorized to prepare postage stamps, which, when attached to any letter or packet, shall be evidence of prepayment of the postage."

Accordingly, contracts were let with the same firm which had produced the City Despatch Post and New York Post Office stamps of 1842 and 1845, to make suitable stamps for the United States. Meanwhile another partner had been added to the firm so that it now was known as Rawdon, Wright, Hatch, and Edson.

The five-cent denomination, which was to be used on letters destined for delivery within 300 miles, featured a portrait of Benjamin Franklin, after a painting by John B. Longacre, while the 10-cent denomination, for double-weight letters within the 300-mile area, or single letters for delivery beyond that distance, was a reproduction of the John Gilbert Stuart portrait of George Washington.

The die was transferred to steel printing plates so that each consisted of a hundred subjects arranged in ten rows of ten stamps each. The stamps were to have been placed in use on July 1, 1847, and while a recently discovered ledger of the Washington Post Office indicated that shipments were made on that date, the earliest known specimen is on a cover which formerly belonged to the late Judge Robert S. Emerson, of Providence, Rhode Island, which was canceled July 9, 1847.

The first two stamps were in use throughout the United States for four years, until rates were reduced by the Act of March 3, 1851.

The second set was produced by Toppan, Carpenter, Casilear, and Company, of Philadelphia, New York, Boston, and Cincinnati, and included values of 1, 3, 5, 10, and 12 cents. In 1857, those same designs were used again, but this time perforations were added.

In the ensuing years, whenever new stamps were required to satisfy postal needs, contracts were let to various firms on the basis of low bids coupled with the ability faithfully to supply adequate quality and quantity. The contracts were let to such firms as the National Bank Note Company, the Continental Bank Note Company, and finally, when these firms were amalgamated, by the American Bank Note Company. In 1893 the Post Office Department decided to turn the production of stamps over to the Bureau of Engraving and Printing, that branch of the Treasury Department which produces paper money and such other government securities which must be recess-engraved. The set of 1894, accordingly, was the first of the government-made stamps, and with the exception of the Overrun Nations stamps of 1943, all our stamps have been made by this agency.

Only one time in the history of United States postage stamps was it necessary to employ any method of production other than the recess, steel-engraved form of printing. That was for the so-called "off-sets" of 1918–1920. Because of war restrictions of that period, the Bureau of Engraving and Printing employed this less expensive method simply because the stamps could be made faster and with less printing ink.

When federal stamps were outlawed in the Confederacy during the Civil War, local postmasters produced provisionals like this one from Alabama.

[3] The Universal Postal Union

In all the world there are few organizations so important to the public and to stamp collectors in particular as the Universal Postal Union, which was founded in Bern, Switzerland, in 1874 and which makes possible an international exchange of mail despite wars, political differences, or disturbances of nature.

The U.P.U. is composed of all the national postal administrations of the world. With headquarters in Bern, representatives of the member nations formulate rules governing the expeditious distribution of letters, postal cards, and printed matter in a manner that turns the world virtually into a single postal district.

Before the introduction of the adhesive stamp in 1840, and the subsequent growth of the use of the mails, a few European countries already had concluded treaties for the handling of communications. After 1840, similar "co-operative treaties" were signed by other nations.

In the first half of the nineteenth century it was possible for Great Britain to have an agreement with France, another with Spain, and a third with the United States, with different rates in each instance. Mailing a letter to a foreign country was a difficult matter, for both the public and the postal employees had to cope with complicated postal schedules. Difficulties were further complicated in the case of a letter to a country with which no postal treaty had been negotiated. If, for example, a missionary in the Hawaiian Islands wrote to a friend in New York, he had to frank his letter with Hawaiian stamps to carry it to San Francisco, and with United States stamps to carry it the rest of the way to New York. In some cases stamps of three or more countries had to be affixed to a single letter. Covers bearing such "mixed frankings" or "combinations" are rare philatelic items today.

The first step toward the formation of the U.P.U. was taken in

1862 by the United States, which suggested that a conference be held to formulate plans for the improvement of international postal service. A meeting was held in Paris in 1863, and thirty-one articles were agreed upon by representatives of various nations. The American Civil War and the Franco-Prussian War hindered adoption of an agreement, but meanwhile Dr. Heinrich von Stephan, a postal reformer in the North German Postal Confederation, undertook to develop and expand the 1863 proposals. Operations began in 1875.

Switzerland, at the instigation of Germany, called a conference in Bern in 1874, and representatives of twenty-two nations, including the United States, attended. The result of this session was the signing of the International Postal Convention, which has endured ever since with comparatively no changes.

The fundamental principle of the U.P.U., formed under this convention, is contained in the provision that for purposes of postal communication the whole territory of each signatory nation become a single postal district. The practical application of this principle lies in the doctrine of liberty of transit, every member nation binding itself to transmit by the best available means all mail entrusted to it by every other member nation.

Membership in the U.P.U. was at first chiefly European, although the United States, Asiatic Russia, and Asiatic Turkey were represented. Within ten years eighty-six countries were members; by 1900 there were 113, and today all but a very few are included. China was the last of the larger nations to join, in 1914, and while Russia dropped out during the Communist revolution, it subsequently renewed its affiliation. All states of the Union of Soviet Socialist Republics now are members of the U.P.U., just as they all signed up as individual entities of the United Nations.

The regulations are simple but effective. Differences between two countries are settled between themselves, but any question affecting a majority of members is arbitrated at conventions held in various parts of the world at intervals of from five to ten years. The last one was held in Paris, France, in May, 1947.

Each country recognizes the postage stamps of all other member nations, realizing that, while it receives no compensation for the delivery of a letter from a foreign country, this concession is reciprocal. Records are kept by each member country to show how much mail from other lands is received, and how much is dispatched for the nation in question. If at the end of the year there is an appreciable difference, claims may be made for payment of handling it. But since almost every letter provokes a reply from the recipient, very rarely does the difference amount to much.

One of the most philatelically interesting regulations of the Universal Postal Union is that stamps which will prepay postal charges on an ordinary foreign letter must be blue; those for postal cards must be carmine or red. The United States stamps that will carry a letter by ordinary mail to a foreign land are of the five-cent denomination, hence they *must* be printed in blue; the blue stamp of Great Britain is the 2½-penny; that of Sweden, the 30 ore, and so on. And since all international postal rates are based on an exchange reckoned in terms of gold francs, it is possible for a stamp collector to compare the blue stamps of any country issued contemporaneously, and through them calculate the current foreign-exchange rates of the currency of the countries under observation.

Tibet, a remote district in the Himalaya Mountains, between China and India, is one of the few remaining lands which have not joined the U.P.U. And because Tibet is not a member, letters to or from it still must be franked with the stamps of two countries: the stamps of Tibet and those of the country of origin. Letters *from* Tibet must contain the stamps of Tibet and those of either China or India, depending upon which frontier is used to carry them to their destination. Tibetan stamps are valid only for use within the borders of that country and are not recognized by any other land. Nor does Tibet recognize the stamps of any other nation. If you wish to experiment and, in the doing, acquire an interesting souvenir, mail a letter to someone in Tibet, putting your return address on the envelope and franking it only with United States stamps. In several months—it takes a long while for a surface-transported letter to get there—you will receive this envelope back, with postal markings to show that although it went to the Tibetan frontier office, it was not accepted for further dispatch.

The existence of the Universal Postal Union also is responsible for a type of stamp that collectors can sometimes obtain. Because every member nation is required to send to the Bern headquarters a definite number of samples of each new authorized issue, so that these samples may be distributed to every other member nation (that these governments will know what stamps have been issued and are good for postage), we have what are known as "specimens."

Although member nations may send either "samples" or actual

postage stamps for such distribution, some countries, especially members of the British Commonwealth, usually overprint or punch the word, "specimen," on the adhesives they submit. This precludes their ever being used to frank mail and thereby kills any postal value they might otherwise have. If, therefore, you come across a stamp imprinted (by type-printing or punched perforation holes) "Canceled," "Specimen," "Muestra," "Sample" or a kindred term, you may be reasonably certain that this once was sent to a member nation of the U.P.U. and that the postal official who got it gave it to a stamp-collector friend. Of course this is not always the case, for sometimes countries print samples for other purposes, and these get into the hands of collectors. In the United States, for example, so many government officials requested postage stamps from the Post Office Department, to send as gifts to their constituents, that during the last portion of the nineteenth century large quantities of "specimen" stamps were especially printed for this purpose. As a general rule such stamps are worth less than normal copies, but there are exceptions, as indicated by the various catalogues that are at the disposal of stamp collectors.

The 1926 and 1942 Universal Postal Union conferences were commemorated by these stamps from Guatemala. The one at the left was diagonally perforated so half of it might be used as a one-centavo stamp.

Part II
History of Stamp Collecting

[4] The Birth of a Hobby

The hobby of collecting postage stamps must have been begun on May 1, 1840. It is impossible to say how many "collections" were made of single copies of the Penny Black and twopence blue of that first set by pure souvenir fans; nor can we say how many of such persons continued to save samples of every other stamp they subsequently saw. There must have been a few at least. However, stamp collecting as we know it today was, of course, beyond conception. In those early days it could have been nothing more than a novelty pursued by folks who had imagination and the time to satisfy it.

In 1841, the London *Times* carried the following advertisement:

A young lady, being desirous of covering her dressing room with cancelled postage stamps, has been so far encouraged in her wish by private friends as to have succeeded in collecting 16,000! These, however, being insufficient, she will be greatly obliged if any good natured person who may have these (otherwise useless) little articles at their disposal would assist her in her whimsical project. Address to E. D., Mr. Butt's glover, Leandenhall-st., or Mr. Marshall's jeweler, Hackney.

In 1842, *Punch* remarked:

A new mania has bitten the industriously idle ladies of England. To enable a large wager to be gained, they have been indefatigable in their endeavors to collect old penny stamps, in fact, they betray more anxiety to treasure up Queen's heads than Henry the Eighth did to get rid of them.

There are a few isolated records of early stamp collectors who indulged in the hobby simply for the sake of getting an interesting variety of different ones. Indeed, one M. Vetzel, of Lille, France, is credited with having reconstructed a sheet of the Penny Black in 1841. In later years, the eminent Belgian philatelist, Jean B. Moens, recalled that he had started in 1848, and when he was nineteen, in 1852, he had begun a stamp business. Dr. C. W. Viner, an early British philatelist, said that he saw the first stamp collection in 1854.

We have it on good authority, however, that a French schoolteacher introduced the collecting of stamps among his pupils to get them more interested in their geography lessons—a method that seems to have been a precursor of our modern pedagogical practice of using projects in addition to regular lesson assignments.

Previously the fellow had had the usual success—or rather lack of it—in getting his students to appreciate foreign countries, their geography, industry, culture, peoples, commerce, and history. According to the story, a pupil came to him one day to ask a number of pertinent questions about a country from which his father had received a letter bearing a queer-looking sticker.

"If a stamp impelled one student to take more interest in geography than he'd ever had before, perhaps stamps might interest others, too," the teacher reasoned. To most children a foreign country was a million miles away, and this was just another reason for disliking lessons unless there was some personal association between that country and the pupil. Accordingly, the teacher suggested that his pupils ask their friends and relatives for stamps from foreign lands and then paste them into their atlases on the pages devoted to the countries from which the stamps came. Almost overnight that teacher had a class of enthusiastic, diligent geography students and subsequently other teachers adopted the idea with no less success.

It is not unreasonable to expect that this collecting idea was carried from the schoolroom to the home. We can visualize one lad who had access to the stamps of a particular country offering to swap a duplicate with another student who had extra specimens of stamps from a different land. We can likewise visualize some youngster getting such personal satisfaction from his pursuit of the best assortment in the class that he continued his quest long after he had finished his geography course. Whether it was this extended interest or whether it was an entirely different motive makes little difference today, but the fact remains that we have records showing that stamp collectors were being born on both sides of the Atlantic. In England, in 1856, a youngster named E. Stanley Gibbons persuaded his father to let him use the back room of the latter's pharmacy as a stamp shop from which the sixteen-year-old lad might do business selling and exchanging postage stamps with other boys. In 1860 one George Oscar Berger-Levrault, a Strasbourg printer, issued a price list of postage stamps. A few months later, in Paris, Alfred Potiquet published the first printed catalogue which chronicled, described, and priced every known postage stamp issued up to that time.

In the United States several dealers set up stamp businesses along Nassau Street in downtown New York, an area which was the philatelic center of this country until only a few years ago.

Until twenty years after the first stamp made its appearance, the folks who got a bit of fun and pleasure out of the collecting of them had either to keep them loose in a box or to paste them down in blank notebooks, for albums were unthought of until Justin Lallier published the first one in 1862 for distribution in England and France. In 1863 the first stamp collectors' magazine was published in England. It carried, in addition to news about stamps, an imposing number of advertisements from persons in various parts of the empire, and several foreign countries, offering to buy, sell, and exchange postage stamps.

As early as 1860, boys and even adults used to meet in Birchin Lane, London, to do their stamp swapping in an open-air bourse. The police eventually tried to interfere because they contended that such "business interfered with and violated" laws requiring licenses to merchandise any commodities. But constabulary prohibitions or no, the enthusiasts, "including at least one cabinet minister and several ladies," continued to congregate in Birchin Lane to pursue their hobby by swapping "a red Prussian for a blue Saxoner or a Russian for a black English."

It is recorded that "one of the ladies contrived to effect a highly advantageous exchange of a very so-so specimen with a young friend of hers, who salved his greenness with the apologetic remark that he could not drive a hard bargain with a lady."

Even several years later the traditional annoyance persisted, and we find in the concluding lines of a poem a description of Birchin Lane after four o'clock:

> When sudden a gruff noise is heard,
> That all the thronging bevy stirred;
> I turned, and fix'd my eyes upon
> A Bobby! Crying—"Stamps, move on!"

We have no definite records to show how stamp collecting became philately, but we do know that the word was introduced about seventy years ago. At about that time some of the thousands of persons who had been bitten by the stamp-collecting germ sought to study postage stamps more seriously and began to differentiate between specimens which had engraving, color-shade, and printing variations: they distinguished between watermark designs and the size of the perforation holes. It may be that the minds of these persons were scientifically trained and therefore they had to have more than an accumulative instinct in order to maintain their interest.

It is not unreasonable, however, to suppose that "advanced" study of stamps was really an excuse to build a larger collection than that owned by a fellow hobbyist. Let us visualize a watchmaker in Paris who had access to a large quantity of Swiss stamps by reason of frequent business mail. Naturally, there was a limit to the number of other specimens he could acquire by swapping his duplicates. His friends, therefore, might have collections that comprised a larger variety of stamps. Having a second- or third-largest collection always is a source of annoyance to any accumulator, whether he saves stamps or butterflies.

"How can I have the best collection?" the watchmaker of our imagination asked. The answer was simple. He must find slight differences in stamps which are superficially identical. Accordingly he took a dozen specimens that he had considered duplicates. He examined them, first with the naked eye and then with a powerful magnifying glass, and found one that was dark red instead of carmine. He placed both in his album; then he examined the rest and found that the perforation holes of one were slightly larger or smaller than the others. This made three "different" varieties. He located another which had a variation in the engraved design due to a printing or transfer fault, and yet a fifth whose watermark was upside down because when it was printed the sheet of paper was put into the press bottom side first.

By the time he had examined his batch of "duplicates," this watchmaker had found some difference in every one of them and soon he had a whole page of stamps which, to the untrained eye, looked alike, but which he could prove were "different." At last his collection boasted "512 varieties," while the next largest collection in Paris had only 493!

Naturally a fellow who studied his stamps with such diligence was not satisfied to be called simply a stamp collector; and, before the average hobbyists of that day knew it, he and scores of others like him were wrangling over a name to set themselves apart from the common herd. One group insisted on calling themselves *timbrophiles* —from *timbre* (stamp) and *phile* (lover). Another group, headed by G. Herpin, dug deep into Greek lexicons and came up with *philately*,[1] a combination of *philos* (fond of) and *ateleia* (exemption from tax). That name stuck; and, while the average person today knows what is meant by it, it was not long ago that radio comedians built gags around the confusion between it, philanthropy, philandering, and Philadelphia.

But whether our imaginary watchmaker developed the art of studying stamps for the sake of our conjectured reason or because he had a more highly trained mind and simply had to do more than add specimens to his collection to get the most fun out of the hobby is of little consequence today. He, and millions of others with a yen to do more than acquire a stamp and arrange it in an album, grew up and eventually so thoroughly studied postage stamps, their method of manufacture, their uses, and their place in postal history that many of them know more about postage stamps than do the postmasters general by whom they were issued.

For thirty years postage stamp collecting crawled through the fad stage and wobbled into universal acceptance. By 1870 the "any old stamp will do" period was as obsolete as exorbitant postal rates, and the golden age of philatelic endeavor appeared on the horizon.

Previous to that time postage stamps had been issued solely to satisfy postal needs, and the number of major varieties had been held down by postal officials to the barest essentials. By 1870 catalogues and albums were being more widely published on both sides of the Atlantic, and so hobbyists could know how many stamps had been issued, how many had to be obtained for a complete collection, and

---

[1] Early in 1946, Leon J. Bamberger, Sales Promotion Manager of RKO Radio Pictures and a widely recognized collector, received a communication from N. S. Iliadis of Athens, Greece, which knocks the definition and derivation of *philately* into the proverbial cocked hat. Mr. Iliadis would have us know that a philatelist is in reality a philotelist, and philately should henceforth be known as philotely. He explains that the derivation is from the Greek words *philos* (friend) and *telos* (stamp), thus, naturally, "friend of stamps." He says the word *ateleia* doesn't enter into it at all, and certainly his explanation sounds very plausible. A piece of mail is taxed, and to say that one is fond of something that is exempt from tax is a rather awkward way of describing a philatelist or, as Mr. Iliadis would prefer to have it, philotelist, when such a simple and logical derivation, meaning "friend of stamps," is available. Mr. Iliadis has asked Mr. Bamberger to "endeavor to have immediate steps taken for the correction of this wrong spelling in the interests of further cementing friendly relations between Americans and Greeks."

how much they were worth in stampdom's markets. Dealers were in business almost everywhere, so it no longer was necessary for a person to have wide personal contacts to acquire the specimens he needed to fill a blank space in his books.

But by 1870 slightly more than four thousand different stamps had been issued by nations all over the world, and as collectors and cataloguers alike wanted to get at all the facts pertaining to the stamps issued so far they had to do a little digging.

Our imaginary watchmaker—and probably hundreds like him— had discovered differences in stamps which governments recognized as the same. To him a pale-green stamp was "different" from a dark-green one; and presently, as the hobby grew in popularity, collectors generally agreed with him. Catalogues accordingly would list, for example, "Switzerland, 1862–63, 5 centime, dark brown; 5c, bistre-brown; and 5c, gray-brown." Collectors knew that those shade varieties existed and now wanted to determine the why, wherefore, and when.

As far as governments were concerned, a stamp was a stamp: printed solely to do its postal duty. They regarded their manufacture as simply a printing job and rarely kept records to answer the questions which suddenly were being posed by the collectors and cataloguers. When they were running short of supplies, they simply ordered more of them from the printers and asked for additional impressions from the existing plates. The fact that in mixing a second batch of ink an exact match could not be possible was of little concern to the government. As long as the requested color was used they were satisfied. They and the vast majority of people who used the stamps recognized a green and were not too particular whether it was chrome or emerald shade.

Governments were likewise unconcerned whether a printer used paper of varying thicknesses or texture; whether the watermark was normal or inverted; or whether certain designs on the plate were slightly different because of transfer flaws. Yet these were the very questions which collectors wanted answered.

Thus, at about the time of the Franco-Prussian War, advanced philatelic study became a recognized specialty. There were dozens of persons in every country who had the training and leisure time to probe the problems and through extensive research to come up with answers to them. Since records rarely could be obtained from government agencies or printing plants, they set out to reason the facts from a thorough examination of the stamps themselves. Some of the research studies that were made by the collectors of this period are as comprehensive as those of medical scientists who discover the causes of disease and the cures for it; and, as we read of their treatises—many of them as long as a complicated biological dissertation—we can but be amazed and impressed. Truly, these men were the fathers of philately!

This was the era when the world's greatest stamp collections were being formed. A surprisingly large number of wealthy persons had become interested in the hobby and apparently set no limits to the amount of money they would pay for any specimen that would add to their collections. Even then the stamps that are the greatest rarities today were scarce; and, when a specimen was found in an attic or a businessman's correspondence files, dealers eagerly purchased it for resale to one of their better customers. Rivalry among these fortunate figures was keen and not infrequently did they vie with one another to obtain an especially rare item, shoving its financial worth up to three and four figures.

Meanwhile the hobby of stamp collecting was being pursued by thousands of persons who had more enthusiasm than cash, and stable market values could be set for even the commonest issues. It no longer was usual to swap stamp for stamp; catalogues were generally distributed, and all but the most inexperienced collector referred to them before swapping a duplicate with a friend for some desired new specimen.

By the time World War I was started, there were few specialists. Almost every collector had a printed album which contained blank spaces, with illustrations and descriptions of every stamp in the world up to that date; and he devoted his interests, time, and sometimes money in the attempt to fill every one of those fourteen thousand spaces. Of course, he knew that he never would be able to fill completely such an album, for even then there were hundreds of items which cost upward of $1,000, but the quest for those which were possible was as thrilling as a big-game hunt.

When war started in Europe, countries were invaded, occupational forces were established, provisional governments set up in parts of lands which formerly had been autonomous, and finally plebiscites and republics were set up all across the European continent, while administrations of colonial territories abroad were reshuffled. All this political and military activity was accompanied by changes in postal administrations and, consequently, in a flood of provisional and new definitive stamps.

Stamp collectors as a whole went berserk. Just as millions of people speculated in the currencies of foreign countries with a naive, inexperienced vision of becoming wealthy overnight, so did the stamp collectors dream that some of these new stamps would become very rare when conditions were settled. They began buying the new European issues so wildly as to start a stampede of speculation. Many of them forsook their regular general collections and started to build specialty collections of Neuropes (New Europes) which came from such places as Carinthia, Karelia, Memel, Fiume, Transylvania, Czechoslovakia, Silesia, Lithuania, Latvia, Estonia, Epirus, Bavaria, and Thrace.

Since communications between Europe and the United States were all but suspended, there was no way of knowing all the facts surrounding these stamps; but collectors did not particularly care: they were blinded by the dream of beating their fellow collectors in getting rich quick. They bought virtually everything that came across the ocean. "We'll buy them now while we can and then when the others wake up and want them too, we'll unload and make a fortune," they talked themselves into believing.

I remember one friend of mine, Raymond Linder, formerly an executive in the foreign department of the Banker's Trust Company, who had a contact in Bavaria. Some of his collector friends and dealers persuaded him to use this contact to obtain quantities of a set of stamps, reports of which had reached this country. Mr. Linder sent funds across and obtained about a hundred sets of these stamps at $55 apiece. He found no difficulty at all in reselling them to dealers at $70. A few years later, when information could be obtained, it was found that instead of being rare, these stamps were as common as wallpaper. Once communications were reopened, literally tons of them came across the Atlantic until they flooded the domestic market; and within a matter of months the price of that set dropped from $80 to about 25 cents.

Virtually the same thing happened to the stamps of the other countries or provinces mentioned. Even today all but a very few of them can be purchased in complete sets for the price of a cheap cigar. The get-rich-quick boys were severely burned, and many of them chucked the hobby for good; but on the whole it thrived more actively than ever.

[46]

By this time about sixty thousand stamps had been issued in the world and general collecting began its decline. The schoolboy, the bank clerk, the industrialist, and the housewife did not have to think very hard to realize the futility of trying to fill all the spaces which now crowded three stamp album volumes. It was not a case alone of being unable to do this financially; it was physically impossible. There just weren't enough of the rarer stamps to go around, even if a person had all the money in the world.

The collecting fraternity therefore began to build specialty fields. Instead of attempting to collect the stamps of the world, they broke up into groups, some concentrated on the stamps of one of the empires: Spain, France, the Netherlands, Great Britain, Germany, and their colonies; Scandinavian lands; United States and territorial possessions; British North America; Canada and its pre-dominion provinces; Australasia, and so on.

The scars of financial loss due to stupid speculation soon were healed or forgotten, and once again stamp collecting became the world's number one hobby.

Then came the boom era with its loose money and carefree abandon. The stamp trade became a prosperous business and one person in every fifteen or twenty in the United States had a stamp collection of some sort. The percentage of collectors in relation to population in Great Britain, France, Germany, Sweden, Switzerland, Belgium, the Netherlands, and Denmark always was a bit larger than here.

In 1929, when the stock market collapsed and suicides due to financial losses in Wall Street were the rule rather than the exception, stamp collecting and dealing experienced an untoward boom.

Men who had lost their jobs turned to their albums for that absorbing recreation which kept them from going mad with worry; men who had collected stamps as a hobby began to turn their avocation to a trade when they could not find work elsewhere. Some opened mail-order stamp firms; others rented small office space along Nassau Street and in the suburbs; and by the middle of the depression there were some five hundred of them within a score of miles from the bucket shops where their owners had been so completely fleeced.

Interest in stamp collecting had reached so popular a stage that around the early nineteen thirties a few of the larger newspapers in the United States were inclined to accept stories especially written for this avocational field on a more or less regular basis. In New

York J. J. Klemann, Jr. (one of the brothers who owned the Nassau Stamp Company) contributed several articles to the New York *Herald Tribune* and the reaction to them from readers led that paper to decide upon a regular column.

Ralph A. Barry, a graduate of Princeton and an engineer by profession, was one of the men whose professional work was badly hit because of the stock crash. As he was a keen philatelic scholar in need of something to do, he offered his services to Mrs. Ogden Reid and was almost immediately engaged to write such a column. On Saturdays he turned out articles that reflected intense historical research and profound philatelic knowledge. Even to this day, those articles are regarded as standard reference works. On Sundays a smaller, more popular column was published as part of the book review section. This carried also a small amount of advertising by stamp dealers.

Other metropolitan newspapers soon realized that stamp dealers could be turned into newspaper advertisers if the papers carried editorial matter to attract readers' attention. The New York *Sun* set up a special division in its classified advertising department under Mitchell Hodges. For a number of months Mr. Hodges produced a "stamp column" based on news which the dealers who advertised provided. In April, 1932, Mr. Hodges resigned suddenly and this department was taken over by his young assistant, Franklin R. Bruns, Jr., who continued to build it up into what is perhaps the most widely read source of new stamp issue reports.

Even before the birth of the New York *Herald Tribune* and New York *Sun* stamp departments, other newspapers had had stamp features of a sort. As early as 1918 Kent B. Stiles, a writer for the Associated Press, decided he would try to syndicate such a feature to papers at $5 apiece. Only one of his prospects responded, but eventually he discussed the propaganda value of such features with the Scott Stamp and Coin Company, and President Hugh M. Clark agreed to hire Stiles and distribute the syndicated columns to any paper who would publish them, without charge.

The New York *Times* frequently published the writings of Frank W. Crane, when such news was of interest to more than collectors alone. Mr. Crane, a writer in the real estate news department, became more or less interested in philatelic news possibilities during 1926, when the second International Stamp Exhibition was staged on the fourth floor of Grand Central Palace. The *Times* now has a regular stamp news department, but this was born only after Mr. Crane retired as a part-time philatelic journalist.

In the late nineteen twenties the radio stations around the country became stamp-collector conscious, not alone because an audience could be built for this subject but rather because they were willing to present any program that would cost them little or nothing. Station KDKA, in Pittsburgh, for instance, allowed the late Eustace B. Power to present a weekly stamp collector's program. During one broadcast, to test his audience, he offered to send a packet of stamps and a small album to any listener who would write and request it. The Scott Company, which agreed to furnish the outfits, Mr. Power, and the station expected some response to a free offer, but they never anticipated the flood of postal cards which swamped the mail room for several days. Realizing that he had a good thing, Mr. Power demanded that the station pay him for his broadcasts. They refused and Mr. Power quit.

At about the same time, still in college, I walked into the office of Margaret Cuthbert, then program manager of the National Broadcasting Company, and told her I should like to present a series of programs for stamp collectors. I explained my own interest and pointed to several small articles I had written for our local newspapers during the past several years. Apparently she was impressed, for she asked me to prepare an audition and, upon its approval, gave me time on the entire network once a week. Subsequently the time available (but without pay) interfered with my classes and I had to quit. The city of New York, however, had a radio station of its own under the direction of Christie Bohnsack, whom I chanced to meet through a friend. He showed some interest and within a few weeks I was given regular time over WNYC. This series, built entirely around descriptions of places I had visited in travels and which were depicted upon stamps, lasted for six years.

Other newspapers all over the country, and radio stations and networks, added stamp features to their programs, and by 1935 the public was well acquainted with the fact that stamp collecting was a highly popular hobby.

But stamps made news in the regular columns, too. In 1932, when the Roosevelt administration came into office, that invincible team of Roosevelt and Farley gave the hobby the biggest boost of its history in this country. Roosevelt himself was a stamp collector and Farley was a shrewd businessman.

When Mr. Farley was appointed Postmaster General of the United States as a reward for having maneuvered the Democratic party into the White House, he knew little or nothing about postage stamps or the hobby of collecting them. But he did know just about everything there was to know about exploitation, publicity, and merchandising. He had successfully sold cement, boxing, and political personages to Americans. Now he was the head of the biggest business in the world and he applied those selling techniques to postage stamps, which had become his new line.

During his first months he authorized the release of stamps honoring the Proclamation of Peace at Newburgh in 1783 and the Century of Progress Exposition in Chicago. In each case he personally was present at not only the ceremonies attendant to the printing of the first sheets at the Bureau of Engraving and Printing, but also at the sale of the first sheets when they were released to the public. A staff of photographers was on hand and the resulting pictures made most of the newspapers, thus providing substantial publicity for these stamps. Publicity always helps a product, and commemorative stamps were no exception. Thousands of persons went to their post offices to get copies of the stamps about which they had read. Commemorative stamps had been issued before, but few of them were so widely announced by the press and so enthusiastically bought by noncollectors. Mr. Farley proved that advertising pays, and subsequent issues were more fully exploited.

In August, 1933, a special stamp was issued in connection with the Blue Eagle fiasco, which then was better known as the National Recovery Act. Advance publicity was distributed, and as soon as the stamps were in stock at post offices all over the country, Mr. Farley instigated a bit of controversy by planting ideas, either directly or indirectly, with prominent journalists. The Communist question was rife, and it was not long before nationally known columnists and radio commentators were denouncing this stamp by saying that the farmer was holding a scythe and thus implying that the United States was in favor of the Soviet ideology. They added that the apron of the "worker" was similar to one used in Russia. Others said that the figure of the businessman really was a picture of Mr. Roosevelt and that he was out of step with the other three vignette companions. Whether their interpretations were true or not, whether the designs were intentionally planned that way or not, made little difference.

The fact remains that the comments got time and space, and the sale of stamps boomed.

The following year Mr. Farley issued a three-cent stamp in honor of the Tercentenary of Maryland and, instead of using the normal violet, had it printed in carmine. Again columns were devoted to mention of this deviation from postal regulations, for the Universal Postal Union regulations specify that carmine be used for stamps that will prepay postage on post cards to foreign lands. As the then-current rate was two cents, Mr. Farley's new issue was a technical violation of the international regulations. Again there was a rush to buy the stamps.

But the biggest publicity campaign for a new stamp accompanied the Mother's Day issue of 1934. No sooner had the design been issued than regular columns, art features, and critiques were jammed with comments. Some of the writers and commentators lambasted the stamp as being an insult to "Portrait of My Mother" by James Abbott McNeill Whistler because "her legs were chopped off." Others stated that the composition had been improved by the postal adaptation of the internationally known painting. Some found exception to the addition of a vase of carnations to the design; not a few even went so far as to suggest that the vase had not cost more than a dime. Another camp favored the use of the flowers. And so it went for weeks. Each time such Farley-instigated comments were uttered, postal clerks were stormed with requests for copies of the Mother's Day stamps.

Similar campaigns accompanied the appearance of almost every new postage stamp, and each time tons of them were bought because most folks wanted copies of stamps about which they had heard or read so much. Some no doubt suspected that a stamp that caused so much controversy would certainly become a rarity, especially since some of the comment intimated that the stamps would be withdrawn from use because of "mistakes" in their designs.

But Mr. Farley did more than simply exploit the sale of his stamps. He followed the first precept of salesmanship and made it a practice to open the doors of his office to any stamp collector who desired to discuss postage stamps with the postmaster general. Before his administration, the postmaster general usually remained aloof and referred all inquiries to the third assistant postmaster general, under whose jurisdiction the actual distribution of stamps was entrusted.

Mr. Farley made it a point to attend philatelic exhibitions and meetings whenever he was invited, and before long he was called "the stamp collector's friend." He heightened his popularity even further by building up a philatelic list. Each time a new stamp was issued, he would send to each person on that list a letter enclosed in an envelope to which the new stamp and a first-day postmark were affixed.

I distinctly recall my first visit with Mr. Farley. Within a few weeks after his installation I was in Washington, visiting with the deputy third assistant postmaster general. Before we finished our discussion of new stamps he suggested we go downstairs and meet Mr. Farley, who wanted to make the acquaintance of everyone connected with stamp collecting.

We were admitted to the office immediately and Mr. Farley was most cordial in his welcome. "I want you to feel free to call on me any time at all, and if there's anything we can do to make your work easier, just say the word."

Our friendship grew and soon his letters were signed, "Jim." In 1934, after the National Parks issue was authorized, I was leaving for the Canadian Rockies and I mentioned it to Mr. Farley.

"As long as you're going to be up that way, why don't you come down to Yellowstone Park on July 30, because I'll be out there in connection with the sale of the five-cent denomination," he invited.

A week before the appointed day, I was hospitalized because of an automobile accident just below Glacier Park, and did not return home until several weeks later. But there was a letter from Mr. Farley.

When I opened it, I expected to find only the regular note which accompanied a first-day cover. Instead, it read:

I read about the accident which prevented you from being with us here at Yellowstone Park for the sale of the "Old Faithful" stamp, and am glad it was not more serious. I hope you'll be up and around again real soon, but to be sure you have a first-day cover, I'm sending you this one for your personal collection.

Mr. Farley's frequent issues were the object of considerable complaint from various quarters in the philatelic press. Charges that he was exploiting stamp collectors by keeping the presses at the Bureau of Engraving and Printing rolling day and night were heard. So anxious were some writers, who couldn't see beyond the ends of their philatelic noses, to compel their own limited judgments upon their readers that they did not realize the actual good Farley's prolific stamp production did for the hobby.

It is impossible to estimate the number of new stamp collectors whom James A. Farley must be credited with developing, but today as I chat with young and old men and women in all parts of the country, I invariably am told by an amazing number of them, "Why, I started to collect when the National Parks set came out"; "I was so interested in the territorial stamps, I decided to collect all United States stamps"; or "The Army and Navy series got me started."

It was an amazing thing, this Farley influence. Every time a stamp was issued, the accompanying publicity must have compelled thousands of persons to buy one of the stamps that made the news, just as folks in England bought a Penny Black on May 1, 1840!

These persons had no particular reason for buying the stamps, except perhaps a naive notion that some day those stamps might become valuable. Perhaps it was only because a particular stamp had some personal association and represented a tiny paper souvenir. But whatever it was, people of all ages and in all walks of life were putting a stamp into a secretary drawer or in the corner of a desk.

Eventually Farley issued a second and a third and a fourth stamp that aroused the interest of these souvenir accumulators, and before they knew it a great many of them had the nucleus of both a stamp collection and the enthusiasm for stamp collecting. The first thing they realized was that they were stopping to take a second look at some of the other United States stamps displayed in the window of a dealer's shop on the way to work. Usually it took only a few days or weeks before they ventured inside and purchased a few stamps and an album in which to mount them. From there on it was easy sailing on the course to the greatest hobby in the world.

And just as stamp collecting was in its heyday, clouds of unrest were gathering over Europe. Refugees were coming over in droves, and while it was said that they were driven out of their homes without funds, few of them arrived without trunks full of stamps, jewels and cameras—especially stamps. A fortune could be put into rare postage stamps, which could be put into a small parcel. That made stamps the refugee's ideal commodity. Hundreds and thousands of persons put francs, marks, zloty, and korunas into tiny pieces of paper and carried them through Switzerland, Spain, Portugal, and England to the United States. When they arrived they either liquidated them in the established market or set themselves up in their own stamp businesses here.

Many of the more or less active European professionals emigrated to American cities, too, and by the time Hitler marched into Poland, more than half of the world's stamp business had already settled in New York. Stocks of stamps which had not been abundant before suddenly became plentiful, and because most of the refugee dealers had to eat and live, they undersold the American traders to satisfy the yearning of collectors to fill blank spaces.

By this time the country was steeped in the defense project; men and women were in war factories earning more money than they had had before, and those of them who were collectors were spilling some of that extra income into their stamp albums. The market went up and up to set new records. But then the Japs bombed us into the conflict which had been European and Asiatic, and the wheels of industry were geared to all-out victory. Long hours of overtime at the lathe, at the bench, on the assembly lines, and in the offices forced virtually every sensible person to seek a form of relaxation that was absorbing and interesting. Stamp collectors already knew that source of recreation, and they turned to their albums with renewed enthusiasm.

By 1942 our boys were heading for the four corners of the earth to drive the enemy from its strongholds. They went to Australia and North Africa; New Guinea and Newfoundland; Morocco and New Zealand. And, as was inevitable, those boys became acquainted with the postage stamps of those places that before had been but vague memories of a classroom lesson. They did not have to buy them, for they had the franking privilege to send letters to the folks back home; yet they did visit the post office and buy assortments of those in stock "for Johnny next-door, who collects them."

Postage stamps usually have an amazing ability to influence folks, so many of these boys who never collected stamps themselves, nor had the inclination to do so, wound up with a modest collection of their own. Any interest in postage stamps, however small or slight, eventually fascinates a normal person. Our men in uniform were no exception, and as they purchased a set here and a set there they invariably examined the colorful adhesives themselves before they put them in an envelope and sent them to their friends back home. By the time they made a second or third purchase, they were buying an extra set for themselves.

Ray Kershner

Anatomy of a postage stamp: (*A*) Figure of value. (*B*) Margin. (*C*) Frame of margin, upper panel. (*D*) Inner frame line. (*E*) Printing flaw due to poor inking or presence of dirt or dry ink in recessed portion of plate. (*F*) Postmark, or cancellation. (*G*) Vignette. (*H*) Inscription of value, bottom panels. (*I*) "Nibbed," or missing, perforation. (*J*) Lathwork, or background of vignette. (*K*) Perforation "tooth." (*L*) Perforation "hole."

Mulready envelope.

Penny Black.

First Swiss issues: Geneva, Zurich, Basel stamps.

Brazil's Bull's-
Eye.

Ray Kershner
New York
Provisional of
1845.

First United States stamps.

Ray Kershn

Hawaii.

Post Office
Mauritius.

Cape of Good Hope Triangle.

The story was universal. In North Africa, in New Guinea, the Solomons, the Philippines, and finally throughout Europe and Japan, the post offices ran out of stamp supplies simply because so many GI's were buying them for collections or just souvenirs. By the time our forces were in foreign lands three to six months, not only the post offices but the stamp dealers were doing a land-office business. It has been said that GI's spent well over $20,000,000 for postage stamps which they purchased for friends back home and for themselves.

Meanwhile collecting trends in Great Britain and the United States veered from a pure hobby pursuit to a mad wave of speculation and "investment." A certain amount of speculation has characterized philatelic circles ever since the collection of postage stamps became a universal hobby, but the wide indulgence of this practice set staggering records during the war years.

Some persons who were collectors no longer were satisfied with a single stamp to fill a blank space in an album. When new stamps were issued, they rushed to the post office and purchased as many full sheets as they could afford—and in some cases more than they could afford. Their reasoning, perhaps, went something like this: "I need a stamp for my collection. It was issued only thirty years ago and cost but ten cents at the post office then. Today I have to pay five dollars for a single copy. If I buy a stamp today and put it aside, I can later get a couple thousand per cent profit. Besides, the United States doesn't demonetize stamps, so I can always use them for postage."

And so these get-rich-quick boys bought full sheets of every new issue and jammed bank vaults with them with such enthusiasm that a printing of several million special issues was usually absorbed in a matter of months.

Meanwhile, normal collecting activities were in a boom era and millions of men, women, and children built an unprecedented demand for these recent issues, forcing prices up and up until the collector's value of stamps was doubled within a year or so after a stamp was current. The "investors" grinned as they saw their holdings accumulate paper profits.

"But if the stamps that I bought at face value in full sheets constantly are rising in the stamp market, how can I lose money?" the naive "investor" asks. The answer is not too difficult, for the whole idea is one based from the very beginning on a false reasoning.

Take any arbitrary stamp of the past which has risen in value—for example, the five-cent stamp issued in 1907 to commemorate the tercentenary of the founding of the Jamestown colony of 1607. That stamp in unused condition today is worth around $5 a copy, although slightly fewer than 8,000,000 of them were printed and issued.

On the basis of those figures you calculate that if you had bought only 100 of those Jamestowns forty years ago and held them you would have made a $495 profit on a $5 investment. And, when the United States issues a new special stamp, you're going to be very wise and get your share of them. You're not satisfied with buying as many as you can afford; you dig into the bank account which you'd built to guard against emergencies and sink $1,000 (a modest amount compared with some sums individuals and syndicates spend on modern commemoratives) into a supply of full sheets.

The fly in the reasoning ointment is an oversight in your comparison between the Jamestowns—or any other United States commemoratives issued before 1930—and the ones into which you're putting your money "for a rainy day."

Before 1930 folks generally bought only those stamps which they needed for their collections or, if they were legitimate dealers, for stock. Since the rest of the stamps were bought at post offices to frank regular mail, they were lost to philatelic channels unless they happened to be addressed to stamp collectors who salvaged the used copies. And so, although nearly eight million of the Jamestowns were issued, it is a safe guess that only ten per cent of that number exist today, and of those a certain small percentage no longer are in collectible condition. Stamps are delicate items, and unless extreme care is used in handling them they are likely to become torn or otherwise damaged.

Since 1930, and especially since 1937, exactly the opposite is true. Usually fewer than ten per cent of any special issued actually do postal service. The remainder have been and are being carefully put aside by persons with the get-rich-quick hallucination; and considering that nowadays printings run to 100,000,000 of every new issue, you do not need a comptometer or an abacus to figure the number that is in existence.

But from the "investor's" point of view the situation is quite different. Pete Peters, for example, drained his bank account to put $1,000 into a supply of full sheets two years ago. "I can always get face value for them," he argued himself into believing. Today he suddenly needs that money, and he's a happy man as he looks at the advertisement that quotes those stamps at exactly twice what he paid for them. He goes to his tin box, takes out his $1,000 worth of sheets, and begins to peddle them. "If dealers are selling the stamps at double face value, I ought to be able to get at least $1,250 for this lot," he tells himself as he starts out.

The first dealer he visits gives him his first jolt. "I've got enough of them in stock to take care of my customers," he is told.

Another dealer offers to take the lot for $900. By the time Pete has tramped around New York and offered his supply to dozens of dealers he has not found one who will give him a profit. He concludes, therefore, that all of them are crooks.

Perhaps you who read this feel the same way about the professional. But let's analyze the situation. Every legitimate dealer in the country is well aware of the speculative trend. They know that millions of stamps are hoarded by the profit prophets, so they maintain a stock only large enough to satisfy their immediate needs. "Why should we tie up our working capital when 'investors' do it for us," they will tell you in all honesty. "Certainly we sell at six cents a stamp that you could buy at a post office for three cents two years ago. We're in business and have to make a legitimate profit. But how many of those can we sell in a year? A thousand dollars worth?" There just aren't that many stamp collectors around, for the ones who patronize dealers don't buy in sheet lots. They purchase only singles, or blocks of four, at most. The sheet buyers patronize the philatelic agency of the Post Office Department where they buy at face value while the issue is current. Considering that the dealers would be tying up capital for several years on stock that cannot be turned over immediately, they can afford to pay only less than face value.

But what about the "they're always good for postage at face" illusion? The Post Office has a regulation against the redemption of postage stamps, so Pete cannot take them to the clerk from whom he bought them. The big firms, which could use $1,000 worth of three-cent (or any other value) stamps, cannot afford to involve themselves in a possible stamp-theft case, and so they have rules about buying their postage only from the post office.

If Pete is like most folks, $1,000 worth of postage would satisfy a lifetime of letter writing, so he cannot use them himself. Besides, he needs $1,000 immediately. And so, after he has approached every person to whom he thought he could sell his hoard at a profit, he finds that he can get only about ninety per cent of his money back.

By 1930 so many postage stamps had been issued around the world that general collecting was impossible, and even the specialists had to develop new specialty fields if they were to complete their endeavors. The results of that situation were amazing. From all corners of the country came original collecting ideas. The vast majority of men, women, and children began concentrating on the commemorative issues of our own country, for in addition to philatelic pleasure, these colorful adhesives did much to acquaint them with the history of our country.

But another large group of collectors expressed their individualism through their albums, and an entirely unheard-of crop of specialty collections was soon being built.

There is no way in which we can credit the actual "inventors" of the varied types of collections of which we speak, so we shall mention only those who built the first ones that came to our attention.

Father (now Monsignor) Ferdinand Cech, a parish priest of La Cross, Wisconsin, never had very much money to devote to his avocation, so he concentrated on making a stamp collection which depicts subjects relating to religion. His "Philatelic Litany of Saints," he calls his album. Among his specimens are stamps from Greece and Crete that depict mythological gods such as Zeus, Hermes, Apollo, and Poseidon. On the stamps from Oriental lands, he has pagan conceptions of the Supreme Being. Among them is the goddess, Siva, with six arms, on the issues of Indo China, and Phoenix, the god of wisdom and the symbol of revitalization, on the stamps of Japan and Hongkong. This entire collection was recently given by Monsignor Cech to Pope Pius, and now forms a part of the Vatican Library's treasures.

Under the heading of Christianity there are stamps from many lands portraying Christ, the Madonna, and even the various outstanding popes. Other countries portrayed their patron saints, such as SS. Rose of Lima, Elizabeth, Cyril, Peter, Paul, Francis, and others.

The most interesting of this group is the set issued by Portugal in 1895. The front of this stamp, which is philatelically worth less than a dime, shows a picture of St. Anthony of Padua preaching to the fishes, an incident familiar to all of us. The back of these stamps, however, is very unusual. On each one is an inscribed prayer, which, when translated, reads, "O Blessed Tongue, which always didst bless the Lord and cause others to bless Him, now it is evident how highly thou were esteemed by God." This, as you perhaps know, was what St. Bonaventure exclaimed when the body of St. Anthony was unearthed thirty-two years after his death. His entire body was crumpled into dust, but his tongue, says tradition, remained as incorrupt as the day he died. The prayer on these stamps reminded the Portuguese of this miracle each time they affixed one to a letter. By it they were admonished to refrain from "sins of the tongue."

In Albany, New York, Mrs. Carl Wichmann built a collection that is unsurpassed in interest and fascination. Mrs. Wichmann always had been interested in animals and stamps, and when she was confronted with the impossibility of fulfilling her latter avocational ambition, she decided to combine it with her other interest.

The collection of animal stamps she has amassed is amazing. On her adhesives she has so many strange beasts from the far corners of the earth that none but a zoologist would be able to identify them all. In fact, she has a collection of animals on stamps that would turn a zoo or menagerie curator green with envy.

You may recall the newspaper articles about the first Okapi that was brought to this country. It was a sensation at the Bronx Park Zoo, and even today people come from the far corners of the country to get a glimpse of this strange combination of antelope and giraffe from the jungles of darkest Africa. But if you examined Mrs. Wichmann's collection of stamps you would find *two* Okapis. One is on the stamps of the Congo and another on the stamps of Belgian East Africa.

Mr. Philipp Murray, an insurance executive of Merion, Pennsylvania, likewise is interested in animals. Mr. Murray, however, specializes in stamps picturing only elephants. He has made a collection of many stamps from Africa and Asia upon which are delineated pictures of the world's largest quadruped. He has pygmy pachyderms from Liberia, rogue bulls from Abyssinia, and ceremonial elephants from India; even a sacred white one from Siam.

The Steinway family of New York was another leader in the building of subject collections. Theodore E., president of the piano firm, long has been one of the philatelic peers of our generation; but even he realized the limitations imposed by the never-ending release of postage stamps, and he gradually turned from his collections of the classics to a type collection. As was natural, he selected stamps relating to music and has accumulated every stamp which depicted musical instruments, composers, or actual music scores.

The rest of his family sought other subjects. His son, Fritz, started out with a collection of stamps relating to railroads and trains; his daughter, Elizabeth, concentrates on stamps showing maps.

Harvey E. Fisk, a maritime insurance broker of New York, is particularly interested in stamps showing ships and boats. He has everything from birch-bark canoes to Egyptian quinqueremes and modern ocean liners.

Fay Jordon, a New York socialite, began a collection of stamps printed in violet or shades thereof. When she began she did not realize the scope of such a collection, but today she has nearly forty volumes of violet stamps, including some that are extreme rarities in their own right.

Mrs. Edith Adams Brown, also of New York at the time and now a resident of Cleveland, Ohio, concentrated on stamps showing babies and small children. Some of those in her collection are pictures of just babies; others are pictures of famous personalities when they were children: Princesses Elizabeth and Margaret Rose; Prince Jean, King Michael, and others.

The popularity of subject or type collecting has no limits other than those bounded by the ingenuity of the persons who make them. Subject collecting includes trees, industries, fruits, vegetables, plants, airplanes, balloons, birds, sports, literature, mountains, war, exploration, and flags, in addition to those subjects mentioned before.

As stamp collecting, then, has marched down through the years, even though trends have changed, the basic hobby has only become more popular. Internationally it is first in the ranks of avocational pursuits, and in the United States it is second only to photography as a personal hobby. It has been beset by many undesirable encroachments and by racketeering, but in spite of these it still stands high above its nearest competitors. Collectors may vary the types of material they want, but they will collect postage stamps as long as there are stamps to collect. It is a hobby which has already proved that it is here to stay.

If we survey the continental European situation we get a pretty good idea of how firmly this fascinating hobby has entrenched itself upon the life of man. As these folks dug themselves out of the ruins of war they lost wealth and limb, home and hope, but never their love for stamps and stamp collecting. For example, after our armies had vanquished Germany, about the first thing many Central Europeans wanted to know was what stamps had been issued by the

United States during the years when communication between the countries had been denied them. Within a month after our occupation forces had been established in Munich and Frankfort, the State Department called upon me to supply an article devoted to this subject, because "next to food and clothing about the only thing the Germans who had been stamp collectors before the war wanted now was news about stamps." I wrote that article and it was published in *Heute* for distribution in the zone occupied by Americans. Even before a copy of the magazine reached me, I was literally deluged with letters from German philatelists who sent me sets of German war issues in exchange for copies of the stamps that I had described.

In this country interest cannot help but wax stronger. In 1946 we had about ten million collectors. During 1947 the nation observed the centennial of the first United Stamps stamps and, in connection with this anniversary, the established collectors' societies staged exhibitions in every major city. Since newspapers and magazines publish numerous articles devoted to stamps, the hobby will likely be adopted by further millions of persons who never before thought they could think more of a stamp than its utility as the prepayment of postal charges.

The manufacturers of meter stamps have been putting on intensive campaigns to install machines that will stamp and postmark mail, thereby eliminating the need for adhesives. Mailomats have already appeared in post offices in the larger cities, and they will continue to be made and distributed; but the idea that they eventually will replace the postage stamp is inconceivable. Persons who now are collecting, or who may begin in the future, therefore, need not fear that they are taking on a decadent hobby.

What is this fascination that has made the collection of postage stamps so universal a hobby? What is there in an avocation that knows neither race nor creed, social rating, age, or professional rank? One can pick up the membership roster of any stamp collector's society of any country of the world and on a single page find listed bankers and diplomats, clerks and tradesmen, college students and retired businessmen. Certainly, then, it *must* be something more than a superficial bond that can hold such a diversified group of persons in a common pursuit.

Stamp collecting is so popular, first, because it has no hard and fast rules: it is possible for a thousand persons to be stamp collectors, and yet each of them may have a particular stamp collection through which to express his own individuality. It is possible to build a collection without spending a dime for a single specimen, yet it is likewise possible to spend a million dollars and still be far from the attainment of a self-set goal. It is possible to be a *stamp collector* or a *philatelist:* to collect stamps simply according to design and endeavor to get as many distinct varieties as were issued, or to take any selected single stamp and study it so thoroughly that a lifetime is passed and still questions remain to be answered.

Stamp collectors are a unique clan. They care little whether a fellow hobbyist shares their particular specialty or has one of his own; the fact that another person also is a *stamp collector* is enough to rank him as a friend. When they correspond, or when they meet in a stamp club room or at an exhibition, they forget their professional prestige and social standing and concern themselves only with discussions of stamps, and watermarks, and perforations, and the like.

Stamps that qualify for subject collections: a supply ship, musical notes of a funeral dirge, a polar bear, and a mythological phoenix.

[5] Uses and Abuses of Postage Stamps

Could Rowland Hill today examine an ordinary album of postage stamps and see to what extent his original idea had been used—and sometimes abused—his amazement would be no greater than that of Orville Wright, who lived to see the day when his invention had been so improved that it is possible to fly over oceans and continents with greater ease than he had enjoyed even by surface transportation.

When Rowland Hill suggested the use of a label, he had but one purpose in mind: to facilitate the handling of mail and thereby enhance the service the government might render to its citizens. During the first decade or two after Great Britain introduced the world's first postage stamp, a stamp was intended solely as an adhesive sticker to indicate to clerks that the payment of postal charges had been received and that the letter franked with one or more of them could be forwarded to its destination without further charge. Accordingly, those early philatelic pioneers were devoid of any extraneous imprint and usually featured only the head of the ruling monarch as a sign of traditional respect. Postage stamps still serve their original purpose: they still indicate the prepayment of postal fees and expedite the handling of mail; but they also have come to foster many other projects. They have been employed as grindstones upon which many an opportunist in office has sharpened his personal axe.

The use of postage stamps was rapidly adopted throughout the world, and since folks used their brains as well a hundred years ago as they do today, it is not especially difficult to realize that it did not take long for some nations to visualize the postage stamp as an advertising medium.

For, what other medium could be so effective? By its very nature a postage stamp must reach every corner of the world. Its design must be seen not only by the person who buys it at a post office and the person who ultimately receives it, but also by the persons who handle the letter on its journey from one place to another.

And realize the potential propaganda value of postage stamps they did, those early postal officials. As we go through our albums we can see the change that developed. Gradually the designs used to ornament the faces of postage stamps veered from a set pattern, which satisfied only the utilitarian purpose for which they were originally intended, to miniature advertising posters. Since then the stamps of the world have served to exploit national industries and political ideologies. They have been used to advertise domestic products and arouse spirits of nationalism. They have promoted travel and incited wars. They have recounted history and immortalized heroes.

Since the economy of any nation depends largely upon the industries it has and the products it can export to boost its foreign exchange, it is but natural that many nations of the world think of these assets and seek means of bringing them to the attention of world marts and the potential buyers therein. In many lands a single natural resource may determine the difference between prosperity and starvation, so that the entire populace of a given nation thinks in terms of the sale of its sugar or tobacco, its timber or coconuts. In other lands, where nature has provided an abundance of crops or deposits, the dependence upon one is not so critical. But whether a country has one or a score of industries, the advertising of native products is invariably to be found upon its postage stamps.

In Cuba, for example, tobacco is an almost vital crop, and even though we did not already know it, her postage stamps would tell us that fact; for since the first Cuban Republic stamps were designed and issued, we find tobacco prominently featured on her postal paper. Upon various Cuban stamps we see tobacco plantations, tobacco crops, tobacco plants, and even a finished cigar.

Coffee and sugar are two other crops that have been very important to the economy of several nations, and we need but look at their stamps to appreciate the extent of that importance. It is especially interesting to examine the various "coffee" stamps and note how each country boasts, through its postage stamps, that *its* product is "the best." We can, for instance, look at the stamps of Costa Rica, Guatemala, Colombia, Venezuela, and Brazil and at once read in Spanish or Portuguese, "ours is the finest coffee in the world."

Practically every nation and colony in the world has at one time or another used its postage stamps either to advertise its industries or pay postal tribute to them. The industries we find depicted on these color-ful adhesives run the gamut of variety, for as we may reasonably sup-pose, many remote places have crafts and products that are as indi-vidual to them as are the Alps to Switzerland. The Congo, French Guiana, and the Netherlands East Indies advertise the weaving of baskets which natives use in their everyday chores and tourists buy as gay souvenirs. Peru has advertised its guano deposits, and Chile, its nitrate fields. Rubber has been advertised on the stamps of the Cameroons, Ceylon, the Congo and Mozambique, and the making of salt from evaporated ocean water is depicted upon the stamps of the Turks and the Caicos Islands. Newfoundland has postally exploited its cod fisheries and paper-pulp mills; Honduras, its mahogany and chicle; Colombia, its emeralds, oil, bananas, and gold; Egypt, its cot-ton; Switzerland, its cheese, watches, and embroidery; the Philippines their rice, and Dahomey, its dates.

There really is no limit to the number of products which have been advertised upon the miniature billboards that have carried letters across the seas and continents. Indeed, several enterprising collectors have begun collections upon which are depicted the products of the world's lands, and so vast is this specialty that I know no one who has yet been able to complete it.

Several years ago one prominent New York collector gave a private party for a group of her friends at the Warwick Hotel and, instead of having the menu printed in the conventional manner, listed every item served according to numbers given in Scott's "Standard Postage Stamp Catalogue." Besides providing the guests with an unusually interesting menu, this novelty did much to impress upon me the great variety of things to be found upon stamps. Even pepper was identified by a postage stamp from Liberia, upon which that seasoning is depicted.

Exploitation of tourist attractions has been another conspicuous job of the postage stamp. Almost every country has some natural phe-nomenon or wonderland to lure victims of wanderlust and seekers of adventure. To the natives these are sites of domestic pride and assets which have paid off in many a tourist dollar, franc, or mark.

Industries, also, have been reproduced on postage stamps just as they have been in the folders of tourist propaganda. At first, when ordinary modes of transportation limited the number of people who could travel beyond their country borders, only the highlights ap-peared. Switzerland exploited her Alps and lakes; Egypt her Pyramids, Sphinx, and monuments of antiquity; New Zealand, her Mt. Cook; Turkey, her Golden Horn; and Greece, her classic ruins.

But as travel became more convenient to the citizenry and more lucrative as a business for foreign lands, both the number of sites and the quality of their reproduction as postal vignettes were stepped up. Lands that were within reach only of expeditions before the airplane abbreviated vacation times to hours instead of months, began to bid for the tourist trade by devoting enormous efforts to the production of travel-poster stamps. And in many cases, when there were not a sufficient number of stamps in a regular set, extra stamps were issued to do the job.

Belgian East Africa—a remote section of darkest Africa which formerly was visited only by the DuChaillu's and Dennis's—began putting in a bid for popular visits early in the nineteen thirties. Her stamps began to depict portraits of spectacular native types, native scenes, native flora and fauna—and, as though to give the stranger an assurance of security, even a member of the native constabulary!

Islands in the Pacific, which to most folks were once merely names in the books of explorers and adventurers, suddenly issued stamps to advertise their exotic charms. In many instances, places which never before had had a legitimate need of postage stamps began to issue them. We find the Gilbert and Ellice Islands luring tourists by stamps that show seascapes and coconut trees, pandanus trees and Frigate birds, thatched huts and outrigger canoes, to paint pictures envisioned by anyone who had ever heard of the South Seas. Pitcairn Island, about which the story of the *H.M.S. Bounty* mutiny was centered; Nauru, an insular speck in the broad Pacific; Niue and Penrhyn; Papua, New Guinea—and in 1947, Norfolk Island, all of them sought their share of the travel business through the medium of stamps.

Even those places that formerly had enjoyed a regular influx of sightseeing vacationists put on an all-out campaign to proclaim their right to spread out the welcome mat for the members of Cook's tours. They not only employed the standard views with which every globe trotter was already familiar, but they showed glamorized views of the same places and depicted some new ones a little more distant from the harbors. When a Caribbean cruise was a full two-week proposition, what with a five-day ocean voyage involved, tourists could hit only the highlights on their brief on-shore stops. But now that it takes but a short eight hours by air to reach these islands, the time saved can be used to visit the hinterlands. And knowing this, the islands began exploiting their inland attractions as well. Cuba, for instance, added Matanzas and the Bellamar Caves, the Yumuri Valley and Rio de Piñas, to stamp designs, whereas formerly only Havana sights were featured; the same tactics were employed by Jamaica, Haiti, and the Dominican Republic. The United States went tourist conscious along about 1934 when we began to exploit our vacation lands with ten special stamps honoring and advertising the highlights of ten of our national parks.

So comprehensive has been the use of tourist scenes upon the postage stamps of the world that the average collector could challenge even Burton Holmes to name a site or place anywhere on this earth which has not appeared upon the design of at least one postage stamp.

The advertising of industries, products, and tourist attractions, flora and fauna and historical events, upon the postage stamps of the world is a perfectly legitimate procedure and attests both to the shrewdness of postal officials and the value of postal paper. But Rowland Hill—could he see them today—would be even more astonished at the uses to which postage stamps have been put that are entirely extraneous to their original purpose.

The use of stamps to swell the financial coffers of financially weak countries at the expense of collectors is more than half a century old. It developed within a decade after the hobby of stamp collecting became securely established in continental Europe and the United States.

Such tiny places as North Borneo, Liberia, Labuan, and Persia were the first to prostitute their postal paper. And so thoroughly did they do their job that today very few serious collectors will recognize the stamps issued by these countries as legitimate, except when they can be found on original letters with the proper postmarks to prove that they served a genuine postal purpose.

All of these countries were so commercially and socially undeveloped that under normal circumstances a single ordinary issue of stamps would have satisfied their needs for years. Instead, postal officials authorized the production of numerous sets at frequent intervals. There is some controversy among philatelic students today to determine whether the postal officials were the instigating culprits or only the instruments of conniving operators. There is ample evidence to support both sides; it is not my intention to champion either camp, but simply to relate the results.

[67]

Liberia is typical enough, so there is little need to go into detail about the rest of the countries which have abused their postage stamps. This tiny republic, which was founded in 1847 along the West Coast of Africa by freed American slaves, was—until the Firestone Rubber Company developed its rubber industry—just another corner of Africa which enjoyed only a rather ordinary ivory, timber, and native crafts trade during the nineteenth century. A very small percentage of its population of approximately 1,500,000 souls was literate, and for about two decades its postage stamps honestly reflected a limited amount of correspondence. By 1892, however, stamp collecting had developed, and because they were relatively rare, every collector sought to obtain specimens from Liberia.

The demand for stamps boomed to such an extent that some of the smart boys in Liberia decided to pluck a few plums. Suddenly this small republic, which had discovered that three or four stamp denominations at a time were more than adequate to serve all postal needs, obligingly issued a set of a dozen of the most colorful and fascinating adhesives that were ever designed. One depicted an elephant; another, a hippopotamus; a third, some native jungle scenery; and others, equally striking vignettes. These stamps ranged in face value from one cent to five dollars. The cost of producing the stamps was but a few cents per thousand, regardless of the face value, and since millions of them could be sold to stamp dealers at the price that was inscribed, the revenues received through their sale were substantial. Of course a person who so wished could go to Liberia and get five dollars worth of postal service for the stamp he owned, but most of the adhesives for which hard cash was paid by a hobbyist never were presented to do their duty, and so the difference between the insignificant production cost and the money that had to be paid to the post office was pure profit.

The first made-to-order set was so lucrative that Liberia went into the stamp business. Each succeeding set was more colorful than the last. In addition to depicting subjects that could not help but lure the collectors—and especially imaginative youngsters—those stamps were printed in combinations of colors that made them more vivid than the gaudiest of circus posters.

And then Liberian officials found another way to step up sales. After all, there was a limit to the number of sets they could sell in unused conditions at face value, although the demand was apparently

[68]

unlimited. Unused stamps had to be sold at the value that appeared on the stamp, for the officials could not afford to sell below face lest somebody who had legitimate trade, and therefore a cause to send mail from Monrovia or one of the other towns, might buy his stamps through the stamps trade at a discount and use them for their full face value.

The Liberians solved the problem by taking full sheets of the brilliant stamps and applying a neat cancellation in such a way that a complete strike hit four stamps. As these were obliterated and could not be presented for postage, they could be offered to wholesalers at a fraction of their face value. Such canceled-to-order stamps were sold by the millions at prices that varied according to the number any one dealer bought at a time. For many years complete sets—from one cent to five dollars—could be bought from nearly any dealer in the world by youngsters who had 25 cents to spend. Youngsters were so anxious to own those gaudy stamps from a land whose very name conjured up the wildest adventure stories that they ignored the possibility that someday those stamps would be scorned for what they were.

Today you will find collection after collection with these stickers that were made and obliterated by postal officials, but which are no more "postage stamps" than the labels that are made today by dairy, gasoline, and aviation companies. You can recognize them by looking for one thing, although there sometimes is a second give-away. If the stamp you have has a neat cancellation across one corner of its face, you can bet your best magnifying glass that it is one of those undesirable "cancel-to-order" culls. And if it is in a collection of the person who bought it originally, you can turn it over and see that the gum still is on the back, for those officials were so anxious to peddle their wares that they did not even bother to wash off the gum to give the stamp at least the superficial appearance of having once been affixed to a letter. Of course it is best to have a stamp still affixed to the envelope which it franked, to prove that it was legitimately employed in the mails, but this is not absolutely essential, for a stamp that did postal service was nearly always obliterated with a cancellation mark in such a manner that an almost complete obliteration is struck over it.

But philatelically abominable though Liberian, Persian, North Borneo, and Labuan issues might have appeared, they were lily pure as compared with some of the moneymakers that were foisted upon the collecting world during the ensuing years. In our own United States one Nicholas F. Seebeck promoted a deal which perpetuated his name in the annals of nefarious philatelic rackets.

As the head of the Hamilton Banknote Company, Mr. Seebeck knew a little about stamps and the hobby of collecting them. More than half a century ago, he approached the postal administrations of several Central and South American countries and offered to print their postage stamps on such terms that the countries would not have to pay him anything for his work. His contracts stated that he would supply the desired number of postage stamps that would fill the needs of the governments if they would order a new set every year, and that, once an obsolete set had been replaced, then he might be allowed the use of the plates. His proposition was reasonable from an official point of view and the contracts were signed.

Within a few years Seebeck had manufactured four sets for Ecuador, five for Honduras, and ten for Salvador. As soon as the issues were replaced the plates were cleaned and thousands of sheets were run off from each one. These then were peddled at a fraction of their face value to stamp dealers, who in turn sold them to collectors. Everything went well, and Seebeck did a substantial side-line stamp business that more than repaid him for his efforts until the details of his operations became more widely known in philatelic circles.

A wave of protest disturbed the otherwise tranquil realm of stampdom and damnation was heaped upon not only the Seebeck reprints but also upon the legitimate issues of the countries as well. During the last several years, however, serious students began crusading in behalf of the original stamps made by Seebeck and sold through the post offices of the countries that fell victim to his scheme, thus in some measure re-establishing their original favor. Fortunately there are differences in the type of paper used for the originals and the reprints: the latter are on thick, porous paper that may be identified even by the beginner when he holds it against a strong light. The paper, of the reprints, held in this manner, reveals a sievelike appearance. So abundant was Seebeck's reprint production that even today some dealers can supply all 252 stamps at a fraction of a cent apiece, while some of the originals are worth one dollar or more, especially when they are still affixed to original envelopes with proper postmarks.

But never in the history of postage stamps were these tiny bits of paper put to such sanctioned revenue-raising and propaganda-spreading use as during the global war and prewar years by Germany, Italy, and especially Russia.

Shortly after Mussolini got control of the Italian government and began his campaign to rouse the nationalistic spirit of his countrymen, the designs that carried the "Poste Italiane" banner were modified. No longer were normal size stamps with the effigy of the reigning monarch sufficient. Instead, the area of the stamp doubled or trebled, and suddenly every person, every incident, that once had contributed to past glory was placed upon Italy's postal paper. Within a matter of years there was no Italian capable of reading the testimonial inscriptions and understanding the striking pictures who could not be led to think he was a personal descendant of Virgil, the Caesars, Ferrucci, Garibaldi, and Philibert.

Mussolini honored warriors and the immortals of science and culture to serve his purpose. He paid tribute to Boccaccio, Machiavelli, Dante, da Vinci, and Sarpi to impress upon Italians that they were stemmed from men of culture. He recalled Romulus and Remus, Augustus and Julius, to recall their Roman heritage. And when he had saturated his followers with legends of two long centuries ago, his more direct propaganda messages were placed upon the postage stamps Italians had to use to mail letters to their relatives across the seas. He glorified babies who saluted à la Fascist. He showed children harvesting wheat; infants in the Fascist Youth Movement; adolescents brandishing rifles; and himself as the invincible military *Duce*.

Similar stamps were issued for his colonial "empires"—Cyrenaica, Eritrea, Tripolitania, Lybia, and the Aegean Islands. The adhesives were large and gaudy, to appeal not only to the natives but to the millions of collectors around the globe. They were distributed through every known channel to serve their double purpose. They made an impression upon collectors who did not immediately recognize the propaganda for what it was worth. The lire and centesimi for which they were sold did much to buy the uniforms worn by the soldiers who marched toward Addis Ababa and the bullets that killed helpless Ethiopians first and Allied soldiers later.

Adolf Hitler employed his postage stamps in much the same manner but did a more thorough job of it from the propaganda point of view. He began his stamp campaigning in 1934, when the swastika first appeared in a design that featured the Nuremberg Castle; a few weeks later, when the Saar plebiscite was due for vote, German stamps conveyed the claim that this rich coal land belonged to the "greater Reich."

Steadily, rapidly, new stamps, each with a more striking design and message than the last, were issued. Many of them were regular stamps proclaiming the benefits and righteousness of the New Order, and they could be bought at face value. But most were semi-postals, the premiums for which were used for "winter relief," "child welfare," "charity," and "culture funds." The designs were carefully planned, artistically arranged, and exquisitely executed. Looking at them from a graphic point of view, no stamps in the world are more beautiful or more perfect examples of miniature engraving. But as instruments of a vicious ideology, none are more lethal. Every subject was selected to tell Germans and the world that the land of the Nazi supermen was superior in art, culture, music, industry, and commerce; invincible in military and aerial might.

Hitler, however, did not operate a vast foreign export business in these labels. He did not need to. Almost from the inception of the hobby Germans were enthusiastic stamp collectors. For generations German stamps enjoyed a popularity which not even the treachery of the Nazis could suppress. Hitler's own populace absorbed as many of these issues as rapidly as they came from the presses, and even after his hordes marched into Czechoslovakia and Poland, collectors over here continued to so clamor for "those beautiful German stamps" that the market for them continued brisk until December 7, 1941, when all enemy issues or stamps from enemy-controlled countries were outlawed by the United States' "Trading with Enemy Act."

But of all the nations of the world who have exploited the faithful postage stamp and the millions of enthusiastic hobbyists who collect them for fun and pleasure, none can surpass the Soviet Union for racketeering.

For over sixty years Russian stamps were without the slightest taint of extra-postal production stigma. The stamps issued were made solely for postal purposes; the designs were beautifully conceived, finely executed, and always highly sought after by serious philatelists.

Then came the revolution and the birth of the red regime. Until the turmoil of riot and civil strife was subjugated, the stamps of the new nation reflected the cataclysmic conditions that must have prevailed in Moscow and other large cities of Russia. They were crude, poorly made, and cheaply printed. But as the revolutionists entrenched themselves more strongly in the Soviet government, the postage stamp became a propaganda instrument of the most spectacularly vicious type.

The regular postal series featured three classes of Soviet men: the soldier, the worker, and the peasant. But in addition to the stamps that were needed to frank what relatively few letters were mailed in Russia, special sets were produced to publicize the red cause. There were labels that delineated portraits and the mausoleum of Vladimir Ilich Ulyanav, alias Nicolai Lenin. By propagandizing this disciple of Karl Marx, the Russians furthered the ideology of the present administration. There were pictures of revolutionary scenes, mass meetings of socialist followers, and kindred subjects that were shrewdly calculated to impress upon the public mind the subordination of man to a state based on godless militarism and communistic principles.

And when a stamp of ordinary size was inadequate to carry the nefarious message, the size of the stamp was enlarged until virtually all stamps became in fact small posters. At first these labels were intended for domestic consumption: in those days Communist literature was not welcome in the United States and other nations where democracy still was held in high esteem, but there was nothing to prevent sending messages through in the form of franks on mail. Later, however, as officials became better acquainted with the philatelic market, means were found to distribute, in tremendous wholesale quantities, the stickers which the Soviet called "postage stamps." They soon learned that their treasury might be enriched as well, for, like the Liberians, Russian postal officials got good American dollars, English pounds, and Latin American pesos for their gaudy paper. No sooner had they become aware of this double utility of postage-stamp production than the presses were kept rolling in record-breaking speed. They not only issued Russian stamps with unceasing regularity, but they also produced dozens of sets for some of their outlying Asiatic territories, notably Tannu Tuva, a portion of Northern Mongolia the Soviets appropriated from the Chinese in 1926.

When stamps first appeared from this remote spot of which few Americans had ever heard, specimens were eagerly bought by young collectors who were entranced with the pictures of unusual animals and the strange shapes and vivid colors in which they were issued. How many thousands of dimes and quarters were spent out of weekly allowances will never be known, but spent they were, for the wholesalers did a brisk business all over the stamp-collecting world. Always the stamps appeared in unused or canceled-to-order condition, until presently serious philatelists began to investigate the postal status of these strange labels.

Letters were written to postal officials in Kysylchuto, the "capital" of this country of nomads and caravansaries, asking for data to establish the authenticity of these postage stamps. Invariably the queries went unanswered; in one or two recorded cases the replies came from Moscow and were so ambiguous that doubt prevailed in the minds of philatelic students. The late Eugene Michel, a postal historian of wide repute, made the investigation of Tannu Tuva and its stamps a personal project and was tireless in his efforts to establish the facts. When he finished he found that there never was a postal service that could be honestly called such in this desolate outpost of northern Asia. He learned that the stamps were printed in Moscow and distributed from that city to stamp wholesalers "as a convenience." In short, they were made expressly for collectors, and especially the young, inexperienced collector. As a consequence, the editors of the *Standard Postage Stamp Catalogue* made a bold statement to warn future victims of this racket:

> We purposely omit listing various pictorial sets, perforated and imperforate, of triangular, diamond, square and oblong shapes inscribed, "Postage," "Air-Mail," and "Registered," which appeared in 1934 and 1935. We do not consider them to have been issued primarily for postal purposes.

But since Russia *did* and *does* have an established postal system, nothing could be done to prove that the stamps issued by the Soviets were nothing more than labels. Once a member nation issues a stamp and sends specimens of it to the Universal Postal Union as samples, they must be recognized as such regardless of the real purpose for which they were produced, however scandalous that may be.

And so the Soviet program not only went on, but was stepped up to a pace that never before was, and probably never again will be, matched. Portraits of Russians whose names are familiar to students of music, science, socialism, the arts, and the military were placed upon huge, brilliantly inked stickers; drawings of scenes on farms, in industry, and in rural communities extolled the success of the Five Year Plan and its extensions. There were pictures of the buildings and civic splendors of the Soviets—some that exist and some that are but the dreams of architects. There were pictures of huge airplanes and lighter-than-air craft; pictures of schools and universities—all in all a grandiose job of publicity to show the rest of the world how wonderful is life and work and play in the Union of Soviet Socialist Republics.

As Europe began to arm for the conflict that started when Hitler invaded Poland on that tragic day of September 1, 1939, the Soviets began a campaign to glorify their military might. There were labels that paid tribute to the infantry and artillery; the navy and the air force; the cavalry and the mechanized troops. When war came to the Russians, collectors here had been so impressed by these stamps that no one would believe that the Germans could withstand this nation of might. And even as they were pressed farther back on successive Nazi onslaughts before American weapons and Allied support came to their aid, Soviet stamps still proclaimed their own valor. Their stamps paid tribute to heroes of Stalingrad, Leningrad, and Odessa; they showed pictures of Russians bayonetting Nazis, tanks in action, and soldiers tossing grenades.

These stamps began flooding the American market at the rate of a new set almost every week or two. They were offered by dealers in used and unused condition; but like the Liberian stamps of the nineteenth century, the "used" specimens were neatly canceled labels with the original gum still on the back. During the war Russia was an important "ally," and the dealers who handled the material were reluctant to expose these labels for what they were lest official offense be taken.

That none of these stamps ever were intended to serve a postal purpose is evidenced by the fact that, as far as I could learn, sets never were on sale in any given post office. We have had access to the commercial mail of several large firms whose correspondence was substantial, yet in all the years during which so many hundreds of new stamps were issued, the envelopes were franked with only the regular "soldier" and "workers" types introduced a quarter of a century ago. When the Russian correspondents were asked to obtain these "commemoratives" and use them instead of the ordinary issues the answer was invariably the same: "We know of no such stamps as you request"; "Our post office has no such stamps"; or "We understand that these sets are available only through the philatelic agency." Of the more than one thousand different stamps issued in Russia since 1930, I have seen fewer than perhaps twenty or thirty different ones legitimately used on commercial mail.

According to the Soviet methods, an agency in Moscow has charge of the production of stamps, and as soon as an issue is ready supplies are sent to a number of accredited wholesalers in strategic parts of the world, together with a release describing the person or event honored by them. The wholesaler first distributes the releases to the editors of stamp columns in metropolitan newspapers and the chroniclers of philatelic magazines in much the same manner as a press agent publicizes a circus that's coming to town. A week or so later, the stamps appear on the market.

Since editors of philatelic publications always are anxious to receive copy for which no payment need be made, publicity concerning the Russian stamps has been widely published—invariably verbatim—so that the collector has been primed to want a set when it is available.

The Soviets have even gone further than this. A few years ago one of the outlets controlled by an American distributor for Russian issues announced that a limited number of imperforate sheets of obsolete issues was available to specialists. According to his advertisements, these sheets had come from the archives of the Russian Post Office and were being offered as a special favor to American collectors—at three-figures prices.

What will happen to these labels remains to be seen. Thousands of collectors have paid face value for them—at the established rate of exchange, plus a normal dealers' profits; thousands of others have paid slightly less by purchasing the stamps from merchant mariners who had been on the Murmansk run during the war and who were able to obtain quantities from sources there at the lower domestic rate of exchange. Reliable sources reveal that all the plates from which Soviet stamps have been printed during the last twenty-five years still are in Moscow. If the Soviets remain content to have sold so many stamps, perhaps a market value can be established for those that exist. But if, at some time in the future, values should rise in stampdom's markets—because of a greater demand than existing supplies can satisfy—the Soviets should suddenly get an idea that reprintings would be profitable, then collectors would be left holding the "sucker's bag."

The stamps we have discussed so far are "regular" issues, which were sold in unused condition at the prices which were inscribed as the "face value" of the adhesive, and for which amount postal service would be rendered. But there is another form of postal paper through which many a nation has raised revenue for either a genuinely charitable project or just another scheme for which there was no provision in the national budget. These are called semi-postals and are in a class by themselves.

Back in 1897, when the whole British Empire was marking the diamond jubilee of the reign of Queen Victoria (under whose administration the world's first stamp was issued), New South Wales issued a pair of stamps for which buyers had to pay one and two-and-a-half shillings respectively. Depicting an allegory of charity, and printed in two colors and gold, these stamps had an actual franking value of only one and two-and-a-half pennies.

The festive mood of folks in New South Wales had inspired the Post Office to solicit funds to help pay for a desperately needed home for consumptives. According to existing records, it was a grand idea, because a great many folks were more than willing to pay a premium to show their respect for Her Majesty and at the same time to aid in a charitable cause by franking domestic and foreign letters with either of these two special stamps. The difference between the franking value and the sales price of the stamps was turned over to the cause for which the stamps were issued and did much to make the tuberculosis sanitorium possible. And thus were born semi-postals.

The idea was a good one, and for three years these two stamps remained unique. In 1900, Queensland, a neighboring Australian colony, copied New South Wales' novelty and issued a pair of stamps to swell a patriotic fund in connection with the Boer War on the other side of the world. The two stamps sold for one and two shillings apiece, but had a franking value of only one and twopenny respectively. The difference between the sale price and the franking value was contributed to the fund.

It took a long time for this postal means of serving charity to catch on. In 1906, the Netherlands prepared three stamps which were sold at double face value (1-plus-1, 3-plus-3, and 5-plus-5 cents) for its campaign in behalf of the Society for the Prevention of Tuberculosis. That same year Romania issued twenty different semi-postals to raise funds for victims of the Balkan wars and featured pictures of Queen Elizabeth in the role of social worker and nurse. Each of these was sold at a premium above its face value. During the ensuing few years Barbados surcharged its then-current twopenny stamp to help care for the victims of the Kingston, Jamaica, hurricane; and Belgium issued two dozen semi-postals for the benefit of its tuberculosis control campaign.

In 1913, Switzerland produced an attractive stamp which was sold during the Christmas holidays at 10 rappen, although it had a franking worth of but half that amount. The premium was put in the fund which aided various charities. From that time forward semi-postals were established as a regular means of getting extra funds through the exploitation of those who collect stamps as a hobby.

Today there is hardly a nation in the world which has not regularly or spasmodically produced semi-postals for purposes that strain the imagination in their variety. The notable exceptions are the United States and Great Britain, who never have employed this means of harvesting surplus cash at the expense of those of us who use the mails. Appeals have been made to both governments to forsake tradition and get into the swim.

As early as 1917, when our country was soliciting funds for many charities in connection with the World War, Congress and the Postmaster General's office was literally besieged by petitions to authorize semi-postals for the benefit of the American Red Cross, the Salvation Army, the Liberty Loan Drive, the Boy Scouts, and the like. "Folks would be delighted to pay an extra cent or so when they mail a letter if they knew their premium contribution would aid a worthy cause," the petitions pleaded. The Post Office condoned the sale of Christmas seals in post-office lobbies, but they refused to do more.

In 1930, the late Ernest R. Ackerman, United States senator from New Jersey and one of the country's eminent philatelists, revived the semi-postal appeal when he petitioned that such stamps be issued to raise funds for the victims of the drought. Again during World War II the idea was broached in behalf of the National War Fund, the Red Cross, and the U.S.O., but still the Post Office would not yield. But if the United States and Great Britain have maintained the purpose of the mails, other nations have not. Some have used semi-postals with restraint and integrity; others have turned them into a racket. Especially since 1930, semi-postals have been dumped upon the patient public—and the philatelic market.

Among the foremost examples of semi-postals that have done an immeasurable amount of good and have been exceptionally popular with collectors are the annual sets issued by Switzerland since 1915 and known as "pro juventute" stamps. These have been released around the first of December and have remained on sale until the end of that month. They are valid for postage until the following May, when they are demonetized and declared obsolete. The premium collected is turned over to that branch of the government which cares for child-welfare institutions and, as the cause is so worthy, almost every Swiss makes a practice of franking all mail during the holiday season with these colorful adhesives although he can, if he wishes, use regular stamps for which he has to pay no premium.

Swiss officials, who take their stamp designs and production very seriously, were especially careful to make these pro juventute stamps outstanding examples of graphic art. The first several sets featured pictures of the various cantonal costumes; then followed a series which depicted the coats of arms of each of the twenty-two cantons; a series of famous scenic spots; and currently, series showing some of the more famous Swiss flowers.

Many nations issue annual sets for the benefit of antituberculosis campaigns, war-victim funds, cancer-control projects, and kindred humanitarian endeavors, but others have exploited semi-postals for numerous other causes that can hardly be called charitable. In 1931 Austria produced six semi-postals whose double-face value helped finance the international Rotary convention held in Vienna that year. Belgium issued several sets to pay for the restoration of the Orval Abbey; Czechoslovakia, to pay for its participation in the Olympic Games; Finland, to finance a national ski meet; Germany, to provide a stake prize for a horse race; Hungary, to finance a propaganda campaign to regain control of Transylvania; Jugoslavia, to pay for a national stamp show.

Spain issued a set to pay for the restoration of the Catacombs of Saints Damasus and Praetextatus at Rome. In our own hemisphere, Ecuador, Guatemala, and Nicaragua issued stamps to pay for the construction of new public buildings, the cost of which was greater than the national treasuries could stand. At one time the proceeds from the sets of stamps paid for the erection of a new fence around the palace of a Latin American president!

During the Hitler administration of Germany, that country issued great numbers of semi-postals, the premium on which was greater than the franking value; and while these were ostensibly for "charity," subsequent information shows that what was collected was used to help pay for martial activities.

But of all the nations of the world, France has set a record for the number of things that can be done with money obtained through the sale of semi-postal stamps. France has had issues for the benefit of victims and relatives of victims of World War I; for the benefit of children of the unemployed; for "unemployed intellectuals"; for a "recreation fund for employees of the Department of Posts, Telephones, and Telegraphs"; for monuments in honor of Pierre Loti, the Army Medical Corps, civilian victims of World War I; to finance celebration festivities related to the fiftieth anniversary of the Eiffel Tower; to aid political refugees; to decorate the Louvre; to aid the Versailles Concert Society; to assist French volunteers in the Spanish Civil War; to aid France's repopulation campaign; to buy cigarettes for French seamen; and to aid indigent musicians.

This 25-pfennig stamp cost a 100-pfennig premium which amount helped provide a stake prize for a horse race.

Norfolk Island began issuing stamps in 1947 more for collectors than for postal needs.

The 25-franc premium of Belgium's semi-postal was used for "winter relief."

One of the Soviet Union's war propaganda designs.

[6] Postage Stamps as Big Business

Even those countries that have not turned the production of postage stamps into a major industry realize the importance of postage stamps as collectors' merchandise, and they, together with the exploiters, have set up special divisions to handle the sale of stamps to philatelic channels and to produce the kind of stamps collectors will want.

Great Britain, for example, has been so determined to maintain a traditional aloofness in its postal business that to date this great nation has neither air-mail, special delivery, nor semi-postal stamps; and only on fewer than ten occasions was more than the effigy of the ruling monarch allowed to decorate the face of its stamps. Yet Great Britain does a philatelic business that runs into the millions of pounds sterling. They have got around hoary tradition in the British Isles by exploiting colonial issues and setting up an office in London where wholesalers can purchase stamps of possessions all around the globe and which have never left England from the time they came off the presses.

Before World War II such places as the Gilbert and Ellice Islands, Papua, New Guinea, Pitcairn, Basutoland, Aden, Ascension, Bechuanaland Protectorate, British Solomon Islands, South Orkneys, Grahamland, South Shetlands, and South Georgia were but names which a cartographical student might have recognized; for with the exception of a few literate natives and a handful of foreign residents, none of these places had a sufficient number of people to require stamps of their own. For years they had been more than satisfied with the adhesives of neighboring colonies and, in some cases, the stamps of England.

But suddenly the crown agents for the colonies decided that the continued policy of issuing only such stamps as postal needs demanded meant a loss of potential revenue. Possessions from which not a hundred pounds of mail a year had been dispatched suddenly were given complete sets including values ranging from a halfpenny (or its equivalent when other than the shilling scheme of currency prevails) to the high shilling denominations. The stamps were carefully designed and handsomely produced by the better engraving and printing firms of England—Bradbury-Wilkinson, Harrison, Waterlow and Sons, and Perkins-Bacon. A small quantity of these new stamps was sent to each of the colonies; the rest of the printed supply went to the London office of the crown agents, where wholesale orders were filled. Many a collector, seeking the fun of getting his stamps from the source, wrote to these colonies, inclosing payment for the stamps requested. All most of them ever got was a brief note from an "obedient servant" stating either that the stamps ordered no longer were in stock or that British postal regulations prevented colonial postal clerks from filling special requests from stamp collectors.

When the series of British and British colonial stamps was issued in honor of the Silver Jubilee of King George V and the coronation of King George VI and Queen Elizabeth, the bulk of them (like the aforementioned pictorials) never left England until they were shipped to wholesale dealers in the United States and some other countries. In 1946, when the Peace stamps were produced, less than ten per cent of the printed supplies ever reached the colonies whose names appeared on them.

Of course, a majority of collectors prefer their stamps in unused condition, for since the stamps are so magnificently produced, they do not wish the design marred by a postal obliteration and, as long as the stamps are legitimately authorized, they care little whether the specimens they own ever were in a post office. Perhaps, then, they themselves are to blame for the current willingness of postal officials to cater to their demands.

During the 1930's and 1940's many other nations have set up special divisions in their post office departments which do nothing but sell stamps to collectors. Known as "philatelic agencies," these divisions are in fact government-operated stamp stores. Foremost among these is that operated by our own government in Washington.

Founded in the early 1920's under the direction of the late Michael Eidsness, then Superintendent of the Division of Stamps, the Philatelic Agency consisted of a supervisor, his secretary, and a clerk occupying the corner of an office in the city post office. Together these men handled the smattering of orders that came to the department from collectors in small towns who could not obtain all the various issues and denominations in their third- and fourth-class post offices, and from larger cities where collectors desired out-of-the-ordinary specimens. By the end of the decade stamp production was stepped up by the emission of new regular air-mail and commemorative sets. News of the agency's service became more widely known, and by 1930 literally thousands of hobbyists were sending mail orders to it when they could not obtain these stamps in their local offices. So substantially did the agency's business boom that within ten years it was an important adjunct to the Division of Stamps and its head, Herbert Chamberlain (now Assistant Superintendent of the Division), had a staff under him that occupied several rooms in the post-office building opposite Union Station.

The Philatelic Agency renders a definite service to collectors. When new stamps are issued, a certain portion of the complete printing is deposited with it for sale to collectors. This fraction is "picked stock." Before the sheets leave the Bureau of Engraving and Printing experienced clerks go through the press run and pick out those sheets which are well centered and otherwise above average from the philatelic point of view. Orders are filed in order of receipt and distributed to clerks who have been trained to satisfy philatelic needs to the best of the department's ability, whether the collector has remitted a dime or a five-figure amount.

The clerks in the agency are tireless in their efforts to please and usually go far out of their way to fill such orders as specify particular plate numbers or plate positions. When orders for blocks arrive, they are not given just the first that happen to be torn from a sheet; instead the clerks scrutinize the sheet and pick out that one which is most perfectly centered in a manner that leaves a visitor with the impression that each of the clerks is the personal agent of the collector who has placed the order.

When Postmaster General James A. Farley took office and began his prodigious stamp-issuing program, the business done at the agency was staggering. At one time so many orders were received that it took five months to fill them. Finally, when the new Post Office Department was built, a portion of one entire floor was turned over to the agency. Special windows were included where a brisk over-the-counter trade was done every day. Inside, a long line of wire cages accommodated clerks who filled the mail orders in the best Sears-

Roebuck manner of efficiency. At its peak, a hundred employees were on the payroll of the agency, which then was under the supervision of Otho Larkin Rogers.

Sales figures set new records quarter after quarter, and the annual take grossed well into the millions. Much of this increase was due to the general increase in philatelic interest, but some of it was due to the interest that Mr. Rogers took in the service to "his" collectors. So efficient, so personable was Mr. Rogers, that collectors, dealers, and officers of philatelic societies rarely referred to him in terms other than "the collector's best friend in Washington."

Trained for law, Mr. Rogers was a career man in the postal service and a reserve officer in the United States Marines. But always he was a champion of postage stamps and service to those who collected them, although he himself did not have a collection of his own. He took his position seriously enough to devote spare evenings to the study of handbooks and catalogues until he became as familiar with the hobby as any philatelist. His door was always open to visiting collectors, and before he had been agent a year, he was personally acquainted with many of the agency's customers. He was keenly sought after as a speaker for philatelic meetings, and when he attended functions not associated with this field, he invariably preached the gospel of stamp collecting. When new stamps were issued and placed on sale in distant places, Rogers invariably would be there personally to see that every envelope submitted by collectors was given a perfect "first-day-of-issue" postmark. By reason of his position and his interest, Mr. Rogers was an ambassador of philatelic good will, the likes of which has never been seen before or since.

When war threatened, Mr. Rogers was given a leave of absence to assume active command of a Marine battalion, first in this country, then in Guantánamo. After the attack at Pearl Harbor he served in New River and was among the first to go to the Pacific.

He was killed in one of the earliest Solomons landings in September, 1942. Philatelists all over the country mourned his loss. Several societies honored him by memorials and plaques, and even today no mention of the Philatelic Agency can be made without associating it with the late Major Otho Larkin Rogers, the first United States Post Office Department executive to give his life during World War II.

The war made its inroads on the service rendered by the agency, which was headed by James Bell after Rogers' entry into service, but not into the business it did. The war called many of the clerks into uniform or more vital jobs, and so orders piled up to a point where it became necessary to handle only commemorative issues as they appeared. The speculative trend (which is discussed elsewhere) was responsible not only for more orders, but also for those that seemed like wholesalers' orders. Many an individual and investment syndicate began buying more stamps at the agency than at most community post offices. The condition became so critical that an appeal had to be made to Congress to authorize the employment of an additional staff of clerks; and only recently were they well enough caught up with the deluge to enable them to replace regular issues and airmails to the list of material available from the agency.

Doing business with the agency is a simple matter. A collector simply writes a note, requesting a copy of the current list of stamps that can be bought—a list that includes every stamp currently used by the United States Post Office, and many types and denominations that cannot be bought at any but the largest regular offices. The collector uses this list as an order blank, indicating which stamps he wants and the quantity of each variety. He incloses a money order or certified check to cover the face value of the requested items, plus the cost of return postage (and registration on orders above $5), and mails it back to Washington.

No fee is charged for this specialized service, for although the salaries of the staff must be paid by the Post Office, the department figures (and rightly so) that the majority of stamps sold through the agency never will be used for postage, so that the money received for them is pure profit and more than pays for this expense.

Before the war, agencies of a similar nature were maintained by most of the large foreign countries, but many of these were discontinued and never re-established. Today a collector can obtain unused stamps from such places as Canada, Australia, New Zealand, Sweden, and Switzerland, all of which operate agencies whose service is just as good as that of our own country.

Unique among government-operated philatelic services is that at the Pan American Union, in Washington. Some years ago Albert F. Kunze, an enthusiastic collector and philatelic journalist, conceived the idea of a philatelic agency through which the stamps of all Latin-American nations might be obtained in the United States. Heretofore, service had been mediocre at best, and although all of the Latin-American nations had produced a great many stamps for which there had been a most substantial demand, collectors here had encountered the most disappointing experiences when they ordered stamps for their albums directly from the post offices of those countries. The differences in language and temperament, the slowness of ordinary mails, and the expense of air-mail service united to set up an almost insurmountable barrier between the postal officials of our Latin neighbors and collectors here.

Mr. Kunze accordingly submitted a plan to the late Dr. Leo S. Rowe, Director General of the Pan American Union, whereby each member of the union would deposit a supply of stamps at union headquarters. These stamps would be placed on sale at a price in American currency that would approximate the exchange rate of the face value. The stamps would remain on sale six months, and collectors might obtain as many of them as they desired within that time. After the six-months period the stamps would be removed from the union's list and the surplus stock returned to the nation in question. Dr. Rowe was impressed with the idea, for he had often expressed an interest in philately and appreciated that the stamps of foreign countries inspired many a collector to a better understanding of the nation issuing them. That alone was worth while, for one of his main missions in life was the extension of the Good Neighbor policy.

Mr. Kunze was hired and with a secretary established the Latin American Stamp Section for the Pan American Union. His office consisted of a desk in the corner of a room in the accounting department. The project was placed before the diplomats of the twenty republics who resided in Washington, and a long exchange of official correspondence ensued between them and their governments. Finally a few of the countries risked a trial of the system and submitted some of their specimens. The stamp section was in business. But the going was rough. Dealers here complained bitterly, indicating that a government agency was cutting into their business; they justifiably pointed out that the very difficulty in obtaining stamps directly from the Central and South American countries made it possible for them, who had agents there, to supply a demand which could not be filled in any other manner.

Mr. Kunze answered them all. He pointed out that he and his office planned to sell new stamps only over a six-month period. He argued that the union, by virtue of its wide nonphilatelic connections, could reach a great many persons who ordinarily might not buy from dealers; that the union's service would "make" new collectors who

An original "flimsy" carried by pigeon post between Great Barrier Island and New Zealand in 1900.

During the last century stamps often were split to make them valid for lower denominations when stocks ran low. This is a twelve-cent stamp used to pay six cents postage.

Letters salvaged from wrecked planes are postally marked and become philatelic gems. This one was aboard the *Yankee Clipper* when it crashed at Lisbon in 1943.

Extremely rare Hawaiian Missionary on cover found by a boy in a Massachusetts library.

One of the letters carried by air across the Atlantic in 1919.

German stamp honoring Wagner's opera *Parsifal*, autographed by Lauritz Melchior, who sings the role and who is himself a famous collector.

Stamps frequently were used for money when metal was scarce. The back of this Russian stamp was imprinted to make it valid for three kopeks.

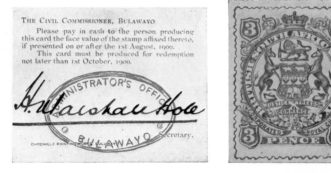

Rhodesia also used stamps as money, as shown here.

Where printing facilities are inadequate, stamps are crude, as witness this one from Bundi.

Five methods of mail transportation used since 1847 were featured on this three-cent stamp commemorating the centenary of our first stamps.

ultimately would become customers for the obsolete issues which the union did not handle. The controversy continued, but eventually Mr. Kunze won his point.

At first only a handful of countries took advantage of the service on a trial basis. To promote both the sale of the stamps they had, and to further the aims of the union, the Pan American Union published many releases to the philatelic press and books about the subjects depicted upon stamps of the past which collectors might purchase for a dime. In addition, Mr. Kunze was instrumental in making up educational stamp displays which were circularized to schools, libraries, and stamp exhibitions. His program aroused an interest in Latin American stamps which few philatelists had ever believed would be possible, since these stamps had fallen into disfavor as a result of the Seebeck operations described on page 70.

Today the Pan American Union's stamp section occupies a large portion of the ground floor and consists of a spacious counter and any number of display frames. The project has of course been invaluable in spreading the gospel of philately, because so many noncollectors who visit the union's palatial building as a sight-seeing highlight in the nation's capital are inspired to buy some or all of the various sets available. All twenty nations have not as yet made final arrangements with the Pan American Union, but Mr. Kunze asserts that it will not be long before American collectors can obtain from him, at face value, any stamp that is current from Mexico to Chile and the Argentine—with the exception of Dutch, French, and British possessions within that area.

Some governments have become so cognizant of the power of the philatelic market that they have engaged philatelic consultants to work with their postal administrations in order to exploit to the fullest extent the sale of postage stamps for which no postal service would have to be rendered and which would represent huge net profits. Only recently Liberia, who again decided to get its share of collectors' money after a period of philatelic hibernation, engaged the services of a professional philatelic advisor whose office is in New York, and through whom issues are planned, produced, and distributed to American wholesalers.

Just before the war the government of Luxemburg sent an agent to this country to engage an American who might serve as an advisor and whose prime job would be to survey the market and tell the government how many Luxemburg stamps could be sold here. The actual outbreak of hostilities, however, prevented the fulfillment of that idea.

A number of other countries engage qualified and recognized philatelic students to aid them in their work, not so much with a view of capitalizing on the sale of unnecessary issues, but in the hope of establishing a better service for collectors. The stamp collector is by nature a most inquisitive fellow. The search for answers which are not immediately available is much of the sport of the hobby, so that virtually every postmaster general is besieged by letters requesting data on recent and obsolete issues. Some of them dismiss the query with a blunt, "We don't know." Some dig into the records, find them missing or inadequate, and must reply, "Sorry, but we haven't the information." Still others take a more co-operative attitude and really try to help the philatelist, for they have learned that he can sometimes become a useful source of assistance when the government itself happens to need help.

Switzerland was one of the first to offer an almost perfect service. In conjunction with the philatelic agency they established in Bern, where current stamps may be bought at face value, they set up an information service under the guidance of a well-known Swiss philatelist. Every record and document relating to stamps was dug from the archives and placed at his disposal for the prompt, accurate answering of any questions that might be sent to the Swiss Department of Posts. For a number of years now, every new issue is accompanied by a handsomely printed leaflet which describes the design and explains its significance if there is an allegorical vignette; which gives every detail of paper, inks, and printing method employed, the name of the artist who drew the original design and made the finished engraving, and even biographical information about such individuals as were selected for postal honor but who were not always listed in standard encyclopedias outside of their native land.

In 1943, when Switzerland honored the centenary of its first adhesive postage stamp, this division of the Post Office produced a handbook which not only illustrates every stamp design ever issued since 1843 (many of them in original colors), but which describes the production methods and the history of Swiss stamps during the century.

Sweden has pretty much the same arrangement, but unfortunately most of the records before 1920 are missing, so that information is available only about stamps issued since then. Meanwhile, they have purchased the philatelic library of Nils Strandell, an eminent Swedish student who has been in this country on a number of occasions to judge international philatelic exhibitions. They subsequently engaged him, and through his efforts soon will be in a position to furnish answers to any stamp issued by Sweden since 1855, as based on the original researches of living or deceased specialists.

Canada, Australia, New Zealand, and South Africa have a similar service. The United States does not, but since both postal officials and the director of the Bureau of Engraving and Printing are aware of philatelic efforts and the importance of the hobby to their receipts, they furnish answers to most questions asked of them when it does not require too much effort. When they are approached by a person of some reputation, they are generous in opening to him the archives and allow him to dig for the information he seeks; but beyond that they do not venture.

A few years ago the Cuban postal administration set out upon a stamp-producing program which was not particularly welcomed by collectors in the United States. In fact, even Cuban collectors themselves were opposed to it as a project intended solely to separate them from their centavos and pesos. A group of them—the leaders of the Club Filatelico de la Republica de Cuba—voiced its protest with such vigor that the scheme was squelched almost before it had a chance to blossom. Because these men who complained most bitterly were all citizens of such means and high professional and social standing that they did not have to use their hobby to advance financial ambitions, the Director of Communications gave them an audience.

Together they worked out a program of issuing postage stamps that represents an ideal spirit of co-operation between a government and stamp collectors. Their arguments pointed out that stamps were a reflection of a country and that therefore none but the finest examples of graphic art should be accepted for reproduction on postal paper. They insisted that stamps be issued only for legitimate postal needs or to commemorate historical events and honor individuals only when the events of persons were of outstanding international importance.

By the time the conferences were over the Director de Comunicaciones set up a project whereby every proposed stamp would be submitted to a committee for consideration. The committee consists of three recognized art critics. Any stamp suggestion which is not approved unanimously is discarded. Once a stamp is approved, the

Cuban government announces the fact to the public and invites native artists to submit design ideas. These essays then are examined by the committee and the best ones given to engravers for execution.

Egypt is another country which solicits and accepts the opinions of a stamp organization which has proved by its past actions that it has the interest of its native land at heart. All prospective stamp suggestions are discussed with members of the group. For some time Egyptian dealers, by virtue of their residences there, were able to buy up entire issues of stamps and hold them for substantial profits. This condition made for many complaints from dealers abroad who did not have an "in" and therefore had to become victims of the professionals in Cairo and Alexandria. The Egyptian Philatelic Society explained the foolishness of such action, and as a result it was cleaned up. Today, when an issue is proposed, every dealer—whether he lives around the corner from the main post office or ten thousand miles away—has an equal chance of buying at face value the stamps he orders. Sometimes the quantity precludes the filling of a complete order, but when that happens all wholesale requests are pro-rated in an equitable manner.

Fancy postmarks enhance philatelic interest in a country's stamps.

[7] Stamp Dealers

As soon as people expressed an interest in postage stamps, pioneers appeared who were willing to undertake the job of providing hobbyists with what they wanted. Three of the earliest European dealers began as modest collectors in their teens and, envisioning possible profits, set themselves up in the business.

Jean B. Moens always will be regarded as the granddaddy of the great philatelic tradesmen; he began in 1852, and soon was in business for himself in a small shop in Belgium.

E. Stanley Gibbons used a table in the rear of his father's chemist shop, at 13 Treville Street, Plymouth, as his stamp emporium, and a portion of the window for displays to attract customers. This youngster got his real start in 1863, when a pair of sailors who had just returned from Cape Town dropped in to sell some stamps. While there, these tars had been persuaded to buy a shilling raffle ticket from members of a ladies' bazaar, and as winners they had been handed a sack full of canceled Cape of Good Hope triangular stamps for which they had no use at all. They brought them back to their English port and, on seeing the Gibbons display, decided to sell their bag of colored paper. Gibbons got the lot for £5 (about $25) and sold them wholesale to fellow dealers for many years to come. His rates were 20 cents a dozen for the 1, 4, and 6-penny values, and 75 cents a dozen for the woodblock issues. The famous errors, which today are listed at $1,500 and $1,750 apiece, were offered by Gibbons at $1 each!

In London, a William Lincoln set up business, while in Paris a Madame Nicholas added selections of postage stamps to her stock of books, magazines, and newspapers. By 1862 the names of Mount Brown, Edward L. Pemberton, H. Stafford Smith, Henry R. Victor, and J. J. Woods were known as dealers of recognized reliability.

On the continent there were François Berger-Levrault, Alfred Potiquet, M. Herpin, Senf, and a few others, and although we have no definite record of them, there were probably some more dealers scattered in the farther corners of the earth where postage stamps were in use, and from whom the established European and American dealers obtained supplies as demands for foreign material waxed.

The United States at the time was in the midst of the Civil War, and most folks were more concerned with its problems than with the avocation of philately. Nevertheless, this pioneer period found the first foundations of the trade set in New York by William P. Brown and John Walter Scott; F. M. Trifet opened a shop in Boston in 1865, and S. Allen Taylor entered the business in Albany, and later in Boston, to sell not only genuine postage stamps, but a large quantity of counterfeits and bogus issues to plague hobbyists for many years to come.

While I still was in grammar school I used to pass an old gabled house completely surrounded by tall hedges and a garden that was crammed with lilac bushes, rows of vegetables, and corn stalks. Its inhabitant was a tall, stately man with a full white beard who looked like Santa Claus but who acted like a demon when children carried their games too close to his property. One day I decided to brave a visit to this "haunted" house and its eccentric owner in the pursuit of my hobby.

I went straight up to the door, shivered a bit as I rang the bell, and asked the old man whether he had any old letters in his attic from which I might find some stamps for my collection.

"So you're a stamp collector, eh?" the old man mused. "Sure, I've got some stamps. C'mon in." I followed the man as he limped through a cluttered kitchen and upstairs to a room that was dominated by a roll-top desk and three huge safes. "I used to be a stamp dealer, but I've still got some of my stock. Here's my price list," he said.

He handed me a small folder that had been printed in 1919, just before he retired. It was imprinted, "William P. Brown, Postage Stamps for Collectors."

That was how I met William P. Brown, who was unquestionably the most colorful figure in philatelic history in this country; and while I learned his identity only after his death, I entered into a "business deal" with him that provided me with quite a number of good stamps.

My father would not permit me to buy stamps, and old man Brown wouldn't give me any gratis. I did arrange, however, to "invest" $1 to purchase some sets which he offered me in 1923 at 1919 prices according to his list. I then sold these to some of my friends at school and used the profits to buy the ones I needed. But to get back to Mr. Brown.

"Willie" Brown, as he was known to his contemporaries, started his career as a coin dealer in a small Nassau Street shop which was demolished and replaced by a tall office building more than half a century ago. He moved into a ground-floor store at 65 Nassau Street about 1875, and operated a stamp and coin exchange until his retirement in 1920, after which he moved to the large house on the corner of 103rd Avenue and 120th Street, Richmond Hill, Long Island, where he lived until his death on December 30, 1929.

He gave the details of his entry into the stamp trade in a letter written to Samuel W. Comstock, a numismatist of City Island, the Bronx, on June 20, 1919. He wrote at that time:

> About who and when was the first stamp dealer in New York there is no question about that. About the year 1860, as near as I can figure it, I went into the coin business in N.Y.C. At that time there was no one in the United States offering to purchase postage stamps of various nations. A few people, notably Captain Pretle, of Portland, Me., were making collections of them for their own amusement.
>
> During that year the fever of stamp collecting struck New York City, but for about three months there was no monetary value. It was all done by exchanging item for item, when suddenly collectors began offering money for them. I was then requested to keep some of them as a dealer by the city boys, but held out for a week or more until I finally bought a few of a Dr. Bond at Cortlandt and Essex Streets. I picked about 100 of them from a boxful, at one cent each, and that started me in the business. Probably other dealers started in London and Paris at about the same time.[1]
>
> About a year or so later J. Walter Scott came over, a boy from England, and sold me his collection for $10, and a short time later he was out of funds and I started him in the stamp business.

A few years after he began dealing in postage stamps Mr. Brown supplemented his store trade with a sidewalk business. The demand

[1] Jean-Baptiste Philippe Constant Moens, a bookseller at the Gallerie Bortier, Brussels, Belgium, began dealing in stamps in 1852, in much the same manner as Mr. Brown. A Mr. Hanciau, a young bibliophile, asked Mr. Moens to accumulate postage stamps for him, and that led to the development of a stock which was unquestionably the finest in Europe until Mr. Moen's death. The Walter Scott, to whom Mr. Brown refers, was the founder of the business which later was incorporated as the Scott Stamp and Coin Company.

for perfection in postage stamps was unknown in those days, so he took several large boards and fastened a large assortment of foreign and domestic stamps to them with pins and thumbtacks. He took these to the corner of Broadway and Fulton Street and hung them on the iron fence in front of St. Paul's Church so that people working in the vicinity might make selections during lunch hour.

As the demand for stamps increased, Mr. Brown developed his stock to such an extent that he had a large variety to meet the requirements of all his customers. During the last two decades of his business career he realized a considerable profit, but as a large portion of it was given to church charities he rarely spent money for anything except personal necessities. Although he had a home, he frequently slept and cooked in a small mezzanine above the shop. He was fond of fishing and often brought his catch directly to the store and fried it there, filling the shop with piscatorial odors. Whenever his flowing white beard grew too long, his sister, working with him at the Stamp and Coin Exchange, trimmed it.

In 1876 he established Brown's City Post, to carry letters between the post office and offices of his clients. To prepay the one-cent charge he made for this service, Mr. Brown issued a set of five stamps [2] showing a man pushing a wheelbarrow and inscribed, "City Post— One Cent." The vignette represented the manner in which he carried on this service.

His religious interests were almost as widely known as his philatelic activities. Regardless of weather or business engagements, Mr. Brown devoted a certain number of hours each week to teaching a Bible class at the Five Point Mission near the wharves of the East River, endeavoring to convert the seamen who came there for meals and lodgings.

After his retirement he moved to the Richmond Hill house where he raised vegetable crops for his own use. Excess crops and the flowers were donated to the three churches in the neighborhood. He could not remain aloof from his philatelic interests, which included the writing of many philatelic articles, and in 1920, he even published a booklet, prefaced by a history of Richmond Hill, containing a summary of postage stamps that had been issued to that date. He distributed these to church organizations, schools, and stamp clubs to promote interest in the hobby.

[2] Some students of local stamps of the United States contend that Brown issued the stamps solely as a joke.

After his death the Chatham Phoenix National Bank and Trust Company, executor of his will, removed the contents of the three safes and sold the remaining stamps and coins. The house was allowed to fall into disrepair and ruin. Today the building is entirely gone and weeds have covered the property. And while the cellar hole is almost completely filled in, portions of the three safes, which tumbled into it, still are visible to represent the last tangible relics of America's pioneer philatelic tradesman.

After the birth of the stamp trade with William P. Brown and John W. Scott, and a few others whose names are but vague memories, the United States gradually became one of the most active stamp marts in the world. The men who entered the field during the transitional period of the last quarter of the nineteenth century did more than anyone else to develop not only the framework of a lucrative business, but also to lay the foundations for the hobby millions of us so enjoy today.

These men so loved postage stamps that almost all of them had personal collections; they were active researchers and contributed a major portion of our philatelic literature. They so cherished stamps that they treated each one with a generous measure of love and devotion. In many cases when they obtained a real gem they would either keep it for their own satisfaction or, if they did sell it, would hold it for a customer who would regard it for what it was, rather than turn it over to the first person who would offer them a profit. In those days dealers considered as sacrilegious the idea that a postage stamp was just a commodity to be sold at a standard mark-up over its cost, like a bolt of cloth or a spool of thread. To them every stamp, except the commoner ones, had a soul. It has been said that if these old-timers had been more practical in their trade; if they had been merchandisers instead of dealers with a strong connoisseur's spirit, more of them would have retired with substantial fortunes. But those dealers, perhaps fortunately for us who appreciate their self-sacrifices, devoted a lifetime to their vocation and left it with but a wealth of reputation and memories of affection.

These old-timers virtually lived in their shops, not only to arrange their stocks, but also to delve deep into the literature of the day to explore the problems which an unusual philatelic piece posed. In those days the dealers explained postal history and contributed generously to the magazines which students of this generation use as the basis of modern research. As we read the pages of our half-century-old periodicals, it is amazing to note that no less than seventy-five per cent of our facts and figures have been the works of those dealers.

In those days the shop or office of a stamp dealer was usually an upstairs corner of a low-rent building. It was cluttered as an alchemist's laboratory; as cobwebby and dusty as a sorcerer's den. Of all of them, the one of the late Percy G. Doane, in the Tribune Building on Nassau Street, New York City, was a landmark until the "grand old man" of the stamp trade died only a few years ago. Crammed into this small office were several roll-top desks, three safes, huge mountains of albums from which stamps had been taken for auction sales, monstrous piles of old magazines and philatelic handbooks. The great Percy could hardly be seen behind the narrow counter, and not even he knew everything that was betwixt the heaps of dust-covered accumulations. Yet stamp students from far and wide, millionaire philatelists and ordinary collectors, beat a path to the office of Percy Doane like pilgrims to a shrine. They came not alone to browse through the material that he offered in his auction sales, but rather to partake of the wealth of information he always had at his tongue-tip and which he always willingly shared with serious collectors. It was said that if a person sat in Percy Doane's office for one month he would meet every important philatelist in America, for all of them came there as often as opportunity would afford.

Similar to Mr. Doane in habit and experience was Arthur Tuttle, of Philadelphia; but unlike Percy, Mr. Tuttle was more of a hermit: he had little patience for anyone except a very small circle of friends, and if he were not in the mood, he would without hesitation ask an unknown customer to leave and come back some other time.

The last of the old-time dealers, the Burger Brothers, held out on Nassau Street. Arthur died in 1949, August in 1952. Their tiny office was the last relic of three generations ago; their dealing habits were as unchanged as they were in 1890. They handled only the classic issues, and many of the stamps they owned—and their safes bulged with gems for which a modern collector would give his right hand— were acquired half a century ago. In the tattered envelopes, in the small black stock books, a browser would be likely to find items that cost a few dollars when they were purchased, but which since had leaped to four-figure values.

Old, bent, and gray, the Burger Brothers lived and worked at a pace that was as unhurried as was a buggy of the gas-light days. They *knew* stamps, and if they were convinced that a customer shared their appreciation for a rare specimen, they would pass half a day hunting for one they remembered having obtained years before, but which was hidden in some corner of one of their safes. If a stranger dropped in with the impression that he could buy a bargain for resale, they would decline his business.

In 1932 "Herr General Gus" and I were discussing some early Egyptian official adhesives about which little was known. "Oh, we have some of those around. When I find them, I'll let you know," Mr. Burger told me. Subsequent inquiries disclosed that he had not had time to look for them. "Don't worry, we'll find them one of these days." After two or three years I gave up hope of ever seeing those round adhesives; but along about 1944, I received a package from the Burger Brothers with a note explaining that while looking for something else they came upon the material for which I had waited. The small collection had cost them $50 in 1904. If I wanted it, I might have it for $55!

Then there was William Handshaw, another of the old Nassau Street dealers, who used to buy stamps from banks and import houses and retail them to friends who came to his back-of-the-building shop. There were Henry Calman and Hiram Deats, who are best known for their association with the discovery of many of the United States Postmaster's Provisionals of the 1845–1847 period. There were Rudolphus R. Bogert, and L. W. Durbin, and P. M. Wolsieffer. But the peer of them all was John Murray Bartels, who often is referred to as the schoolmaster of philately.

A member of a prominent family, Bartels began business as a youngster and, after operating small stores in Washington and Boston, migrated to the heart of the stamp trade in New York. More of a philatelic scholar than a businessman, Mr. Bartels devoted a major portion of his time to the study of the stamps in which he was most interested. He made the first organized attempt to classify the beautiful cancellations used by New York clerks of the seventies to postmark mail passing through the foreign post office. His book on the stamped envelopes of the United States long remained the standard reference work and was used as the basis of Prescott Holden Thorp's Crawford Medal-winning work. His books on the stamps of Panama, the Canal Zone, and the Philippines, his articles on the stamps of Guam, Puerto Rico, and many other countries, have been unsurpassed in their scope and completeness of research.

The J. M. Bartels Company was nicknamed "the school of stamp dealers" because of the number of his clerks who subsequently left to establish their own businesses. Coming to Mr. Bartels as neophytes or inexperienced clerks, they soon learned so much about stamps and the stamp business that they soon decided to engage in the same business. Mrs. Catherine L. Manning, curator of the Smithsonian Institution's stamp collection, was one of his first employees, when he still had his Washington, D.C., shop. The late Herman Toaspern, who made quite a reputation for himself in his short lifetime, and George B. Sloane, the eminent United States stamp dealer and appraiser of the Roosevelt Collection, both were "Bartel's graduates." Others whose names are well known in trade and collector circles today are Ed and Sophie Buser, Irwin Heiman and Eugene N. Costales, Christian Dull and Edwin Mueller. Donald D'Amato, today one of New York's more popular philatelic auctioneers, was a postal clerk around 1935 when he applied for a job as bookkeeper with Mr. Bartels. The only thing he knew about stamps was their postal purpose; yet, during five years of employment with the veteran, he left the company, obtained an auctioneer's license, and has come up the ladder of success in this field.

Most of his "students" left only with the knowledge they had acquired and with Mr. Bartels' blessing. One of them, however, left not only with this invaluable asset, but absconded with the Bartels customer list, a substantial portion of his stock, and other tangibles with which to go into business.

Another of the old-timers who will always be remembered is J. J. Klemann, Jr., who early in 1947 was made the first honorary life member of the American Stamp Dealers Association in recognition of his contributions to the trade. With his brother, John, "Jake," as he is familiarly known, formed the famous old Nassau Stamp Company, through whose hands passed many of the greatest stamp collections of the past eras including the Earl of Crawford and Mason accumulations. When the brothers decided to retire a few years ago, the entire Nassau Company was sold. The name and some of the stock was purchased by Lesgor and Reel, and another portion was purchased and auctioned by Harmer, Rooke and Company, of London. John retired to a whirl of travel and entertainment. Jake moved to Georgia to be nearer his son who was an Air Force officer, and there established just a small stamp business to keep himself occupied.

As late as the nineteen twenties, stamp dealers still were hermited in the upper floors of ancient office buildings and, more often than not, a customer risked life and limb as he climbed up dark creaky stairs to reach the cluttered back room of the dealers whose stock he wished to examine in search of new additions to his album. The notable exception was the ground-floor shop of the Scott Stamp and Coin Company, near Grand Central Station in New York. A few other dealers, realizing that cleanliness was an inducement, had offices that were reasonably attractive, stocks that were neatly arranged in file cabinets and safes, but in those days the collector had to know where he was going, for neither window displays or ground-floor stores attracted the passer-by.

But with the advance of the hobby, progressive dealers envisioned the wisdom of merchandising principles, and soon the street-level shop and attractively arranged lobby displays (for those firms which could not get down-stairs stores) began to appear all over the city.

All of a sudden, it seemed, the stamp business became as entrenched a trade as candy stores, dress shops, and drugstores. The modern merchandising principles used by merchants of other commodities were employed by stamp dealers. Advertising increased; walls were laden with well-lighted displays of the latest sets, packets, and bargain offers; stocks were arranged according to professional systems to save time and labor in filling orders. In short, the tradesman had replaced the collector-dealer.

The stock of the dealers changed, too. Relatively few of the newer tradesmen endeavored to stock stamps of the entire world. Like collectors, who realized the futility of trying to fill an album with *all* the stamps of the world, they specialized to handle only the material of several countries or groups of countries.

Today there are those dealers who maintain specialized stocks of stamps and the collector who confines his own albums to a certain few countries will do well to contact these supply sources, since stocks usually are much more complete and prices a little closer to actual market values.

There are firms that deal exclusively in stamps of the United States and possessions, in those of British North America, of Latin America, Switzerland, the Netherlands, Scandinavia, the British or French colonies, and so on. With the increase in topical collecting [3] a certain number of dealers have gone into this field, offering

[3] The American Topical Society, 3306 North 50th Street, Milwaukee, Wisconsin, publishes a monthly magazine and numerous handbooks for this specialty, and dealers featuring such stocks advertise therein.

"thematic" stamps selected according to the subjects depicted in the designs, rather than the lands which issued them.

Other dealers specialize in air-mail stamps, still others in first-day covers or postal stationery (stamped envelopes, postal cards, air-letter sheets, newspaper wrappers, and so on).

Back in the 'twenties, two brothers, H. Ellis and Stephen F. Harris, decided to enter the stamp business as a career. But instead of accepting the traditional manner of doing business, as was customary in those days, these young men applied to their new venture the principles they had learned in commercial schools.

Engaging in mass production schemes and Sears-Roebuck methods of mail-order trade, they set up a stamp business that was unlike any one of the established firms in existence at the time. Issuing well-illustrated, annotated, and descriptive price lists, they sought and found business in the far corners of the United States. At first they offered only sets in the low-priced and medium range; but so successful was their campaign that today they enjoy an enviable record throughout the world.

Today the H. E. Harris Company occupies three entire floors of the large Transit Building in Boston, where some two hundred employees are engaged in various departments of the business. In addition, they have a building in New Hampshire, where rent is lower, enabling them to make up sets and packets in mass quantities for sale at the lowest possible overhead. Their advertising is carried not only in English-language publications, but in stamp magazines published for French, German, Spanish, Portuguese, and Arabic-speaking peoples abroad. Their present price lists are printed and distributed by the millions, and so accurate are the prices quoted that many collectors use them as actual catalogues for their own reference.

Unusual as it may seem, the chief concern of the firm today is not getting more customers, but rather getting enough material to keep their present clientele supplied. Because they have such an extensive business they offer to buy collections and accumulations of any size.

Not too long ago, when one stamp dealer had to give up a well-established business of British colonial issues, Harris purchased the entire stock outright at a sum which ran into six figures! The firm also keeps in touch with foreign postal administrations and often buys remainders of stocks of old issues just before they are taken off sale and replaced by new issues.

Most phenomenal firm that has made international philatelic history is Gimbel's Stamp Center, in New York. In 1931, Jacques Minkus, who had come from Germany and Paris, persuaded Gimbel Brothers to set up a stamp department to cater to the needs of many persons who had become enthusiastic collectors.

The store was somewhat skeptical, but it risked a trial by allowing Mr. Minkus and his wife to set up his wares on a concession basis on the corner of a counter in the book department. At first Mr. Minkus sold stamps only to youngsters whose mothers had to buy something to compensate their offspring for having trailed them on shopping expeditions. Presently, however, indefatigable efforts and constructive ideas established Gimbel's Stamp Center as a popular rendezvous for more advanced collectors, too.

When Mr. Minkus realized that available stamp albums did not fully satisfy the demands of new collectors who were entering the hobby in such huge numbers, he decided to publish his own. At first he produced specialty books for stamps portraying Franklin D. Roosevelt, stamps issued for the Pan American Union, United States commemoratives, and other popular specialties. Finally he entered the general field and turned out albums for stamps of the world. His greatest achievement was the "Supreme Master Global Stamp Album," a set of two massive volumes with spaces for 76,000 different stamps of the world.

Still later he decided to get out a specialized United States Stamp Catalogue which describes, illustrates, and prices stamps, and can be used as a price guide. He then produced a world-wide catalogue and now, for the first time in nearly a century, the United States has two standard price guides.

All of the Minkus publications have experienced immediate success, not only because each of them presents a modern approach, but because annual supplements are regularly and promptly published so that each of them always is right up to the moment.

Today the stamp department of Gimbel's in New York covers a huge section of the main floor and is one of the store's most lucrative departments because of its constantly large number of customers. In addition Mr. Minkus has established similar stamp departments in the Gimbel stores in Philadelphia and Milwaukee; in

Marshall Field & Company, Chicago; Jordan Marsh Company, in Boston; Rich's, in Atlanta; Kaufmann's in Pittsburgh, and the J. L. Hudson Company, in Detroit.

Mr. Minkus always is ready to purchase important material from large collections. He was one of the big buyers at the sales conducted by H. R. Harmer, Inc., to dispose of the holdings of the late President Franklin D. Roosevelt and ex-King Farouk, of Egypt. His large purchases then were broken up into small lots so that even a youngster with a limited budget might purchase at least a single stamp that once was owned by such famous philatelic personalities.

But of all the firms that have developed in recent years those specializing in auction sales have been the most spectacular. Auctions have been with us many years, but this form of disposing of stamp holdings was usually restricted to the clearance of collections by estates to whom they were left by deceased collectors because that seemed the only way in which fair-sale values could be established for tax purposes. Within the last two decades, however, it has seemed that almost every person who had a collection to sell offered it under the hammer. In some cases, dealers offered their own stock in this manner, hoping to move material which they could not sell in the normal retail way.

Until the popularity of auctioneering reached its present all-time peak, we had comparatively few dealers who were exclusively philatelic auctioneers. Among these few were the late Percy G. Doane, Max Ohlman, Max Pool, and Hugh C. Barr, all of New York; Daniel Kelleher, of Boston, and one or two others in Chicago and San Francisco.

With the threatening clouds of war hovering over Europe in 1938–39, the British Government encouraged several established English auctioneers to migrate to the United States and procure desperately needed American dollars for foreign exchange credit. Accordingly, just before Hitler moved into Poland, New York Offices were opened by H. R. Harmer, Ltd., Harmer, Rooke & Co., Ltd.,[4] and Robson Lowe, Ltd., all of whom had important auction businesses in London.

Their entry into the American market at first was tolerated as a gesture of Anglo-American amity. Later, however, some American

[4] While the names of the firms are similar, they have no connection with each other.

dealers considered it an intrusion. It was easier to say that the British firms were taking away business than to admit that they really got the business because they offered more experienced service than the firms who were here.

The H. R. Harmer Organization's rise to the fore of American auctioneering has been nothing short of sensational. During the war years, when the sons of the founder were serving in the British Armed Forces,[5] the New York branch was operated by Mr. H. R. Harmer himself. Following V.E.-Day, however, the old man retired and his place was taken by Bernard Harmer, who really put the firm on the map in this country.

In galleries on Fifty-seventh Street and Madison Avenue they built auction premises that were unprecedented in size and decor. Because they offered unexcelled service they were selected to sell some of the most important collections in existence. Most notable was the disposition of the vast accumulation built by the late President Franklin D. Roosevelt, the sale of which attracted more people than any other stamp auction in history. The firm also was selected by the Egyptian Government to sell the collection built by the late King Fouad I and continued by ex-King Farouk. The greatest of the H. R. Harmer triumphs was the disposal of the fabulous Alfred H. Caspary collection of great classic rarities of the world, following the owner's death, in January, 1955. Appraised at "about $2,000,000," this most valuable lot of stamps ever offered was broken into sixteen sections that would be put under the hammer over a period of nearly three years. The first three sales, held at the Hotel Ambassador, in New York, surprised even the optimists, for the stamps offered brought in excess of $730,000, considerably more than had been expected.

Even though its original galleries were planned to accommodate "business for the next twenty years," the firm's sales were so great that in 1955, it had to move to even larger quarters, at 6 West 48th Street, where it now occupies an entire floor. The premises are completely air conditioned and scientifically designed to handle nothing but philatelic auction sales.

[5] Cyril Harmer, an officer of the Royal Navy, was taken prisoner during the Battle of Crete and was confined to a Nazi prison camp from which he was released in 1945 by American forces in Germany.

[8] Philatelic Philanthropy

Stamp collecting is rich in therapeutic value, and collectors as a rule are generous humanitarians, for long before the global war, many of them, as individuals or as members of stamp societies, worked to bring the pleasure, relaxation, and recreation of the hobby to persons less fortunate than themselves.

In Brooklyn for example, DeWitt Frankel used to devote every Saturday to visits with youngsters who were at the Brooklyn Hospital for Incurable Diseases, bringing with him envelopes full of duplicate stamps which he distributed to the patients and which they mounted in their albums (which he also provided) during the week.

In California, Garner Curran, a former newspaperman, began a correspondence club for shut-ins, and over a period of several years built up a regular association through which invalids and the bed-ridden exchanged stamps and letters to absorb the time that hung so heavily on their hands.

The Association of New Jersey Stamp Clubs organized what they called a "Rainbow Division." This group of volunteers from the various clubs that form the association regularly visited local hospitals and orphan asylums aiding folks, young and old, to collect postage stamps as an avocation.

The Masonic Order regularly sends substantial supplies of stamps and accessories to its home for invalids and indigent aged. The Metropolitan Life Insurance Company Stamp Club, comprised of employees who are philatelists in the home office, made a special feature of distributing stamps among the inmates of the sanitorium which the company maintains for tuberculars in the Adironacks.

Some collectors even visited penal institutions and converted many a prisoner to the hobby. On one occasion Warden Lawes of Sing Sing told me that the organization of a stamp club among the men in that prison had done much to redirect the men's minds along proper channels. In fact, one fellow who had been sentenced to a rather long term had become so interested in stamps that he not only was paroled before his sentence was up, but obtained a position with a stamp firm after his release. I have met that man at Sing Sing and since, and a better reformed criminal never left any jail.

But the greatest humanitarian project ever undertaken by organized philately and the men and women who make it up is Stamps for the Wounded. Soon after war was declared in 1941, Charles J. Heck, a member of the New York Stock Exchange Stamp Club, proposed that stamp collectors should send their duplicates to various hospitals so that men who were interested in the hobby before they entered service might resume the collection of stamps while recuperating from wounds or disease. His idea was not readily accepted, but several individuals on their own initiative began visiting hospitals near their homes and doing just that. The Teaneck Stamp Club of New Jersey was the first philatelic organization to undertake a stamp collectors' program as a group project, and for more than two years volunteers visited Camp Shanks to supply men there with the tools of the hobby.

In 1943 *Life* Magazine carried a mention of how I was independently working at Halloran Hospital (on Staten Island), and as a result Charless Hahn, then editor of *Weekly Philatelic Gossip*, published an editorial in that magazine, urging the two largest stamp societies in the United States to investigate the possibilities of undertaking this project on a national scale. The officers of both the American Philatelic Society and the Society of Philatelic Americans appointed committees which were asked to study the possibilities and report back at the 1944 conventions.

The Society of Philatelic Americans held their conclave first, and in Chicago the committee resolved that it should be tried. This committee went to Milwaukee the following week and met with the other committee, and when they found that all were in favor of the idea, the matter was brought to vote and unanimously carried on the convention floor.

And so, on August 19, 1944, Stamps for the Wounded was born. Within a month nearly eight hundred stamp collectors and dealers, and some persons who were not philatelists, but who had read of the project in the press, had volunteered to do the work.

A national office was set up in New York, where Mrs. Ogden Reid provided, without cost, office space and telephone and mail service, in the Herald Tribune building. Regional offices were established in the twenty largest cities of the country, and local units were set up in virtually every town which had a naval or military hospital.

Drives were initiated to collect stamps and philatelic material for hospitalized servicemen. Collectors volunteered to take the contributions to the hospitals and work closely with the American Red Cross to distribute them among the patients who either had been interested in stamp collecting before their confinement or who sought an escape from the long hours of staring at white ceilings and black futures.

Within a year stamp collecting was an established branch of recreational therapy programs in nearly eighty hospitals. Within two years over twelve million postage stamps had been distributed along with thousands of albums, catalogues, hinges, watermark detectors, perforation gauges and other accessories without charge to a single servicemen, the Red Cross, or the hospitals. The stamps were contributed by individuals and firms which usually have a large volume of business mail; the accessories, by stamp collectors and dealers; the cost of printing, postage, and express shipments was paid by stamp clubs, societies, and individual donors. Never once was a single cent solicited!

When hospital jurisdiction passed from the Red Cross to the Veterans Administration, the therapeutic effectiveness of the work was considered so important that Stamps for the Wounded was asked not only to continue, but to expand its services. "No other recreational project in any hospital has done so much to rehabilitate our patients," General Carl Gray, head of the VA, declared. By the end of 1955, this group had distributed more than sixteen million stamps and fifty tons of albums, catalogues, and other accessories to some 50,000 servicemen, seventy per cent of whom had never collected stamps before. Today Stamps for the Wounded has volunteer workers in every VA hospital in the nation.

But even while this worthy permanent project has continued in operation, stamp collectors have used their avocation to assist in other patriotic and civic causes. On several occasions national groups have sponsored benefit auction sales of donated stamps in order to raise welfare funds.

When the Red Cross needed extra funds following World War II, $11,768 was obtained for a group of stamps which collectors had generously donated to a special auction sale. In England the Royal Philatelic Society and the British Traders' Association raised about £50,000 ($200,000) through a series of similar sales between 1939 and 1945 for the benefit of the St. James Fund.

Most spectacular was the Atlas Sky Merchant cover project. In

1948, when the Atlas Corporation planned a global flight to build foreign sales, of its products, I was asked to arrange for the carriage of 5,000 air-letter sheets for the benefit of the Cancer Fund. The famous DC-4 visited thirty countries on five continents on a 100-day, 50,000-mile journey, and at each stop each of the covers was specially postmarked. One of them was offered to every person who made a donation of "$1 or more" to the fund. By the time all were distributed we were able to send a donation of $20,000 to the fight against Cancer.

In 1953, when the Herald Tribune Fresh Air Fund needed more money to send underprivileged city youngsters to summer camps, director Frederick Lewis asked me whether philatelists might be called upon to help. An ordinary auction seemed too prosaic. We wrote one hundred letters to as many of the world's most famous collectors, asking each one to contribute a single stamp from his personal collection, attaching it to a calling card or letterhead (to establish its source). Never before had so many celebrities contributed to a single human need. Donations came from such persons as Prince Bernhard, Grand Duchess Charlotte, Cardinal Spellman, the Duke of Windsor, General Mark Clark, Jascha Heifitz, President Perón, ex-King Carol (whose donation of nine lots arrived two days before his sudden death), and numerous others. The only person to whom a request was sent but who did not reply was Queen Elizabeth II! These lots were offered at a gala auction sale in the ballroom of the Hotel Astor and enough money was raised to send several hundred children to camp that summer!

Sweden's stamps honor King Gustav's birthday, poet Esaias Tegner's death, and the eight hundredth anniversary of the Lund Cathedral.

Part III
Stamps and Collecting

[9] Sources of Postage Stamps

Usually the first question asked by a person who thinks he may become interested in the collection of postage stamps as a hobby is, "But where can I get stamps?"

The answer is simple: "Almost anywhere."

That is the answer I would give without the slightest hesitation to anyone who might ask me, for I can speak from experience. Perhaps I began the hobby a few years earlier than many readers of this book, but those same sources still are available to anyone who cares to seek them out. My father before me was a collector during his school days, and it was largely he who encouraged me to use a bit of effort to acquire new specimens.

Just a few months before I entered my first grade at grammar school I was sent to a small laundry shop on Grand Avenue, just off Second, in Astoria, Long Island. As I watched Charlie manipulating his abacus to calculate the cost of the shirts he had ironed, my eye was attracted by an envelope to which two blue stamps were affixed. The design of a very strange ship on them intrigued me, and in a few moments the whole envelope and the stamps were mine and I took them home as carefully as I would have a new Sweet Caporal picture card portraying Ty Cobb. Some time later, on an errand to Landers' hardware store across the street, I spied an envelope with some more stamps on it. When I asked for it, old Mr. Landers seemed tickled. "Of course you can have it," he told me. "But, my you're a small fellow to be a stamp collector."

My father had never shown me his album before, so I never knew that stamp collecting was already an established hobby. To me these were just something unusual which the other fellows on the block did not have. Before I left I had been given a short salestalk on the fun of collecting stamps. "I'm busy now," Mr. Landers said as I left, "but if you'll tell your father to bring you around here some evening I'll show you how to collect stamps."

Getting back there immediately became the most important object in my life, and as Dad had been a collector I had little trouble in convincing him that he ought to take me to see Mr. Landers that very night. The old gentleman first showed me his album and opened an entirely new ambition in my life. He then pulled envelopes from various corners of the room, picked out a couple dozen stamps, and gave them to me. That was the nucleus of my collection, and soon, under the guidance of my father, I got my first lessons on how to learn from what countries the various stamps came.

From then on, every neighbor, every friend, every shopkeeper became a victim of my request for stamps from mail. Our Bohemian janitor, our Spanish street cleaner, our Italian fruit peddler, our Greek candy-store owner, and the Englishman next door—all of them, and every visitor to our apartment, were asked for postage stamps. And everyone of them usually came through with one or two each time I asked. With remarkable speed the five-cent notebook into which I placed each new specimen began to fill up. Within two years it could hold no more and I had to begin a second.

By the time I was ten or eleven years old, I was devoting more time to my stamp album than to my homework, and many were the times that I was threatened by my father, who insisted that if I continued at that pace my album would be consigned to a locked closet. But on the other hand, when report cards came around and my geography and history marks were up around the top of the class, there was no limit to the amount of encouragement I received. There was only one hitch to Dad's encouragement. While he urged me to procure more stamps, he never once allowed me to *purchase* stamps from the few dealers who were in existence then.

"If you want really to appreciate postage stamps, you've got to get them yourself."

Every birthday, every Christmas, and on many other occasions, among my gifts were stationery and two- and five-cent postage stamps, with which I could write letters to domestic and foreign firms who might be likely to help me along.

Sunday after Sunday was devoted to the arduous task of writing those letters, telling presidents of corporations, consuls, ambassadors, and even royalty about my juvenile interest in this hobby and asking whether they would mail me some stamps that had reached them on mail. The response was tremendous. None of the returns was large, but the number of small contributions to my collection must have run into the hundreds. When Queen Marie of Romania was the subject of a magazine article and mention was made of her interest in postage stamps, Father suggested her name, and of course I wrote. Almost by return mail I received not only a small packet of canceled stamps, but a kind letter and a complete unused set of every Romanian stamp in use at the time.

I once wrote to our own Department of State. A short while later I received a large manila envelope which contained a swell letter signed by Secretary Charles E. Hughes himself and an assortment of stamps which had me in clouds for days. There were large pictorials from African nations and high denominations from European lands, the likes of which I had never believed I would ever own. I replied immediately to thank Mr. Hughes, and from that time until he relinquished his post, the mailman delivered a similar envelope every third Tuesday.

The collection grew steadily and my correspondence with foreign lands amazed even our postmaster; and, though I frequently went far beyond my allowance to pay for the postage and had to do a sales job on Father, he always kept me supplied. He would give me fifty cents to buy stamps for ten foreign letters, but never a dime to send away for some colorful pictorial that I thought I must have.

By the time I was in high school my craving for stamps had developed even further. During the summer holidays I would go into the city and canvass one large building after another. I began at the Battery and methodically worked my way uptown, starting at the top floor of a building and descending until I had entered every office whose name suggested that foreign mail might be received. The receptionist of some firms promised to save the stamps on incoming mail; some said they were already being saved for another employee; still others told me bluntly that they could not be bothered. I obtained Persian, Syrian, and Lebanese stamps from rug importers around Madison Square; German and Czechoslovakian stamps from toy merchants in Union Square; South-American issues from rubber companies around Columbus Circle; Asiatic stamps from banks in Wall Street.

By that time I had joined a stamp club comprised chiefly of adult collectors [1] and I found no difficulty in swapping off my duplicates

[1] When I was but fourteen years old a member of the Brooklyn Stamp Club, second oldest philatelic organization in the country, invited me, at the suggestion of a member friend, to visit a meeting. Before the evening was over the president told me that although the club was intended only for adults, he

—I had many of them—for material which either was obsolete or which did not come on mail addressed to firms who kept me supplied. By 1926 my collection boasted over 35,000 different stamps and not one of them had cost me a single cent! Donors to that collection included such names as Martin Johnson, who used to send me stamps from his camp in Kenya; Admiral Richard E. Byrd, who carried a letter from New York to Ver sur Mer on his trans-Atlantic flight; Dr. James Clark of the American Museum of Natural History; Charles Denzau, assistant to the president of the National City Bank; Carl Hagenbeck, the animal dealer of Hamburg; Baron Kurt von Gonthard, the German sportsman; Sven Hedin, the explorer; and a multitude of similarly distinguished persons.

But even if you find it impossible to exploit such sources of supply, consuls, government agencies, business firms, and banks still help youngsters along by giving them stamps from incoming mail. And there are many other ways in which to obtain the items you need to begin a stamp collection of your own.

Today there are stamp dealers in every city in the country; department stores and even the branches of national chain shops usually have assortments of stamp sets and packets. If you live in a small town where none of these may be found, advertisements published in general magazines published for youngsters, and such others as *Good Housekeeping, Collier's* and *Popular Science* will give you the names of reliable stamp dealers.

Stamps are sold in mixtures, packets, sets, and individually. A *mixture*, no matter what adjectival name is given to it, still is exactly what its name implies. It is a lot of stamps, usually still affixed to the paper on which they were mailed, which is made up according to weight. Since no attempt has been made to sort the stamps, in a mixture packet of, say, 1000 stamps, you may find only a few dozen varieties with a number of duplicates. For a beginner, or a person who enjoys hunting for shade varieties or unusual postmarks, this is an exceptionally economical way of obtaining the beginning of a stamp collection.

A *packet* consists of an assortment of postage stamps, all of which are different varieties; so when you purchase a packet of 1000 different stamps of the world, you will get just that. Packets are made

was convinced I knew enough about the hobby to be eligible provided I could obtain my father's permission to join. For nearly twenty years I was the only juvenile ever to be a regular member of that club.

up according to stamps of the world; stamps of a certain country or groups of countries, or according to subject—for instance twenty-five different animal or ship stamps. In the early stages of the hobby this is an economical way to procure specimens. But since packets are made up by large firms who must hire inexperienced philatelists, you can rarely expect to find specimens which are perfect enough to merit a permanent place in your collection. They are either the cheapest varieties or poor specimens of better types: the kind whose condition does not warrant their being used to make up sets.

Sets consist of stamps issued at one time by a postal administration to serve some postal need. The current set of United States stamps, for instance, comprises all denominations from the half-cent to the $5. Sets are made up by stamp dealers and are offered as "complete" or "broken."

In making up such sets the dealer is usually honest about it and will advertise only what he has to sell. Therefore you must be careful in purchasing sets, lest through your own misinterpretation or understanding of an advertisement you are disappointed when you get something less than you expected.

When the word *complete* is used, it means that the set contains every stamp issued at the time, or as it is listed in the standard catalogue. Sometimes, by chance, a single denomination of a set is quite rare, or perhaps the higher denominations of the issue are too expensive. A set then will be offered as "complete except for the two-penny," or "complete to the 25 cent."

If you live in a city where a stamp dealer has a shop, you can visit him and look through his stock for specimens you need and want. Invariably the dealer will have an album on the counter in which the spaces are kept filled with the proper issues. You look through this volume, pick out the stamps you need, and pay for them. Or you can make a list of the stamps you want to fill spaces in your own album, submit it to the dealer, and let him supply them. In submitting such a *want list* it is always important that you specify whether you would prefer used or unused specimens and the condition [2] you will accept. It is wise, too, to submit a supplementary list, because relatively few dealers have *all* stamps in stock at one time and this will enable them to send a larger selection.

By far the most convenient and popular method of purchasing postage stamps, especially for persons who live in small towns or

[2] Condition of a stamp is most important and is discussed in Chapter 11.

suburbs of larger ones, is through what is generally called *approval service*. Many dealers realize the importance of filling the needs of rural residenced collectors and so offer a mail-order form of business. Approvals, as they are popularly known, are sheets or small booklets filled with postage stamps, each one of which is marked with a catalogue number to identify it and a price at which the collector may purchase it. These are sent to persons who may select the stamps they desire and return the rest, together with a remittance for those taken, within ten days.

To obtain such business, many firms that specialize in it offer premiums to those collectors who express a willingness to order stamps on approval. The premiums usually range from a hard-to-get postage stamp, which is offered to "approval applicants" without charge, to a regular stamp or set of stamps that is sold at a substantial discount from the normal price.

When sending for approvals in answer to advertisements, there are several things the collector should do to obtain best service. He should specify both the types of stamps he is most likely to buy and the amount of money he can afford to spend in a given period of time. If he does this, the dealer will send him—on approval—those items which will fit into both album and budget. Unless a dealer knows these facts he is likely to submit Belgian stamps when you are interested in only British Colonies; or he may send you items that are beyond your immediate financial reach. This naturally results in a waste of time and effort to the dealer and a disappointment to you.

After you have received your first selection from the dealer, you will be wise to examine it immediately and make returns promptly, at least within the time allowed you or even sooner if possible. If for some reason you are not sent the type of material that appeals to you, explain the situation. There is nothing a dealer dislikes more than dunning his customers for delinquency in returning material that was sent on approval in good faith. Promptness results in better service and treatment; delinquency will ultimately lead the dealer to refrain not only from sending more material, but also to place your name on a "black list," which is circulated among the trade to protect other dealers from trusting their stamps with collectors who fail to keep up their end of the implied bargain.

Yet another method of purchasing postage stamps is the auction service. Philatelic auctions have been an established form of sale for many decades; but during recent years this phase has become most popular simply because both vendor and buyer know that they are getting all that is possible.

Virtually every important stamp firm has an auction service. In fact, several philatelic auctioneers confine their activities to this form of business.

When a person has a collection or a large accumulation of postage stamps to sell which cannot be disposed of to a single buyer for one reason or another, he may offer it through an auctioneer. The auctioneer will accept the lot on consignment and undertake to sell it on a flat, pre-determined commission: usually twenty per cent of the gross receipts.

Once a large lot is handled by an auctioneer, he and his staff break it up into *lots* of single stamps, sets, or the stamps of a whole country which experience has taught him will sell best. These lots then are described briefly—the condition of the stamp, the catalogue number and quotation, and such other details as will give the prospective bidder a good idea of what he may expect if his bid obtains the material. These descriptions are published in a catalogue, copies of which are mailed to persons who have previously bid on the particular dealer's sales, or who have requested a copy in answer to an advertisement. Except in special cases, auction catalogues are available without cost to serious collectors.

The dealer then makes up a *book* in which all mail bids on every lot may be entered as soon as they arrive from collectors. In the meantime you have received a catalogue, perused the descriptions of each lot, and determined which of the material you want and how much you are willing to pay for it. You then fill out the *bid sheet*, that accompanied the catalogue by writing in the number of the lot and the highest price you are willing to bid for it. The completed bid sheet is then mailed to the auctioneer. If you are known to the dealer, nothing further is required. If this is the first time you are bidding, you should also include the names of other dealers with whom you have done business or that of the bank with whom you deal.

When your bid sheet arrives at the dealer's office it is given a number, and each of your bids is entered in the aforementioned book like this: "64/$5." By the time the auction is actually held, all of the mail bids have been entered in the same manner so that at one glance the dealer can tell how much has been bid by out-of-town customers for each lot in the sale.

When the auction is staged in the auction room of the dealer's place of business, or in a hall hired for the occasion, a clerk keeps track of the book bids, acting as a personal agent for each of the mail bidders.

When the auctioneer announces the lots, the keeper of the book announces the price at which bidding is open. This figure is determined by the clerk: if there are two or more bidders on the same lot, the starting bid is usually a slight advance over the second highest bid, regardless of how much the top bidder has submitted as his limit. If only one mail bidder has made an offer, the clerk starts the bidding at what he considers a fair price for the lot in question. If no bid has been received through the mail, the clerk so tells the auctioneer.

The bidding is then thrown open to the *floor*—to those collectors and dealers who have come to the sale to offer their bids in person. If the price at which the lot is started is higher than that which any floor bidder is willing to pay, it is knocked down to *order*. If, however (and this usually is the case), the floor bidders advance the starting price, the clerk will continue to bid in behalf of the mail client until he has reached the limit of the figure specified. At the end of the sale, those lots which have been procured for mail bidders are dispatched together with a bill and the bidder is expected to make full payment for the lots within three days of receipt of the material.

All of the larger auction firms—especially those that are only philatelic auctioneers and do no counter or approval business—are meticulous in acting in behalf of the mail buyer. At all times they will treat with absolute integrity the confidence of the client, so that the collector in Pocatello, Idaho, will have the same advantage as the person who attends a New York sale in person.

Many times I have found offered at auction sales some Egyptian item which I knew to be very rare and which I needed to fill a gap in my collection. I have never hesitated to submit a substantial bid to the auction firms with whom I deal, even though I knew that none but a fellow specialist would even approach that figure. At one time I remember seeing a rather common stamp—one that retails at about $3—in an auction sale of the late Percy Doane. This stamp was particularly interesting and valuable to me because it was obliterated with an exceedingly rare type of post mark. To me that stamp was worth up to $15, and that was the bid I mailed to Mr. Doane. After the sale was over, I received the stamp for $3.50; apparently no other mail or floor bidder had wanted it as badly as I. Mr. Doane opened the bidding at $3, a floor bidder raised it by 25 cents, and Mr. Doane, acting on my behalf, raised it another 25 cents and obtained it for me.

But what about the vendor, you ask. If he had sold that same stamp to me he would have obtained $11.75 more than the auctioneer obtained. That is true, but how is any person who sells a collection of postage stamps to know where he can sell a single item that is of particular interest and value to a fellow collector who is an advanced specialist? The stamp was valuable to me only because it had a rare type of postmark which only an Egyptian student would recognize or want. It was sold for even a price above the normal retail market of the *stamp*.

When you bid at auction, however, do not expect to get bargains. Occasionally you can buy certain stamps a bit cheaper in this way than you could at a dealer's counter, but this is due solely to the fact that the stamps offered at an auction *must* be sold and you may just happen to be bidding for material without competition. As a general rule from five to ten thousand collectors and dealers have received the catalogue and, like yourself, have entered bids on popular items they want. Some will enter *piker* bids; others will make offers that closely approximate market values; and still others will bid a trifle more. I have seen collectors bid 50 cents for stamps that any dealer would gladly buy for $5. Perhaps one time in a thousand such a ridiculous bid will be successful, but if you want a stamp which you know is regularly worth $10, you are wasting your time and the auctioneer's by sending him a bid of only a fraction of that amount.

Because auctioneers try to break a large collection into individual lots that will bring at least $2, there is usually a large portion of the collection left that is composed of stamps so common that they cannot be offered as sets or single items. These are usually left on the original album pages and bunched into "lots by countries." These are the lots that will most interest the beginner, for they are of marvelous value in forming the nucleus of a collection quite cheaply. They are offered with but brief descriptions, such as the following, which is taken from an auction catalogue: "Foreign, 19th and 20th Century, miscellaneous accumulation of 445 stamps (105 are unused), majority Asiatic countries. Catalogue value is $95."

If such a lot seems to be of interest to you, you can do either of two things: (1) ask the dealer to let you examine the lot, or (2) sub-

mit a *blind* bid consisting of a figure you would be willing to pay
All auctioneers will send lots for inspection provided you stand th
cost of postage *both* ways and agree to return the lots within one da
of their receipt. In bidding blind, you may rest assured that ordinaril
such mixed lots sell for about half catalogue value if the stamps i
them are in very fine condition.

Cachet postmarks are prepared for special events. At left is one used b
Egypt during the First Philatelic Exhibition at Cairo, in 1946. Upp
right: Applied by Curaçao to commemorate first air-mail flight. Low
right: One of Switzerland's cachets to advertise its resorts.

[10] Stamps with Personality

Stamps are much more than pretty, delicately designed pictures or bits of paper imprinted with colored inks which will fetch definite cash values in the philatelic market. Every stamp in your album, whether it is a common current one or a great classic gem, reflects a chapter in the history of mankind or a dramatic episode of its own, and a study of the stories behind it will open vast vistas of other lands and peoples, and thus become the gateway to endless hours of absorbing interest.

For into every design that ever was conceived to decorate a small piece of paper as a frank to transport mail went reason and calculated purpose; and however crude the product, it portrays world events, power, and sometimes even pathos. Stamps indeed have not only human interest but also character and personality.

Because the quest for the stories behind stamp designs is a pleasure the collector should enjoy for himself, we shall not attempt to compile a compendium of such stories. Indeed, we could not do so if we tried, because a lifetime would not be long enough to do even a partially complete job. We shall therefore merely touch upon a few of the stories.

The One-Cent British Guiana

There are other stamps as rare, others with a more definite pedigree, and others much more attractive, but to the stamp collector and layman alike, the one-cent British Guiana error of 1856 is the aristocrat of stampdom. This tiny stamp, crudely imprinted on magenta-colored paper, initialed EDW (E. D. Wright, Clerk of the Colonial Post Office), and postmarked, "Demarara," has been so widely publicized that almost everyone has heard of it at one time or another. Actually it is an imperfect ugly duckling, the history of whose issuance is shrouded in doubt and uncertainty.

Located in the northeast corner of South America, British Guiana had a postal system of sorts dating from 1783, and postage stamps were adopted on July 1, 1850, just a decade after the birth of the motherland's Penny Black. This first issue, known as *Spool Tops*, were but impressions of a handstamp, inscribed with "British Guiana" and the denomination, on paper of various colors. Subsequently a set was lithographed by Waterlow and Sons, England, and shipped to the colony for use. In 1856, however, supplies ran low, and the Baum and Dallas firm, a local printer in Georgetown, was engaged to produce provisionals for use until fresh supplies could be obtained from London. The result was primitive, for in those days art was only a secondary factor in making postage stamps. "British Guiana Postage" and the denomination were placed around the framed center at top, bottom, left, and right respectively. The center, inclosed in a single frame line, showed the picture of a sailing ship and the colony's motto, *Damus Petimusque Vicissim* (We Seek and We Give in Turn).

Collectors knew of four-cent values of this set, for a number of them were found; but reports of a one-cent value, printed on magenta-tinted paper, were not published until 1873, when a fifteen-year-old lad named L. Vernon Vaughn (perhaps Vaughan) located the stamp in question while going through old correspondence in his native Georgetown. History does not record whether Vaughn clipped the four corners of the stamp or whether he found it in its present mutilated condition. At any rate, he had it in his stamp album when a more advanced collector, named Neil McKenner, spotted it and offered him the equivalent of $1.25. Certain that he would uncover another, Vaughn sold this stamp, and shortly afterward the entire McKenner collection was shipped to Glasgow for sale, where it eventually was purchased by Thomas Ridpath, the Liverpool dealer, for £120, including the unique one-cent error.

The stamp was then removed from the collection and sold at an undisclosed figure to the fabulous Count Ferrary. From that day to this, no other copy of a one-cent printed on magenta was ever located,[1] nor have records of the post office or printer disclosed

[1] In the October, 1938, issue of the *Stamp and Cover Collectors Review*, Colonel August Dietz published a letter which he had received from an anonymous writer who mailed it in New York City on October 1, 1938. The letter stated that it was written by "an old man" who agreed to "Mr. Arthur Hind . . . that he would keep his secret," and went on to relate a story that he, too, owned a copy of the British Guiana one-cent of 1856—He had had one in his album "for many years," and that, after debating what to do, he had taken his specimen to Mr. Hind in 1928. He had offered the stamp to Mr. Hind for "a big sum." According to the letter, Mr. Hind had said, "If it's worth that much to you, it's worth twice that to me, provided this is never known."

whether such a denomination was authorized or knowingly produced.

About the time the Ferrary hoard was offered for sale in Paris, Arthur Hind, a textile manufacturer of Utica, who had been spending a considerable amount of money for postage stamps, either on his own initiative or upon the advice of his philatelic secretary, William Kennett, decided to buy the most expensive stamp at the Paris auction, just for the sake of the publicity that was certain to accrue.

Stamp after rare stamp was purchased, but each time the price went higher. Finally the British Guiana came up, and when the auctioneer's hammer fell, Gerard Gilbert, the Parisian dealer to whom the sale had been entrusted, announced that Arthur Hind had purchased it for the equivalent of $32,500 in American money.

The news of such a figure being paid for a single postage stamp was cabled to the world. Overnight Arthur Hind became an internationally known figure. Perhaps owing to the imagination of a reporter who wanted color for his story, perhaps, to an honest mistake, the story added that King George V was the under bidder; this, however, was entirely erroneous. The agent representing the royal philatelist did make a few bids when the stamp was offered, but as the price soared higher only Mr. Hind and M. Burrus, an Alsatian industrialist, vied with each other. It was M. Burrus, whom the Utica collector beat.

Mr. Hind owned that stamp for many years and on several occasions exhibited it at important national and international shows. In fact, after he purchased it he had facsimiles made up in faithful color reproduction which he distributed to intimate friends from time to time. Mr. Hind died in 1933, and Mr. Kennett and Charles J. Phillips were retained by the estate to liquidate the stamp collection he had left behind. When it was examined, the famed British Guiana was not to be found. Subsequent investigation disclosed that his widow had the gem in her possession. When questioned, she insisted that some time prior to her late husband's death, he had given it to her as a personal gift.

Mrs. Hind married Pascal Costa Scala on Nov. 8, 1933 and, as she

---

The following morning the writer had returned to Mr. Hind's home, agreed to say nothing more about the transaction, and accepted the money. A few moments later Mr. Hind lit a match and burned the duplicate to ashes. "There still is only one magenta one-cent British Guiana," he said. The entire letter was written in so sincere a manner and so accurately described Mr. Hind, his home, and the incidents that philatelists who have read this report cannot bring themselves to believe that it is entirely fantastic.

had benefited little from the Hind will, made arrangements to sell the valuable stamp. It was sent to London for auction, but in the absence of any bid topping the reserve price of $40,000 it was returned to Mrs. Scala unsold. Knowledge of its being on the market was known by the trade and potential buyers, but she failed to receive a satisfactory price through her own efforts. Finally, in October 1938, the Kenmore Stamp Company published an advertisement offering the stamp for $37,500.

Little more was heard of the stamp until April, 1940. About March of that year I began work as director of the International Stamp Exhibition at the New York World's Fair, and among the unusual displays I sought, in order to make this show a fitting substitute for the exhibition originally planned in London to mark the centenary of the Penny Black, was the British Guiana. I called upon Ernest Jarvis, owner of the Kenmore Company, whom I had known for several years, to see if he could arrange the loan of this rarity. Within a week he and I visited Mrs. Scala and her husband during a trip they had made to New York. We were received in her Hotel Ambassador suite and discussed the terms under which she would loan it. We agreed that the New York World's Fair would insure the stamp for $50,000, publicize it as being worth that much, and use Mrs. Scala's name whenever a story was released concerning it.

During the weeks between the agreement and the time the stamp was to be delivered, Mrs. Scala abruptly severed her relations with Mr. Jarvis and consigned the sale of the stamp to Emil Bruechig, a well-known stamp dealer who happened to be related to the Director of Publicity for the Hotel Ambassador.

The fair's publicity department worked up a campaign that was to start three days before the Fair opened. The stamp was brought down by train as far as Harmon where Mrs. Scala, the stamp, and half a dozen World's Fair guards, fully armed, got aboard an armored truck. At the city limits a police escort, with sirens blazing, met the truck and raced to the Hotel Ambassador.

The hotel had arranged for a reception to the press before the truck's arrival, and pictures and stories literally flooded the New York newspapers, news reels, and radio. Two days later, arrangements were made to have Mrs. Scala deliver the stamp, again in an armored car, to the Stamp Exhibition at the British Pavilion, which was to open the following Saturday. Grover A. Whalen and Cecil Pickthal, Commissioner of Great Britain to the World's Fair, were with me when Mrs. Scala arrived. Several photographers shot flash guns at us as Mrs. Scala handed the stamp to Mr. Whalen and myself, with Mr. Pickthal looking on. Later Mrs. Scala was asked to pose individually with each of us, and while she stood with Mr. Whalen and Mr. Pickthal, I had the stamp in my hands. It was in a black card with a transparent protective covering. I looked at the stamp, and while I could not be absolutely certain without a more careful examination, I thought that it seemed to be a shade different from the one I had seen at the exhibition of 1926.

On the way to the Administration Building, where Mrs. Scala was to get the insurance policy that had been obtained, she and Mr. Whalen rode in the first car and I found an excuse to follow with the fair's attorney and one other person whom I do not now recall. In the ten minutes it took to get there, I suggested that it might be a good idea to have some guarantee from Mrs. Scala that the stamp she was giving us actually was the original specimen. Suppose that this was not the genuine stamp, and that after we returned it at the end of the fair, Mrs. Scala could prove that what we gave her was a counterfeit or reproduction? The insurance company would have to pay her $50,000 and someone would be suspected of having made a substitution.

The attorney saw my point and when we got to his office, he asked Mrs. Scala to personally seal the card and affix her signature so that there could be no way in which the seal could be opened without destroying it. This she refused to do. As an alternative, the attorney requested that Mrs. Scala sign an affidavit that the stamp being handed to us was the original British Guiana. Again she refused without consulting her counsel. Accordingly the attorney said that he would wait until the following morning and would transmit the insurance policy as soon as he had the affidavit.

The next day passed well into the afternoon, but Mrs. Scala did not show up, and when we phoned to the hotel, we learned that she had "checked out." For the following days I devoted most of my time to long-distant calls in a vain effort to reach Mrs. Scala.

The fair opened, and for nearly two weeks we had to offer apologies for the absence of the stamp that had got so much publicity and that so many people wanted to see. Finally I reached Mrs. Scala, who said she had had an attack of arthritis and had been under the doctor's care ever since. She was sorry about the trouble she had caused, but said that, upon further reflection, she would loan the stamp to the fair only if, in addition to the insurance, we would pay her a four-figure amount for its "rental." This I refused to do, and we never got the stamp.

On August 7, 1940, R. H. Macy and Company announced that they had acquired from Mrs. Scala the British Guiana stamp for an unnamed client, but refused to disclose either the purchase price or the figure at which it was sold.

Rumors ran rampant. *The New York Times* announced that the figure was $40,000 and that it had been purchased by "an Australian who could not take it home while the dominion [2] was at war . . . and for that reason the owner preferred to let the stamp stay in the United States until the European conflict ends."

Other rumors reported that the stamp had been given to President Roosevelt as a gift, but he personally told me that if this were true he never knew of it and that perhaps some secretary had put it into a lot of mixed stamps. This report proved untrue after the president's death, for it was not found among his possessions.

The stamp now belongs to a wealthy American collector who at present is building up what will be the finest collection of British Guiana stamps ever assembled. He has been buying rare items at every auction sale in which stamps of that country are offered, and in 1944, when the famous "A.P." collection was offered at public auction by Robson Lowe, Ltd., of London, a catalogue was air-mailed to this person just a few days before the sale. He telephoned his agents in London, and in a matter of hours before the sale was to have taken place—on December 20 at 2 P.M.—the entire lot was withdrawn and sold to him intact.

This unique stamp was featured as the high light of the Centenary International Philatelic Exhibition at Grand Central Palace, New York, in May, 1947. The loan of the stamp was arranged with the owner through Finbar Kenny, who now is general manager of the J. and H. Stolow Company, stamp wholesalers and auctioneers. It was placed in an elaborately constructed jewel-case display, and faithfully reproduced facsimiles were freely distributed as souvenirs by the Stolow firm.

Post Office Mauritius

All fields of special pursuit have their zenith, their greatest of all gems. To the philatelist the greatest of all stamps is the *Post Office*

[2] Australia is a Commonwealth, not a Dominion as the *Times* said.

Mauritius. The British Guiana one-cent of 1856 has brought a higher price. Other specimens are rarer in terms of quantities known to exist. But none of these is so garbed in the traditional aura of glamour and prestige as are the two stamps that came into being on a September morning of 1847.

The fact that Mauritius, a tiny insular speck on the vast Indian Ocean, should have been the fourth spot on the earth to have distinctive adhesive postage stamps is enough to make philatelic history; but the legend surrounding these two stamps is so dramatic that they long have been recognized by philatelists as the foremost aristocrats of stampdom.

Little is known of the postal history of the island prior to December, 1846, when the postal system of Mauritius was completely reorganized and rates fixed for inland and overseas mails. It is clearly stated that stamps were about to be issued for the prepayment of carriage charges on outbound letters, since this regulation was made compulsory under the reorganization.

The story that is accepted by philatelists the world over is dramatic, and certainly never since have rare postage stamps been associated with the whims of a woman.

According to the traditional account, Lady Gomm, wife of the governor of Mauritius, was staging a formal ball for the night of September 30, 1847; and, wishing to demonstrate that she was as modern as her social equals in London, she decided to copy the idea of having her invitations franked with adhesive postage stamps. She had seen specimens of the Penny Black and two-pence blues of England and thought well of the idea. Lady Gomm took samples of the English stamps to one J. Barnard, a jewelry engraver in Port Louis, and asked that he copy the designs and print the necessary stamps in time to send out her invitations.

It is said that Barnard worked all night at cutting the vignette into a piece of copper such as is used to engrave calling cards. But by the time he had finished everything except the inscription, he had forgotten the exact wording, and so entered the words "Post Office" in the lateral panel. The legend goes on to state that Lady Gomm immediately noticed the mistake—the wording should have been "Post Paid"—but, as there was insufficient time to correct the plate, accepted the stamps, franked her invitations, and only afterward was a correction made in the stamp.

Although students have discovered no facts to disprove this story, researchers do make the serious collector wonder if the Lady Gomm legend is not an exaggeration of the actual circumstances.

According to Major Edward B. Evans, who was stationed in Mauritius for several years until 1879, he was given access to the government archives and thus became the first philatelist to unearth some details that had been mysteries until then.

Among other things he came upon a letter dated September 20, 1847, and written by the Mauritius postmaster to the colonial secretary in London. This letter states that "700 copies of the first stamps were struck off." Eight months later, the same person wrote another letter in which a report of "1000 stamps" is given. The difference of 300 stamps can be logically explained only by the fact that the Lady Gomm ball came between the time the first and the second reports were written; and it is reasonable to suspect that Lady Gomm simply obtained a sufficient number of stamps for her invitations.

Evidence that perhaps her request for additional stamps led to the association of Lady Gomm with the actual issue is further strengthened through an examination of the plate from which the stamps were printed. In 1912 the effects of the governor of Mauritius were examined by his grandson, who found among them a small ladies' visiting card copper plate measuring 53 by 36 millimeters. Upon this small plate were engraved the designs for the two stamps, one in each upper corner. The plate was acquired by David Field of England and sold by him to Sidney Loder. Finally this plate, for which Barnard had received £10, was sold to Mr. Burrus.

Considering the amount of work that is necessary to produce a copper engraving of this quality, and considering that Barnard made *two* engravings on the single copper plate, we may assume that he could not have made it in a single night, and that if "Post Office" were substituted for "Post Paid" it certainly would not have been impossible for him to check with officials before he finished the job.

That "Post Office" should have been due to the "forgetfulness" of the engraver is another source of bewilderment to stamp collectors. According to the *Regent Empire Stamp Encyclopaedia*, Mauritius used several types of handstamps to mark mail before the introduction of adhesives, and as most of these were inscribed "Post Office," we may reasonably assume that Barnard had a sample of one of these markings and *deliberately* copied the inscription. At any rate, in less than a year the first stamps were withdrawn from circulation and replaced by similar adhesives inscribed with the more appropriate

"Post Paid." It is said that the original printing became exhausted and for a time the colony was without stamps because Barnard had to undergo treatment for his eyesight and could not make new plates until May, 1848.

Whether Lady Gomm was responsible for the Post Office stamps to satisfy her vanity, as the prevailing legend states, or whether they were just a natural outcome of the aforementioned postal reforms, the stamps nevertheless still are bright with the glamour of philatelic appreciation among the connoisseurs.

Actual knowledge of the Post Office issue was not recorded until about 1865 by continental collectors. The earliest European and American albums and catalogues published up to that time made no mention of such issues. In a way they are similar to the British Guiana one-cent magenta, for, as we explained, this stamp, too, was not "discovered" until long after it had become obsolete.

About eighteen years after the Post Office stamp was in use, one Madame Bauchard chanced upon copies of the one-penny orange-red and the twopence blue; but because there was no space for these in her album, she traded them with M. Coutures, a fellow collector in Bordeaux, France, for specimens of Uruguay's Montevideo stamps, which she could mount in her Lallier album. Coutures later submitted them to J. B. Moens. The latter sold them on February 15, 1866, for £20, to Judge F. A. Philbrick, who bought them only after haggling for six months to see whether he could not obtain them for less. The Philbrick collection was sold to Ferrary, but no mention is made of an individual pricing on these two classics. When the Ferrary collection was auctioned, this pair went to Mr. Burrus for 116,000 francs.

Once the existence of these stamps was known, collectors hunted for copies and philatelists searched for information concerning them. Within a few decades their true status was uncovered and their fame spread to such an extent that the demand for specimens became phenomenal. To date, fewer than thirty copies of both are known: Charles J. Phillips—whose memory so failed in his later years that all his writings cannot always be relied upon—published a "pedigree" of these stamps before he died and listed twenty-seven copies; other reports put the number at twenty-nine. But all of these extant stamps were found among correspondence by ardent collectors.

The two finest Post Office gems are the covers now owned by Mrs. John D. Dale and Mr. Burrus. The former has a letter written to Bombay which is franked by a pair (two singles) of the one-penny stamps in superb condition. This item was purchased by a Mr. Howard for £50 in 1897, in a local Indian bazaar.

A year later, on a visit to London, Howard sold it to W. H. Peckitt for £1,620. He in turn sold it to Vernon Roberts for £1,800, then bought it back for £2,000 and sold it to the late George Worthington, of Cleveland, Ohio, for £2,300. When Alfred F. Lichtenstein, Mrs. Dale's father, purchased the Worthington collection,[3] this item was in it. Mr. Lichtenstein used to say that it did not cost him a cent. It seems that he figured out what the stamps that he wanted from this large collection were worth, then sold the rest through the Morgenthau auctions, and the difference between what he received and what he paid, less his estimate of retained portions of the collection, left him with this cover.

The second cover is franked with one specimen of each value and was sent to Bordeaux. Early in 1903, a Marseilles schoolboy found a few stamps among his father's correspondence, and among them was this cover. With friends he went to Paris and sold it to Theodore Lemaire for £1,600. This dealer turned it over almost immediately to M. A. B. L'Argentiere, a well-known French collector, for £1,800. Mr. Lichtenstein purchased this collection in 1917 and later parted with the cover to Arthur Hind. The cover was sold by H. R. Harmer, Ltd., at their auction of June, 1934, and was purchased for $27,500 by Edgar Mohrmann, a Hamburg dealer, in behalf of Mr. Burrus, by whom it still is owned.

On several occasions reports have come from various parts of the world that additional copies of either of these two stamps have been found. A recent report, from a Central American republic, was accepted by the press, but after investigations were made it was learned that the "find" consisted simply of an album illustration painted the color of the stamp. During the International Exhibition of 1947, Frank Godden, a dealer and British Commissioner to the show, announced that his firm in London had purchased an old-time collection in which was found another specimen of the one-penny Post Office Mauritius, and that after the item had been expertized and guaranteed by the Royal Philatelic Society, "a substantial price" had been paid to the fortunate owner of the otherwise worthless collection.

On April 17, 1946, the Berlin radio reported that the two-penny "Post Office," which had been purchased by the Berlin Postal

[3] See pages 233–234.

Museum some years ago, had "disappeared from the Berlin Museum after having been stored underground in western Germany for safe-keeping during the war." Subsequent reports from American Occupation officials confirmed the report but also stated that it had been recovered.

Considering that there were 1000 of these printed, and apparently used on mail, and realizing that only thirty (at most) are known to exist today, it is not too unreasonable to suspect that some day one of us may be going through a bundle of forgotten and century-old correspondence and come upon one of these philatelic gems which we will sell for enough to take that holiday flight around the world.

Hawaiian Missionaries

When a philatelist speaks of *missionaries* he refers to examples of four of the great classic rarities of the stamp world, and not to peregrinating apostles of the Lord. But he speaks with as much reverence as he would when referring to the nineteenth-century ministers of the Gospel after whom these dramatic, precious paper flimsies were named. For they rank next to the Post Office Mauritius as the outstanding gems of our hobby.

Less than a hundred years ago, when Hawaii was more commonly known as the Sandwich Isles, the need for a postal service was manifest, and on June 18, 1851, King Kamehameha signed a decree which called for the establishment of a post office in Honolulu, because "the 15th article of a treaty with the United States rendered indispensable the establishment of a post office."

The official act designated that "for the time being the *Polynesian* [4] office is declared to be the post office." It continued to designate the duties of a postmaster who was subject to the minister of interior; to stipulate the prevailing rates of postage and the authorization for the preparation of postage stamps by the postmaster.

In 1851 stamps were in use in only a few scattered countries around the globe; and as mail to the Hawaiian Islands from those places was extremely scarce, it is probable that H. M. Whitney, the first postmaster, never saw more than a dozen different designs to inspire him in his creation. Furthermore, even if he had had a desire for better examples of graphic art, the facilities in Honolulu were not up to the job of producing them.

[4] The *Polynesian* was one of the leading newspapers in Honolulu and the official organ for announcements of government orders.

The first set—the missionaries—accordingly, were type-set, and made up entirely of loose type and a few decorative printing slugs. Among the first mechanical devices brought to the islands by the early white settlers was the printing press, primarily shipped over to produce the literature necessary in spreading the Gospel and converting natives to Christianity. Later, as literacy increased, the number of printing shops waxed proportionately. The job of producing the first stamps was assigned to the Government Printing Office in Honolulu, while Mr. Whitney himself created the design by piecing together sample impressions of existing print jobs in much the same manner as some kidnappers quilt ransom notes. The "Hawaiian Postage," which appears in the top panel of the stamps, was set from type in the front of the American Missionary Press, which had previously been used in printing *The Friend*, a temperance magazine edited by one Mr. Damon.

The fancy border design used to inclose the numerals of value had previously been used by the Catholic Mission Press in printing *Te Aniani (The Mirror)* and later to make up a frontispiece in the *Manual for the Catholic People of Hawaii*.

Mr. Frank C. Atherton and Lieutenant Colonel Charles C. Gill, both of whom have done tremendous research on these stamps, have so far been unable to identify the source of the numerals used for the stamps. Nor have they been able to determine the reason why the Government Printing Office should have been compelled to "borrow" type from these other shops, except that perhaps Mr. Whitney could find no more appropriate type and design slugs in the government plant. The American Mission Press' printing equipment and type had come from the eastern United States; that of the Catholic Mission Press, from France.

The three stamps—two-, five-, and thirteen-cent denominations—were issued on October 1, 1851, only eleven years after the birth of the Penny Black and but four after the first United States postage stamps.

A month after the stamps were issued the top panel of the thirteen-cent value was changed from "Hawaiian Postage" to the more appropriate "H.I. & U.S. Postage," for this denomination was produced and issued to pay charges on mail from the island to the portions of the United States beyond the Rocky Mountains. The two-cent was for local newspapers, and the five-cent, for domestic letters.

Originally the stamps were known as *numerals*, but because most of the extant copies were found on letters addressed by missionaries sent to the islands under the auspices of the Park Street Congregational Church of Boston, the more appropriate nickname was given the adhesives by philatelists.

Among the 150 examples of all the missionaries discovered so far, only two types of each denomination exist; therefore experts conclude that two basic forms were set by hand and locked in a chase to provide the printing surface. How many impressions were struck on each sheet of paper still is a mystery, for the largest known multiple is a strip of three of the thirteen-cent value. Students suspect that the type for the two-cent denomination was set up in this manner and supplies printed. The central numeral and the bottom inscription then were changed to produce the five-cent stamps, and when finally supplies of these were made, another alteration was made to print the thirteen-cent values.

The two varieties of the latter stamp are the most common, as they were used on mail which happened to be saved by the original recipients. That some still may be hidden away in attics or closets, waiting to be found by collectors, is evidenced by the fact that one turned up in 1938. It is seldom that any further examples of great rarities should be discovered at this late date, in view of the spotlight of publicity which has been focused on the value of stamps. We shall let the late Spencer Anderson, a dealer who eventually acquired this gem, tell about the find in his own words:

In the year 1852, Miss Fidelia Fisk, of Shelbourne Falls, Mass., was sent out to Persia as a missionary from Boston. While there, she received a letter from a friend in Honolulu, franked with a perfect specimen of the 13-cent H.I. & U.S. stamp. Miss Fisk retained all correspondence, and at her death around 1900, her personal effects were willed to her home town library. They were stored in a sea chest which remained in the basement of the library until May, 1938.

A young boy, given permission to rummage through the basement in quest of stamps, uncovered a packet of letters in the chest. He called the attention of the librarian to them. Her sister, who is a stamp collector, told the Library Board of Trustees that one of them was quite valuable. After some negotiations, the writer acquired the cover, the result being that the library is richer by a substantial sum and philately has another choice specimen of one of the world's classic rarities.

All of the four missionaries are rare, but the two-cent value is the most valuable, for this stamp usually was affixed to newspapers, which generally were thrown away after they had been read. These stamps are so scarce that for a while after they became obsolete and until a few copies found later could be authenticated, some philatelists, even in Hawaii, refused to believe that there was such a stamp.

It is said that only fourteen copies of this denomination are included in the 150 total. On May 11, 1943, an auctioneer who handled the Charles A. Wilson (of Aberdeen, Scotland) collection, sold for $7,200 that copy which is listed in the *Kohl Handbuch* reference as "No. 2." It was first purchased by William P. Brown, America's pioneer dealer, and sold by him to the fabulous Count von Ferrary, in whose collection it reposed until June 27, 1922. At that time it was auctioned to Arthur Hind for 80,000 francs. After the latter died, the collection (all except the United States section which had been previously sold at the Waldorf Astoria Hotel) was shipped to England for sale, and it was there that Mr. Wilson purchased it. This one, and one each of the other three stamps that Mr. Wilson owned, brought $18,000 at the 1943 sale. Truly a nice fortune for four tiny bits of crudely printed and fragile paper.

The Two-Cent British Guiana

There are hundreds of stamps whose designs reflect adventure or whose issuance suggests fabulous tales, but none has a history quite so unusual as that of the two-cent stamps issued by British Guiana on February 22, 1851.

The postal system of British Guiana dates from 1783, when England's only colony on the South American continent was confined within the boundaries of Demarara. Poor transportation facilities and bad management caused the initial mail service to fail until the General Post Office in London sent an agent to reorganize it and establish regular packets between British Guiana, adjacent colonies, and the mother country.

On July 1, 1850, according to the *Royal Gazette*, the first set of regular postage stamps was produced by a local printer in Georgetown, the capital of British Guiana. The product represents one of the crudest of philatelic designs, for it consists only of a rough circle inclosing the words, "British Guiana" and the figure of value (4, 8, or 12 cents).

All three denominations were printed in black ink, but on flimsy paper of different colors for each value. Before they were sold, however, they were initialed by James Belton Smith, a clerk, or E. T. E. Dalton, Deputy Postmaster General.

The following February the postmaster at Georgeton had a two-cent denomination added to the series to be used for the prepayment of extra postage on a local delivery which took place at 10 A.M. and 2 P.M. This stamp, which today is one of the world's rarest, was not heard of in Europe until 1877, when the first known copy was sold to Thomas Ridpath of London. Since then, nine additional copies have been found. The story of two of these is a potpourrie of luck, charity, circumstance, and profit.

Christ Church in Demarara was in financial difficulties in the Spring of 1896; a mortgage was due on the small school, there was an overdraft of more than £100 (about $500) at the bank, and there were numerous other small debts. The congregation, anxious to meet these obligations, collected £75 and contributed it to their minister, Canon Josa.

Stamp collecting was already a popular hobby by that time, and the demand for canceled copies of the early Guianas was so great that the minister gratefully accepted stamps from those parishioners who could not afford cash. A Miss Preston, a Negress, donated two four-cent blue circulars of 1850, and when $33.60 was realized from their sale, Canon Josa went to her home to thank her and ask her whether she had any additional copies. A thorough search revealed a folded letter sheet, among her old receipts and papers, to which was affixed a pair of the two-cent circulars. The letter was addressed to "Miss Rose, Blankenburg," and as Miss Rose was present at the time the cover was found she not only consented to give the valuable stamps to Canon Josa, but danced with joy and exclaimed, "Thank God! I am at last able to give something worth while."

The cover was sent to England, where E. C. Luard paid £205 for it. It has since been owned by such eminent philatelists as Henry J. Duveen and Arthur Hind. When Mr. Hind's collection was broken and sold at auction by H. R. Harmer, of London, the two circulars on the original envelope went to Theodore Champion, of Paris, for £1,300. The cover still is in Mr. Champion's collection, even though it had to be sent to Switzerland during the years of the Nazi occupation to keep it from being looted.

The Pony Express

The greatest financial failure and the most glorious chapter in the history of the United States Postal Service—that was the Pony Express. In 1860 the eastern section of our growing nation was commercially well established and the west coast was the center of extensive mining projects, but the area between the two represented only a barren, desolate expanse of danger and hazard. The East and the West needed rapid communication: the stage lines were too slow; the telegraph and railroads had not yet been completed.

The Pony Express was conceived by Senator William M. Gwin, of California, in 1854, when he was taking a leisurely trip across the country by stage. The many disadvantages of the idea were obvious, but six years later, when it seemed possible that the government would subsidize the venture when its effectiveness was demonstrated, Russell, Majors, and Waddell, who already were operating an express service, instituted the Pony Express on April 3, 1860.

In the East, rail and telegraph communication reached as far as St. Joseph, Missouri, so it was in that city that the eastern terminal of the Pony Express was established. Between the Missouri River and Sacramento, California, relay stations were built at intervals of forty to a hundred miles, at each of which food and fresh horses were kept in a manner not unlike the ancient posts of Rome and Persia.

As soon as the mail was taken off the train at St. Joseph, it was placed in a mochilla—a four-pocket saddle bag—and the rider mounted his pony, dashed to the ferry across the Missouri River, and continued on to the next station.

There the mochilla was transferred to another horse and the rider went on, always conscious that speed was the most important part of his job.

Although the schedule called for relays of only forty to a hundred miles, there were many instances along the route when riders had to do more than that. Several times relay stations had been raided by Indians; a rider reaching the place and finding the relief man slain would have to go through on an additional leg of the trip. There is a record of one Jack Keetly who rode 340 miles in thirty-one hours because three of his relay men were unable to take the mail off his hands.

During the Indian wars—as well as at other times—there were thrilling episodes in this service. One night when Howard Egan, a Pony Express rider, was threading a canyon west of Salt Lake City, he saw the faint gleam of a campfire on the rock walls ahead: a band of Indians in ambush, but evidently not expecting him quite so soon. He would not turn back. He approached stealthily, and then, suddenly spurred his pony and galloped through the band, yelling and shouting. The whole Indian band scattered and Egan went through safely.

The government never supplied the financial aid that they had expected, so Russell, Majors, and Waddell were forced to turn over their route to Wells-Fargo. But even with reductions of rates, heavy losses punctuated the enterprise.

At last, on October 20, 1861, the telegraph joined the stage route at Salt Lake City and the use of the Pony Express was no longer necessary. It operated for another four weeks and then folded up.

Because the rates were very high—$5 a half ounce—only the most important mail was sent in this manner, and consequently the operators could not meet their expenses.

The installation of the line cost at least $100,000, and maintenance cost an additional $650,000. Total receipts were less than $500,000. That left Russell, Majors, and Waddell holding a $200,000 bag.

By reason of their human interest and historical significance, as well as their relative scarcity, letters carried by the Pony Express are sought today by collectors who are willing to pay high prices for specimens in fine condition.

Flimsies

Pigeons were known to carry messages long before white men ever settled New Zealand; they were used to fly mail across areas that made regular service impractical before copper was mined on Great Barrier Island; but it was not until 1898 that special stamps were made for letters carried through the air by these winged messengers.

Great Barrier Island, where extensive copper deposits were developed toward the end of the nineteenth century, is situated north of Cape Colville and across Hauraki Gulf about sixty-five miles east of Auckland, New Zealand. Regular mail service brought letters back and forth about once a month, when ships called at Great Barrier for cargoes of copper.

A pigeon fanciers' club of Auckland at one time took a number of birds to Great Barrier for a race. The results of that sixty-five-mile hop across water inspired the organization of the original Great

[137]

Barrier Pigeongram Service in November, 1897. This private enterprise, owned by S. Holden Howie, had the sanction of the New Zealand Post Office. For the sum of one shilling, small letters written on thin tissue sheets called "flimsies" were carried from Great Barrier to Auckland.

Within twelve months the service became so popular that postage stamps were zincotyped at the printing plant of the *Auckland Observer*. They were made in sheets of four, with wide perforated margins separating the two pairs, which were set tête-beche to each other. Two varieties, one on thin and one on thick paper, may be distinguished in this first issue.

Apparently these stamps were not entirely satisfactory because in January, 1899, another variety was surface-printed by *The New Zealand Herald*. The design was similar, but an ornate border was added. They were on sale only a few weeks when the New Zealand government objected to the inscription, "Special Post," which was placed just below the central design showing a pigeon in flight, and so the existing stock of 960 greenish-blue adhesives was overprinted, "Pigeongram," in black, in May, 1899.

In August of that year a new printing of 12,000 stamps was made in which the inscription "Special Post" was replaced by "Pigeongram." These were used until the service was discontinued in 1901.

Success develops competition, and in July, 1899, a rival company, called the "Great Barrier Pigeongram Agency," set up a similar service and issued its own stamps in the form of distinctive triangular adhesives, designed by a Mr. Wiggs of the Department of Public Works. At first their rate was two shillings a letter a pigeon, but later when it was found possible to send four letters by each bird the rate was reduced to sixpence. The return rate was one shilling, and for that reason the new design appeared in two denominations: six-penny blue (10,000 copies) and one-shilling carmine (5,000 copies).

It is interesting to note that Mr. Wiggs made the design about three times larger than he planned to have the actual stamp, but the printer misunderstood instructions and made them the size of the drawing, so that the pigeons were carrying stamps that were heavier than the letters—or flimsies—themselves. The letter headings bore the royal coat of arms in recognition of the patronage given by the governor of New Zealand, Lord Ranfurly.

In September, 1899, a service to Marotiri (Hen and Chicken) Island was operated by the Copper Mines Syndicate, which was working mines in that archipelago, as a branch of the original Great Barrier Pigeongram Service under the supervision of J. W. Mackay. Two hundred copies of the "Pigeongram" provisional of January, 1899, were overprinted "Marotiri" for initial service, but in October a distinctive design was produced by lithography in sheets of six red stamps of one shilling apiece.

By this time the pigeon air-mail service had become so popular that it rivaled the ordinary postal service, and in 1901 the New Zealand officials decided that there was too much competition and forced both firms to cease operations. However, they did prove that rapid communication was necessary between Auckland and Great Barrier Island, so the government laid a cable across the sixty-five-mile gulf that separated them. The cable service started only a short while after the post office asserted its monopoly over the mails, so that the pigeon service probably would have been put out of business by 1903 anyhow.

All the pigeongram stamps are scarce in either used or unused condition, and the collector who is so fortunate as to have a complete "flimsie" in good condition, owns a real philatelic gem.

Three types of postmarks are recognized, according to the following types:

1. A circular blue cachet with the inscription, "Original Great Barrier Pigeon Service."

2. A two-line dated cancellation in violet and black, inscribed, "The Original Great Barrier Pigeongram Service."

3. A double-lined circular cachet similar to Type 1, but inscribed "The Original Great Barrier Pigeongram Service."

Air-Mail Stamps

Air-mail service across oceans and to every distant place in the world has progressed to the point where the posting of a letter that will be delivered in Australia within sixty hours is as routine as mailing a statement to your customer down the street. But William Krinsky, of Brooklyn, has traced the development of this service in so striking a manner that everyone who has ever seen his collection at philatelic exhibitions has little but superlative adjectives to describe his enthusiasm.

Almost every pioneer aviator who attempted to span oceans has carried mail since the days when Harry G. Hawker and Major K. MacKenzie Grieve tried to fly from Newfoundland to Ireland; and it is the collection of these postal souvenir envelopes, many of which are exceedingly rare, that Mr. Krinsky has undertaken. This collection is not simply an accumulation of valuable envelopes and post cards. Assisted by his brother, Ben, Bill Krinsky has made up a vivid and colorful display which is a complete record of trans-oceanic air mail up to the present day. Each cover is supplemented on a black album page by a map of the route over which it was flown, a photograph of the plane and aviators who made the trip, and a concise sketch of the flight itself.

In 1913 the *London Daily Mail* posted a prize of £10,000 for the first flight across the Atlantic Ocean in less than seventy-two hours. The war forced cancellation of the offer, but in 1919 it was renewed, and four teams of flyers prepared to enter the contest. John Alcock and Arthur W. Brown left St. Johns, Newfoundland, in their Vickers-Vimy biplane, *Atlantic*, on June 14, 1919. In order to gain altitude they were forced to drop their landing gear, which meant that if they spanned the ocean they would have to crash-land on coming to earth. The flyers encountered severe weather conditions off Newfoundland but managed to pull through it and finally made a triumphant landing at Clifden, Ireland, on the morning of June 15. Each of the envelopes Alcock and Brown carried across the sea was franked with a regular 15-cent Cabot stamp that had been provisionally overprinted in St. Johns, "Trans-Atlantic Airpost-$1."

Another treasure in the Krinsky collection is a cover flown from England to the United States on the last leg of the United States Army around-the-world flight of 1924.

Three planes flown by Captain Lowell H. Smith and Lieutenants Henry H. Ogden, Leigh Wade, Eric H. Nelson, Leslie P. Arnold, and John H. Ogden, left Seattle on April 6, 1924. Covering Alaska, Siberia, Japan, China, Malaya, India, Arabia, and Europe, they reached London three months later. On July 27 they took off from Brough with three envelopes franked with the then-current 1½-penny stamps of England. They made intermediate stops at Greenland and Labrador and finally returned to Seattle on September 28, completing the course of 27,553 miles in fifteen days, eleven hours, and seven minutes flying time.

The record flight around the world, made by the late Wiley Post and Harold Gatty,[5] in 1931, also is represented by a cover they car-

[5] Wiley Post later was killed in an accident, in which Will Rogers flew with him as a passenger, at Pt. Barrow, Alaska. Harold Gatty is today an executive of Pan American World Airways, in charge of Australasian service.

ried from New York to New York in the famous *Winnie Mae*.[6]
Signed by the aviators, the envelope is franked with an ordinary
two-cent stamp of the period and is postmarked at Mineola, New
York, June 21, 1931; Berlin, June 24; Moscow, June 29; and Mineola,
July 1, to show that it had been carried over two oceans and three
continents.

The Amelia Earhart section is particularly interesting, for it contains letters carried on all of her important trips across two oceans.
The first of these is one flown on the *Friendship* when she accompanied Wilmer Stutz and Lou Gordon on the trip from Trepassy
Bay, Newfoundland, to Burry Point, Wales, which was covered
in twenty hours and forty-nine minutes. The cover is franked with
ten cents' worth of Newfoundland adhesives and a British 1½-penny
stamp. Mr. Krinsky also has covers which Miss Earhart carried on
her solo flight from Harbor Grace, Newfoundland, to Londonderry,
Ireland, on May 20-21, 1932, and her two successful Hawaii–United
States trips.

When Rear Admiral Richard E. Byrd flew from New York to
Ver-sur-Mer in the *America* with Bernt Balchen, Bert Acosta, and
George Noville, he carried a number of letters,[7] all franked with the
regular five-cent stamp of that year; but the crash into the sea on
the coast of France caused most of the stamps to be soaked from
their envelopes. The cover which Bill Krinsky has, however, still
has the stamp affixed.

In 1937 France issued a set of special postage stamps in honor of
Jean Mermoz, who made the first successful flight from Paris to Rio
de Janeiro in a hydroplane between May 12 and 14, 1930, as a pioneer
in behalf of Air France, the French national airline. Mr. Krinsky has
a cover which was actually flown in this plane. Signed by Mermoz,
it records the pioneer conquest of the South Atlantic by air.

While the collection is almost unequaled[8] as a postal history of

[6] The *Winnie Mae*, a sleek white monoplane with a single engine, now is in
the Smithsonian Institution, Washington, D. C.

[7] Richard Byrd was the first trans-oceanic pilot to be sworn in as a mail pilot,
so that the approximately two hundred envelopes which he carried to France
in the America were in fact the first United States-to-Europe air mail. While
the covers carried by previous flyers were franked with postage stamps as a
matter of form, they cannot be considered as actual mail, but rather as souvenirs. Aero-philatelists, however, overlook this technicality and regard all
envelopes as relics that trace the development of over-ocean air-mail service.

[8] Mr. Krinsky's collection is perhaps the most widely known specialized assortment of trans-oceanic covers in existence. John V. P. Heinmuller, president of
the Longines-Wittnauer Watch Company, however, was a stamp collector long

air-mail across oceans, it is also interesting to note the difference between current rates and those established on such early flights as were authorized to carry United States mail overseas. Letters carried by the Graf Zeppelin had to be franked at the rate of $1.05 per half ounce, for instance, while those carried on the first regular flight of Pan American Airways in 1939 cost 30 cents a half ounce; today the rate to Europe is but 15 cents.

Puffin Stamps

The *Standard Postage Stamp Catalogue* does not recognize the local adhesives issued for "postal service" between Lundy Island, the geographical division of the Atlantic Ocean from the Bristol Channel, and the nearest British post office at Barnstaple on the southwest coast of England; but John D. Stanard, of Chattanooga, Tennessee, has made an intensive study of these queer "puffin stamps" and assembled an extensive collection of them.

In a book about the history of these stickers, which is based on his collection and which was published by the American Philatelic Society in 1938, Mr. Stanard presents a complete history not only of the stamps, but also of the small, privately owned island as well.

During the nineteenth century and up to 1927 an English post office was maintained on the island, and all mail dispatched thence was franked with regular English postage stamps. In 1927, Martin Coles Harman, a London financier, who had purchased the island from Augustus Langham Christie in 1925, advised the English postmaster general that "a post office on Lundy is not required" but that he would personally carry mails from the island to the mainland in his private vessel without remuneration.

With an eye to emphasizing his jurisdiction over the island, Mr. Harman decided to issue his own currency and postage stamps on November 1, 1929. Instead of using the conventional "pence" currency of England, he established a new unit of money called the "puffin." He selected this because a century before Lundy Islanders did a brisk business in the sale of feathers from this native sea parrot,

---

before he was interested in watches and became official timer for the National Aeronautical Association. It was only natural, therefore, that he should have combined his professional and avocational interests by making a collection of covers carried on *all* sorts of record flights. By virtue of his official position, he personally knew the early pioneers of aviation and invariably persuaded them to carry souvenir envelopes along. His collection of these recently was donated to the Institute of Aeronautical Sciences in New York, after he had used them as a basis for his book *Man's Fight to Fly.*

called the puffin, and used them as a medium of exchange for such necessary commodities as butter, cheese, and shoes. The first token coins and postage stamps, then, depicted a puffin and were inscribed "half-puffin" or "one puffin."

At a later date the British government challenged Mr. Harman's right to infringe upon a royal prerogative of issuing currency. Mr. Harman, holding that he had a right to do as he pleased on his private island, refused to entertain the command of the crown agents to "stop issuing private coins." The matter was finally brought into the higher courts and official records indicate that Mr. Harman "lost the day." His right to issue and use postage stamps also was questioned, but he was permitted to continue the practice. However none of his privately issued labels was allowed to be affixed to the face of any envelope or to be placed anywhere near the British stamps which had to be used to frank the mail to any place beyond the island itself.

The first issue of Lundy Island stamps was printed by Bradbury, Wilkinson and Company, of New Malden, Surrey, England, in sheets of 120, divided into four panes of thirty stamps apiece. The half-puffin depicts the head of a puffin and is printed in red. The one-puffin shows a full picture of the queer bird and is executed in blue. Five hundred thousand copies of each value were delivered to Mr. Harman on May 13, 1929, and were sold to the natives, all of whom were his employees, and to tourists. A large quantity of them were exported to wholesale stamp dealers who bought them eagerly, since there was no way of knowing at the time whether they would stick or whether they would be condemned—as later they were—by postal officials and catalogue editors.

In his collection Mr. Stanard had the original photographic designs of the issued stamps as well as a set of die proofs in black. In May or June, 1930, Mr. Harman, pleased with the successful sale of his first adhesives, increased the set by adding a six-puffin in mauve, a nine-puffin in brown, and a 12-puffin in green. Two hundred and fifty thousand copies of each were delivered on July 11, 1930, and August 11, 1930.

The Stanard collection contains a canceled copy of the six-puffin stamp printed in blue instead of mauve, and, according to its owner, this was the original color of the stamp. It seems that shortly after the stamps were ordered the color was changed, so that specimens of the original color are scarce. Unused copies of the blue stamp are unknown and the only other canceled copy is in the collection of an

English collector who refuses to allow his name to be mentioned.

Although Mr. Harman has been admonished to desist from selling these labels as postage stamps, he has nevertheless continued. He has issued quite a number of special sets since then, and in spite of the fact that the standard catalogues do not recognize them, and wide publicity in the philatelic press has admonished collectors of the true nature of the labels, it seems that there still are persons who insist on buying them. But then, again, that is not surprising, for as we mentioned before, stamp collecting has no rules; it may be enjoyed exactly according to personal preferences of the hobbyists.

V-Mail

Millions of people in the United States and the British Empire used V-Mail during the World War II years to communicate with members of the armed forces in all corners of the earth and marveled at the efficiency of "this modern wonder of science." Only a few historians and some philatelists realize that V-Mail was the result of an idea introduced by the French photographer, Dagron, in 1870, and that only slight modifications were necessary to bring up to date the principle first employed during the Franco-Prussian War.

V-Mail is a microphotographic process. The sender writes his message on a special printed form issued by the government. A number of these are photographed on tiny film strips which are sent to their destination. There they are enlarged and individual prints are delivered to the addressee. The saving in transportation space is tremendous and permits the shipment of thousands of messages that could not be carried if sent in the form of regular letters.

When the Prussians laid siege to Paris, not even trained dogs could get through the lines with news to or from the outside world. On September 23, 1870, the "Neptune," a free balloon, was released from Paris with a cargo of letters. The success of this flight, which ended in Eure, led Parisians to make and release sixty-four other balloons, each of which carried letters. This solved the problem of getting news out of Paris, but provided no means of obtaining replies. A postal employee who had a number of homing pigeons suggested that his birds be taken with the balloons and released with messages after the airship landed beyond the Prussian lines. This was helpful, but because one bird could carry only a single thin piece of paper, messages back were scarce.

Dagron had experimented with microphotography before the

siege, and when the need for news in Paris became acute he conceived the idea of copying dispatches on microfilm at great reductions, thereby increasing the amount of intelligence that could be carried by a pigeon. Accordingly he embarked with an assistant and his equipment in a balloon and, after many vicissitudes, escaped to Tours. Arrangements were made there to have all public and private letters or dispatches printed on large sheets of paper each of which could contain 300,000 characters. These were reduced photographically to a *pellicule* measuring 50 by 70 millimeters, or an area smaller than the average postage stamp.

Twenty such pellicules, incased in a quill and fastened to wing, tail, or leg, could be carried by a single pigeon. Upon arrival at Paris the films were projected on a large screen and transcribed by copyists. Later photographic enlargements were made on paper. In all, more than 100,000 of these dispatches were sent to Paris in this manner, and it was the practice to make up and send forty sets of each, as the mortality of pigeons from cold, enemy rifle fire, and trained hawks was great.

Though this process was practicable during times of war, it was too expensive to compete with normal communications services in peacetime, and Dagron's idea remained an intellectual plaything and a challenge to experimenters until 1941.

Actual examples of these pellicules of 1870–1871 are extremely rare, although George W. Angers, of Springfield, Massachusetts, has what is believed to be the only complete collection of them in existence.

Tin Can Mail Service

Modern postal systems have replaced primitive methods in all but a few remote districts of the world. Until 1946, the Tin Can Mail of Niuafoo, a tiny isle of the Tonga Group in the South Pacific, used one of the most unusual methods of dispatching letters ever devised. Tin Can Mail service was retained so long not so much because it was practical as because it provided tourists and stamp collectors with souvenirs of adventure.

Niuafoo seldom is visited by ships which operate between New Zealand, Fiji, and other ports of the South Pacific. Reefs and barriers make it impossible for any ship larger than a canoe to come within less than a mile of its shore. Even smaller craft find it difficult to navigate the choppy seas and tie up alongside steamers offshore.

The handicap was overcome about 1910, with the inauguration of the Tin Can Mail Service. By this method letters from Niuafoo to the outside world were sealed in a five gallon can and given to a native who swam out to a steamer whenever one stopped offshore, pushing the can before him across more than a mile of choppy waves. While the native floated alongside, the mail was removed from the can, letters for the island were resealed in it, and the can was tossed back for the return trip to the island.

The service was discontinued after several years because sharks occasionally attacked the swimming postman. About 1930 stamp collectors started a demand for envelopes that had been carried in the original Tin Can Mail Service, and when substantial sums were offered for the few that existed, the service was resumed as a souvenir enterprise.

Walter George Quensell, a resident of Niuafoo, became the Tin Can Canoe Mailman by self-appointment, and with the co-operation of several steamship lines, who distributed publicity about the service throughout the world, established a business that was successful for several years.

Operation of the new service was somewhat different from that of the original. To minimize the shark hazard, the can was carried by Mr. Quensell in an outrigger canoe, propelled by two natives. When the canoe got to within a few yards of the ship a native dove into the ocean and pushed the can the rest of the way so that crew members could fish it out and haul it aboard.

In the meantime mail from the ship, which generally had several hundred envelopes from stamp collectors all over the world and from passengers who wanted souvenirs, were sealed in another can and tossed into the ocean. The native retrieved it, swam to the canoe, and climbed aboard to help his partner navigate Mr. Quensell back to Niuafoo.

The few envelopes addressed to residents of the island were delivered in the regular manner by postman Quensell, but self-addressed covers for stamp collectors were postmarked, stamped with numerous gaudy cachets, and held for dispatch when the next ship called. These cachets were unusual in themselves; Quensell, as we have already mentioned, received requests for Tin Can Mail from all over the world, and as was to be expected, these letters were written in many languages: Greek, Cyrillic, Slavic, German, Dutch, French, Italian, Spanish, Portuguese, and several others. Each time Quensell received such a letter he copied the native wording of "Tin Can Mail" and reproduced it with rubber stamps, so that a cover mailed during the last days of the service might have as many as fifteen cachets, each in a different language!

The demand for these covers was very heavy during the years immediately preceding World War II and for the few months between its end and the announcement by Quensell that he was retiring. And as Quensell collected a few cents on each one he serviced, the venture was moderately profitable. In addition, it gave the island international publicity. However, in a letter to one of his correspondents, Mr. Quensell explained several difficulties in connection with his position as Tin Can Mailman. He said, "There are many silly questions asked by some people about banks, churches, religion, and if the Tongans are headhunters. Well, I can grin at all these matters, and it is only natural for people to ask questions, but I haven't time to answer them all. Correspondents should send me a dollar bill and half a dozen envelopes by registered mail, and I will oblige everyone. Some have been very decent and sent me stamps for my son, American newspapers, and pictures of your president, who is a stamp collector, too."

Vanity Stamps

There have been some men of consequence who marched through the pages of history devoting one day of every week to the accomplishment of great things, and the other six to the vain glorification of those deeds, that posterity might not forget their names. Charles Connell was not exactly in a class with Rameses, or Alexander, or Napoleon, but he was so vainly concerned with his own importance that he flaunted royal British tradition, placed his own portrait upon a postage-stamp design, lost his job, and then did not even get the satisfaction of seeing himself immortalized.

Connell was postmaster of New Brunswick in 1860, when it still was a separate British possession in North America. At that time the colony's currency was changed from shillings to dollar units and a new set of stamps valued in the new money was decided upon. For nine years the strikingly attractive diamond-shaped postage stamps had served their purpose, but Connell made arrangements for entirely different designs. Contracts were let with the American Bank Note Company of New York to produce stamps featuring the portraits of Queen Victoria, Edward, then Prince of Wales, and finally Postmaster Charles Connell.

The designs were drawn, the dies engraved, and the plates prepared from which the stamps were printed. But even before they could be placed in regular use, news of Connell's brashness reached the crown in London.

British subjects—especially obedient servants—just don't place their own pictures in the same class as the Royal Effigy, and get away with it. Connell accordingly was dismissed from office and the stamps which he had printed were withdrawn and destroyed. Somehow a few of them escaped and subsequently found their way to philatelic markets in unused condition. While some specialists have paid substantial amounts to obtain the few that do exist, the standard catalogue admonishes the average collector, "this stamp was prepared but not issued."

Another set of stamps which are evidence of a man's vanity is what philatelists commonly call the "Bomba Heads" of Sicily. In 1859, before Italy was unified, the various states had their independent postal services and their individual postage stamps. King Ferdinand II prepared a series of nine different stamps during that year, in which a portrait of himself was featured as the main vignette. Lest the royal effigy be defaced by the obliteration then in vogue, Ferdinand ordered that an entirely new type of cancellation be devised. Artists prepared a fancy obliterator which was the shape and size of the frame design of the stamp so that when it was struck only the outer portions of the stamp would be "killed" and the bulky, bearded portrait of the king would be left unmarked.

When the first United States–Africa air-mail route was inaugurated, the Post Office Department marked covers with this design.

[11] Condition of Stamps

No single factor so influences the monetary value of postage stamps as *condition*. In the early days of philately folks collected just stamps and did not care too much about this quality. So long as a stamp was of a variety he did not already have, a collector would add a new one regardless of whether it was *off center, heavily canceled, thin,* or *slightly defective.* But later, as the hobby advanced, its followers became more and more discriminating until now the matter of condition is almost a fetish. Collectors and dealers alike classify postage stamps according to certain set standards as follows:

SUPERB—the finest possible condition. The color of the stamp is bright and fresh. If it was issued without perforations, all four sides have wide, even margins around the imprinted design. If it is a perforated specimen, all the *teeth* are complete. There are no creases, tears, or thinnings. If it has been postally used the postmark is distinct and light.

VERY FINE—A stamp that merits this description has the same qualifications as the preceding type except that they are not quite so perfect. The margins may be slightly uneven. The color may be a trifle faded. One or two perforation *teeth* may be a bit short, but none may be missing. The cancellation may be either indistinct or a little heavy.

FINE—A stamp that is not quite very fine, but that still is without defects or blemishes.

GOOD—A stamp that is free from defects, such as tears, creases, or thin spots, but that is *off center*, heavily postmarked, or noticeably faded. One that a collector will accept as a space-filler—if he *must* have a particular stamp—until he can replace it with a better specimen.

POOR—A defective stamp. One that has a tear or thin spot. Unless a stamp is a great rarity, such a specimen has absolutely no value and does nothing except detract from the appearance of a collection as a whole. Wise collectors will throw poor stamps away as rapidly as they get them.

Since condition in some cases is relative, the collector must come to know how to apply the preceding standards to certain issues. In the very early days of stamp manufacture the engravers placed the stamp designs of a sheet so close together that when the perforations were punched the holes frequently cut into the actual design of the stamp itself. It is therefore virtually impossible to find specimens whose imprinted design is free and clear of perforation holes on all four sides. The issues of the Australian states, Egypt, and New Zealand are outstanding examples. In these cases, even a closely perforated variety may still be called *very fine* provided the stamps are free of tears and creases and, if used, are lightly postmarked.

The standards you set for the specimens in your own collection depend chiefly upon your own personal preferences. Some collectors have what is called *conditionitis:* they are so discriminating that they will accept no specimen unless it is absolutely perfect in every detail. In fact, Otis Beal Kent, a Washington philatelist, is so meticulous that he will measure with a millimeter rule every specimen offered and, unless it is mathematically centered on all four sides, will refuse to accept a new specimen for his collection. Naturally persons who are so discerning will have many, many empty spaces in their albums because stamps are, as we have mentioned often before, made to serve postal needs, and only a comparatively few of each printing are perfect enough to meet these high standards. And because they are rare, such specimens command a high premium when they are offered for sale by a dealer or fellow collector.

The continental European collectors have a much more practical set of standards to guide them in the matter of condition. They consider as very fine any stamp which is in as good condition as when it was issued by the post office. They pay little attention to centering and do not care whether the perforation holes touch or even cut into the imprinted design, so long as all the perforations are still on the stamp and none of them is torn.

This manner of determining condition standards is a sensible one, and the person who seeks to collect for the sheer joy of owning stamps that will give him the satisfaction of possession coupled with the fun of learning many things which a postage stamp has to teach will be able to build a much larger collection if he does not set his standards too high. This does not mean that he will collect only off-center stamps; rather it means that he will accept an off-center specimen only when he cannot get a perfectly centered one in those cases where the specimen is worth more than a few cents apiece.

The collector should never compromise in other respects. The sooner he learns to abhor a specimen that is creased, torn, or thinned through careless handling or very heavily postmarked, the sooner will he be proud of his collection; for, as in every other field of endeavor, a thing of beauty is a joy forever. Perhaps a stamp that is thin because it was peeled from the envelope on which it was used as a frank, or because a previous hinge was carelessly removed, may look well on the face and may even deceive a fellow collector who examines the collection; but the owner himself knows of the defect and will never be absolutely happy about the specimen if he is the least bit honest with himself.

Paper

One does not have to be a stamp collector or a book publisher to know that the word *paper* covers a multitude of printing surfaces. One doesn't have to be a Dard Hunter to recognize the difference between the pages of this book and a sheet of newsprint, nor does one have to have years of training to see that there is a difference between the pages on which the text and the illustrations of this book are printed.

When postage stamps are ordered by governments, the only specifications for the type of paper that should be used are based upon utility and security. The paper must be cheap enough to make tremendous printings possible, durable enough to stand up under the wear and tear to which postage stamps are subjected, and uncommon enough to make it difficult or impossible for dishonest persons to counterfeit it.

When the Penny Black was suggested, one of the safeguards employed by the British Post Office Department was the use of a paper made to specification so that each sheet had 240 watermark designs in the shape of a small crown so arranged that one of them would appear on the back of every stamp. The use of watermarks [1] for postage-stamp paper was widely used thereafter and even today some governments insist that such paper be used whenever it is possible to do so. In many, many other cases postage stamps were and are printed on whatever type of paper happens to be available, whether it has a watermark or not.

In our discussion of paper we shall not endeavor to enter into a technical discussion of paper as a subject. Entire books have been

[1] The subject of watermarks is another technical phase of philately and will be covered more thoroughly on pages 164-166.

written on this subject alone, and if a reader wishes to delve into a more serious study he is urged to read Dard Hunter's *Papermaking* (published by Alfred A. Knopf, Inc., New York), which is without question the best, for it covers the matter most thoroughly and yet makes enjoyable, interesting reading. Here we shall merely point out the importance of paper as it affects the collection of postage stamps.

Again we must remember that to a government the production of postage stamps is a printing job, nothing more. In the larger countries of the world a postal administration or the government printing plant (if postage stamps are not ordered from a private firm) will generally specify minimum standards for the paper to be used. In other instances the selection of paper is left up to the printer to whom the contract is let, for, like any other business, a post office realizes that the specialist to whom a job is given should know his business and, when left to his own resources, will invariably do the best work with the best materials at his disposal.

In virtually every instance both governments and printers endeavor to provide uniformity in the paper used, but frequently they have to employ substitutes simply because stocks of the identical paper cannot always be procured on a moment's notice. You need only recall some of your own experiences to understand this. Suppose you had ordered some letterheads that pleased you very much and that filled your needs for a definite period of time. But now your supply of them is running low, or has been already exhausted, and you want some more. You go back to the same printer who made the original ones, give him a sample, and ask him to duplicate them. How often will he say, "Sorry, but I have no more of this paper on hand and it will take six months to get a new supply." Or, "Sorry, but the factory from which I got this paper no longer stocks it." To the average person exact duplication of paper stock is not too important; so long as the one he gets is approximately the same texture and quality, he will accept a substitute. And so do governments. It is only because philatelists are keen students that they take such a deep interest in paper and classify stamps according to it.

The distinction between papers can mean that a stamp you own may be a common or a rare variety, and unless you are able to tell the difference yourself, you cannot know if the specimen in your album is worth $200 or just $2. As you scan the pages of the standard catalogue you will come across hundreds of examples where the same design was imprinted on two different kinds of paper, in which case that same design is listed as *two* different stamps.

Take for example the Threepenny Beaver of Canada's first issue. When that stamp was issued in 1851 it was printed on a laid paper. A year or so later more such stamps were needed to serve postal duty and the plates were put in the press again, but this time only "wove" paper was available. The former have a collector's value of about $20 while the latter are worth less than half of that.

There are many paper-making processes, but fundamentally all paper is produced by pulping the fibrous ingredients into a mashlike liquid form and screening it into a thin, flat surface so that the fibers will interlock, dry, and come out as a solid sheet. Because the ingredients will vary, there are rag and wood-pulp papers; because paper is made by hand and by various types of machines, and because different screens are used, the finished product may be anything from a thick, brownish wrapping paper to an extra-thin, highly glossy tissue. A brief description of the types of paper encountered by the stamp collector will be given here, but let it be said that verbal descriptions can be used only for a guide and that the collector must actually examine specimens of stamps printed on each type before he can become familiar with their characteristics.

All machine-made paper—the kind on which most of today's printing is done—is *wove*. It derives its name from the pattern of the paper's fibers, which look very much like the weaving in a piece of cloth simply because the screen on which the pulp was spread to mould was very finely woven with thin wires. All current United States stamps are printed on this type of paper, so it might be a good idea to take any one of these, hold it against a good light, and examine it with a strong magnifying glass until you can see this "weaving" in the actual body of the paper. While the examination of paper can be made by an expert regardless of what has been printed on it, the novice would do well to study those portions of a stamp that bear no printing —the space between the design and the perforations or, better still, the selvage margins around the margins of a full sheet. In this way he will not be confused by such printing as is on the stamp, which may give the paper itself a different appearance.

When a screen consists only of fine wires stretched only in one direction, the paper produced from it has a pattern of straight lines and is called *laid*. When the paper is made the lines run in a single direction; but when stamps are printed on such paper after it has been cut into sheets, the lines may run from top to bottom of the design, in which case philatelists refer to it as *vertically laid*, or from side to side, in which case they call it *horizontally laid*. Actually these are misnomers, and although this terminology is universal, it would be better to say that they are horizontally or vertically printed on laid paper.

When a screen, especially one made of very, very fine wires, is expected to be subjected to hard wear, the manufacturer often reinforces it with stronger wires in much the same manner as a construction engineer places steel rods in concrete to give it strength and support. Paper made from such screen, whether the fine wires run in one direction or are woven like textiles, will therefore reveal heavier lines where the reinforcements have been placed. If the strengthening wires are webbed in two directions across the screen to form squares, the paper is designated as *quadrille carré*, or to form rectangles, *oblong quadrille*.

Paper used for the manufacture of stamps is also classified as to thin, thick, hard, soft, and as to color—bluish, grayish, yellowish, and so on. Such designations, however, are seldom standard but rather are relative, depending upon the stamps to which they refer. A complicated scientific gauge must be employed to determine the exact thickness of any piece of paper, and as such gauges are quite expensive and not likely to be available to stamp collectors in general, such vague terms "thick," "thin" or "medium" are used by catalogue editors. The collector need have no worry about distinguishing these, for if he has any specimens of a certain issue which come on a variety of paper thicknesses he can easily see which are relatively thin, medium, or thick, for these differences are perceptible to the ordinary touch or feel.

The colored papers, too, will identify themselves. They are merely mentioned in the catalogue to let the collector know that the stamps come that way. Just one word of caution, however. Not infrequently a regular stamp printed on white paper will have been used on an envelope made of colored paper, and in the course of soaking the stamp, the color of the envelope washes into the paper fibers of the stamp and dyes it. It is possible, therefore, to find a "bluish" stamp in your album, although the catalogue makes no mention of such a variety. If the specimen is a canceled one, you can be pretty sure that this dyeing has taken place.

As a security measure some papermakers have employed a number of methods to produce a paper that cannot easily be counterfeited, among which the addition of silk threads or fragments to the paper pulp is especially predominant. In some cases long silk threads have been stretched across the pulp before it has had a chance to dry and harden so that these threads are actually impregnated in the paper itself. A stamp printed on such paper will have a single thread running horizontally or vertically through it.

More often, however, the papermaker simply takes a quantity of silk rags of the same color or of colors that differ from the color of the paper pulp itself and chops them so thoroughly that only wee bits of thread are left. These are mixed in with the pulp just before the paper mash is spread on the screen to harden. When the paper is dry, these fragments, almost microscopic though they be, can be seen in the texture. This type of paper is commonly called *granite paper*.

For the benefit of the collector who desires personally to examine the various types of paper mentioned, the following list of common stamps is presented. The collector need only get specimens of these and within a few minutes become familiar with what is meant in each case:

Wove:	Any current United States issues.
Laid:	Brazil 1882–84 issue, all values.
Batonné (quadrille):	Mexico, Guadalajara, 1867, 68.
Colored:	Great Britain, 1887, 2½, 3 and 6-penny.
Silk-thread:	Switzerland, 1854–62, all values.
Granite:	Switzerland, 1905 and nearly all after that.

Printing Methods

Like papermaking, the graphic arts employ a wide variety of printing methods; and while an advanced philatelic student will study every available book dealing with those methods, and often visit printing plants to watch personally how they are used, the average collector need merely know how to tell the differences between stamps that have been printed from steel-engraved plates, or lithographed or typographed surfaces. Again, the novice who watches an expert pick up a stamp and identify it by a single glance may marvel at this person's ability; but with only a little practice he himself may soon duplicate that feat, for there are several characteristics that betray the method by which a stamp was produced.

Basically, stamps may be made from recess-engraved plates or they may be typographed, lithographed, or embossed. Each of these printing methods has several subdivisions. For example, the term "engraving" covers such specific printing processes as steel or copper engraving by virtue of the metal upon which the design is cut. It also covers the modern mass-production processes of heliogravure, photogravure, and rotogravure. Typography includes printing from hand-set type, electrotypes, and stereotypes. Lithography may designate the method of printing from a design drawn on stone or from a zinc offset. Yet, subdivided though each of these general processes may be, the principle is the same in each.

The principle of engraving involves the cutting of a design *into* the metal printing surface so that the *recessed* lines will be filled with ink when the printing operation begins. After a plate has been inked the surface is wiped clean, either by manual or mechanical power, and a sheet of paper (frequently moistened beforehand) is then placed against the surface and subjected to enough pressure so that the ink in the engraved lines will adhere to the paper and produce the desired design.

Because the colored portions of a design made from an engraved surface represent ink that has filled recesses cut into metal, there is a visible "thickness" to it which stands above the paper; and this is the clew for which the collector must look in determining whether his specimen has been engraved. The *thickness* of the ink is relatively small, and except in very, very few cases can it be *felt* by one's finger; so never make the mistake of trying to determine this manually, for the chances are that you will thus soil the stamp itself.

To learn how to distinguish an engraved stamp, select a specimen which you know has been made by this process—all recent United States stamps, with the exception of the Overrun Nations or Flag series, have been recess engraved, so these are perfect and easy-to-obtain samples—and study it through a magnifying glass. First pick out a portion of the stamp that has a solid mass of color either surrounding or surrounded by a strong white area: the figures of value or the inscription "U.S. Postage" make excellent samples. Examine the selected portion of the stamp (through a good magnifying glass) at an oblique angle rather than straight down and then notice how the ink of the colored portion seems to stand *above* the white of the design. In some cases—the New York World's Fair issue of 1939 is an excellent example—you can actually see the thickness of the ink. Now for a second "test" select an area of the stamp which is composed chiefly of fine lines and look at these through your glass. The eyes or hair of a person, if a portrait forms the main subject of the stamp's vignette, or the distant background, if a stamp has a pictorial subject, usually offer the best examination area. In an engraved stamp these fine lines are clear and sharp, no matter how tiny or how close together they may be. They are not fuzzy or jagged when you look at them through a glass. But they will be weaker and appreciably lighter than those areas you examined first, and so the ink will appear to have no *thickness* at all. This is due to the fact that in engraving the design the craftsman must cut the heavier areas much deeper than the fine ones in order to achieve that "three-dimensional" effect which can be obtained only through this graphic process.

Typography involves exactly the opposite principle. Whereas in engraving the colored portion of a design was cut into the metal, in typography the colored area was produced by the actual surface of the metal or other material used to make the design. The pages of this book were typographed: that is, each of the letters and each word were made in such a way that the inked portions stand above the white area. An inked roller is passed over the printing surface and then pressed against a piece of paper to make the impression. And since the layer of ink passed over the surface is even, it is impossible to notice any *thickness* at all. Were a surface, prepared for the typography of this book, inked in the same manner as one for recessed engraving and then printed you would be reading a black page with white letters.

To recognize a typographed stamp you examine it in the same manner as outlined before; but in the doing, you will notice that the colored areas will be flat, and even though you have an "eagle" eye, you will perceive no difference in *thickness* between the colored and the white areas. When you examine the fine details of a design you will notice two things. The lines will be a bit ragged and not perfectly sharp. The white area between them will not be too perceptible. The reason for the latter characteristic is that the metal of the printing surface which imprints these fine lines is only slightly raised above the recesses that are not intended to be inked. Under the pressure required to transfer the ink from the printing surface to the paper, the ink is "squashed" and spreads a trifle (unevenly, of course) to the white area that surrounds these fine lines. When examined under a very strong glass, these thin lines look not unlike those you make with a fountain pen upon a piece of newspaper.

Lithography is based upon the principle that water and oil will not mix. Originally the printing surface was a stone polished to a high degree of smoothness, and it is because of this fact that the process has derived its name from the Greek *lithos* (stone), and *graphein* (to write). Today the surface may be a metal, but whether it is metal or stone, the principle is the same. The desired design is drawn on the surface with a greasy ink and allowed to dry. The face of the surface then is wetted with water in which an acid mixture has been dissolved. This mixture will settle over those portions of the surface that have not been painted with the drawing ink. Now a mixture of greasy ink and water shaken together is flowed over the surface. The wet part of the surface will not take the greasy ink, and the inked parts of the surface will not take the water but will accept the ink. The paper is then pressed against the surface and the ink that was flowed on comes off, reproducing the design.

Nowadays lithography is produced by the offset method. The surface (usually a zinc alloy) is inked as described, but instead of placing the paper against it directly, a fine rubber roller is passed over it. The paper is then set against the roller, upon which the design has been transferred, and thus accepts the printing.

Lithographed stamps closely resemble engraved ones, except that the ink is not raised above the surface of the paper. They are usually very dull and flat in appearance as compared with those made by either typography or recess engraving.

In the early days of postage-stamp manufacture, a process known as embossing was used to make postal paper, but today about the only general use of this method is employed in the production of our stamped envelopes. To make an embossed design, the design is cut into steel *male* and *female* dies in such a manner that the raised portions on the male die are recessed on the female. A piece of paper is then placed between the two and the dies are pressed together, thus forcing the paper to take the shape of the design. Embossing may be colorless or a combination of color and colorlessness. It cannot ever be completely colored, for it is impossible to ink the embossing dies. An examination of any United States envelope will reveal in a moment the characteristics of stamps made by this method much more easily than will any study of a written description; and as there never can be any confusion between these stamps and the ones made by previously described processes, the collector need never worry.

In the beginning of this section we mentioned that each of the general printing principles was subdivided. As these branches of the graphic arts may be recognized by distinctive characteristics, the most important and most frequently met ones will now be mentioned.

Type set. As the name implies, the printing surface of this process is made up from letters, figures, and symbols usually in stock at a print shop. When stamps are required by some small place which does not have the more advanced printing facilities, entire stamps are made up by this method. The early Hawaiian and British Guiana stamps are excellent examples.

More frequently, however, typesetting is used to make provisional stamps by overprinting ones in stock. Examples of these can be found all through the stamp album. Most countries today order their regular stamps from the large banknote companies in the United States and Europe, but not infrequently a change of postal rate, or the failure of a new supply to arrive in time to meet a need, results in the lack of proper stamps. Government officials therefore take stamps they have on hand, send them to a local print shop, and instruct the printer to change the value originally inscribed by overprinting a new one. In some cases an event or a new service warrants the preparation of distinctive stamps, and again, when regular stamps cannot be made in time, the local printer does an overprinting job. That is why we find regular stamps overprinted *Correo Aereo* or *Gobierno Revolucionario* or kindred words and phrases.

Local print shops rarely have a very large supply of type of any specific font, and so in such an emergency, when they must overprint entire sheets of stamps so that each stamp in the sheet is overprinted, they set up whatever type they have on hand. As a consequence, stamp collectors will find a number of minor varieties in the overprints that have been applied in this way. The individual letters or figures may not be identical; the spacing of the overprint may not be exactly the same; punctuation marks may be present or absent, and so on. One of the best examples of the varieties that can be found on such stamps is shown by the stamps of the Cape of Good Hope, overprinted in 1877 for use in Griqualand. In making up the printing form with which these stamps were overprinted with a *G* the printer used no fewer than twenty different fonts!

Stereotyped. In larger cities, where print shops have more advanced equipment, uniformity can be achieved through a process known as stereotyping. This process involves the setting up of a desired design with type and then placing a piece of specially prepared papier-mâché over the single design and subjecting it to tremendous pressure. The raised portions of the design are then sunk into the paper, which then becomes a mould. Molten type metal is then poured into this mould as many times as necessary to make up a surface that will print a number of stamps at one time. Since all the stereotypes have been made from the same mould, all of the stamps in the sheet are alike except for such minor variations as may be caused by faulty casting.

Photoengraved. While this name may cause a bit of confusion at the outset, one should remember that photoengraved stamps fall into the category of *typographed* stamps and not recessed ones, simply because the colored portions are made from the *surface* and not from the *recesses* of the printing form. Photoengraving is most generally used in the printing of pictures which appear in modern newspapers and books, and to learn the fundamentals of this process the collector is urged to pick up the nearest newspaper, select a picture printed in it, and examine it with a magnifying glass. He will see that the picture consists of a series of dots of varying sizes and density.

To make a photoengraved design, an artist's original drawing is photographed at the engraving plant. But this will not be an ordinary photograph such as you or I could make with a regular camera. This special camera has a device which allows the photoengraver to place a piece of glass between the bellows of the camera and the film upon which the image is to be reproduced. Even the glass is extraordinary. Known as a *screen*, this glass has been precisely and finely ruled with tiny squares, so that when the image is photographed the film will not have a full picture but one broken up into small square dots. The size of the dots will depend upon the gauge of the screen used, and it is determined by the type of paper used to make the finished picture. When a cheap quality paper is used, the screen will be coarse (from 65 to 85); the finer the paper, the finer the screen.

Once the film has been exposed and developed, it is placed on a metal surface that has been coated with photographic emulsions and again exposed. This metal plate (zinc when a coarse screen is desired, and copper when a fine one is needed), after it has been exposed to the negative in a manner similar to that used in making a print of a snapshot, is then etched in an acid bath. The dots are not affected by the acid, so that only those areas that will be white on the finished stamp are eaten away.

In making up a surface from which sheets of stamps will be printed, the same negative is exposed time and again until the whole sheet has been photoengraved.

Several other processes employ the photographic principle, and among these are rotogravure, heliogravure, or rotoprint. While these are fundamentally the same, the differences represent simply technical devices developed by individuals with a view of improving the finished products made from them and to protect their patent rights.

These methods, although the principle is the same as photoengraving, however, fall into subdivisions of recess engraving because, in the printing, the *recessed* areas are filled with ink and the surface is wiped clean before the paper is pressed against it.

Even experts have been known to be unable to tell whether a stamp was helioengraved, rotoengraved or rotoprinted; and so the collector need not worry about a lack of ability to distinguish between these processes. His only concern will be to tell the difference between one of these subdivisions and typography, lithography, and recess engraving. This, however, is very simple, since the aforementioned dots can be seen without difficulty when examined under a good magnifying glass.

Methods of Separation

When postage stamps were first introduced they were delivered to post offices in full sheets so that clerks had to separate them by using a pair of scissors or a knife, or simply by folding them and tearing them along the creases. In some cases, either intentionally or by accident (when a sheet happens to be put in a stack of finished stamps before it has been perforated), stamps still are issued without any way of separating one from the other. All such stamps are commonly known as *imperforates* or the shortened *imperf*.

If you can imagine yourself going to a post office today and waiting until a clerk has snipped a stamp from a sheet, you may readily realize that those fellows back in the 1840's were likewise annoyed and sought methods of simplifying the separation of individual stamps.

In 1847 an Irishman by the name of Henry Archer invented a device that would "pierce the sheet of 240 stamps with slits so that each sheet might be torn apart." He offered this invention to the Postmaster General, who liked the idea well enough to pay him £4,000 for the model and patent. The first model was actually a rouletting machine which later proved to be unsuitable, for it did not punch holes *from* the paper, but merely *incised* the paper with tiny cuts. Archer himself and several others experimented further, and finally, in 1853, a machine was developed which cut tiny holes all along the sides of each stamp in such a manner that under ordinary circumstances the stamps would hold together and yet be easily separated. The Post Office was satisfied with this device and put it to use on January 2, 1854.

The rouletting method (derived from the French word meaning *small wheel*), has been used in various corners of the world because it could be done on an ordinary printing press by setting up printing slugs, padding the bed of the press, and then running the stamp sheets through without putting ink on the rollers. Roulettes come in a variety of forms, depending upon the design used on the printing press. There is the *line roulette* (— — — — —), which consists of dashes in a straight line. The *scalloped roulette* (‿ ‿ ‿ ‿ ‿) is formed by using a half-circle design in a straight line. The *serpentine roulette* (‿ ⁀ ‿ ⁀ ‿ ⁀) is formed by using half-circle designs in an alternating succession, one normal and one inverted. The *sawtooth roulette* (vvvvvv) is formed by using a row of v's.

Perforations are more commonly used today because machines for doing this job are manufactured and available nearly everywhere. These machines all work on the same principle, although some are more developed than others, especially in countries where stamp production runs into the billions each week. They consist of rows or *combs* of metal rods set in wooden or metal blocks in such a manner that the rows will strike a stamp sheet right between the individual designs. Some machines will perforate stamps along one direction at a time, others will perforate in both directions at the same time. In the former instance it is quite possible for a workman to perforate a sheet of stamps horizontally and, through error or carelessness, forget to turn the sheet around and add the vertical perforations, or vice-versa. This results in what is philatelically known as a partially perforated stamp, or *part perf*. Such varieties normally are rare and worth much more than a fully perforated specimen.

Since the size of the rods used on a perforating machine are not always the same in diameter, the holes they punch between the margins of stamps are consequently different. In the United States, for example, we have stamps that are perforated with holes of a wide variety of sizes, each one of which was used for a specific purpose. When vending machines were introduced, stamps were made into coils rather than sheets, and these were perforated with very large holes to make them easy to dispense from one of the nickel or dime automatic salesmen such as you see in drugstores or railroad stations today.

In the regular sheet stamps there are differences, too. At one time the Bureau of Engraving and Printing used perforating machines that punched a great many small holes close together around the stamps; but this resulted in a problem for postal clerks. They found that the sheets broke apart much too easily, for the slightest handling of the sheets would result in their falling apart. It seems that the paper "bridges" were too weak. Accordingly the Bureau made the hole slightly larger but placed them farther apart. Even this was not practical, for unused stamps in a full sheet have a tendency to curl in the direction in which they were gummed. The larger holes were all right for the direction opposite that to the curl, but they were too strong for the other direction, so finally the bureau got around to making the perforations larger on one side and smaller on the other. Stamps with different perforation sizes vertically and horizontally are called *compound perforations* by philatelists.

If you have ever heard collectors talk about perforations, or have looked at a catalogue, you will have heard or seen such terms as "Perf. 10" or "Perforated 12," and probably wondered what was meant by this mysterious parlance. If you're like most folks who have never had the terms explained, you will have decided that a stamp identified as a "Perf 10" has ten holes along one side, and then become perplexed when you counted the perforation holes and found that there were more than ten on the stamp you owned.

Almost as soon as this method of separating stamps from a sheet was adopted, philatelists devised a system of measuring the sizes of the holes. The inventor of that system, a continental collector, used a two-centimeter rule as his basis and then measured all perforations by it. If there are seven holes within that two-centimeter distance, the stamp is said to be perforated 7; if there are fifteen holes, the stamp is said to be perforated 15, and so on. But naturally counting holes would be a tedious and often tiring job, so the matter of measuring a stamp's perforations has been simplified by the introduction of a *perforation gauge*. This is a piece of cardboard, metal, or plastic upon which are printed dots of color in rows, each of which is a different size, ranging from the smallest to the largest found on any stamps of the world. Each is marked with the size of dots contained in the row. You can buy one of these for anywhere from a cent to a dollar, depending upon the quality of material on which the gauge is printed. But most dealers will give you one for the asking, and so there is no reason why any collector should be without one of these very important tools of the hobby.

To measure the perforation of any stamp you own, you simply run the stamp up and down the gauge until you reach a row whose colored dots exactly fit the perforation holes of the stamp. You then look at the number printed alongside the row and you have the gauge. That is how simple it is.

Watermarks

The watermarks that have been used on various postage stamps is yet another technical factor which every serious collector must understand to more fully appreciate his hobby. As we mentioned before, Great Britain introduced watermarked paper as a final measure to prevent counterfeiting. Since that time many governments have employed the same precaution in the making of their postal paper. But the absence of a watermark on a stamp does not mean it is not genuine, for a great many stamps of the world have been printed on paper without such a device.

Then too, a stamp design, its color, and its perforations may be similar, yet the watermark may be different. So again this provides the collector with two or more spaces in his album to fill instead of just a single space.

For years the British colonies printed their stamps on paper watermarked with a device consisting of a crown and the letters "CC," an abbreviation for "Crown Colony." In the eighties this was changed to "CA," for "Crown Agent," and although the designs, colors, and perforations were unaltered, philatelists recognize stamps printed on each of these watermarked papers as separate items.

This truth applies to stamps all over the world. Many times an original order is printed on specially watermarked stock, but when a reprinting is necessary the paper is not on hand and unwatermarked stock must be used. In some cases the design or inscription of a watermark is purposely changed. When Egypt was under Turkish administration its stamps had a watermark showing a crescent and one star; later, as it gained its independence and altered its national flag, a triple crescent and star replaced the Turkish emblem.

In 1898, when the Sudan issued its first definitive stamps, which were printed by Thomas de la Rue and Company, of England, a lotus flower was selected as the design for the watermark. However well intentioned the selection of that particular design was, the watermark itself looked so much like a Christian cross that natives who used the stamps almost staged a revolt. Being fervent Moslems those of them who noticed that watermark refused to use the stamps lest they violate their religious scorn for the "infidels." So widespread was this protest that the watermark had to be changed to a crescent and star, an undeniable symbol of Islamism.

Watermarks may mean substantial price differences, too. The New Zealand stamps of 1855 and 1864 are similar in all respects except watermark designs. A onepenny stamp of the first issue, with a large star watermark, is worth about $350; one of the second, with a watermark consisting of the letters "NZ," is worth but about $10!

But what are watermarks? Surely every reader has seen a watermark at one time or another. Paper on which good stationery is printed has a watermark to identify it as the product of a definite manufacturer. Government letterheads are usually watermarked with either the United States seal or the seal of the agency using it. On such large sheets of paper you need but hold the letter to the light to see the watermark, which appears as a lighter figure in the texture of the paper. Some stamps' watermarks can be seen in the same manner; some are more difficult to behold. We shall discuss examination methods later; for the moment we shall endeavor to explain the process by which watermarks are made so that we may better understand what they are.

In our description of papermaking we mentioned the screen on which pulp is spread to dry and harden and explained how these are made up of tiny wires either laid or woven. One type of watermarking is produced by soldering designs, made of fine wires, right to the wires of this screen; another and more widely used method consists of soldering the wire designs to a "dandy-roll," which is rolled over the paper after it has been *formed* on the screen but before it has been completely hardened. In either case, the fine wire designs—

shaped into letters of the alphabet or any desired figure—are impressed into the paper so that the paper itself is microscopically thinner wherever the watermark design has been pressed.

When a watermark cannot be seen by holding it up to an ordinary light source, the use of a philatelic watermark detector will prove valuable. Such a detector is a simple affair and its operation is even simpler. Stamps to be examined are placed in the detector—a small black dish made of enameled metal or glass—face downward. A drop or two of benzine, Carbona, Energine, or kindred fluid, will cover the area of the stamp, and before it evaporates the watermark design usually will become visible as a neon light on a dark street.

There are more advanced watermark detectors on the market with which no liquid need be used. These consist of a box in which a small electric-light bulb sends illumination through a glass-covered opening at the top. The stamp is placed on this and examined through a filter which absorbs the color of the ink with which the stamp has been printed. The watermark can then be seen without difficulty.

Plating

When a government of today issues a new postage stamp, collectors can obtain for the asking, directly from the post office or the printing firm, almost all the technical information they require for a full knowledge of the issue. But it was not always thus. When postage stamps were first issued there were no philatelists, and such details as "who made the design," "who engraved the die," "how the stamps were printed," "when certain stamps were issued," "how many stamps comprised a full sheet," or "how the subjects were arranged on the full sheet," were rarely put into the permanent records. Accordingly, later, when stamp collecting waddled from the stage of a simple acquisition hobby to a serious, advanced avocation, these questions could be answered only through arduous study on the part of the philatelists themselves. The quest for answers to the last two questions formed the basis for some of the most brilliant sleuthing of our hobby and resulted in what philatelists call *plating*.

"But why is it necessary to know such details?" you may ask.

Frankly, the average collector is no more concerned about such information than is a general practitioner about details of the technique of curing cancer. But there are many physicians to whom such knowledge is valuable, and so determined research is going on all the time. This concern or lack of it is chiefly what distinguishes a stamp collector from a philatelist. The former simply *collects* stamps; the latter *collects* and *investigates* them and the circumstances surrounding their issuance.

Twenty or thirty years after some of the early issues came into being, then, philatelists began asking the questions listed, and when they could not get answers from the officials, they set out on their own hunt. The plating of the Penny Black and subsequent British issues offered no problems, for, as we have already mentioned, each stamp on a sheet had control letters on each of the 240 subjects that were on the full sheet, so that all one had to do was read the letters in order to know the exact position on the sheet from which that particular stamp was originally placed.

Working on the premise that no matter how carefully a craftsman may do his job, it is impossible to duplicate any design without leaving a clew, however minute or tiny, even if a plate is made from the same master design, philatelists set out to discover those variations. They studied every stamp of a single type that they could find under high-powered magnifying glasses. They scanned every square millimeter of the design and made notes of every difference they discovered, whether it was a variation in the length or breadth of a fine line, the shading of a portrait, or the shape of a tiny curlicue.

After examining several hundred or perhaps several thousand stamps of the same issue, they could pretty well tell which of the variations recurred again and again and thus knew precisely how many such variations existed. This, in turn, gave them an almost accurate idea of how many stamps were in the original sheet. But now came the problem of *reconstructing* the sheet.

For, suppose, they knew that there were a hundred variations, and that therefore the original sheet must have contained a hundred stamps, they still had to know whether the sheet consisted of ten rows of ten stamps each, four rows of twenty-five, two rows of fifty, or any other combination to make up a total of a hundred.

The second step of plating consist of once again examining each specimen and finding evidence that will betray its position on the sheet. If a stamp has a right-hand margin still attached, we know it must have come from the right-hand side of the sheet. If it has both top and side margins, we know it must have come from a top corner. That information narrows down our search.

The third step is the examination of multiple pieces such as pairs, strips, or blocks and checking the variations which are found on each stamp of the piece until we have determined the relative position of each of our classified variations. Eventually, after we have studied enough multiple pieces, we can arrange our hundred copies, reconstruct the entire sheet, and know exactly how the sheet was arranged and the position of everyone of the hundred specimens.

The job is very much like a difficult jig-saw puzzle. Suppose we have classified an identified hundred differences in any given stamp and numbered each one consecutively for our own preliminary guidance. Now we find two pairs of that stamp and examine them further. We see that one pair contains varieties which we have called 1 and 15. The other contains varieties which we have called 15 and 37. We now know that our varieties 1, 15, and 37 were printed from adjoining positions on the original plate. We continue this until we have irrefutably located every one of our one hundred variations and have completed the plating of the sheet.

This procedure is simple if the number of a definite stamp issue was small and only one plate was used. It becomes more involved if the stamp was a common one and millions of them were issued, for then the chances are even that more than one plate was used for the printing job—either at one time or at a later date, as supplies of the initial printing were exhausted. It means that we shall have to study each stamp even more carefully and check a large number of multiple pieces to be absolutely sure that our deductions are flawless. Suppose again that we find two pairs of stamps and notice that the right-hand one of each pair shows the variety we classified as 15, but that the left-hand one of one pair is our 37; the other, our 75. Immediately we know that these must have come from two different plates or other printing surfaces. Accordingly we shall have to reconstruct *two* sheets. Assuming that the printing surfaces were made up at different times,[2] we are aided by the fact that the shade of printing ink

[2] In recess-engraved and lithographed stamps the printing surface is usually stored in the vaults of the printing firm and may be used again and again until the surface is worn out. When a new plate or stone is made up, the same variations rarely if ever occur. Therefore a variation we classified for the first printing will not recur in the second, and our problem resolves itself into merely placing an additional number of variations in their proper positions.

In typographed issues a certain number of individual clichés are made, each of which usually is characterized by one of the variations we identified, and then is assembled into a printing surface. When the initial printing is completed the clichés are usually disassembled and stored. Now, if a second printing is required, the workmen reassemble the clichés into a second printing surface, so that the chances of the same arrangement being made are very, very slim. In

cannot be exactly matched and the chance that different paper was used to print from the original and the subsequent surface. By sorting out our specimens according to shade of color and paper, if, in fact, there is such a difference, we can estimate almost exactly which ones belong together.

Errors

In the whole field of philately there is no more thrilling subject than that of *errors*. There are errors due to the carelessness of an artist who made a mistake in the drawing that was used by a government in creating a postage-stamp vignette. There are errors that are due to imperfect production. And there are errors that were intentionally produced in order to exploit collectors.

The first category is particularly interesting, and the number of stamps with such errors increases annually. If you wish to have an endless amount of fun, you can examine the various stamp designs in your own collection; examine them carefully and see how many you can find which do not agree with fact.

In 1903, for example, the British possession of St. Kitts-Nevis, in the lesser Antilles, issued a set of stamps that featured a portrait of Christopher Columbus peering through a telescope. At first glance, this is a very fine design; but if you check your dates of inventions, you will discover that the telescope was developed only a century after Columbus lived, so that he could not possibly have used one in sighting land in 1492!

That same year France issued a set of stamps which show the picture of a sower, while in the background you can see the sun rising against the horizon. Again, this is a very attractive design, but if you begin figuring it out, you will see that the front of the sower is illuminated while the back—the side facing the sun—is in the shade! Now, who ever heard of such a phenomenon? Certainly this is an error, yet those stamps remained in use for over thirty-five years, and none of them is worth more than $1! Most are worth only a cent or two apiece.

In 1922, Gambia obtained a new set of stamps in which an elephant is shown against a "native scene." It is quite obvious that the artist

the case of Egypt's third issue, those clichés were assembled six or seven different times, and so we have that number of *settings*, or the arrangement of the same number of variations in six or seven different combinations. In this case the slight differences in the shades of ink used in the printing and the type of paper employed are the clews that distinguish among the several *settings*.

who made this design never used a real animal as a model, or even consulted a zoological reference or actual photograph, for in drawing the hind legs of the elephant, he gave the pachyderm the knee-joints of a horse. If an elephant had hind legs as the artist made them, the animal could not walk!

The person who studies United States stamps can find similar errors in astounding numbers. In 1893, for instance, our government issued belatedly a set of stamps to commemorate the quatro-centennial of the discovery of America. The one-cent denomination features "Columbus in Sight of Land." The two-cent value features "The Landing of Columbus." If you consult your history books you will discover that the great explorer reached the shores of San Salvador one night and made his landing the following morning. But if you look at the stamps you will see Chris clean-shaven on the first stamp and with a full beard on the second. In this case you cannot blame the stamp designer, for these pictures were copied from famous oil paintings: the first one by William H. Powell, the other by Vanderlyn. When these artists painted the masterpieces, they had to imagine Christopher Columbus as he looked back there in October, 1492; there are no records that prove whether he was clean-shaven or bearded. Individually they are wonderful pictures, but when you look at them side by side in a stamp album, the inconsistency is indeed striking.

Of late, United States postage stamps—especially the commemorative issues—have been produced under considerable pressure. In many cases the Post Office Department decides upon a stamp or set of stamps only a few weeks before they must be issued, and so the Bureau of Engraving and Printing does not have a chance to check all detail designs for fact and accuracy. When a stamp engraver must turn out a vignette in a matter of weeks, he is so busy doing the actual engraving work that he cannot accomplish the necessary research, and so errors in details are bound to creep in.

Take, for example, the stamp that was issued in 1927 to mark the New York-to-Paris flight of Colonel Charles A. Lindbergh. That stamp shows a map of the route over which the Lone Eagle flew the Spirit of St. Louis. If you check the stamp map against a real one you will see that the engraver made a number of cartographical mistakes. Nova Scotia is attached to the Gaspé Peninsula, Newfoundland is badly misformed, and Paris is shown at the mouth of the Seine instead of far inland.

In 1932, when we had a Winter Olympics commemorative stamp, the engraver depicts the ski jumper in a pose that is as unorthodox as can be. Such a pose, if undertaken by a skier, would result in a serious fall.

The Pony Express stamp of 1940 was severely criticized by equine experts because the engraver has a horse in full gallop while the foreleg of the animal is crooked, a posture which is entirely impossible.

In 1944 we had a special stamp to mark the seventy-fifth anniversary of the completion of the first transcontinental railroad at Promontory Point, Utah. The engraver produced a very nice vignette, but the day he portrayed must have been most peculiar, for if you look at the stamp more than casually you will see the smoke of the engine blowing to the right, while the flag beside the iron horse is blowing in the opposite direction.

In 1945 we had the army stamp which was supposed to depict the United States army entering Paris. The artist copied rather faithfully a picture supplied by the War Department—an actual photograph showing long columns of troops parading under the Arc de Triomphe, but he added a flight of B-29 superforts to fill up a blank space in the sky overhead. Dramatic as that stamp design looks, it is a complete error, for according to the War Department's own records, none of these planes were used in Europe at the time.

Errors such as these are interesting indeed, but they rarely increase the value of a postage stamp unless the postal administration takes steps to correct them before the printed supply is sold. In 1937, France issued a stamp in honor of René Descartes, and in addition to this philosopher's portrait, the design included the front page of his famous book. It was inscribed, "Discours sur la Méthod." Shortly thereafter the error was noticed, the stamps were removed from sale, and the plates altered to have the correct, "Discours de la Méthod." As it happened, about the same number of stamps of each variety exist, so there is little difference in their value.

On September 16, 1946, Canada issued a stamp for the combination air-mail–Special Delivery service, and the engraver placed a circumflex accent over the French "Exprès." This "error" was noticed almost immediately by French officials. The printer was immediately asked to correct the incorrect accent to the accurate grave one and as soon as new stamps could be printed the old ones were removed from sale without advance notice. As a result, dealers and collectors did not have an opportunity of stocking up on the stamps with the false accent and now can get only the correct ones. It is quite probable from what information is on hand that these "error" stamps will be rare in days to come; therefore, if you happen to have one, be sure to keep it to one side.

Errors in stamp designs have had serious consequences in some parts of the world, and these have usually been errors in the designs of maps. In 1900 the Dominican Republic issued a stamp showing the island of Hispaniola, which is occupied by both the Republic of Haiti and the Dominican Republic. Border disputes there have been the cause of numerous uprisings, and when this stamp came out, and the inaccuracies of the artist who drew the dotted borderline between the two countries were noted, Haiti looked upon the stamp as a direct challenge to its territorial rights and lodged a protest that resulted in another conflict in the mountains along the border.

In 1936 the Argentine Republic had a similar experience, although the offending stamp caused nothing worse than a heated exchange of diplomatic notes between Buenos Aires, Santiago, and London.

The stamp in question featured a map of South America in which Argentine territory was indicated in dark ink. When English officials looked at it they were quick to notice that the Falkland Islands—tiny bits of land that have caused not a few contests between the Argentine and Britain—were colored. Chile also noted that some color was included on a tip of the continent which was actually Chilean territory. These protests were so strong that the Argentine had to remove from sale all those stamps and make up a new one which was more accurate in its cartographical delineations. Today the first, erroneous stamp is worth about twice as much as one that was subsequently corrected.

Nicaragua was not quite so fortunate. In 1937, at a time when the feeling between that country and its neighbor, Honduras, was not too friendly, Nicaragua issued a set of air-mail stamps which showed a map of Central America. Here again the engraver showed border lines which included a portion of land claimed by Honduras. When those stamps were placed on sale in Managua, a group of Hondurans (mostly students) took the design as a deliberate challenge to their country's claim and started a riot which lasted several days and resulted in the death and injury of several hundred persons.

Back in 1941, the Philippine Islands sought a new design for their regular postage stamps and staged a contest in which artists of the world were invited to submit suggestions. As a friend of Elaine Rawlinson, who won a prize for her design of a one-cent stamp which subsequently was accepted and used for the Presidential series of United States issues, I was asked by the Philippine Committee personally to ask her to enter a sketch for this contest.

The only stipulation was that a portrait of José Rizal, the national hero of the islands, be featured. After searching through libraries and inquiring at the Philippine Resident Commissioner's office in Washington, the only portrait that could be located (other than that which had been previously used on Philippine stamps) was one printed on an old menu for a Philippine celebration. It was not a particularly good design; moreover, Rizal was facing to the right, whereas Miss Rawlinson needed a picture facing the other way. But since none was available, she photographed the menu card and made a reverse print from which she drew the Rizal portrait. That design ultimately won the contest and the stamp was printed. Only later did scrutinizing Filipinos protest because Mr. Rizal's hair was parted on the wrong side! In turning the print around, Miss Rawlinson had neglected to compensate for the part. Rumors that the stamp would be removed from sale and the design corrected may have been true; we shall never know, because just about that time the Japanese attacked Manila and future stamps were issued under their occupation.

Of course these may be called *errors*, inasmuch as the stamps in question are not accurate; but in a philatelic sense, *errors* consist of mistakes made in the course of production of postage stamps, and these are the ones in which most collectors are most seriously interested. Most errors are worth more money because they are scarcer than normal stamps and therefore are governed by that omnipresent law of supply and demand.

Errors may be produced in all stages of production. They can be made through careless engraving, transferring, printing, overprinting, or perforation, as will be shown here.

Errors in engraving. When entire printing surfaces are hand engraved, the craftsman is quite likely to make a serious mistake in one or more of the individual subjects. When J. Barnard made up the plates from which the second Mauritius stamps were printed, he hand engraved, on copper plates, twelve individual stamp designs. In one of the designs he allowed his graver to cut a little too much copper away so that the inscription, which normally reads, "Two

Pence," actually says, "Two Penoe." This *error* is worth about twice as much as the normal stamp.

Errors in transfer. As we explained before, most stamps are designed and one master die is hand engraved. This is then transferred to a *secondary matrix* by mechanical means and used to make up the printing surface from which the stamp sheets are impressed. It makes little difference whether the *matrix* is a transfer roll (in the case of recessed-graved stamps), a transfer tissue (in the case of lithographed designs), a film negative (in the case of rotogravures), stereotypes or electrotypes (in the case of typographed stamps); the fundamentals are the same.

In making up the full sheet surface the siderographer (the workman to whom is intrusted the job of transferring the master design to the printing plate) can make a mistake if he is the least bit careless.

During World War I, at a time when the Bureau of Engraving and Printing was under terrific pressure and shifts were on a twenty-four hour a day basis, a new plate for the then-current two-cent Washington stamps was being made up. In the course of transferring the designs to the printing plate, the siderographer rocked in the design of the five-cent value into three of the four hundred positions of the plate. How this mistake ever remained unnoticed until the full sheets were printed and distributed to post offices, we shall never know, but we may suspect that inspection was a bit lax and no one observed that these three were inscribed, "5-Cents-5" instead of "2-Cents-2." The plates were put to press, and since they were intended for rose-colored ink, even the three five-centers were printed in that color rather than the blue which would have been normal for the higher denomination.

When stamps are typographed from stereotypes or electrotypes, we can get similar errors. In some cases, each subject for a printing surface is an individual *cliché* or *cut*, mounted on a block of wood, and a number of these are assembled into a complete printing surface. Such was the case in 1877, when the stamps for the various colonies of the Portuguese Empire were produced in Lisbon. At the time a universal design was used for all of the colonies' stamps: it showed a crown surrounded by fancy designs and carried the inscription "Correo" and face value. The only difference was the name of the individual colony. Now, as it happened, the workmen were preparing the printing surface for stamps intended for use in Cape Verde, a group of islands off the West Coast of Africa. They took a lot of individual clichés and arranged them in the desired form, but by mistake one of the clichés which had been made for the stamps of Mozambique got into the layout of the Cape Verde sheet and was printed along with them.

If, therefore, you have one blue 40-reis stamp of Mozambique, issued in 1877, you have no way of telling whether it is one of these errors or not; but if you have a *pair*, or a *block* of stamps, one of which is inscribed "Moçambique," while the others of the multiple piece are inscribed "Cabo Verde," you have an error worth $100.

A similar accident happened in the Cape of Good Hope nearly a century ago. The famous triangular stamps had been made in England, but at one time a new supply had not reached the post office in time, so a local shop, Saul Solomon and Company, had to print up a provisional supply. The printer did not have the recess-engraving facilities, so he made line cuts and stereotypes to be used for the printing job. In making up the printing surfaces for the one and four-penny stamps he got one of the cuts of each value mixed up so that the sheet of the one-penny has one four-penny value in it, and the four-penny sheet has a one-penny value. As these were printed in red and blue, respectively, it is possible to find each value printed in both colors. You may check the Cape of Good Hopes you have, but don't expect to find one of these errors for they are extremely scarce and worth upward of $1,500 each!

A much commoner example of errors caused in this manner may be found among the third issue of Egypt. In 1872, the Egyptian government placed a contract for new stamps with the firm of V. Penasson, of Alexandria, and they made up clichés from which the set was printed. Two years later, as the financial condition of the government grew ever weaker and economies had to be effected, the postal administration asked Penasson to turn over all the clichés to the government printing office in Boulaq. There they had local printers make additional supplies.

As most of the men were natives who knew little or nothing about this form of printing, and besides could not read the inscriptions, they took the clichés and put them into the printing form any old way. Some were placed correctly; others were put in upside down, locked up, and put to press. When the sheets were printed, therefore, we find some normally printed, while others are inverted in relation to the surrounding stamps. A pair of such stamps, one of which is upside down in relation to the adjacent design, are commonly known as

Tête-beche, a term introduced by the French. While they are affixed to each other, they comprise an error; once two such stamps are separated from each other, they no longer are anything but two individual postage stamps and have no premium value or interest.

Printing Errors—Inverts. When a stamp is to be printed in two or more colors, or when two portions of a stamp are printed in the same color, but in two separate printing operations, we may expect another type of error that is very popular and, in many cases, quite rare. The most widely known error of the "invert" species is the famous 24-cent air-mail stamp of the United States issued in 1918. This stamp consists of a red frame design and a blue center in which the picture of a then-popular Jenny airplane was featured. To make this printing, then, the Bureau of Engraving and Printing had to have two separate plates, one for the frame, the other for the vignette. After the first plate was printed and the sheets dried, the sheets were imprinted with the second plate's design, in the second color. One single sheet was put into the second press upside down so that the finished product shows the vignette inverted in relation to the frame design. [It is possible that more than one sheet was printed this way, but at least only one ever got out and found its way to philatelic circles.] Today that is an outstanding rarity and even a single stamp is worth a few thousand dollars.

Whenever two or more plates are used to print stamps, the possibility of similar errors is ever present; and as you thumb through the catalogues you will find numerous references to them. In some cases, a sheet of stamps printed from one plate is overlooked and never gets into the second press so that an intended design is entirely absent. These are mentioned in the catalogue as specimens with "frame omitted" or "vignette omitted," as the case may be.

Printing errors—Multiple impressions. Not infrequently in the course of printing, a sheet of stamps cannot be removed from the press by the workman in time and it is run through twice, resulting in a *double impression;* sometimes even a *third impression* is made. If such a sheet passes the inspectors for one reason or another, is sold through the post office and finds its way to the philatelic market, the stamps showing these multiple impressions are listed as stamp collectors' errors.

Printing errors—Printed on both sides. In some cases a sheet of stamps is printed and through a workman's mistake it is placed on a stack of paper, blank side up, yet to be imprinted. When it goes through the press the second time this sheet is imprinted with the same design on both front and back and is designated as a stamp *printed on both sides*. One word of caution in considering this error. To be *printed on both sides*, a stamp *must* show the design normally in both instances. Frequently we encounter stamps which show a normal design on the front and a design, in reverse, on the back. Such stamps are known as *offsets*.

Such errors are caused in the same way that you will create a sloppy letter-writing job if you place a sheet of paper on top of another upon which you have just penned a message. In printing stamps the workman may not be extra careful, and the finished stamps may be stacked one on top of the other. Now if the ink of the first is not completely dry, the entire design or a portion of it will be offset on the back of the sheet placed above it. The design may be perfectly clear except that it is reversed and looks not unlike the reversed writing on a blotter.

Printing errors—Color errors. Although we have mentioned that it is possible for a stamp of one design to be printed in the color of another because the design was placed in the printing plate through error, we have yet another type of color error that may be caused by a workman who has used the wrong color of ink in printing a sheet of stamps.

We must realize that when a printing firm produces a set of stamps it usually has all the plates ready and on hand so that, except when they are very careful, it is possible to make a mistake in printing one design on a press that has been inked for an entirely different design. This is how the Swiss five-rappen stamp was printed in blue (the color of the 10-rappen denomination) in 1854–1855; and how the Swedish three-skilling was printed in orange (the color for the eight-skilling value). It is also how the four-cent value of the Columbian series of the United States was printed in blue (the color of the one-cent value).

But not all stamps that are in a different color as that in which they were originally printed are errors. Many of them are *changelings*.

If you remember your high-school chemistry experiments you will recall that in some cases it is possible to alter the color of a substance simply by exposing the substance to a chemical. This has happened in stampdom either by accident or intention. Printing inks are chemical in nature and not infrequently it is possible to do a little color-changing of your own. The green United States stamps, for example, are sometimes found in blue. This was caused simply by exposing the stamps to a chemical that eliminates yellow (green is made up of blue and yellow pigments) and leaves only the blue.

Then there is the so-called *lake*, a dark shade of red which is sometimes found on early United States stamps. Students have long considered these as legitimate error, but recently it was shown that either intentional or accidental exposure of a normal carmine stamp to heat over a period of time will darken the color and produce the *lake*, which is a purplish-red pigment prepared from lac or cochineal, for which it is mistaken.

When purple stamps are exposed to strong sunlight, either the red or the blue will be faded, and thus one or the other of the base colors will be left to confound the collector into believing he has an error of color.

Some yellow and orange stamps have a tendency to *oxydize* and become brown over a period of years. This change is quite common and characteristic of such stamps as the six-cent values of the Washington series of the 1908–1919 series, and the 1918 air mails. Such *changelings* are not looked upon with favor among collectors, and if you happen to have any be sure to mark it for what it is and find another copy to fill the space in your album. If you have a stamp that has oxydized, just take a bit of hydrogen peroxide and paint it over the stamp's face. This usually will restore its original yellow or orange shade with little or no ill effects.

Printing errors—Overprints. When a stamp is pressed into service for a postal need other than that for which it has been prepared, a *provisional* results. These most frequently are made by subjecting stamps in stock to a printing that changes either their franking value, commemorate some important event, or makes them valid for a special service.

In most cases the basic stamps have been produced by a good firm in England, the United States, Paris, or Switzerland. But because the need for a provisional is immediate, those basic stamps are given to a printer in a remote place in the world for the overprinting operation.

The same types of errors as were mentioned before can result because a second printing process is required. Accordingly we have *double overprints*, caused when a single sheet of stamps is run through the printing press twice, and *inverted overprints*, caused when a sheet is put into the press topside at bottom.

Sometimes a sheet of stamps is put into the press in such a manner that the overprint type is misplaced or shifted in relation to the basic stamp. Sometimes a sheet is inserted into the press so carelessly that the overprint completely misses a portion of the sheet and some of the stamps are left without the overprinting. This results in what cataloguers list as "a pair of stamps, one without overprint." [3]

Errors—Minor varieties. When one gets into a specialty field one is confronted with the search for minor varieties which are caused by damage to the printing surface through carelessness of the printer or faults in the actual printing operation. Since the number of them that are to be encountered are numerous, we shall endeavor to list only those that are most frequently listed by the catalogues and recognized by philatelists.

Cracked plate. When stamps are printed from recess-engraved plates, the pressure of the presses often causes either the actual plate or the chromium plating (which has been applied to prolong its life) to crack. As a crack (in either case) is a depression which will accept ink at the time the surface is inked, those cracks will show up in the finished postage stamp as tiny colored lines. If the stamp is printed from a typographed surface, any crack, scratch, or dent will show up as a colorless mark. In most cases, such flaws are eagerly sought by advanced collectors who will pay a premium to obtain them.

Double transfer. In making a recess-engraved plate the transfer roll is sometimes rocked into the plate a second time for one reason or another,[4] and when registration is not precisely exact the second

---

[3] Throughout this discussion of provisional stamps we have used the term "overprint." Some collectors prefer the use of the term "surcharge." Actually an overprint consists of *any* inscription that is applied to a stamp which has been produced for one purpose and then is pressed into special service. It includes stamps which are provisionally issued for commemorative events, new service, and so on, as well as stamps of new denominations. This writer prefers to confine "surcharge" solely to its exact meaning, that is, only when the value of a stamp has been changed by the addition of an overprint. In short, the Kansas and Nebraska and Hawaii of 1928–1929 (United States) will be considered *overprints;* the revalued air-mail envelopes of 1945 and 1946 are considered *surcharges.*

[4] In this difficult process the siderographer must frequently examine his work, which requires the removal of the transfer roll from the plate. Frequently when he replaces the roll to continue the transfer operation, the relief design shifts a hair's breadth out of register from the work he has already entered and a *double transfer* results. On other occasions his original entry is incorrect and he must erase the design entered. When this is not absolutely erased before the correct entry is made, the finished stamp will betray traces of the first and incorrect entry, and this, too, is called a *double transfer.*

time, the finished stamp shows evidences of a duplication of all or a portion of the design.

Re-engraved. After a design has been engraved and stamps made from the plate, it may be found that certain portions of the design, while they appeared to be all right on the proof, are not satisfactory on the finished stamp. Accordingly an engraver will make certain modifications on either the original die or on every subject of the printing plate: he may add a little more shading to a portrait or pictorial scene; he may strengthen a background or add clouds to a sky. In any event the resulting impressions from such a re-engraved die or plate may differ very slightly from the original issue.

On the one-cent stamp of Newfoundland's 1923 issue, for example, the map shows Cape Bauld above Cape Norman. Since this is incorrect, in 1929 the plates were altered and the lettering was transposed. In 1900 Switzerland issued a set of three stamps to mark the silver jubilee of the Universal Postal Union. On these stamps the background was weak and the numerals of value were too solid. The plates were altered so that the background is much sharper; the figures of value were lined to give them a lighter appearance. Both of these are examples of re-engraving.

Re-cut. Frequently a recess-engraved plate begins to wear before the entire printing of a certain stamp issue has been completed, but not so badly that an entire new plate must be transferred. Traces of wear are especially noticeable in the finer lines of the design, so the plate is sent back to an engraver and he strengthens these fine lines by going over them with his graving tool. Most often this re-cutting results in a line that is much heavier than the original one.

Pseudo-errors. Frequently collectors come across stamps produced by the recess-engraving process which have colorless specks or dots where ink should be, and immediately imagine that their specimen is an "error." Such variations are most often found in the center of white design, such as the "island" of an "o", 4, 6, 8, or 9; within the hook of the figures, 2, 3, 5, 7; or in certain letters of the alphabet used for inscriptions. Rarely are these errors; they are better described as *pseudo-errors* or *freaks* and are caused by carelessness on the part of the printer. Ink used to print postage stamps from recess-engraved plates is very heavy, and as each line of a stamp design is thoroughly inked before every impression, plates have a tendency to accumulate ink. Perhaps one night a printer finishes his work a bit late and fails to clean the plate sufficiently well. While the plate is stored in a vault overnight, some of the ink that has not been completely removed the night before hardens so well that it takes a while for the heat, applied to printing plates for best results, to melt it down. Meanwhile, when the plate is inked, fresh ink cannot get into the clogged recesses, and therefore the first several sheets printed will have these freaks.

In typographed issues the opposite is true. Sometimes ink lodges itself in crevices because of careless cleaning after a day's work. These harden overnight and the first few impressions show specks of color which should be white.

Another type of nonrecurring pseudo-error is caused by the accidental deposit of a foreign substance on a printing surface between the time the plate is inked and the moment the paper strikes it. If, for example, a small bit of paper, a splinter, or a thread should fall on the plate at this time, the design and shape of that substance would show up in the stamp upon which it lay. In the case of a recess-engraved product it would be colorless; in the case of a typographed stamp it would be in the color of the ink.

Yet a third type of freak is the unprinted paper crease. Not infrequently a collector will find a postage stamp in which a complete strip of unprinted area is found across a postage stamp. Such freaks occur when the sheet of paper upon which stamps are printed is creased at the time the impression is made. After the stamps are finished, the paper is smoothed out; the portion of it that was creased could not have been imprinted and therefore appears as a white streak. Examples of this type, freaks though they be, are sought after by specialists; and if you come across one, remember it is worth a trifle more than a normal copy.

We have already discussed how governments and/or officials of certain lands have exploited the production of postage stamps to enhance their financial incomes at the expense of the stamp-collecting hobby. When stamps are made exclusively for sale to collectors, we can usually suspect them, and it is not very hard for the true reports to become known in a matter of weeks. Stamp collectors are to be found in virtually every country in the world, and as soon as any untoward scheme is cooked up to rig an issue, those persons are quick to scent the racket and notify the philatelic world through the various magazines published from here to Manila.

The philatelic exploitation of made-to-order errors, however, has been more difficult to uncover; and because of this condition, not a few unscrupulous officials have made a career of providing unwary philatelists with "errors." These persons know that errors, legitimately caused by the carelessness of a workman, usually bring premium prices on the market, and so they simply see to it that every so often some of their stamps contain "errors" accidentally produced on purpose. This sort of nefarious operation has been going on for years, and an examination of the catalogue will reveal not a few footnotes warning the inexperienced collector in some such terms as, "All values of this set exist imperforate but are not known to have been regularly issued in that condition." The catalogue editors have been very careful in the listing of all errors, and when facts are discovered that betray some of them for what they are, note of that situation or suspicion can be published. But unfortunately, there are some conditions and some errors which have been so cleverly marketed that they cannot be branded.

Illegitimate errors can reach the philatelic market in various ways: they can be made to order, or they can "leak" out of a printing plant.

The made-to-order ones usually come from countries whose officials are not above using their positions to enrich themselves at the expense of collectors and the reputation of their government. They are made by men who think in terms of dollars instead of integrity.

Suppose Fritz Diablo, Minister of Posts in Costa Blanca,[5] wants to issue a set of stamps to mark the inauguration of helicopter mail service. He is able to or desirous of juggling the actual stamps in co-operation with a speculator without being detected, so he sets about to fill his own purse by creating an error or two. This business is not so dangerous, for usually he can obtain the errors without having to account for them in official records, and anything he obtains can be regarded as pure profit. If he is not conversant with philatelic markets himself, or if he has not been approached by an unscrupulous dealer who wishes to share the profits of underhanded operations, he may contact a fellow whom he knows to be interested in postage stamps and work out a program for the disposal of what can be sold most easily.

As Minister of Posts, Diablo officially requests the printing firm— whether it be a government agency or an outside contractor—to supply him with one or two sheets of stamps without perforations. This can be accomplished very easily. By virtue of his position he can watch the printing plant's schedule, and as soon as he knows the

[5] Any similarity to living persons or existing country is purely coincidental.

[182]

Variety showing "DFU" instead of the correct "DEU."

(*Left*) Rare because horizontal perforations are missing.

Handset overprints using two different fonts of type.

Typographical error caused period to be transposed from "S" to "H."

Details are important: top stamp shows ground under feet and is rare; lower has no ground and is common.

(*Left*) Two stamps appear similar on face yet watermarks are different.

Souvenir sheet issued to commemorate the Pan American Union's Fiftieth Anniversary.

Switzerland marked her 184: stamp's centenary with thi souvenir sheet.

The United States reproduced our first stamps on this souvenir sheet as a tribute to our stamp centenary.

Tiny San Marino honors Lincoln.

Switzerland issued this stam in conjunction with the Cer tenary International Philateli Exhibition, 1947.

stamps have been printed, but before they have gone to the perforating machines, he can find an excuse to ask for the sheets "for examination," "for the records," or for some other reason.

Upon receipt of the unfinished sheets, Diablo carefully puts them aside until such time as the stamps will have been issued. A short while later he releases them through another party who is in the scheme. Supplies are sent to the larger markets with a manufactured story about how they were "found" in the post office among perfectly perforated sheets. The asking price is usually pegged upon a what-the-traffic-will-bear policy. The stamps are offered in places where money is more plentiful than opportunities for philatelic investigation. And because there are unfortunately too many collectors who are so anxious to buy "rare errors" regardless of their pedigree, a couple hundred of them can be sold at substantial profits long before the true facts are uncovered.

The number of such "errors" is staggering. Some countries' issues are so consistently accompanied by "errors" that it is surprising buyers do not yet realize they are but victims of the scheme. The only explanation is that there are relatively many persons who have money to build stamp collections and who do it without the slightest desire to know what they are getting. As long as there are gullible collectors there will be operators who will supply phony philatelic items, just as there always will be crooked art dealers who will sell fraudulent canvasses to uninformed "art connoisseurs."

We have had all sorts of made-to-order errors—imperforates, partially printed sheets, errors of color, and any number of others. There is, however, encouragement in this unsavory situation:

In the first place, the established banknote companies, like the American Banknote Company, Bradbury-Wilkinson, Harrison and Sons, Waterlow and Sons, Courvoisier, S.A., and a few others who have been in the stamp manufacturing business so long that they cannot afford to jeopardize their integrity, realize, too, that errors are philatelic favorites. They also wish to maintain their reputation of turning out flawless work and consequently take every precaution against the production of anything but perfectly made specimens.

In the second place, most dealers are honest and, in their efforts to protect their customers from such swindles, usually delve deep into the facts surrounding the source of any errors that may be offered to them for resale. When one of these dealers suspects underhanded operations, or has uncovered facts to brand them for what they are, he is invariably the first to publish such information for the guidance of serious collectors.

In the third place, made-to-order errors usually command such high prices that only a wealthy person can afford them; and if such a person gets stuck with them it is his own fault for not knowing what he is offered. When a person who knows little about such things wishes to buy a diamond ring or an Oriental rug, he should not buy them from a vendor in a back street without having it checked and appraised by an authority. The buyer who accepts a rare postage stamp without the same precautions deserves to be fleeced.

The second type of illegitimate error can be traced to dishonest persons who work in or have access to a printing plant where postage stamps are produced. As we mentioned, the larger companies have precautions to prevent the leakage of imperfectly printed or unfinished stamps; and so we encounter very, very few instances of trouble in that direction. But as the large banknote companies are so pressed with work that they cannot possibly accept every order, some governments must place contracts with smaller firms who have not yet learned all the ramifications of the business and so have not protected themselves from "thefts" which might yield substantial profits.

To better understand how this can happen, let us suppose the Yumgabia Banknote Company has been selected to produce a set of postage stamps. The firm itself is responsible, and anxious to maintain its integrity; but it is so small that it cannot afford to keep a close watch on every employee or visitor to its plant.

During the course of production of the stamps a legitimate error is made—a sheet is printed upside down; perforations are improperly punched; or any other slip is made that might occur in the normal course of a print job. The workman or an inspector spots the mistake and tosses the imperfect sheet to a waste heap which is to be burned at the end of the day. But before it can reach the destruction furnace, an employee who has some conception of the philatelic worth of errors, or a stamp collector who may be inspecting the plant, sees it, sneaks it into his pocket, and takes it out of the plant.

Some time later that "error," which never so much as got into postal channels, finds its way to the philatelic market, and the first thing we know, the catalogue lists another error.

While illegitimate errors do abound—some philatelists claim that fifty per cent of all those listed in the catalogue today have been the result of dishonesty somewhere along the lines—the novice need not be frightened that he is entering a field where fraud is the rule rather than the exception.

If you would guard yourself against victimization, there is but one word of advice. Never buy a stamp about which you have the slightest doubt. If you are offered a specimen that is not listed in the standard catalogue, investigate the stamp first and buy it only after you have satisfied yourself that it is genuine. If you do not subscribe to a philatelic magazine or journal, the country's leading societies are ever anxious to render what information you desire for the asking. It is cheaper to pass up a "bargain" now and pay a slightly higher price later, when you know the facts, than to buy it now and learn subsequently that you have been stung—whether the person who offered it to you was deliberate or innocent in his transaction. Remember always that postage stamps have such an international market that only rarely will you get a "big bargain" from anyone who knows his business. In no other field of endeavor is the *caveat emptor* admonition more applicable than in stamp collecting.

Four of Canada's "War Effort" set of 1942–1943.

[12] Exhibitions

Stamp exhibitions are a philatelic institution, and nowadays shows of varying importance are staged all over this country and in many foreign lands. They range from simple displays presented at designated times by members of local clubs to the huge international affairs which fill entire exposition buildings, and to which philatelists travel from the far corners of the earth. They are staged to encourage collectors in their efforts and to give the noncollecting world an idea of what postage stamps offer as an avocational medium.

The majority of collectors are satisfied to fill blank spaces in a printed album, for they seek only their own entertainment and pleasure. Others devote years to the specialty of their preference and, in addition to their personal satisfaction, enjoy the admiration and plaudits of their fellow philatelists on their accomplishments. Still others collect stamps and, after a time, desire to know how their work stacks up to that of their neighbors. A competitive exhibition, where qualified judges rate the entries, provides the opportunity for these persons to know exactly where they stand.

While rules are modified to suit conditions, depending upon the size and scope of the exhibition, most of the basic regulations are the same all over the world. Every exhibition is divided into classes, sections, and groups in such a manner that collections of approximately equal philatelic worth can be pitted against one another.

The *classes* are set up for noncompetitive entries, for collections that have won awards at previous exhibitions, and for collections that have been entered at other shows but have not won prizes, or collections that are being entered for the first time.

The *sections* are broad divisions of the show covering the widest philatelic specialty classes such as "British Colonies," "Air Mail" and "Europe."

The *groups* are the breakdown divisions of sections, for it would be basically unfair to judge a collection of "Canada" (which has issued many stamps, has had a tremendous postal history, and includes some outstanding rarities) against a collection of "Pitcairn Island" (which has issued only a few pictorials), although both of them are members of the British Commonwealth of Nations.

The judging is begun with groups, where each entry is scored on the basis of how much effort the collector has put into his albums and how much he has contributed to philatelic knowledge through his studies; the neatness with which his pages are arranged; the condition of the specimens he owns; the completeness of the subject he is covering; and last—almost insignificantly—the monetary value of the stamps themselves. The true philatelist is not concerned so much with the dollars-and-cents value of a specimen as he is with its ability to provide study opportunities, pleasure, and satisfaction.

For example, for many years Charles Lathrop Pack, one of the foremost American philatelist of the golden era, devoted time and money to the accumulation of early classic issues with a view to studying them to learn details which philatelists desired, but which no longer were in postal records. His studies won such awards as the Crawford Medal of the Royal Philatelic Society, London. His collections won prizes wherever and whenever they were shown. But always his honors were challenged by such sour-grapes statements as, "Well, if I had Mr. Pack's money, I could buy rare stamps, too."

Mr. Pack, determined to prove that a student without great financial means could make a serious study of stamps, selected the Dom Pedro head issues of Brazil and the small-cents issues of Canada—two sets of stamps so common that they could be bought at a few cents per thousand copies—and set out to see what could be learned from them. Mr. Pack scrutinized every specimen, and by the time he had concluded his study he had classified the various types of paper on which they were printed, determined the dates on which various shades of ink were used to print new supplies, identified plate varieties, and tabulated the various kinds of postal markings that were used when the stamps were current. Never before had collections that were worth less than a box of good cigars, from a monetary standpoint, got such world-wide honors as the two which Mr. Pack built solely to dispel the idea that a person had to have money to win international honors at stamp exhibitions.

The person who enters a collection at an exhibition must be fully aware of what is expected of an entry or he will be disappointed when the results are announced by the judges. That matter of "philatelic knowledge" is by far the most important, for in most exhibitions this factor is rated at almost half of the whole value of the entry.

Philatelic knowledge is a nebulous thing. Some hobbyists devote days to the perusal of articles written by scholars and published in magazines, journals, and books. They either clip the articles and mount them on pages with the stamps, or they copy them in elaborate penwork; yet the very arrangement of the stamps on the page reveals that they have no personal knowledge of the subject. I recall judging one exhibition in which was entered a collection of Philippine stamps each of which was elaborately supplemented by pages of published information; yet on one of the sheets was mounted a stamp which belonged to an entirely different set than that with which it was included. Obviously the owner had done much reading without learning what he had read, for otherwise he would have known that the one-peso violet stamp was issued in 1909 and not in 1906, as he had it placed.

A great deal has been written about postage stamps by collectors who have studied them, but there is yet much more to be discovered. The person who would earn points at a stamp show, and recognition from his fellows for "philatelic knowledge" and "evidence of original research," is therefore obliged to saturate himself with existing information and then set out to add to it.

Perhaps one of the greatest upsets in philatelic circles resulted from a stamp exhibition held in Newark, New Jersey, less than a decade ago. The show was national in scope and entries came from numerous collectors whose stamps had won prizes all over the country. But when the results were announced by the panel of judges, the grand award for the "best" collection in the entire show was given to Dr. Charles Evans, a physician and surgeon of East Orange, New Jersey, who had been a collector only a short time, but who had built such a collection of miniature sheets of the world and data concerning them that he nosed out completely collections of United States, British Colonial, and air-mail stamps that were far larger than his own collection.

Dr. Evans had not contented himself just with acquiring these miniature and souvenir sheets [1] to the point where he had every one known

[1] In 1906 Luxemburg issued a new set of postage stamps and, in addition to normal-size sheets, produced a small sheet consisting of ten 10-centime stamps surrounded by a white margin, as a special commemorative issue to mark the accession of Grand Duke William IV to the throne. After that, many other countries reproduced stamp designs on small sheets of paper with (or without)

to exist; he had in addition written to government bureaus and to collectors in the countries where the stamps were issued and had obtained authentic data pertaining to each of them. He had learned why and when the sheets were issued, whether they were legitimate or solely a means of exploiting philately, and kindred data which had been hitherto unknown. Until that moment serious collectors had scoffed at miniature sheets as being modern issues prepared to separate hobbyists from their money. Yet the work of Dr. Evans proved that even these fancy sheets of colored paper could lend themselves to philatelic research.

Exhibitions are quite valuable to novice collectors, for at them one finds new ideas that will help the neophyte to move on to more advanced fields. A beginner usually—and rightly—starts with an album in which spaces and illustrations and written descriptions are printed to show him where each new specimen should be mounted. This is wonderful for a time, and some collectors maintain that it is the way to get the most fun out of the hobby, for the sport of filling space after space requires patience and time. But some collectors realize the futility of trying to get one specimen of every stamp depicted in a printed album for there are many stamps so scarce that a lifetime of hunting and a millionaire's checkbook would never assure success.

And so the collector will want to turn his attentions and efforts to a specialty. Such concentrated efforts call for a blank album upon whose pages the hobbyist must make his own arrangements. Unless one is generously endowed with an artistic mind, he is likely to find himself at a loss in this respect. A visit to any stamp show, therefore, is an impressive lesson on the art of mounting a collection and the selection of a field for specialization. By examining and studying the entries that are adjudged the best in group, section, or show, the novice can learn what makes one collection superior to another. Until relatively recently the collection of stamps according to subject or color was unpopular simply because so few persons had the originality required to start such a collection; but as one show after another

commemorative marginal inscriptions in connection with charity drives, stamp exhibitions, and other events. Sometimes these souvenir sheets were sold at a price which included only the face value of the stamp that was imprinted; other times they were sold at a premium. The frequency with which souvenir or miniature sheets were issued after 1930 so increased that philatelists began to complain that governments were going pretty far afield to produce material which was quite obviously made solely for nonpostal use.

displayed topical collections, the idea spread and now is perhaps one of the more widely recognized forms of philatelic endeavor.

Stamp exhibitions have had their missionary value, too. Through the presentation of stamp shows and the attendant publicity given them by local newspaper and radio comments, any number of persons who knew nothing of the hobby before saw how thoroughly absorbing stamps and the collecting of them could be. How many converts have been made through stamp exhibitions alone probably will never be more than a vague guess, but that this number is at least in the thousands cannot be denied.

Today stamp exhibitions in this country are established institutions. All of the national societies and many local organizations have annual shows in cities throughout the land. In Philadelphia, the National Philatelic Museum was established in 1948, by Bernard Davis, retired textile magnate. Here three hundred large, glass-covered frames are used to display the stamps of a single country [2] for a full month.

In foreign countries, too, there are a great many more exhibitions today than ever before. Since 1940, many nations have been able to mark the centenaries of their own first stamps and invariably they observe this important anniversary with an international stamp show.

International Stamp Exhibitions are big business. National collector and dealer groups support them for philatelic prestige. Governments finance them for their importance as promotional projects. Postal Administrations, particularly, and tourist agencies generally feel that stamp shows are unrivaled sources of international publicity to promote sales of the country's stamps and to attract travel income.

Invariably such shows are sponsored jointly between the philatelic groups and the postal administrations. They are staged on a grand style, with superbly appointed displays and dramatic correlative exhibits, such as working models of post-office equipment, mail transportation facilities, and historical relics from postal museums and archives.

The actual programs are planned with the highest standards of

[2] These displays are loaned by owners of the finest existing collections of the countries concerned, by the governments of the nations being featured, or are from the museum's own collections.

dignity and taste, which put philately on a befitting cultural scale.

Because these shows are so important, the ruler of the nation usually attends the opening, and the elite of stampdom throng the halls for the duration of the shows.

The postwar exhibitions were held as follows: 1948, in Basel, Switzerland; 1949, in Paris, France, and Brussels, Belgium; 1950, in London, England; Madrid, Spain, and Buenos Aires, Argentina; 1951, in Toronto, Canada; 1952, in Monte Carlo, Monaco; Luxembourgville, Luxembourg, and Utrecht, the Netherlands; in 1953, in Lisbon, Portugal; 1954, in Manila, the Philippines; 1955, in Auckland, New Zealand; Oslo, Norway, and Stockholm, Sweden; 1956, in New York; Zagreb, Yugoslavia; Helsinki, Finland; and in Buenos Aires, Argentina.

Each of them was a spectacular success, each of them increased the popularity of the stamps of the nation sponsoring it,[2] and each of them attracted thousands of visitors from distant lands. When travelers come to such a show it is not only to see the stamps exhibited, but also to tour the countryside of the land itself.

In the United States, international shows are sponsored by a nonprofit group of stamp dealers and collectors known as the Association for Stamp Exhibitions. It is this organization which staged the shows of 1913, 1926, 1936, 1947, and 1956. None of its officers is salaried; all their work is donated as a contribution towards the growth of the avocation. Because it is a nonprofit group, even the complex financial worries must be faced with not even an incentive for monetary gain. The rental of space, the cost of installation of the frames and booths, the salaries of labor, all have to be met by leasing booth space, advertising in the catalogue, the rental of display frames to competitive entry owners, and admission fees.

The financing of a stamp show in this country is a marvel and an example of the faith collectors have in their avocation. Long before the show can open there are many expenses to be met: rental charges, construction and material costs, and so on.

To meet these expenses, the association puts in a call for "guarantees." Interested persons pledge amounts of from $100 to $1,000 apiece. As bills are submitted and money becomes necessary, the guarantors are called upon to remit a portion of their pledged

[2] In each case special stamps were issued, the sale of which usually paid all expenses of the exhibitions.

amount. In the 1936 show, a call for twenty-five per cent amply paid advance expenses although the show cost $100,000. When receipts were in, this entire amount was given back to those who had guaranteed its success. In 1947, even a smaller percentage was called for and after it had been returned the exhibition still had a net profit of more than $30,000 which was put into a fund with which to finance the 1956 international philatelic exhibition.

There is a considerable difference between the United States shows and those held abroad. Because the ones held here must be self-sustaining, all their features must be planned with a view of getting a rental fee out of every available square foot of space. There is therefore an air of strong commercialism. Abroad, where the shows are treated as expositions and important government support takes care of needed funds, they are things of beauty.

The one held in Holland, in 1952, is a striking example. That show was held in the Trade Fair buildings of Utrecht. An architect was hired to plan the layout with emphasis upon "a hundred years of postage stamps," the theme. The entered collections were displayed in specially built frames that allowed visitors to visit the great treasures with ease and comfort; potted plants were cleverly arranged to provide a garden-like atmosphere, and dramatic displays planned by the Department of Posts told a vivid story of mail service in action. To maintain that spirit of dignity only a dozen dealers were given space in one corner of the show; the others had to find room for booths in an adjacent hall where their business would not detract from the decor of the exposition nor interfere with the comfort of the visitors. It was a triumph and set a record as the finest international stamp exhibition ever staged.

[13] Fortunes for the Finding

There is not a person alive who has read about the value of rare postage stamps without dreaming about the day when he, too, would be rummaging through old correspondence and suddenly come upon adhesives which could be immediately sold for the price of a flight around the world. There is not a collector alive who does not nurse the secret hope of finding a philatelic gem with the same enthusiasm as that of young devotees to Robert Louis Stevenson who envision the location of a pirate's secreted treasure chest.

Nor are such dreams as fantastic as they may seem. Fortunate finds still are being reported in the philatelic press in astonishing numbers and with amazing frequency.

In fact, as this is being written, the report of a fabulous discovery has come from Australia, where R. W. Turk, an English philatelist who moved to the Antipodes, came upon an almost complete sheet of the "enthroned queen" two-penny stamps of Victoria.

The stamps, which were issued in 1851, comprise a sheet, in unused condition, from which two single copies had been snipped. It seems that when he engraved the dies from which the printing plates were to be made, Thomas Ham obtained this sheet as a sample of his work, and, more than ninety years ago, placed it among his personal possessions. Recently, when his grandson was "cleaning house," he came upon the sheet, which, "despite the ravages of silver fish that had been at work on some of the stamps, still is in excellent condition." He sold the sheet to Mr. Turk for an undisclosed price, but considering that a single copy of this stamp costs in the neighborhood of $200, the sheet should, as the Australian report states, "be the sensational discovery of the year."

Just before the turn of the century two janitors of a Kentucky courthouse were cleaning out an accumulation of old, unwanted papers when they came upon some postage stamps. They made a "deal" with a local collector and eventually sold the lot, which consisted chiefly of Postmasters' Provisionals of the 1845–1847 period, for over $23,000. A similar event occurred in Philadelphia in December, 1912, when a paper dealer contracted with Charnley and Whelen to remove refuse from the cellar vaults at a stipulated price. In sorting the waste paper, the dealer found envelopes franked with St. Louis postmaster stamps of 1845–46, which were appraised at about $100,000. The firm, learning of the find, tried every legal trick to share the profit. The dealer stood pat and the firm got nothing but the memory that they had tossed out a fortune.

Some of the material was sold, but forty-two covers were bequeathed for the benefit of the Masonic Home in Elizabethtown, Pa. Only on Dec. 13, 1948, were these covers offered at public auction through H. R. Harmer in New York, and sold for $43,220.

Virtually all the existing copies of the really great classics and stamps with five-figure price valuations have been uncovered among old love letters or business correspondence. Robson Lowe, the British dealer, has uncovered at least a million dollars' worth of stamps and covers within the last decade, simply by communicating with the proprietors of century-old business firms and offering to buy any unwanted correspondence files they might have.

Not too long ago a book publisher and personal friend of my employer came to my office and asked me to look over a bundle of letters which he and his wife had found in the corner of a Connecticut farmhouse they had bought. He had no illusions about finding real treasure, but he simply wanted to be sure he was not going to throw away "five dollars or so."

That bundle of letters included ninety-six communications which proclaimed the love of two nineteenth-century sweethearts, and each was franked with the first five-cent postage stamp of the United States, issued by the Post Office Department in 1847. The sale of these envelopes, through a public auction by H. R. Harmer, Inc., brought the finder a price that amounted to more than a third of the cost of the house in which they were found.

Not long ago, in a radio broadcast, I described the story of how a one-cent stamp, issued in 1923, was worth about $1,000 because of a slight difference in the dimensions of the vignette and because only a few of them had been sold through the Madison Square branch of the New York post office before collectors learned of the existence of this variety. Most of these had been used by tourists who had affixed them to picture post cards telling the folks back home about what a fine time they were having in the big city. Most of them probably went into waste-paper baskets, for only a very few of them are known to exist today.

Even before that broadcast was over a woman telephoned to the studio to say she had a great many stamps of that period. Would I examine them for her? She came posthaste, lugging a large shoe box full of stamps.

She was a sweet old lady and it was difficult to tell her that not a single one-cent stamp she had in the box was worth anything. "But perhaps some of the others in the box might be worthwhile," I suggested.

"O, no," she replied. "The rest are only ordinary stamps Father used on letters when he was stationed in Bangkok."

I looked over this lot and immediately recognized a number of really good items. It seems that her father was in Siam at a time when some of that country's rarest stamps were in use. The old lady had dozens of them—and eventually sold them to a dealer for $750.

At another time I was in Baltimore for the convention and exhibition of the American Philatelic Society, and while I was chatting with one of the dealers who had a booth there, a young lad came up with a handful of letters he had received some years before from a Newfoundland business house. He told the dealer he was so interested in model-airplane construction that he would sell the lot for $1 with which he could purchase some eagerly desired parts.

The dealer casually thumbed through the bundle. Seeing just ordinary stamps from ordinary mail, he figured that they were worth about fifty cents, but wishing to cheer the young enthusiast, he gave him the dollar.

Some minutes later, the dealer discovered in the batch a cover which was franked with a Newfoundland stamp of 1919. Across its face was overprinted, "First Trans-Atlantic Air Post April 1919." The dealer leaped from behind his counter, ran out and located the lad in the lobby of the hotel. In the end the boy received a check with which he could have almost purchased a real airplane.

In 1946 a valuable find of rare early British stamps was disclosed. In rearranging the furnishings of Dalkeith palace, a Scottish ducal seat, Alexander Martin, secretary of the Duke of Buccleuch, found a small writing set, handsomely bound in tooled leather and consisting of a tray in which were several writing implements of a century ago, and a lower compartment in which were found two part-sheets of the rare old postage stamps subsequently caused a sensation in the London markets.

These consisted of forty-eight two-penny blue stamps of Great Britain in unused and extremely fine condition, and which had lain hidden in this box for more than a hundred years. There also were fifty-five one-penny brown-red stamps of the 1841 issue.

It was assumed that these stamps had been originally purchased by the great grandfather [1] of the present owner of the palace, to be used on contemporary mail. How they remained unnoticed until Mr. Martin found them is a mystery, but found they were to prove once again that the days of the surprise discovery of philatelic treasure is still possible.

Recently a great many very valuable stamps have been "discovered" at the regular windows of post offices around the country. Realizing that the sale of imperfect stamps not only casts an undesirable impression upon the government, but that the accidental procurement of such "errors" may lead to huge profits, the Bureau of Engraving and Printing exerts unusual diligence in the inspection of postage stamps to ferret out improperly produced stamps before they are delivered to post offices. The Post Office Department, too, has a rigid regulation that compels a stamp clerk who comes upon an error which slipped by the inspectors to turn it back to his superior. But in spite of these precautions, a number of erroneously printed or faultily perforated stamps have been found by fortunate collectors.

The most famous of these "at-the-post-office finds" was the purchase at face value ($24) of a full sheet of 24-cent stamps whose center was inverted in relation to the frame design, and which was subsequently sold by the finder for $15,000.

In 1938 two dealers "discovered" forty sheets of the then-current six-cent air-mail stamps which were perforated only vertically. They purchased the entire supply at face value—$120—and disposed of them through a syndicate who put them on the market at $100 a pair, or $100,000! Because one of the postal clerks in the office where they were "found" was a collector and friend of the pair who purchased them, postal inspectors made an exceptionally complete investigation. The clerk was dismissed, but the stamps still are in the market although the stigma that perhaps there was some irregularity connected with them has more or less dampened the demand for them.

[1] Walter Francis became the fifth Duke of Buccleuch and the seventh Duke of Queensberry in 1819, and was Lord Privy Seal from 1842 to 1846.

The most sensational such find in recent years turned up on the eve of Thanksgiving Day of 1946, when a man, purchasing sheets of $1 stamps at a Cleveland post office, found one sheet which had only vertical perforations. The sheet was procured by Nelson LaGanke, a Cleveland dealer, who is cutting it apart and offering blocks of them through his own auction sales. This particular sheet's present condition suggests that perhaps it was spotted by an inspector who tossed it aside to a waste heap, for it is noticeably creased. Somehow it must have inadvertently been stacked with OK'd stamps and thus got into a post-office supply. Four blocks already have been sold at the LaGanke auctions, the most recent of which brought $950.

Where rare stamps will be found by you or me is anybody's guess. If charts or codes existed to identify the locations of caches, the hunt would have been ended long ago. Perhaps you will come across some in an old desk drawer; perhaps in the loft of a barn while you are vacationing at a farm; perhaps when you buy your next stamp at the post office; maybe among the love letters of your grandparents. But more stamp treasures *will* be found, and your chances of coming across one of these finds is not as slim as you may suspect. You need but one word of admonition. Never once overlook or pass by an opportunity of exploring a possible old-stamp source, however improbable it may seem. One acquaintance of mine visited an old home in New England not many years ago and naturally asked about old letters. The owner explained that some time previously the attic was "cleaned out by another collector." But just on the chance that something might have been overlooked he made a search of his own and came out with a rather large lot of letters franked with valuable stamps.

Embossed envelope stamp issued in conjunction with the inauguration of the domestic five-cent air-mail rate in 1946, and part of a special postmark applied for the benefit of collectors.

[14] A Guide to Stamp Appraisal

The most frequently asked question when the subject of postage stamps is discussed is "How much is a stamp worth?" The person who has stamps but no knowledge about them usually has an amazing idea about stamp values. They have read or heard about single stamps whose value must be reckoned in five-figure prices, and with the tinge of optimism that is present in every human being, they immediately jump to the conclusion that the specimen they own is one of those priceless gems. In my capacity as stamp-news editor of the New York *Herald Tribune* I receive dozens of inquiries each week from persons who have "rare and valuable" stamps they wish to sell. They submit or describe United States and foreign issues that are exceedingly common, despite the fact that they often are older than the persons making the inquiries.

Items That Have No Sales Value

It is not possible to lay down a general rule about worthless United States stamps, but the following types are most often encountered. None of them is worth more than a fraction of a cent each unless it is unused or has an unusually fine postal cancellation. The types are: the three-cent stamp of 1857, printed in red with a portrait of George Washington; the three-cent blue of 1869, with a picture of a locomotive; the three-cent green of 1870, with another portrait of Washington; the one-cent stamps of 1870–1890, with portraits of Benjamin Franklin; the one- and two-cent values of the Columbian set of 1893, showing respectively Columbus in sight of land and landing in America.

It is even more difficult to generalize on the foreign stamps for which there is little or no sales market. It is well to remember, however, that most foreign postage stamps which have been used for ordinary mail are of little or no value. These include the low denominations of British, German, French, Italian, Swiss, Belgian, South American, African, Asiatic, and Australian ordinary issues.

Items That Have a Sales Value

Covers. A stamp still affixed to the original wrapper or card or envelope on which it was mailed is known as a *cover*. Because such covers often are worth more than the stamp alone, an inexperienced person should never remove the stamp from its cover before consulting a dealer or collector. Envelopes with pictorial advertising designs imprinted thereon are sought by specialists and often bring from 25 cents to $25 each, even though the stamp has a value of only one or two cents. Covers with patriotic designs used during the Civil or Spanish American Wars are worth about $1 each, or more, if they are in perfect condition and properly postmarked. Unused specimens are quite common. Covers that show they have been carried on pioneer air-mail flights or have been aboard wrecked ships or airplanes are worth from $1 to $50 each.

Covers that show censor markings of World War II or previous wars are rather popular and can be sold at prices which vary in accordance with the type of stamp on the envelope and the nature of the censor marking applied.

Stampless covers. Before postage stamps were introduced, letters were sent through the mails without adhesives. The rates paid for the service were generally indicated by manuscript or hand-stamped inscriptions. These are not uncommon and are worth, as a rule, only 10 to 25 cents apiece. There are some rarer types, particularly those that are canceled with a crowned circle or a steamship or railway postmark, a number of which are worth $5 or more apiece.

Revenue stamps. Most revenue stamps, which may be identified by the inscription (many have "I.R." or "Inter. Rev.") are rather common, but higher dollar denominations, if in fine condition, can be sold at prices ranging from ten cents to several hundred dollars.

Official stamps. Stamps that have been overprinted, or specially inscribed to show that they were intended to frank the official correspondence of government employees, are generally worth a little more than the ordinary stamps of the United States and foreign lands.

Such stamps, still affixed to the envelopes of officials like presidents, cabinet members, ministers, and so on, are very popular and are worth more than when they are on letters of lower officials such as clerks, consuls, and the like.

Errors. This is an especially interesting field of philately, and the values for individual errors is governed more than any other specialty field by the law of supply and demand. Some specimens that represent printing errors are exceedingly valuable; others are unpopular and, accordingly, worth very little in a monetary sense. While "errors" are discussed elsewhere in this book, the collector may be guided by the following general rule: if the error is the result of a printing mistake, it is worth more than a normal stamp; if it is an error in the design of the stamp, caused by the carelessness of the artist who drew the design, there is no premium value.

Counterfeits. Toward the end of the nineteenth century a number of unscrupulous persons in Europe and a few in this country made quite a practice of faking postage stamps for sale to unsuspecting customers; and so today many counterfeits exist to confound the unwary or inexperienced hobbyist. Some of these spurious adhesives are crudely made; others are so well imitated that only a trained expert can distinguish between them and the genuine article.

If someone tells you this stamp or that in your album is a fake, do not be too seriously alarmed. It happens to the best of us. If you cannot yourself determine whether a particular stamp is genuine or counterfeit, by checking such details as paper, watermark, perforations, and printing, the best advice we can give is, check with someone who can.

But there is yet another type of fake: the one that was made by criminals who sought to defraud not a collector alone, but rather to cheat the government out of revenue. Such items are relatively rare, and when they still are affixed to the envelope on which they were actually used, advanced specialists eagerly pay fancy prices to obtain them.

This book cannot attempt to serve as a substitute for a standard postage stamp catalogue; but in order that the inexperienced reader may have at least a rough idea of the stamp market at the present time, we shall present the following condensed generalization. It is intended to serve merely as a guide, not only to the market value of those stamps which you may have in an old album, but also to suggest a specialty field if you are inclined to restrict your efforts.

Since the demand for stamps of certain countries varies considerably, a code letter will be placed after the name of each land, as follows:

(p) Popular collecting countries. Stamps from these places are in rather strong demand and therefore prices for them are high and dealers are willing to buy them when they are offered.

(m) Moderately popular countries. The demand for stamps from such places is just fair, and unless specimens are in very fine condition, prices are generally lower.

(u) Unpopular countries. Stamps from these places are generally spurned by most collectors, and so the supply is greater than the demand. Consequently such stamps are sold at substantial discounts for catalogue price valuations.

After each country will be found a short description of those stamps from specific places which command more-than-usual price respect. They are the exceptions that prove the rule.

ABYSSINIA (u)—Several of the old issues and a few of the higher denominations of recent sets.

ADEN (m)—High values, unused and used on original letters, particularly with censor markings.

AFGHANISTAN (u)—Nineteenth-century issues in superb condition. (*Note:* canceled stamps of this country generally have a piece torn out, which is not considered a defect.)

AGUERRA (u)—Only the peseta denominations.

AITUTAKI (m)—Most varieties in superb condition.

ALAOUITES (u)—Air mails and high denominations in fine condition.

ALBANIA (m)—Stamps of Turkey overprinted with a double-headed eagle, high value of regular issues; air mails.

ALEXANDRETTA (u)—High denominations only.

ALGERIA (m)—Franc values and semi-postals.

ALLENSTEIN (u)—Inverted or double overprints.

ANDORRA (u)—Peseta and franc denominations.

ANGOLA (u)—Escudo and angolar values.

ANGRA (u)—High values.

ANJOUAN (m)—Stamps in superb condition only.

ANNAM AND TONKIN (m)—All.

ANTIGUA (p)—All except a few low values.

ARGENTINE REPUBLIC (m)—Early issues in superb condition; high denominations of the other sets; air mails; officials and stamps issued for the states of Buenos Aires, Cordoba, and Corrientes.

ARMENIA (u)—Some of the 1920 sets.

ASCENSION (p)—High denominations.

AUSTRALIA (p)—High denominations; pictorials.

AUSTRIA (p)—Nineteenth-century issues in superb condition; commemorative and semi-postal issues; air mails.

AZERBAIJAN (u)—Comparatively few overprinted issues.

AZORES (u)—Most of the early issues, but only if they are in superb condition.

BADEN (m)—All but a few.

BAHAMAS (p)—Nearly all except a few low values of recent issues.

BAHRAIN (m)—Fine specimens used on original envelopes.

BANGKOK (m)—All.

BARBADOS (p)—Most early issues and high values of the more recent sets.

BARBUDA (m)—Nearly all.

BASUTOLAND (p)—High values in unused condition and used copies on original envelopes.

BATUM (u)—Only a few of the overprinted stamps.

BAVARIA (m)—Early issues in superb condition.

BECHUANALAND (u)—Only those in fine condition.

BELGIAN EAST AFRICA (m)—High denominations and used copies on original envelopes.

BELGIUM (p)—Early issues in superb condition; high values of more recent sets; semi-postals; souvenir sheets.

BENIN (u)—Nearly all.

BERGEDORF (u)—Genuinely used copies.

BERMUDA (p)—Early issues; high values of later sets.

BOLIVIA (m)—Only a few regular issues; air mails.

BOSNIA AND HERZOGOVINA (u)—Only a very few.

BRAZIL (p)—Early issues with only numerals; high values of other sets, if they are very fine; air mails.

BREMEN (m)—All, if they are genuine and in superb condition.

BRITISH CENTRAL AFRICA (m)—Nearly all, especially the high values.

BRITISH COLUMBIA AND VANCOUVER (p)—Nearly all.

BRITISH EAST AFRICA (p)—Nearly all.

BRITISH GUIANA (p)—Nearly all old issues; high values of more recent sets; officials.

BRITISH HONDURAS (m)—Early issues; high values of modern sets.

BRITISH SOLOMON ISLANDS (p)—Nearly all; particularly fine used copies on original envelopes.

BRUNEI (m)—Nearly all.

BRUNSWICK (m)—Nearly all, if they are in superb condition.

BULGARIA (u)—Early issues in superb condition; air mails.

BURMA (m)—High denominations.

CAMEROONS (m)—Nearly all of the German issues; early French issues and modern French issues in superb condition on original envelopes.

CANADA (p)—The stamps inscribed "Pence" are scarce; nearly all unused stamps; the Jubilee issue of 1897; high value of recent sets; high values overprinted "War Tax." (These are not listed in the Scott Catalogue.)

CANAL ZONE (p)—Nearly all, except the very low values.

CAPE JUBY (u)—Only very fine specimens of certain issues.

CAPE OF GOOD HOPE (p)—The triangular stamps; a few of the other issues; all inscribed "Mafeking."

CAPE VERDE (u)—Comparatively few, and then only those in superb condition.

CARINTHIA (u)—None.

CAROLINE ISLANDS (m)—Only the high values in unused condition; used copies in superb condition.

CASTELLORIZO (m)—Nearly all —in postally used condition.

CAYMAN ISLAND (p)—Nearly all early issues and high values of modern sets.

CENTRAL LITHUANIA (u)—None.

CEYLON (m)—Early issues in superb condition and high values of later sets.

CHAD (m)—High values and very fine used copies on original envelopes.

CHILE (m)—Very fine copies of the early issues; high values of other sets; air mails; officials.

CHINA (m)—The earliest issues, commemoratives; high value of recent sets; air mails.

CILICIA (u)—Comparatively few regular issues; air mails.

COLOMBIA (m)—Early issues in superb condition; high values of later sets; air mails.

CONGO (m)—The franc values, very fine copies used on original envelopes.

COOK ISLANDS (p)—Comparatively few.

COREA (u)—Very few.

CORFU (u)—Very few.

COSTA RICA (m)—Air mails; officials.

CRETE (u)—Only the early issues, in superb condition.

CROATIA (u)—Only those used on cover in fine condition.

CUBA (p)—Early issues in superb condition; high denominations of later sets, stamps overprinted "Habilitado" and new values expressed in "Cents"; air mails.

CURAÇAO (p)—Early issues in superb condition; Jubilee issue of 1923; high values of other sets.

CYPRUS (p)—Early issues; commemoratives and high values of later regular sets.

CYRENAICA (u)—Nearly none.

CZECHOSLOVAKIA (m)—Unused high values of others; very fine used provisionals of 1919; semi-postals.

DAHOMEY (m)—Early issues and high values of others; very fine used copies on original envelopes.

DALMATIA (u)—None.

DANISH WEST INDIES (m)—Nearly all except a few varieties.

DANZIG (m)—High values in fine condition; air mails; semi-postals.

DENMARK (p)—A few of the early isues; high values of recent issues; air mails; parcel-post stamps.

DIEGO SUAREZ (m)—Nearly all, if they are fine and genuine.

DJIBUTI (m)—Nearly all, if they are fine and genuine.

DOMINICA (p)—Early issues and high values of recent sets.

DOMINICAN REPUBLIC (m)—High values, air mails.

DUTCH INDIES (p)—The stamps of 1864-1865 in superb condition; high values of other sets; semi-postals and air mails.

EAST AFRICA AND UGANDA (m)—Nearly all except a few of the more recent low values.

EASTERN ROUMELIA (u)—A few of the early stamps.

EASTERN SILESIA (u)—Nearly none.

ECUADOR (m)—High values of recent issues; commemoratives; air mails.

EGYPT (p)—Early issues in superb condition; commemoratives; air mails; nearly all officials.

ELOBEY, ANNABON, AND CORISCO (u)—None unless they are superb.

EPIRUS (u)—Very few.

ERITREA (m)—Comparatively few except superb used copies on original envelopes.

ESTONIA (m)—Some 1920 stamps overprinted "Eesti Post"; semi-postals.

FALKLAND ISLANDS (p)—Early issues; the 1933 pictorial sets and high values of other issues.

FAR EASTERN REPUBLIC (u)—Very few.

FERNANDO PO (u)—Only superb copies.

FIJI (p)—Early issues in superb condition; high values of later sets; postage dues.

FINLAND (p)—Earliest issues in fine condition; semi-postals; air mails.

FIUME (u)—Comparatively few types.

FRANCE (p)—Early issues in superb condition; semi-postals; commemoratives; high values of recent sets; air mails, regular issues overprinted for use abroad.

FRENCH COLONIES (p)—All types, if they are in very fine condition.

FRENCH CONGO (m)—All but the lower denominations.

FRENCH EQUATORIAL AFRICA (m)—High denominations; used copies on original envelopes.

FRENCH GUIANA (m)—Early issues; high denominations of recent sets; air mails.

FRENCH GUINEA (m)—Early issues; high denominations of recent sets.

FRENCH INDIA (m)—High denominations.

FRENCH OCEANIA (m)—High values; used copies on original envelopes.

FRENCH SUDAN (m)—First issue of 1894; high values; used copies on original envelopes.

FUNCHAL (u)—High values in very fine condition.

GABON (m)—Early issues; high values of recent sets; used copies on original envelopes.

GAMBIA (p)—Early issues; high denominations of recent sets.

GEORGIA (u)—None.

GERMAN EAST AFRICA (m)—German issues; Beligan occupation sets; high denominations of British issues overprinted "G.E.A." or "N.F."

GERMAN NEW GUINEA (m)—Early issues, particularly used copies.

GERMAN SOUTHWEST AFRICA (u)—Early issues, particularly used copies.

GERMANY (p)—Early issues in very fine condition; semi-postals; high values of recent sets; commemoratives; souvenir sheets; air mails issued after 1924.

GIBRALTAR (p)—Early issues in fine condition; high values of later issues.

GILBERT AND ELLICE ISLANDS (p)—Fiji stamps overprinted; high values of later issues; used copies on original envelopes.

GOLD COAST (p)—Nearly all except the lower denominations of recent issues; used copies on original envelopes.

GRAND COMORO ISLAND (m)—All, if they are in superb condition, especially used copies on original envelopes.

GREAT BRITAIN (p)—Early issues in very fine condition, except the one-penny red with perforations; high nominations of later issues; regular issues overprinted "I.R.—Official," "Govt. Parcel" "Q.W.," used abroad; "Army," "Board of Education," "Admiralty."

GREECE (p)—Early issues in superb condition.

GREENLAND (m)—Used on cover.

GRENADA (p)—Early issues in superb condition; high values of later sets.

GRIQUALAND (m)—Nearly all, if they are genuine. (Stamps of this country were produced by overprinting stamps of the Cape of Good Hope with a "G.")

GUADELOUPE (p)—Early issues; high denominations of later sets; postage dues.

GUAM (p)—Nearly all.

GUATEMALA (m)—Comparatively few regular issues; air mails.

GUINEA (u)—Early issues when they are in very fine condition.

HAITI (p)—Early issues in very fine condition; air-post stamps.

HAMBURG (p)—Only genuine copies in very fine condition, particularly used.

HANOVER (p)—Only genuine copies in very fine condition, particularly used.

HATAY (u)—Used copies on original letters.

HAWAII (p)—Nearly all, if they are in very fine condition and used copies on original envelopes.

HEJAZ (u)—Only the rarities.

HELIGOLAND (m)—Only genuine copies in very fine condition.

HONDURAS (m)—Very rew regular issues; air mails.

HONG KONG (p)—Early issues in very fine condition; later sets except lower denominations.

HORTA (u)—Only special superb copies, or used specimens on original envelopes.

HUNGARY (u)—Very few regular issues but only when they are in superb condition.

ICELAND (p)—Early issues; high values of later sets; air mails.

INDIA (p)—Earliest issues in very fine condition; high denominations of later sets; air mails; regular stamps overprinted "C.E.F." or "I.E.F."

INDIA—NATIVE STATES (u)— Only comparatively few rarities, and then only when they are in very fine condition.

INDO-CHINA (m)—High denominations; air mails.

INHAMBANE (u)—The St. Anthony stamps of 1895; comparatively few others, and then only those in superb condition.

IONIAN ISLANDS (m)—All, particularly in used condition.

IRAQ (p)—High denominations.

IRISH FREE STATE (p)—Comparatively few.

ITALIAN COLONIES (m)—Only the high denominations.

ITALIAN EAST AFRICA (u)— High values.

ITALIAN SOMALILAND (u)— Comparatively few.

ITALY (m)—Very few of the old issues; high denominations of later sets, preferably in used condition; commemoratives; air mails.

IVORY COAST (m)—Early issues, high values of later sets; used copies on original envelopes.

JAMAICA (p)—Early issues in very fine condition; high denominations of later sets; errors.

JAPAN (m)—Genuine copies of the first few issues; the highest denominations of later sets; air mails.

JUGOSLAVIA (u)—Comparatively few.

KENYA AND UGANDA (p)— High denominations.

KIAUCHAU (m)—Nearly all, particularly very fine used copies.

KIONGA (u)—Only very fine used copies.

KUWAIT (m)—High denominations, used copies on original envelopes.

LABUAN (u)—Only very fine unused copies and postally used copies. Stamps of this country on original envelopes are particularly desirable.

LAGOS (m)—Nearly all if they are in very fine condition.

LATAKIA (u)—Only a few of the highest denominations.

LATVIA (m)—Comparatively few.

LEBANON (m)—Only the high values, commemoratives, and air mails.

LEEWARD ISLANDS (p)—Early issues; high denominations of later sets.

LIBERIA (m)—Early issues in very fine condition; later issues only when they are unused or with genuine postal cancellation or on original envelopes; air mails.

LIBYA (m)—Very few.

LIECHTENSTEIN (p)—High denominations; air mails; officials.

LITHUANIA (m)—The first issue of 1918; comparatively few others.

LOURENÇO MARQUES (u)—St. Anthony stamps of 1895; very few others except when used on original envelopes.

LÜBECK (m)—Only when they are genuine and in very fine condition.

LUXEMBURG (p)—Early issues in very fine condition; high denominations of later sets; semi-postals; officials.

MACAO (u)—Only very fine copies of the older issues; high denominations of later sets.

MADAGASCAR (m)—British consular stamps; early French sets in very fine condition; high denominations of later sets and used copies on original envelopes.

MADEIRA (u)—Very fine copies of the early stamps.

MALDIVE ISLANDS (m)—Ceylon stamps with "Maldives" overprint; used copies on original envelopes.

MALTA (p)—Early issues in very fine condition; high denominations of regular sets.

MANCHUKUO (m)—Almost none.

MARIANAS ISLANDS (u)—Spanish dominion issues; used copies of German issues.

MARIENWERDER (u)—Comparatively few.

MARSHALL ISLANDS (m)—Used copies in very fine condition.

MARTINIQUE (p)—Early issues in very fine condition; high denominations of later sets.

MAURITANIA (m)—High denominations.

MAURITIUS (p)—Early issues in very fine condition; high denominations of later sets; used copies on original envelopes.

MAYOTTE (u)—All, if they are in very fine condition.

MECKLENBURG (m)—Very fine, genuine copies only.

MEMEL (u)—Comparatively few.

MESOPOTAMIA (p)—With "Baghdad" overprint; high denominations of other issues.

MEXICO (p)—Early issues in superb condition; high denominations of other sets; several of the air-mail sets; some of the officials; Campeche, Chiapas, Cuernavaca, Guadalajara, Monterrey, Morelia and Patzcuaro issues.

MIDDLE CONGO (m)—High denominations.

MODENA (p)—Very fine genuine copies.

MOHELI (m)—Very fine copies.

MONACO (p)—The first issue of 1885; high denominations of other sets; semi-postals.

MONGOLIA (u)—Very fine copies of early issues.

MONTENEGRO (m)—Comparatively few, and those in fine condition.

MONTSERRAT (p)—High denominations.

MOZAMBIQUE (m)—Early issues in very fine condition; high denominations of other sets; overprinted "Jornaes."

NATAL (p)—Early issues; higher denominations of later issues.

NAURU (p)—All, if they are in very fine condition.

NEJD (u)—Only a few rarities.

NETHERLANDS (p)—Early issues when in superb condition; high denominations of later sets; semi-postals.

NEPAL (u)—Only very fine specimens.

NEVIS (p)—Nearly all.

NEW BRITAIN (m)—Nearly all.

NEW BRUNSWICK (p)—All, particularly on original envelopes. (Note: Many of these stamps were cut in half by the postmaster. Such items are rare when they are still affixed to the envelope.)

NEW CALEDONIA (p)—Early issues; high denominations of later sets; air mails.

NEWFOUNDLAND (p)—Nearly all except the lowest denominations of recent sets.

NEW GUINEA (m)—Nearly all.

NEW HEBRIDES (m)—All except lowest denominations, particularly used copies on original envelopes.

NEW REPUBLIC (m)—All, when in very fine condition.

NEW SOUTH WALES (u)—The earliest issues; Consumptive Home set.

NEW ZEALAND (m)—Early issues only when in superb condition; high denominations of later sets; air mails.

NICARAGUA (m)—Comparatively few regular issues; air mails.

NIGER (m)—Only the highest denominations.

NIGER COAST PROTECTORATE (m)—Nearly all.

NIGERIA (p)—All except the lowest denominations.

NIUE (m)—Most issues.

NORFOLK ISLAND (m)—Used on original cover.

NORTH BORNEO (m)—Unused or postally used copies on original envelopes.

NORTHERN NIGERIA (m)—Nearly all except low denominations of recent sets.

NORTHERN RHODESIA (m)—High denominations.

NORTH WEST PACIFIC ISLANDS (m)—Nearly all.

NORWAY (p)—Comparatively few of the regular issues.

NOSSI BE (m)—Nearly all.

NOVA SCOTIA (p)—Nearly all (See note after New Brunswick.)

NYASSALAND (p)—Nearly all.

NYASSA (u)—Comparatively few.

OBOCK (p)—Nearly all, particularly used copies on original envelopes.

OLDENBURG (m)—Genuine copies in very fine condition only.

OLTRE GIUBA (u)—Comparatively few.

ORANGE RIVER COLONY (m)—Errors.

PALESTINE (p)—High denominations.

PANAMA (p)—Nearly all except the lower denominations of recent sets.

PAPUA (p)—Nearly all.

PARAGUAY (u)—Comparatively few, and then only those in superb condition.

PENRHYN ISLAND (m)—Only when they are in very fine condition, or used on original envelopes.

PERSIA (u)—Comparatively few.

PERU (m)—Early issues; high denomination of later sets; air mails.

PHILIPPINES (p)—Spanish issues when they are in superb condition; all except the lowest denominations of the later issues; air mails.

PITCAIRN ISLAND (m)—Used stamps on cover.

POLAND (p)—Comparatively few.

PONTA DELGADA (u)—Superb copies only.

PUERTO RICO (m)—Superb copies only in the Spanish issues; United States stamps overprinted.

PORTUGAL (m)—Early issues; high denominations of later issues; air mails.

PRINCE EDWARD ISLANDS (p)—All.

PRUSSIA (m)—Very fine copies only.

QUEENSLAND (u)—Superb copies, on original envelopes.

QUELIMANE (u)—Used copies on original envelopes.

REUNION (m)—Early issues; high denominations of later sets; air mails.

RHODESIA (p)—Almost all, except the lowest denominations of later sets.

RIO DE ORO (u)—All, but only when in very fine condition.

ROMAGNA (m)—All, particularly used.

ROMAN STATES (m)—All, if they are genuine.

ROMANIA (m)—Comparatively few.

RUSSIA (m)—Comparatively few.

SAAR (p)—Nearly all except the lowest denominations.

ST. CHRISTOPHER (p)—Nearly all.

ST. HELENA (p)—Nearly all.

ST. KITTS-NEVIS (p)—Nearly all except the lowest denominations of the later issues.

ST. LUCIA (p)—Nearly all except the lowest denominations of recent issues.

ST. MARIE DE MADAGASCAR (m)—All.

ST. PIERRE AND MIQUELON (p) —Early issues; high denominations of later sets.

ST. THOMAS AND PRINCE IS-LANDS (m)—Nearly all, if they are superb.

ST. VINCENT (p)—Nearly all except the lowest denominations of recent sets.

SALVADOR (m)—Comparatively few regular issues; air mails.

SAMOA (p)—Nearly all, if they are very fine or used on original envelopes.

SAN MARINO (m)—Comparatively few.

SARAWAK (m)—High denominations.

SARDINIA (m)—The first issues, when they are genuine.

SAXONY (m)—Only very fine copies.

SCHLESWIG (m)—Early issues in superb condition.

SENEGAL (m)—Early issues; high denominations of later sets.

SENEGAMBIA AND NIGER (m)—All.

SERBIA (m)—Comparatively few.

SEYCHELLES (p)—Early sets; high denominations of other sets.

SHANGHAI (u)—Comparatively few.

SIAM (m)—High denominations; Boy Scout issues; air mails.

SIBERIA (u)—Nearly all.

SIERRA LEONE (p)—Early issues; high values of other sets.

SOMALI COAST (p)—Nearly all.

SOUTH AUSTRALIA (u)—Only superb copies.

SOUTH BULGARIA (u)—Only superb copies.

SOUTH NIGERIA (m)—Nearly all.

SOUTHERN RHODESIA (p)—All except the lowest denominations.

SOUTH RUSSIA (u)—Only rarities.

SOUTH WEST AFRICA (p)—Nearly all except lowest denominations.

SPAIN (m)—Only superb copies of earliest issues; high values of later sets.

SPANISH GUINEA (u)—Only superb copies.

SPANISH WEST SAHARA (u)—High values and copies used on original envelopes.

STELLALAND (u)—Very fine copies only.

STRAITS SETTLEMENTS (m)—High denominations.

SUDAN (p)—Egyptian stamps overprinted "Soudan"; high values of other sets; air mails; officials.

SURINAM (p)—Comparatively few of the regular issues; pictorials; air mails.

SWAZILAND (u)—Only very fine copies.

SWEDEN (p)—Early issues; high values of later issues; semi-postals; air mails; officials.

SWITZERLAND (p)—Earliest issues; high values of later sets; semi-postals; air mails; early postage dues; officials.

SYRIA (u)—Only rarities.

TAHITI (m)—Nearly all.

TANGANYIKA (p)—Nearly all, except lowest denominations.

TANNU TOUVA (u)—None.

TASMANIA (u)—Very fine copies only.

TETE (u)—Only a few.

THRACE (u)—Comparatively few.

TIBET (u)—Only used copies on original envelopes.

TIMOR (u)—Comparatively few.

TOBAGO (p)—Nearly all.

TOGO (m)—All except the lowest denominations.

TONGA (m)—All except the lowest denominations.

TRANSCAUCASIA (u)—Only the rarities.

TRANS-JORDAN (m)—Nearly all.

TRANSVAAL (m)—Early issues.

TRINIDAD (p)—Nearly all.

TRINIDAD AND TOBAGO (p)—All except the lowest denominations.

TRIPOLITANIA (u)—Comparatively few.

TUNISIA (m)—High denominations; air mails.

TURKEY (u)—Comparatively few.

TURKS ISLANDS (p)—Nearly all.

TURKS AND CAICOS ISLANDS (p)—All except the lowest denominations.

TUSCANY (m)—Nearly all.

TWO SICILIES (m)—Nearly all.

UBANGI (m)—High denominations or used copies on original envelopes.

UGANDA (m)—All.

UKRAINIA (u)—Rarities only.

UNION OF SOUTH AFRICA (p)—All except the lowest denominations.

UPPER SENEGAL (m)—Nearly all.

UPPER SILESIA (u)—Officials, when they are genuine.

UPPER VOLTA (m)—High denominations.

URUGUAY (m)—Nearly all early issues; air mails; comparatively few others.

VATICAN CITY (p)—Nearly all, except the lowest denominations.

VENEZUELA (m)—Rarities of the early issues; high denominations of later issues; air mails.

VICTORIA (u)—Very fine copies only.

VIRGIN ISLANDS (p)—Early issues; high denominations of later sets.

YUGOSLAVIA—See *Jugoslavia*.

WALLIS AND FUTUNA ISLANDS (m)—Comparatively few, except used copies on original envelopes.

WESTERN AUSTRALIA (u)—Earliest issues.

WESTERN UKRAINIA (u)—Rarities only.

WHITE RUSSIA (u)—None.

WÜRTTEMBERG (m)—Rarities only.

YEMEN (u)—First issues on original envelopes.

ZAMBESIA (u)—Comparatively few.

ZANZIBAR (m)—Nearly all.

ZULULAND (m)—Nearly all.

Even postmarks are designed to spread propaganda. This German one proclaims, "Every service to country fortifies our might."

[15] Philatelic Literature

The collection of postage stamps has been called the hobby of kids and kings, because it is possible for anyone to ride this avocation whether he has an allowance of a few cents or an unlimited bank account with which to acquire what he needs. And while it perhaps is possible to get a lot of pleasure out of the unguided accumulation of whatever specimens one can obtain as an individual, and mounting them in an album without the assistance of at least a catalogue, the person who attempts it is likely to miss a great deal of sport.

Nowadays one of the standard postage-stamps catalogues is the *sine qua non* of the hobby. Without a catalogue at hand—whether it is a personally owned copy or one borrowed from a public or philatelic library—the collector is about as lost as a mariner at sea without a compass. It is true that the catalogue's prime function is the quotation of prices "for fine specimens when offered by an informed dealer to an informed buyer." But it has many functions beyond that.

Catalogues list, in chronological order, all the stamps of the world according to the countries that issued them. A specific number is assigned to each stamp, and then follows a description of the color, denomination, and such other details as the watermark which appears in the paper, if it should have one, and the gauge of the perforations or roulette punches. By consulting the catalogue, the collector is immediately able to identify any stamp that he acquires and to get a rough idea of its worth.

The word *rough* is intentionally used, for very few collectors and dealers attempt to use the catalogue quotations as an accurate guide to valuations in a cash transaction. In fact, they cannot so use them. As we mentioned before, the price of any specimen is determined by demand and supply, coupled with the condition of the stamp being offered. The editors of the various catalogues make an honest effort to price every item at a figure that they believe to be fair, but such a multitude of factors enter into any given transaction that they can determine quotations on only a broad, general basis founded upon the information they personally have at hand. The novice, accordingly, is likely to be bewildered by the way in which experienced philatelists employ or disregard catalogue quotations.

The novice, for instance, may read the advertisement of a dealer which states that he is offering 1,000 different stamps, with a catalogue value of $20, for $2 or ten per cent of their listed worth and he may think that he is getting an exceptional bargain. The fact is that the catalogue editors have had to set a minimum price (in the United States it usually is 2 cents) on any individual stamp regardless of how common it may be. This procedure is necessary to protect the professional dealer. The dealer, with an office, equipment, other overhead, and experience cannot afford to sell any single stamp at a fraction of a cent without financial loss, and therefore if a collector needs a stamp which is quoted at 2 cents, to complete a set in his album, the dealer is justified in charging that much to dig it out of his stock books. If a collector made up a list of 1,000 different stamps, each of which had a catalogue value of but 2 cents, and sent it to a dealer, he would have to pay approximately the full $20 for them, even if they were the same 1,000 stamps offered in the packets at $2. The packet represents stamps of a common type, which the dealer has either purchased from wholesalers already made up into packets, or which he himself has made up of surplus stock which he wants to move rapidly.

Because so many stamps have been issued, particularly within the last three decades, it is impossible for every price quotation to be accurate. Some collectors who have the time scrutinize the catalogue page by page and item by item, pick out individual items that they know from experience are far underpriced, and then hunt through dealers' stocks to find them. If the collectors are better informed than the dealers, they are in a position to pick up many bargains, for not even a dealer who is devoting his full time to the professional aspect of stamp collecting can keep abreast of *all* stamp values. In 1906, for example, France issued a 10-centime red stamp showing the figure of a sower with a bit of ground under her feet. A few months later the same design was used, except that the ground had been removed from the design. Today the former is listed in the *Standard Postage Stamp Catalogue* at 25 cents for an unused copy and a dime for a used one. Despite the low quotation, the stamp is a most difficult one to find and has been owned by fewer than three dozen persons whose collections I have examined in over twenty years. The collector who can purchase a copy of that particular stamp, at the catalogue price or for less, is getting a bargain indeed. The same holds true for hundreds and even thousands of other postage stamps listed in this catalogue.

Another source of bewilderment is the custom of selling postage stamps at a discount from the catalogue price. Often dealers will offer specimens at discounts that range from ten to ninety per cent. Again, the factors of supply, demand, and condition enter into the picture, and the buyer must be well informed before he makes a purchase.

Whenever a substantial discount is offered it is only because of one of three reasons: (1) the stamp offered has some defect that impairs its value; (2) the stamp is an item that, because of its general unpopularity, cannot be sold at full value; (3) a dealer happens to have an unusually large supply on hand and wants to liquidate his holdings to turn his invested capital over more rapidly. As a general rule dealers can afford to sell most stamps issued before 1925 at a discount from catalogue quotations because the demand for these is not so strong as for the more recently issued ones, and by the same token, new issues usually are sold above catalogue quotations. Of course there are many exceptions to the general rule which add yet further to the neophyte collector's problem of understanding values.

Many, many times the newcomer to the hobby will hear or read about a stamp which has a catalogue value of $X being sold over the counter, or at auction, for five or ten times that amount. Such prices are justified just as tremendous discount figures are. Only recently one collector paid $165 for a copy of a five-cent United States stamp of the 1847 set, despite the fact that the catalogue listed it at the time at $22.50. But there were reasons. This particular stamp had extremely wide margins, its color was as fresh as the day it had been issued, and it was canceled by a very rare type of postmark. To the average collector it would have been just a very fine stamp to fill a blank space in his album; but to the various persons who bid it up to that astonishing price, and to the man who eventually bought it at the auction sale, it was a specimen the like of which is available only once in a lifetime.

And just as the aforementioned French stamp is an outstanding example of understatement of value, there are not a few stamps that are overpriced in the catalogue. Any number of individual stamps that normally are worth a few cents are listed at many times that value simply because the catalogue editors have not had a chance to make corrections. Often certain stamps are apparently rare because no wholesale quantities of them can be obtained, and accordingly prices are raised. At some later date the holdings of a collector or a dealer, or even the surplus stocks of a postal administration, which formerly were unknown, are dumped into the stamp market. When they are obtained by a dealer before the catalogue editors know about it, it is possible for the dealer to offer specimens at prices that seem like huge bargains.

Not so very long ago, for example, the 2½-penny stamp for Bermuda's 1923 set was listed at 75 cents and sold at about that figure for a number of years. One day I was offered a very nice copy at a bargain price of 20 cents, and I bought it. It seems that a huge supply of these stamps had been hoarded by a private collector who wanted to make a specialized study of them, but who died before he had finished. His estate sold the lot to a wholesaler, and as the supply now could more adequately satisfy normal needs, the sales price dropped. I did not know about this, so assumed that the 20-cent figure was a bargain in view of past difficulties I had experienced in getting it to fill my set. As soon as the catalogue editors found out about the situation, the listing was dropped to 25 cents, and so I did not get such a bargain after all. Today that stamp is listed at only 40 cents, and on occasion it still can be bought at the same 20 cents I paid about twenty years ago.

I remember, too, the time one dealer who advertises widely, but whose reputation for absolute integrity is not too high among philatelists who have traded with him long enough to have been victimized, offered a Turkish stamp of 1913, which had a catalogue value of $50, for $2.50 "to new customers." At the time, the *Standard Postage Stamp Catalogue* listed this item, and according to existing market conditions the stamp was fully worth approximately that figure. The persons who bought it got what appeared to be a very fine specimen, except that instead of a normal postmark this stamp had a *cut* cancellation. Subsequent information disclosed that this dealer had negotiated with the Turkish government when a huge supply of unused stamps was found in a corner of the Constantinople post-office vaults. He obtained a quantity of them, but to prevent them from being used at full face value of 200 piasters, the official ran a knife die over the full sheets. The dealer obtained and sold these stamps before the catalogue editors caught up with the situation. Today, they list both varieties—the normally used stamp, still at the high price, and the "cut cancellation variety"—at $5.

But not every bargain offer need be spurned by the novice collector. Almost invariably stamp dealers hunt through their stock, pick out such items as have a high catalogue value, and offer them to new customers at a discount, which in some cases represents an actual loss. Like the corner drugstore that offers a Saturday bargain, these dealers make attractive offers in the hope of getting more trade, for they reckon that future profits will offset the lack of profit, or loss, sustained in the initial sale.

In the United States we have but one general catalogue, which most often is referred to as the "Bible of philately." Founded soon after the Civil War by John Walter Scott, it originally was but a price list through which this pioneer American dealer offered stamps to the handful of collectors who brought their orders to his small Nassau Street shop. Gradually it became an established annual publication which, in addition to the stamps in Scott stock, makes a sincere attempt to list every postage stamp that has been issued.

All through the years the *Standard Postage Stamp Catalogue* has been maintained as an important and valuable asset of the Scott Stamp and Coin Company as that firm grew and changed hands. Late in the nineteen thirties, Hugh M. Clark and his wife, Theresa, obtained full control and split it into two separate companies: the Scott Stamp and Coin Company, and Scott Publications, Inc. The former continued to buy and sell postage stamps and coins and was sold to Norman Serphos, a collector who started his professional life as a flower dealer, but who became a philatelic broker of no small renown. Mr. Clark retained control of the new company and so became virtual dictator of policies, listings, and prices of the Scott catalogues.

All through the period of Mr. Clark's editorship, he realized that the catalogue could be used as an instrument through which unscrupulous persons could foist upon inexperienced hobbyists items that had been "issued" simply for the stamp trade. And being honestly concerned with the protection of the collector, Mr. Clark exercised an ultraconservative policy to govern whatever was put into the catalogue. So strict were his rules on admittance of new listings that he refused recognition to any stamps that were submitted to him without iron-clad evidence that they were intended primarily to satisfy postal needs.

This policy has unquestionably protected many collectors from buying material that was issued in various parts of the world during the revolutions and uprisings that presaged the war. All through the Spanish Civil War and the Chinese conflict any number of new and provisional issues appeared on the market; and because communications between the United States and the postal authorities were very

(*Upper right*) Monsignor Killian and Cardinal Spellman examine the latter's collection at the Centenary International Philatelic Exhibition.

Alfred F. Lichtenstein Memorial Court of Honor at the Centenary Exhibition.

Collection at the Smithsonian Institution, Washington, D.C.

Genuine stamp: (*A*) The two dashes and "comma" are distinct and well shaped. (*B*) The tail of the Arabic "S" is long, slender, and well shaped. (*C*) The numeral 1 is clear and large. (*D*) The loop of the Arabic "S" is a perfect oval. (*E*) The stroke of the Arabic "A" is almost straight, with a small hook. (*F*) The scroll in the basic design is open. (*G*) The hook of the Arabic "SH" is well formed. (*H*) The long stroke of the same letter is long and tapering. (*I*) The shading of the pearls is on the inside.

First type of counterfeit: (*A*) The two dashes and "comma" are rough and indistinct. (*B*) The tail of the Arabic "S" is curved and has a loop at the end. (*C*) The numeral 1 is weak and too slender. (*D*) The loop of the Arabic "S" is too rounded. (*E*) The stroke of the Arabic "A" is curved. (*F*) The scroll in the basic design is joined. (*G*) The hook of the Arabic "SH" is crudely shaped and touches the adjacent character. (*H*) The long stroke of the same letter is short. (*I*) The shading of the pearls is on the outside.

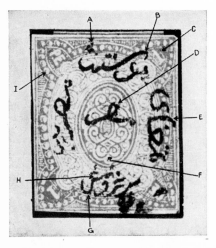

Second type of counterfeit: (*A*) The two dashes and "comma" are joined and broken. (*B*) The stroke of the Arabic "S" is curved and the tail is short. (*C*) The numeral 1 is too slender and large. (*D*) The loop of the Arabic "S" is narrow. (*E*) The stroke of the Arabic "A" curves near the top. (*F*) The scroll of the basic design is joined. (*G*) The hook of the Arabic "SH" is poorly drawn. (*H*) The long stroke of the same letter is incorrectly designed. (*I*) The shading of the pearl is outside.

Genuine and counterfeit stamps: The ability to distinguish between genuine stamps and those made by counterfeiters to deceive collectors is based upon the discrepancy of tiny details.

poor, it was almost impossible to authenticate every one of the stickers which found their way to the stocks of our American dealers. Unless Mr. Clark had adopted such a policy, it is almost certain that he would have given catalogue recognition to thousands of items which are no better than the Tannu Touva labels and some of the other adhesives that were foisted upon collectors during the nineteenth century.

So diligently did Mr. Clark work on editing the catalogue that his health was impaired to a point where he was advised to give it up. For several years he sought a buyer, but not until early in 1946, when he suffered a serious breakdown, did he press the matter. A few months later announcement was made that control of the catalogue had been acquired by Gordon Harmer, an Englishman who had come to this country just before the war to open a New York branch of the London stamp auction house of Harmer, Rooke, and Company in order to raise American foreign exchange credits.

While the Scott *Standard Postage Stamp Catalogue* is the only general catalogue in the country, and the foremost of Scott Publications, Inc., this firm also publishes a catalogue devoted only to United States stamps, and one devoted to air-post stamps of the world. In other countries where stamp collecting is very popular, there are other catalogues. In England there are several: the *Stanley-Gibbons*, the *Whitfield King*, and the *Robson Lowe;* in France there is *Yvert and Tellier;* in Germany, *Senf* and *Michel;* in Switzerland, *Zumstein* and *Müller;* and so on.

But so far we have spoken only of general catalogues, or those that attempt to list all the postage stamps of the world. In addition to these, there are any number of catalogues which concern themselves only with certain philatelic specialty fields. Since the days when general collecting became impossible, collectors have turned their efforts to stamps of one country or a group of countries; to air-mail stamps and covers; to pre-cancels, and the like.

As these specialties developed, the need for specialized catalogues grew, and so within a relatively short period of time we have had (in this country) such catalogues as *The American Air Mail Catalogue*, devoted to a listing, description, and pricing of envelopes carried on historic flights by pioneers and first trips of regularly established air-mail routes; *Sanabria's Air Post Catalogue*, devoted to a listing of all known air-post stamps and correlative material; *The Hoover Brother's Catalogue of Pre-canceled Stamps;* and *The Stampless Cover*

Catalogue, which lists types of markings that were used on letters before we had adhesive postage stamps; and many others.

Since usually the collectors of the various countries place major emphasis upon the collection and study of their own postage stamps, it is natural for each country to have a catalogue that deals at great length with the stamps of that country and to dismiss the rest of the world's postal paper with simplified listings. That truth holds also here, and so we have, in addition to the *Standard Postage Stamp Catalogue*, the *United States Stamp Catalogue*, another Scott publication. This substantial volume lists, describes, and prices not only the regular issues in used and unused condition, but also provides information about such advanced philatelic matters as blocks, plate numbers, stamps on original covers, revenues, postal stationery, proofs, essays, and so on.

In Britain there are catalogues which treat the stamps of England and the colonies in the same specialized manner. New Zealand, Egypt, Sweden, Denmark, Norway, Germany, Austria, Australia, Chile, Brazil, and many other countries all have similar publications; and the collectors here who decide to specialize in stamps of some other country usually obtain copies of these catalogues, not only because the prices quoted are more reliable, but also because they always contain more accurate listings and descriptions of the stamps they treat.

The price lists of many dealers here, too, are valuable reference guides to true market values, and are used by collectors when a matter of prices is involved. The free price lists which the Stanley Gibbons Company (not to be confused with the English firm of the same name) and the H. E. Harris Company distribute to their customers are frequently used by stamp traders in coming to a price at which they will sell or buy United States stamps, simply because these firms so frequently revise their lists that they are almost always up to the minute and not a year or so behind the times, as is true of the Scott volume. Collectors of Scandinavian issues rely upon the Pelander price list in the same manner when stamps of Norway, Denmark, Sweden, and Finland are involved.

But since the matter of values ought to be but a secondary matter to a person who rides the stamp-collecting hobby as a hobby, the standard catalogue still serves his purposes notwithstanding all its failings.

The prime function of this catalogue is to guide the collector in the intelligent arrangement of his collection and the knowledge of which stamps belong to a given set. Yet, beyond that, it forms an almost perfect basis upon which to exchange his duplicates for material that will fill spaces in his album. When two collectors get together in person or through the mails and enter upon an exchange session, the swapping of one stamp for another is futile without a consideration of values.

I can recall the early days of my own activities. I had no catalogue, but through a fortunate bit of luck I had a source of European postage stamps. The fact that some of these stamps were worth considerably more than the ones for which I traded them, stamp for stamp, never entered my mind. I had plenty of duplicates, and I knew that I could swap one of them, for example, for gaudy, interesting Liberian pictorials; and so for many months I had loads of fun trading them off. Only later did I learn that there was such a guide as a catalogue, and that I had been giving stamps worth 25 to 50 cents a piece for material that was barely worth the paper it was printed on. The realization that I could have got all the Liberian stamps for but a handful of my duplicates was eased only by the fact that my transactions had been with a fellow collector who, like myself, was without a catalogue, and that the advantage he enjoyed was purely accidental.

But in addition to the catalogues, many other sources of information are available to the collector who wishes to learn more about stamps and the hobby of collecting them. Foremost among these are the various magazines which are regularly published in this and many other countries. Very soon after collecting began here we had philatelic magazines. Most of them were the house organs of established dealers, or the bulletins of stamp clubs. Many of them were good, so good that researchers still refer to them; others were poorly edited and deserved the failure they suffered. Today magazines are flourishing as they never flourished before. So many new issues are being produced, so many new facts are being learned about existing stamps, that without magazines a serious collector would be lost.

The magazines available must be classified into two groups: those issued to members of stamp societies, and those published for sale to all comers. In the former group we have the *Collectors Club Philatelist*, published quarterly by the Collectors Club, New York, which features the monographs of members who have made exhaustive studies of an advanced nature. *The American Philatelist*, organ of the American Philatelic Society, is a monthly which features serious and semiserious articles about specific stamps and stamp issues.

The S. P. A. Journal is published monthly by the Society of Philatelic Americans, and features articles of a more popular nature with a generous amount of "gossip" news about the society and its members. *The Airport Journal* is another monthly, published by the American Air Mail Society, which devotes its pages to news about air-mail development and history and reports about the stamps and covers relating to aviation's progress.

The Essay-Proof Journal is published by the Essay-Proof Society and presents scholarly articles pertaining to the production of stamp designs before they are accepted and issued.

Many others can be included in this category, but because they are smaller, and usually feature only news about the club and members of the group by which they are published, they cannot be regarded as being of wide general interest.

In the second category we have an entirely different setup, and one which only a veteran philatelist can understand. For years the publication of a magazine for collectors was a labor of love, rather than a profitable business venture. Until recently, when stamp selling became big business, dealers had to weigh their pennies in advertising so that rates had to be held to a minimum if a publisher wished any at all. Subscribers habitually shared their copies with other collectors, and so circulation never was too high. In fact, many clubs or groups of collectors had a community arrangement whereby each would subscribe to a different magazine and at a meeting would exchange their copies so that every member could read five or six magazines regularly, although he personally had to pay for only one.

This lack of income hampered the publishers and they had to get along on the proverbial shoestring, which was reflected for many years in their editorial columns. Publishing a weekly periodical is a tough job, even under the best of circumstances when payment can be made for contributed material. But since income was just about enough to cover the cost of publication, editors of philatelic magazines could not afford to pay for manuscripts or news reports. They had to depend upon the contributions of collectors who wished to share their knowledge with their fellows; of dealers who had an axe to grind; and of persons who would write simply for the questionable pride of seeing their name in print.

As a whole, philatelic periodicals were mediocre or poor for a long period of time. Only once in a while would any of them publish articles that had permanent reference value, and even these were usually the products of a few men and women who were so purely interested in the advancement of the hobby that they reported the results of their studies without hope of remuneration or even reimbursement of the postage it cost to submit them. In fact, the number of articles of this nature was limited, and those scriveners who produced them were induced to contribute them to magazine editors solely on the basis of personal friendship. Therefore the bulk of each of the various magazines was filled with "feature stories" which would have been better off in a waste-paper basket. Editorial columns were generously filled with articles about stamps which dealers contributed as a build-up to create a demand for the stamps in question, which later were offered through advertising media.

Among the many instances of this type which I vividly recall is the "campaign" presaging the Cuban set of 1929, issued to mark the inauguration of the Capitol in Havana. For several weeks all the magazines of the time carried articles and stories about the stamps: about the edifice in connection with which they were being issued, and reports of the "scarcity" of the issue. By the time supplies of these five stamps arrived in this country collectors had been so thoroughly saturated with propaganda about them that they flooded the dealer who had authored the publicity with orders and he found no difficulty in selling thousands of sets at from $2 to $4 each. It was only months later that we learned the stamps were not as rare as they had been announced to be, and the price was slashed to the truer 75 cents.

The inability to pay for material has placed a great handicap upon philatelic editors. To retain their advertisers they had to accept virtually all contributions which dealers sent for publication in the editorial columns, and in some instances they worked on a five-to-one basis. For every inch of advertising a dealer bought, he might obtain five inches of editorial mention. Some dealers were fair about exchange propositions and contributed really constructive information based upon their superior experience and knowledge; some few prostituted the opportunity by exploiting that material that lay dormant in their stocks.

But the editors were handicapped even by the material that was submitted by persons who had nothing to sell, but merely wanted to write for the sake of having their journalistic endeavors published. A few such contributions advanced philatelic knowledge; most, however, were either rewrites of other persons' material or, when originally produced, were full of mistakes and inaccurate statements.

They were published in good faith by editors who were so busy trying to find material with which to fill each week's columns that checking was impossible. Some of these errors were so careless as to be amusing. One of them, for instance, gave an account of a phase of the Anglo-Egyptian Sudan's postal history and placed Khartoum as the capital of Egypt; another placed the highest mountain in the world in Chile.

The philatelic periodical situation has improved considerably within the last decade, chiefly because both advertising and circulation incomes have jumped because of the great increase of interest in the hobby. It thus became possible for editors to offer writers at least a semblance of pay for material.

No longer need most editors accept everything that comes along; they can now select what they want, and they often ask a definite person to write a specified article or regular feature column. There are no fewer than a dozen weeklies, and each of them caters to a definite class of reader by presenting material that will interest him. All have new-issue columns in which postage stamps are chronicled as they are officially announced or placed on sale. For the sake of the collectors who may want to subscribe to a stamp collector's magazine, we shall tabulate the most popular ones here, with the sincere recommendation that no person can intelligently collect postage stamps without reading at least one of them regularly. This writer subscribes to each of them and derives both valuable information and enjoyment from all. The reader is urged to request a sample copy of each and determine which will most likely satisfy him and and his individual needs.

Chamber's Stamp Journal
Chamber's Publishing Company
Detroit, Michigan

Linn's Weekly Stamp News
Sidney, Ohio

Mekeel's Weekly Stamp News
Portland, Maine

National Stamp News
Anderson, South Carolina

Stamps
Lindquist Publications
153 Waverly Place
New York 14, New York

Weekly Philatelic Gossip
Holton, Kansas

Western Stamp Collector
Albany, Oregon

Philatelic literature also embraces a multitude of handbooks, monographs, and volumes covering the entire subject of stamps, stamp collecting, and postal history. They range in variety from books to assist novices to the recorded findings of the most profound studies.

There are pamphlets and sets of several volumes. A listing of all the titles of philatelic publications would require a book as large as this one, for one need only realize that the Collectors Club has over 100,000 different works on its shelves and that the job of cataloguing it, although started several decades ago, still is in process of being completed.

Finland's stamp of 1929 commemorates the seven hundredth anniversary of the founding of the cathedral at Turku.

A torch of liberty, V for victory, and flags of the American nations were used on this stamp issued by Costa Rica in 1942.

Part IV
Some Famous Collectors

[16] The Patriarchs of Philately

The history of every human enterprise, whether it be military, political, social, or cultural, has been studded with the names of those leaders who have laid the foundations upon which success and enduring reputation have been erected. Philately is no exception, and today we look back with pride, honor, and almost reverence to those patriarchs who are the cornerstones of our universal hobby.

Of course, we have had our multimillionaires whose collections set new records in terms of the amount of money that could be spent for tiny bits of postal paper. We have had wealthy persons who spent fortunes for postage stamps, and who used the stamps not alone to satisfy their egotistical pride, but rather as a means of studying them and the conditions under which they were issued. And we have had our scholars who have delved into the postal history of less valuable specimens and have come through with information that would otherwise have been lost to posterity. It is these latter whom we may call the cornerstones of intelligent postage-stamp collecting.

Of all of the forefathers of philately *Paul Mirabaud* stands well in the fore of our annals. Born in 1848, Mirabaud was the famous offspring of a famous family of France. His brother was head of one of the largest and richest banks in Paris; he himself was a regent of the Bank of France, a director of the Suez Canal Company, and a director of the Paris-Orleans Railway. His conversion to stamp collecting was indirect, for he first developed an interest in the few that had been issued only as a sort of diversion for his son who was wasting away as the result of a spinal affliction.

After the death of his son, Paul Mirabaud continued the collection and decided to concentrate on the stamps of Switzerland, Hawaii, France, Japan, and a select few of the British colonials. Each of these specialties he developed to the point of perfection. First he obtained the gems necessary for completion, and then he studied each item until he had discovered the answers to every philatelic problem which confounded the students of his day and which formed the basis for further research of modern scholars.

Switzerland was his favorite country, and together with Baron Alex de Reuterskiold he wrote and published a book dealing with the cantonal, transitional, and regular issues of that country up to the 1862 issue. This book, published in 1899, was so complete as to facts, details, history, and illustrations that even today it is the standard reference work for the subject it covers. Philatelists regard it not only as the best work treating early Swiss stamps but as the finest contribution to all philatelic literature.

In his collecting activities Paul Mirabud would settle for nothing less than superb condition and never was known to compromise for an inferior copy of a stamp he required or wanted.

A dealer who had occasion to introduce the late F. W. Ayer, one of the old-time great of American stamp collectors, to Paul Mirabaud emphasizes this quest for perfection. Ayer had gone to London to dispose of his collection, and knowing that Mr. Mirabaud might be interested in several outstanding items, the dealer accompanied him to Paris.

In the Mirabaud mansion Ayer displayed a page of the extremely rare Missionary stamps of Hawaii while his host literally squealed with excitement. He examined copy after copy until he had selected a complete set of four—the two, five, and both types of the 13-cent denominations. The two-cent—by far the rarest of the issue— looked superb, but a few pieces of paper still adhered to the reverse side as though the stamp had not been properly taken from the envelope it had franked. Mr. Ayer had purchased this gem some years before and was not quite so fastidious as Mr. Mirabaud. The latter, however, asked permission to remove the offending scraps before purchasing the stamp. With the owner's permission he immersed the delicate stamp in some warm water and in a few moments staggered with disappointment as the stamp itself floated into three separate pieces. All three men were horrified to think that the stamp had previously been repaired. Mirabaud exclaimed, "And that was such a beautiful stamp! Now I must select a less attractive copy."

In later years Mirabaud suffered from a heart ailment and died in 1908. His collection, which his estate elected to sell in different sections, brought a total of more than $150,000; his Swiss stamps alone were sold to Zumstein & Cie., stamp dealers of Bern, Switzerland, for the astounding sum of $62,500. And that was nearly half a century ago when prices were but a tiny fraction of prices today.

Another of the patriarchs was *Frederic Breitfuss,* son of the court jeweler at St. Petersburg, Russia. Through the fortunate circumstance of parentage, Breitfuss started collecting postage stamps early in life, about 1864–1865. His father gave him most of the stamps that came on mail addressed to the royal household, but also ordered substantial lots from the few dealers who were in business on the continent in those early days.

As he pursued his professional career, Breitfuss allowed his philatelic proclivities to follow him to Marseilles, to London, to Odessa, and back to St. Petersburg. In each city he accumulated more additions to his albums and an ever larger circle of friends with whom he could discuss the more advanced aspects of the hobby; for in his days the shelves of philatelic literature were narrow indeed.

Continually buying stamps, Breitfuss eventually built a collection which was surpassed in quality and scope only by the Ferrary and Tapling holdings, which will be discussed later. He inaugurated a practice which should be a valuable hint to every collector alive. Whenever Breitfuss bought or traded a postage stamp, he usually made a penciled notation on the hinge with which he mounted the new specimen in his album, recording the name of the person from which it was obtained, the price he paid for it, and the date of acquisition. Through this habit he was always able to furnish that information which so frequently slips from the mind of the average hobbyist.

When his collection was sold these notes were dramatic testimony to the increase in postage-stamp values. He noted, for instance, that in 1874 he had purchased the 27-parale Moldavia issue of Romania for $12.50. Today that stamp is worth $1,000. A pair of the four-rappen Zurich stamps of Switzerland cost him $20 in 1881. Today fifty times that amount could not buy it. The British Guiana type-set stamps of 1862 were purchased in 1877 for less than 25 cents apiece, and the halb-neugroschen blue of Saxony was purchased from a Dr. Kloss in 1879 for $15.

While his predecessors had already set up the principles of advanced stamp collecting and had built the fundamentals of philately, *Sir James Ludovic Lindsay, K.T., Earl of Crawford,* was the real father of philatelic research. The Earl of Crawford was an astonomer by inclination, a bibliophile and philatelist by avocation. A prominent socialite, the Earl was a man of highest literary and scientific attainments. He built what is considered one of the finest astronomical observatories in the entire British Empire and subsequently donated it to the University of Edinburgh in 1888. He used his yacht, Valhalla, to set out on expeditions to unexplored seas in order to bring back marine information and specimens to be donated to the British Museum, of which he was a trustee.

When he became interested in stamps he was not quite content with the manner in which the hobby was generally pursued. His scientific training along other fields of endeavor had given him the practice of delving further into the whys and wherefores of stamp issues. He developed a new kind of historical collection, for, as has been said, "his was a collection which forms a history of the stamps it contained."

The Crawford collection contained not only the actual stamps of countries in which he was interested, but also the results of his correspondence with banknote firms, engravers, printers, postal authorities and everyone else who could give him first-hand information pertaining to the manufacture of the stamps. Wherever and whenever he could do so, he procured the original drawings from which engravers had made their dies and plates; he obtained impressions from those dies and plates in trial colors and in the accepted shades. He investigated the reasons why certain issues had been produced and kindred correlative data until he had every scrap of information relating to them.

When he completed his work, the Earl of Crawford usually knew more about the stamps than the officials under whose authority they had been produced.

As one of the most active members and later, president of the Royal Philatelic Society, he was instrumental in raising it from the level of a club for just stamp collectors to an organization of advanced students and scholars, a status which no other hobby group has been able to match.

So tremendous was his influence upon the philatelic hobby that in 1920, when the Royal Philatelic Society decided to present an annual award to the person who had contributed "the most valuable and original piece of work toward the study and knowledge of philately, published within two years preceding the award," they named it the "Crawford medal." The contribution might consist of a "book, article or series of articles on any subject of philatelic interest," and so far the award has been made as follows:

1920	Hugo Griebert	"The Stamps of Spain, 1850-'54."
1921	Sir Edward Denny Bacon	"The Line Engraved Postage Stamps of Great Britain."
1922	C. Nissen and B. McGowan	"The Plating of the One Penny Black Postage Stamps of Great Britain."
1923	Charles L. Pack	"Half-length Portrait of the Two-pence Queen Enthroned of Victoria."
1924	Lt.-Col. G. S. F. Napier	"The 1843 Issue of Brazil."
1925	Justus Anderssen and H. Dethloff	"The Postage Stamps of Norway, 1855-1924."
1927	F. J. Peplow	"The Postage Stamps of Buenos Aires."
1928	C. F. D. Marshall	"The British Post Office."
1929	A. M. Tracey Woodward	"The Postage Stamps of Japan and Dependencies."
1930	Dr. Carrol Chase	"The Three Cent Stamps of the United States, 1851-'57 Issue."
1931	G. J. Allis	"The Stamps of the Cape of Good Hope."
1932	E. A. Smythies and Capt. D. R. Martin	"The Four Annas Lithographed Stamps of India, 1854-55."
1933	E. J. Lee	"The Postage Stamps of Uruguay."
1934	Dr. Emilio Diena	"I Francobolli del Regno di Napoli."
1935	Carl Schmidt	"Die Postwertzeichen der Russischen Landschaftsaemter."
1936	Dr. Herbert Munk	"Kohl-Briefmarken-Handbuch."
1937	Stanley B. Ashbrook	"The United States Ten Cent Stamp of 1851-57."
1938	Max Johl	The 4th Volume of "The United States Stamps of the 20th Century."
1939	Dr. H. Osborne	"Great Britain, Twopence, Plate 9, A Study of the Plate and its Repairs."
1940	J. H. Curle & A. E. Basden	"Transvaal Postage Stamps."
1944	Albert A. Jurgens	"The Hand-struck Letter Stamps of the Cape of Good Hope from 1792-1833 and the Postmarks from 1853-1910."
1945	Prescott H. Thorp	"The Stamped Envelopes and Wrappers of the United States and Possessions."
1947	Winthrop Boggs	"The Postage Stamps and Postal History of Canada."
1948	A. Tort Nicolau	"Guia del Coleccionista de Sellos de Espana, 1855-'69."
1949	Dr. F. E. Wood	"Straits Settlements Postage Stamps."
1950	L. E. Dawson	"The One Anna and Two Annas Stamps of India."
1951	D. A. Stevenson	"The Triangular Stamps of Cape of Good Hope."
1952	J. Schmidt-Andersen	"Postage Stamps of Denmark, 1851-1951."
1953	Sir John Wilson	"The Royal Philatelic Collection."
1954	J. R. Purves	"Half-lengths Victoria."

Also in 1920, the Royal Society offered another award to be offered annually and named it in honor of a second eminent patriarch of the hobby. This man was *Thomas Keay Tapling, M.P.*

Born in 1855, Tapling began collecting stamps before he was ten years old, so he actually got into the hobby "on the ground floor." His avocation followed him through Harrow and Trinity College, whence he was graduated with honor, and although he was also active and proficient in such sports as cricket, riding, and shooting, his stamp album claimed many hours of his spare time. Soon after school he joined the London Philatelic Society (before it was given crown recognition and allowed to use the prefix "Royal") and so became acquainted with the leading British stamp collectors of the day. Within a year, in 1882, his father died and Thomas Tapling had to foresake a promising law career to guide the destinies of his family's carpet business.

His serious study of postage stamps began at about the time when hobbyists were originating philatelic investigations, and during the ensuing years he worked out many of the problems related to the difficult issues of Afghanistan, Turkey, Tasmania, New South Wales, and many others. His contemporaries appreciated his philatelic knowledge, but it is said that none of them actually knew the extent of his studies and collections until after Tapling's death in 1891.

His will left his entire collection to the trustees of the British Museum on the condition that it never would be broken up or sold, that it would be kept in a separate section of the library, and that it always would be accessible to the president and secretary of the London Philatelic Society. After conferences with Sir Edward Denny Bacon, another scholar and friend of Tapling's, the British Museum officials decided that this collection should be displayed in a manner that would not only allow the specified officers of the society to view it when they so desired, but that any stamp collector visiting the museum might behold its treasures for reference purposes or for just the sheer joy of seeing unique and rare specimens.

In due course Sir Edward, who later was appointed philatelic curator of King George's collection, arranged and mounted the Tapling collection, and now they are on permanent display in "The King's Library" of the British Museum, set in upright cases and covered with glass in such a manner that they may be pulled out and examined with ease, yet will remain in dark cases when not in use, and so be safe from fading. The museum never published a catalogue of the Tapling collection, but the late Gordon Smith, an associate of Stanley Gibbons, made a list which was published in that firm's *Monthly Journal* between May, 1895 and December, 1901.

Unfortunately Smith died before he had completed his self-appointed task, and so only those sections devoted to the stamps of Mauritius, the West Indies, the United States of America, India, France, and one or two others have been recorded. The collection is vast and replete with the finest examples of the greatest rarities, which makes it one of the most important collections in existence to-day and certainly the best of the publicly owned stamp treasures. It is impossible to place an accurate market value on it, but as early as 1934 an appraisal of over $2,000,000 was offered by an accepted expert.

The Tapling medal, which was mentioned, is a silver plaque which is annually awarded "for the best monograph written by a Fellow, member or associate of the Royal Philatelic Society of London, and read before the society during the two years preceding the date of the award." To date its recipients have been:

1920	Charles L. Pack	"The Two-pence Half-length of Victoria."
1921	W. D. Beckton	"Romania Issues of 1866–68 and 1870."
1922	R. B. Yardley	"Virgin Islands."
1923	Capt. H. R. Oldfield	"The Early Issues of India."
1924	Benjamin Goodfellow	"The Four-skilling Norway of 1863–66."
1925	C. J. S. Jewell	"Plating the Rivadavias 5c, Plate D, and the Identification of Each of the Four Plates."
1926	L. Meinertzhagen	"Bordeaux Issues of France."
1927	Percy de Worms	"Ceylon Surcharges of 1885."
1928	Major T. Charlton Henry	"Lithographed Stamps of Trinidad."
1929	Dr. Emilio Diena	"Newspaper Tax Stamps of the Duchy of Parma."
1930	George Ginger	"Diadem Issues of New South Wales."
1931	Dr. W. Byam, O.B.E.	"Egypt, First Issue, 1866."
1932	T. W. Hall	"The 1858 Issue of Peru, with Particular Reference to the Plating of the Medio Peso Rose, Error."
1933	Sir Edward D. Bacon, K.C.V.O.	"The 1d. and 6d. Stamps of Victoria, 1860–66."
1934	Capt. M. H. Penfold, C.B.E.	"Norway 24sk Brown of 1863–66."
1937	H. W. Edmunds	"Tuscany."
1938	J. W. R. Purves, LL.M.	"The Postage Stamps of Fiji, 1878–1902." (Published in the *London Philatelist* during 1936–1938.)

1939	Senator J. A. Calder	"Some Phases of the Canada 1859 Issue." (Published in the *London Philatelist,* 1939.)
1940	Dr. F. E. Wood, M.B.	"Straits Settlements and Native Protected States. With special reference to stamps of doubtful catalogue status."
1941	Eric W. Mann	"The Victorian Postage Stamps of Natal."
1943	E. A. G. Carde	"Iceland: The 1902–03 Overprints."
1944	A. F. Bassett Hull M.B.E.	"Western Australia; The De la Rue Printings 1864–1902."
1946	Dr. Martin Button.	"New Zealand. Type I. The Issues of 1864–67. First Three Values."
1947	Major K. M. Beaumont	"Great Britain: Surface Printed Issues."
1948	F. T. Bolton	"New South Wales, 2d Diadem, 1855."
1950	Sir John Wilson	"British Guiana, 1853–'60."
1951	James Andrews	"Papers on Falkland Islands."
1952	W. R. Forrester-Wood	"First Issue Sarawak."
1953	Ian T. Hamilton	"Isabel the Catholic Issues of Spain."
1954	Arthur Linz	"Settings of the 5-piaster of Turkey, 1863."

Alfred F. Lichtenstein

The unquestionable peer of philatelists in the world today was the late Alfred F. Lichtenstein, first president and then chairman of the board of the Ciba Company. Mr. Lichtenstein's profound knowledge of postage stamps and postal history can be expressed only with superlatives; his personal collections only in adjectives in a press agent's vocabulary. Beginning his collection when he was a boy at school in Brooklyn, his interest in and knowledge of everything philatelic was keen to the point of perfection.

Mr. Lichtenstein was a philatelist in the fullest sense of the term. He collected postage stamps, but he devoted most of his time to the study of them and the conditions under which they were issued. In the years that he collected, Mr. Lichtenstein, or "A.F.L.," as he was most widely known in stamp circles, built up specialized collections of Mauritius, British Guiana, Newfoundland, Canada, the French colonies, Uruguay, Argentina, the Cape of Good Hope, Switzerland, and United States issues of the Pony Express and stagecoach period. Each of his collections was highly specialized and included some of the world's greatest rarities.

The most amazing thing about the A.F.L. collections was the prime condition of every item in them. Mr. Lichtenstein had no use for inferior material and would never place a torn or otherwise less-than-very-fine copy in any of his albums. Evidence of the perfection of his collections was the number of trophies he won during his lifetime. He would exhibit in competition only at international shows and never won less than a first gold medal in any of them. In 1926, at the International Exhibition held in Grand Central Palace, his collection of Uruguay issues was judged to be the finest one of the entire show and to rank above those entered by collectors all over the world.

But in spite of the importance of these specialized collections, which he kept up to date at all times, Mr. Lichtenstein's favorite was housed in a Lallier album published in 1870, so that it has spaces for no stamps issued after that date. He often told his friends that stamps issued after 1870 were "junk," however rare they might be.

The Lallier album was filled only with "pups," or the finest examples of stamps that he was able to find in more than sixty years of collecting activities. Unless a stamp was absolutely superb in all respects—centering, freshness of color, interest of postmark—it could not be mounted in this album. The result was that every specimen was a philatelist's dream which could not be duplicated for love or money.

Of course Mr. Lichtenstein was envied by many a philatelist, and primarily because he possessed so many great rarities. "If I had his money, I'd be able to have a good collection, too," a few persons would say scornfully at every show in which his material was displayed. It is true that Mr. Lichtenstein spent fortunes to obtain the material he owned. An example of the size of his purchases was the sum he spent to acquire the famous Worthington collection in 1917. At that time George Worthington, a Cleveland industrialist, was compelled by circumstances to sell what was then one of the truly great stamp collections. News of the liquidation quest reached Mr. Lichtenstein and, on his way to a business meeting, he stopped in to see Alvin Good, Mr. Worthington's philatelic secretary. Mr. Good recounts the subsequent deal in his memoirs:

Mr. Lichtenstein came to my office and asked whether he might bid for the Worthington lot. I told him he might but that it would cost roughly $500,000. He told me he was interested if the value was there and would I take the matter up and have an answer ready when he returned in two days.

Lichtenstein arrived as promised. I took him to the bank . . . and it did not take him long to convince the gentlemen that he meant business and could produce the necessary cash . . . we spent the following four days going over the stamps . . . and Lichtenstein made a cash offer of $445,000 for all except the United States envelope collection which I later sold separately to the Nassau Stamp Company for $15,000.

I will never forget the proceedings in the Board Room of the bank when Lichtenstein came to make payment for the stamps. There were half a dozen of us sitting around a table. Lichtenstein handed out some New York drafts and certified checks for a certain amount and announced he had $165,000 in cash. The lawyers looked over the checks and then inquired about the cash, expecting to see Lichtenstein empty his suitcase full of bills on the table. Instead, he reached into his inside vest pocket and pulled out a small package of bills with a rubber band around it and tossed it onto the table. There were sixteen $10,000 bills and one $5,000.

Mr. Lichtenstein picked what he wanted out of this collection and sold the balance through the J. C. Morgenthau Company at a public auction staged in the old Murray Hill Hotel, in 1917.

My own acquaintance with Mr. Lichtenstein began in October, 1926, at the time he was chairman of the Second International Philatelic Exhibition in Grand Central Palace, New York. My interest in stamps was great but my collection small, and I was more than bewildered to see the long line of frames filled with material that represented the cream of the philatelic world. I recall pausing in front of a huge collection of Cape of Good Hope triangulars and literally gaping at many of these queer-shaped stamps which are the goal of every young collector. I checked the catalogue and found they were owned by "Alfred F. Lichtenstein, N. Y." Just about that time a tall gentleman with rosy cheeks and a broad grin passed behind me and stopped for a moment. "Are you having fun?" He asked.

"Gee, yes. I sure like seeing these stamps. I always wanted one for my own collection." I replied.

"If you come down to my office sometime, maybe I can find a duplicate around somewhere," the gentleman said as he handed me his card. He had already rounded the corner of the frames before

I realized who he was. The card was engraved, "Ciba Company, Cedar and Washington Street, New York. Alfred F. Lichtenstein, President."

During the Christmas holidays I gathered together absolutely the best duplicates I had and went to Mr. Lichtenstein's office. The receptionist was reluctant to let me in, until I produced the card and assured her that Mr. Lichtenstein had asked me to come.

Finally his private secretary, Gail Creedon, came out and ushered me through the wide doors to a private office where Mr. Lichtenstein sat behind a desk piled high with papers and letters. I explained that I had brought along duplicates, and he assured me that perhaps I might have something he could use. He pored over every specimen with enthusiastic interest and picked a stamp here and another there —stamps I had received from several friends who worked in import houses and got much foreign mail. Finally, when he had a small pile set aside, he said he would be willing to swap those for a Cape of Good Hope triangular. He pulled out a very fine specimen of the one-penny red and asked if I were satisfied with the deal. Of course I was. I would have given the entire lot of duplicates to get one of those coveted three-cornered stamps of South Africa.

In the mail the following morning I received a letter from the Ciba Company: "Dear Ernest: I find on checking over my collection that I already have all the stamps I selected when you were here, as I think you might be able to swap them with some other friends, I inclose them herewith. Good luck in your collecting."

After that time I came to know Mr. Lichtenstein more intimately, and of all the collectors whom I have met in this country and abroad, none was ever more inspirational than he. His entire credo was built upon a few down-to-earth principles: Stamp collecting, the hobby, should be followed purely for fun and never with a thought of financial return, for then one's stamps become objects representing so many dollars or cents, and not "friends." When studying philatelic problems, as in every other form of sincere research, first check every conclusion and then double-check it twice more to be sure that philatelic records and literature will not be cluttered with false statements to lead others astray.

Mr. Lichtenstein wrote little about his personal studies and discoveries, but he never hesitated to assist those of us who wrote about postage stamps and postal history. His personal collections were always available to the sincere student, and on many occasions the material he accumulated over the years was placed at the disposal of persons whom he wished to help.

On dozens of occasions he allowed me to come to his office, go through his albums, and then take notes as he discussed various problems with tongue-tip familiarity. On one occasion I required two types of covers which could not be found elsewhere in New York. I phoned his secretary, explained my quest, and asked whether she would mention it to Mr. Lichtenstein at a convenient moment. I was told that he would be tied up in conferences most of the day, but an hour later Mr. Lichtenstein himself phoned and told me to come down, pick up an album which contained the material I sought, and bring it back at my leisure.

Several years ago, Winthrop Boggs, now secretary of the Philatelic Foundation, wrote a book on the stamps of Newfoundland. It was a sincere effort which reflected honest research attempts, but when Mr. Lichtenstein examined a copy he laughed at its incompleteness. "But how could Boggs have done better?" I asked him. "You have virtually all the material which a student would require."

Some months later, Boggs undertook the preparation of a similar handbook on Canadian postage stamps, and this time a meeting was arranged between Mr. Lichtenstein and Boggs.

At first Mr. Lichtenstein gave Boggs carte blanche to have access to his Canadian albums—unquestionably the best in existence—and later, as his manuscript began to take shape, sat down with him and gave him information that he had accumulated over the years. He dug into his files and came up with documents that shed light upon early Canadian issues which philatelists formerly had believed completely lost when the Ottawa archives had burned down. Boggs had originally planned a 100-page handbook for general distribution. So thoroughly did Mr. Lichtenstein aid him that by the time it was published, nearly three years after it had been expected, it filled two volumes and stands today as one of the most comprehensive studies ever made of the stamps and postal history of a single land.

As may be expected, Mr. Lichtenstein had an innumerable number of experiences in the acquisition of the gems he possessed. At times he would purchase through an agent, but at no time did he employ a philatelic secretary as do so many other wealthy collectors. He attended the great auction sales in person, whether they were staged in New York, London, or Paris. When an item was offered that he knew to be rare, he would stop at nothing to obtain it; but by the same token he would not go beyond his bids if he felt certain that he could obtain another specimen later.

Mr. Lichtenstein went to many countries to seek rare stamps at their source and came back with some very good material; but none was obtained under more unusual circumstances than a lot of covers he found in New Brunswick.

Some years ago he went up to Fredericton and made the round of houses that had been standing since 1850 and which appeared to have been owned by the same families, asking each owner whether any old letters might be lying around in attics or trunks. At one house he met an ancient fisherman who said that he did have some family correspondence. He finally was persuaded to haul out the letters, and Mr. Lichtenstein's eyes almost popped out when he saw the specimens with which they were franked. Apparently the mariner noted the surprise, for he withdrew the lot and began setting down the terms under which he would sell them.

"I want so-and-so much for each letter, depending upon the face value of the stamp on it," he declared.

Mr. Lichtenstein tried to interrupt to explain that some might be worth more, but before he could give voice to his first words, he was stopped. "Either you accept my terms or you don't even look at the stamps." The fisherman said. "I know you Yankees. Ye'll tell me the stamps are no good and try and get them cheaper."

He began showing Mr. Lichtenstein one cover at a time, stating a price he wanted for each one, reckoning it on the basis of a fixed price for a three-penny stamp, twice as much for a six-penny, and four times as much for a shilling denomination, regardless of how many combinations of stamps were on the envelopes.

Finally he produced a number of envelopes that were franked with "splits." Back in the 'fifties, New Brunswick ran short of the lower denominations and the postmaster used to cut existing stamps in halves or quarters and use them as fractional values.

When used and still affixed to letters which they carried, such "splits" are exceedingly desirable; but apparently the fisherman who knew all about Yankee "tricks" was not to be outsmarted. When he came to them he stated flatly that he was aware of the fact that collectors would not pay anything for "damaged" stamps, and that if Mr. Lichtenstein wanted them he would have to pay just as much for them as for the ones that were not "defective." A quarter-of-a-shilling stamp would cost just as much as a three-penny stamp, and so on.

There just was no other way out of it, and again, when Mr. Lichtenstein wanted to explain that these stamps were much more valuable than the others, the fisherman put in a firm "Take it or leave it."

Mr. Lichtenstein took the entire lot at the vendor's figure, having obtained some of the really great rarities which are known to exist today at but a small fraction of their true worth simply because a New Brunswick fisherman insisted that he would not be duped by a "smart Yankee."

Mr. Lichtenstein's intimate knowledge of classic issues made him the foremost judge in the world, and wherever an important exhibition was staged he was invariably invited to head the jury that was responsible for the selection of the winning entries. He headed each of the three international exhibitions that were staged in the United States—1913, 1926, and 1936. He was the last of the truly great figures in philatelic history, and the peer of all collectors until his death just before the fourth International Stamp Exhibition of 1947, which he was to head. Fortunately, his daughter, Mrs. John Denny Dale, was well tutored by him and will carry on the collections that he amassed.

Theodore E. Steinway

Second only to Alfred F. Lichtenstein, we can without hesitation set Theodore E. Steinway at the head of American philatelic leaders. He is unquestionably the keystone upon which our hobby is founded. We have had scholars who devoted their lifetimes to the study of specialty fields: Dr. Carroll Chase, who explored everything there was to be learned about the three-cent stamps of 1851 and 1857; John N. Luff, who compiled the monumental work concerning early United States issues; Beverly King, who treated the early twentieth-century issues; John Murray Bartels, who produced the permanent references about United States stamped envelopes, the stamps of United States territorial possessions; Jere Hess Barr, whose researches on the stamps of the Ionian Islands is regarded as tops; John Klemann, Elliott Perry, Henry C. Needham, Laurence Mason; John H. Hall, J. J. Klemann, Jr., B. H. Homan, Edward Stern, Edward Knapp, and scores of others. But eminent though each and all of these may have been in the specialties of their choice, none had the broad, thorough knowledge of general philately that Mr. Steinway has accumulated. As head of the firm of piano makers which bears his name, Theodore Steinway is as internationally famous as a stamp student as he is in the world of music. He is one of those men whose financial means enabled him to own great rarities, but who preferred to build collections that would contribute to philatelic knowledge.

In his earlier days, Mr. Steinway concentrated his efforts to the study of the classic issues of New South Wales and the various German states. His work with the "Sydney Views," a set of stamps issued by New South Wales and so named because their vignettes feature scenes of that Australian city, won recognition and fame wherever stamp collectors gathered.

His collection of Hamburg, Baden, Brunswick, Hanover, Saxony, Thurn and Taxis, Lübeck, and Mecklenburg won prizes wherever they were shown by reason of the study that had been put into their classification and arrangement. But while he did an Herculean task in research along those lines, his enthusiasm for and knowledge of *all* the stamps of the world has seldom, if ever, been matched, and never surpassed. It can be said that Theodore E. Steinway knows more about general stamp collecting than does any other collector in the United States today, amateur and professional included.

As one of the men who was responsible for the growth of the Collectors Club of New York until it attained a reputation almost as famous as that of the Royal Philatelic Society of London, he is an avid researcher and reader. He was one of the first men in the country to advocate the creation of a complete philatelic library to which stamp students might turn for the published information about their hobby. And to this end he puchased, in 1922, the tremendous philatelic library which had been formed over a period of many decades by the late Victor Suppantschitsch, chief justice of the Austrian Supreme Court, and donated it to the club as the nucleus of a library which now is housed in two rooms.

Before the war, the Collectors Club devoted most of its regular meetings to the entertainment of a distinguished collector, who would display his albums and tell members about the philatelic history of the particular country in which he specialized.

During such meetings Mr. Steinway always was to be found in one of the frontmost seats so that he could see every item on the display stand and hear every word spoken. He not only wanted to saturate himself with all information he could absorb, but was willing to share with the guest what knowledge he had learned in his own lifetime. Time and again a man who had devoted many years to the study of certain specific stamps would admit that he was stumped by a problem in connection with stamps or postal history. Invariably Mr. Steinway, without referring to a note or book, could give the answer.

One evening the Collectors Club entertained a collector whose researches into the stamps of Afghanistan are recognized from here to the Khyber Pass. At one point he discussed the shahi issues of 1872, and made a statement to which Mr. Steinway took exception. The guest backed his opinion up with the corroboratory findings of two Englishmen, but still Mr. Steinway insisted he was in error. Without another word he went to the library and found a small treatise which had been written by a German philatelist during the nineteenth century and which was based on actual investigations in the archives at Kabul. Mr. Steinway translated the monograph verbatim to prove that he was right. The manner in which he did it offended no one, for his contradiction was made not in a spirit of officious vanity but in that of a teacher who delights in steering a student to the correct logic. The book to which he was referring was rare and probably had been read by neither of the men who had studied Afghanistan's stamps, so that Mr. Steinway's intimate familiarity with its contents was all the more remarkable.

Mr. Steinway has been known in international philatelic circles for several decades. His acquaintance with stamps in general has qualified him as a judge on international stamp exhibition juries on several continents, and on many occasions he has traveled abroad for that solitary purpose. He has been one of the motivating forces and treasurer of the Association for Stamp Exhibitions, Inc., in this country and guided each of the *big* shows we have had in the United States: the International Exhibitions of 1913, 1926, and 1936. When the 1947 show was planned he insisted that "younger men" take over; yet despite his retirement from active obligations and responsibilities he still contributed as much as anyone else on the committee to the success of the show.

At the time of this writing (1947) Mr. Steinway has relinquished his more serious collections and concentrates on such specialties as provide "fun to satisfy his personal fancy." Among these is a collection "without rhyme or reason," and into which go only such stamps as are "socked on the nose." To qualify for inclusion in this album, a stamp must have a complete cancellation applied to the exact center of the adhesive. It is not a large collection, for incredible as it may seem, not one postage stamp in ten thousand is postmarked so perfectly!

His second favorite is his collection of postage stamps, stamped envelopes, and postmarks that relate to music. If the design or inscription of a stamp or postmark has something to do with a composer, musical instrument, a bar of music, or a musician, Mr. Steinway is interested in it. The collection he has built is a masterpiece and one that has won many honors and prizes. His gem is a cheap stamp that was issued by Poland when Ignace Jan Paderewski was president of his native country in 1919.

Since the composer-pianist used a Steinway concert grand exclusively, he was a personal friend of Mr. Steinway, so it was not difficult for the collector to approach Paderewski at a propitious moment and ask him to autograph the stamp, which is so common even today that two cents will buy one in a stamp shop. After signing the brown-red stamp with his portrait upon it, Mr. Paderewski promised Mr. Steinway that he never again would autograph another one so that this would remain as a unique piece. Many years later, Paul W. Savage, chief photographer for the Worchester, Massachusetts, *Telegram*, had occasion to take a picture of the virtuoso, and, being a stamp collector, prevailed upon the celebrity to put his signature across a block of four of the same stamp. Mr. Steinway never complained to Paderewski for having broken a promise, nor begrudged Mr. Savage's acquisition, but rather complimented the latter in having gotten a truly unusual philatelic item.

He has one habit which has endeared Mr. Steinway to the hearts of fellow collectors from Sydney to Sussex. In his visits to stamp shows and clubs, he usually makes a mental note of collections which impress him as being unusual and then, whenever he comes across an item that would fit into that collection, he will forward it, whether he knows the owner personally or not. Just before the war Germany used fancy cancellations which related to the scenic attractions or industries of the various cities throughout the land. One day he called to ask if I happened to know the address of Mrs. Edward Lewandowski, whose collection of "stamps depicting fish" he had seen at a Philadelphia exhibition two years before. "I just got a letter from Germany which was postmarked with a couple of fish on it, and I think she ought to have it."

How many such thoughtful gifts he has made is known not even to Mr. Steinway himself, but in my travels around the country I have seen or heard of literally thousands of them, each of which was accompanied by a simple white card inscribed, "With the Compliments of Theodore E. Steinway." In the upper corner is a small lyre, and at the bottom you will usually find a penned "TES."

That, like his phenomenal conversance with stamps and postal history, is typical of one of the patriarchs of philately in America.

Colonel Hans Lagerloef

Of all the outstanding figures in the world of stamps, none is more colorful than Hans Lagerloef. There have been general stamp collectors and specialists, but Colonel Lagerloef has built what is unquestionably the greatest collection of specialized collections that any one person ever got together.

A Swede by birth, Colonel Lagerloef came to this country in 1904, burning with two ambitions: to make a fortune and to amass a great stamp collection. He succeeded in both and is internationally known in the professional and philatelic world not only for his achievements, but also for the benefactions which his success made possible. Professionally Colonel Lagerloef was an importer of paper pulp from the Scandinavian countries and, before he retired in 1939, was recognized as one of the peers of that industry. Colonel E. V. Moore, of the Moore-McCormick Lines, once publicly stated that it was only Colonel Lagerloef's tremendous trade with Sweden and Finland before the war that enabled his firm to do so profitable a shipping business with Scandinavia.

But it is in the realm of philately that we know Lagerloef best. For years his activity was known, and dealers vied with one another to supply him with the material he needed. Endowed with a physical makeup that allowed him to work with a minimum of sleep, Colonel Lagerloef devoted days to his business and long nights to his stamp collection. Night after night the light in his Weehawken, New Jersey, home would punctuate the otherwise black street, and neighbors coming home late from a social engagement would look up and say, "Lagerloef's still at his stamps."

Until 1939, Hans Lagerloef was but a name in the stamp world. He devoted so much time to his albums that he never visited stamp clubs and only rarely put in an appearance at the exhibitions where his entries were on display. The job of looking after his exhibits was entrusted to his chauffeur, William Watson, who got to know the albums almost as well as did his employer.

Colonel Lagerloef collected stamps in a spectacular fashion. Instead of attempting to fill one album, space by space, or selecting

[242]

one specialty and devoting his interests only to the pursuit of it, he made a specialty of every country in the world. He usually purchased a modestly begun collection of any country which happened to be available and then set out to build it into a truly worth-while one. At times he might be working on half a dozen or more specialized collections at the same time, always striving to hunt for and acquire such philatelic pieces as would enhance its interest. He concerned himself with stamps and covers, essays, proofs and blocks—in fact anything that was needed to tell the complete story of the postage stamps. In some cases he obtained original drawings from which stamps were made and which had leaked out of the back door of some archive. Once a collection was, in his estimation, ready for competition, he would exhibit it at a national or international show where it had to meet other collections of the same classification. If it was awarded only a second or third prize, the collection would go back to his home for additional work until it could win a first. Once a collection was awarded a first prize, it was consigned to his "disposal" shelf where it remained only until he found a worthy recipient.

For two decades before the war, and since 1945, the Swedish government was the beneficiary of his philatelic philanthropies. Almost the entire Swedish Postal Museum consists of stamps collections which he has donated to his native land. It is now so vast that it is housed in a specially built wing of the Stockholm post office and described in seven large catalogues. At one time he learned that the German Postal Museum in Berlin had acquired specimens of the famous Post Office Mauritius stamps and felt that Sweden, too, should have these rare stamps in its collection; and so, although fine specimens are worth around $15,000 apiece, he went out and bought one of each of the two values and sent them to Stockholm.

Colonel Lagerloef had built a collection of stamps issued by Emilio Aguinaldo in 1898 and 1899, when the Philippine Islands were in the hands of the native forces. The two albums, full of rare items, had been "retired" some years before the war; but it was only in 1943 that he found a fitting, permanent home for them.

Because Bataan and Corregidor had been strongholds of the Aguinaldo forces during the Philippine insurrection half a century before, Lagerloef decided that the stamps would make an appropriate memorial to "General Douglas MacArthur and his heroic defenders of Bataan and Corregidor." He got in touch with the Smithsonian

Institution in Washington, which already had a philatelic display of no mean value and interest, and offered his collection. Since acceptance could be made only if Colonel Lagerloef would provide a suitable display case, he gave not only the stamps but also cash to cover the cost of constructing the exhibition frames.

Colonel Lagerloef has donated complete collections to stamp clubs and libraries all over the United States and in many foreign countries besides his native Sweden. He had even given stamps to private persons, but usually only after he has teased them for a while. Not infrequently he acquires a rare specimen which one of his collector friends covets. Colonel Lagerloef will keep the item, will on every occasion gloat over it in the presence of the friend, and then after a time—often as much as five or ten years—will send it to him as a gift. At other times he will visit a stamp exhibition, see a collection which impresses him, and, without knowing the owner, will felicitously send him some unusual stamp or stamps which will fit in with the stranger's collection.

For fifty years he has collected stamps, and the astounding scope of his work can perhaps be best described by saying that he has filled over 900 albums in that time. Their binders, pages, and mounting alone cost nearly $80,000.

Since 1939, when his importing business was upset by the European war and he decided that this would be a propitious time to retire from active work, stamps have consumed the major portion of his waking moments. He has continued to work on those collections which he still had at that time, but has not seriously begun any new ones. Instead he has devoted more time to actual participation in philatelic activities such as conventions, exhibitions, and club meetings. He has attended nearly all of the conclaves of the national societies and has made it possible for many a smaller stamp group to stage exhibitions or do other constructive work.

Each year he offers life memberships in all three of the national societies to persons who have done what he considers outstanding work for the good of the hobby. Invariably he donates a sterling silver trophy which an exhibition committee may offer as the grand award for the best stamp collection entered. These donations have enabled many a national and local group to get truly wonderful collections to attract visitors, for usually prizes consist of only certificates and ribbons, which do little to encourage collectors to submit their best material.

Colonel Lagerloef has been a benefactor to stamp exhibitions in other ways, too. The aim of every exhibition chairman is to put on a show that includes the stamps of every country in the world; but ordinarily when entries have been submitted it is found that there are gaps simply because so few collectors in the United States tackle the "difficult" issues. So widely are the collections of Mr. Lagerloef known that there is a general saying in stampdom, "You name the issue and Lagerloef will have it." Accordingly, at the last minute, exhibition chairmen will put in a rush call to Mr. Lagerloef, explain that even though they have received his competitive entry they still lack an exhibit of this or that country's stamps, and can he help them out? He not only obliges by sending the desired entry, but submits it as a noncompetitive display, and usually sends a check to pay for the frames in which it is to be shown. In 1940, when the stamp world observed the centenary of the Penny Black and the originally planned London exhibition had to be canceled because of the war, the Collectors Club in New York decided to put on a token display in which were mounted used and unused specimens of every postage stamp issued in the world between 1840 and 1870.

Simple though the presentation of such a display might seem, it was a tremendous task, because of the extreme rarity of many of those early classics. Naturally Colonel Lagerloef was called upon, but instead of submitting what he thought would add to the show, he told the chairman to get as many specimens as he could from other collectors and then tell him what the exhibition lacked. The entire country was combed, and five days before the show was due to open the chairman sent a list of missing items to Mr. Lagerloef. That night he dug into his albums and the following morning every desired specimen was delivered.

In 1943, the National Stamp Exhibition staged in Newark, New Jersey, wanted something unusual as a central theme. The committee decided that, in view of the Pacific campaign, they would feature the stamps of the tiny islands on which the Japanese were being taught that American forces were not as decadent as Nipponese propaganda had painted them. Again Colonel Lagerloef was called upon, and the display of stamps from the Marianas, Marshalls, New Guinea, Guam, the Solomons, and Papua not only made news but philatelic history as well, for never before had so comprehensive a showing been made in public.

Perhaps his greatest contribution to philatelic circles was the group of Barry Awards he initiated in 1940 to encourage philatelic writers to turn out better work. Although he put up the money to pay for the awards, Colonel Lagerloef named them in honor of the late Ralph A. Barry, former stamp-news editor of the New York *Herald Tribune* who shortly before his death was named the dean of philatelic journalists in America because of his profound researches and articles. After they had been established, the awards were placed at the disposal of a group of judges who each year perused all philatelic columns published in the United States for a given period of time. The awards then were given to the authors of the best in the realm of news value, general interest, evidence of original research, typographical appearance, and so on.

No other incentive did so much to improve the quality and accuracy of what was published, for the improvement of philatelic writings could be noticed overnight. Knowing that their writings would be judged and the results published throughout the stamp world, authors did their absolute best to turn out superior work.

John V. P. Heinmuller
Another of the more colorful figures on the international scene—a man who is as prominent in stampdom's hall of fame as he is in the world of aviation and accurate timekeeping—is John V. P. Heinmuller, president of the Longines-Wittnauer Watch Company. Mr. Heinmuller was a student in Geneva, Switzerland, when a friend sent him a souvenir card carried on one of Graf Ferdinand Zeppelin's early airships on a short flight from Frankfurt am Main. That single card was the nucleus of a collection that can never be duplicated. It was like the momentary smile of a strange damsel which eventually leads to romance, passion, and lifelong happiness. It was the spark that kindled the flame of collecting and the fires of philatelic pursuit.

From the moment when he first obtained the card, Mr. Heinmuller was intrigued by Zeppelin mail and he set out to accumulate cards and letters carried as postal souvenirs of all future airships built at the Friederichshafen hangars. He obtained many by watching European newspapers, and whenever a new flight was announced, by writing to Count Zeppelin and asking him to dispatch a souvenir.

Mr. Heinmuller obtained his first few stamps through personal endeavor. We must remember that the building of these large dirigibles was primarily an ambition of Count Zeppelin and that the terrific expense was borne by public-spirited individuals who envisioned a future in aviation. In fact, after the first one was built and had made a few trial flights, it crashed, and so great was the public's sentiment that voluntary subscriptions were sent to Count Zeppelin. Even schoolchildren in Germany, Switzerland, and Austria contributed pfennigs, rappen, and hellers toward a fund with which a second Zeppelin could be constructed. The idea of souvenir post cards and letters was conceived as a means of raising money to carry out the Zeppelin dream. Hundreds of persons willingly paid a small fee to get these luftpost mementos, and virtually every trial flight carried a sack or two full of mail.

But Count Zeppelin envisioned his big airships as something more than a novelty; he saw in them a means of speedier communication between the peoples of Europe; and to prove his point, whenever one of his ships made a flight over a number of towns and cities, he would drop a few cards in a small container to which was affixed a message instructing the finder to deliver the cards to the nearest post office for dispatch.

These "drop cards," because there were not too many of any single type, are today among the real aero-philatelic rarities. Meanwhile, Mr. Heinmuller's interest in Zeppelin mail grew ever stronger and his quest for specimens which he did not own became his life's ambition. He communicated with other collectors who shared his specialty and offered to enter into exchange arrangements for material he did not possess. He pored through library newsracks and German postal records to determine how many flights were made by the various Zeppelins, and when. By the time he finished he had compiled a list of dates and routes that served as a catalogue of all existing Zeppelin covers. So intensive was his search for covers and data that Mr. Heinmuller soon became known to Count Zeppelin, and, after that pioneer's death, to Dr. Hugo Eckener and Dr. Ernst Lehman. When the Graf Zeppelin and the Von Hindenburg made their regular trips to Lakehurst, Mr. Heinmuller almost always was on hand to greet the stocky, goateed German captain. And stepping from the gondola, Dr. Eckener invariably would ask Mr. Heinmuller first for a cigar, which he evidently had missed during the trip, and then about any new information which his watchmaker friend had uncovered about Zeppelin history.

Since 1909, Mr. Heinmuller has amassed a collection of over 5000 pieces of Zeppelin mail. He obtained them one by one, or in lots when someone else's collection was offered for sale. In 1946 he paid $1,750 for a collection that had been seized by the United States government under the Trading with the Enemy Act and that had been put on sale by the Alien Property Custodian.

Today Mr. Heinmuller's Zeppelin mail collection is regarded as the finest in existence. But once he tasted the pleasure of stamp collecting Mr. Heinmuller did not confine his prodigious efforts solely to mail carried by lighter than aircraft. His entire collection fills several rooms of his Park Avenue apartment and his Katonah home. It includes postage stamps and covers carried by air.

The most interesting and the most historically important portion of his collection consists of covers which Mr. Heinmuller obtained through a combination of his professional work and his avocational interest. As president of the Longines-Wittnauer Watch Company, he naturally is concerned with timing instruments. For years he has been the chief timer of the National Aeronautical Association, and during the days when aviation records were being set by pioneers like Byrd, Chamberlain, Post, Gatty, Pangborn, and Lindbergh, John Heinmuller was at the airfield with his watches to make official note of the minute and second of departure or arrival. He knew most of the birdmen personally, so he could ask them to carry a souvenir letter even when they did not have enough room in their ships to accommodate such items for the public.

So well did most of these men know that Mr. Heinmuller was a collector that even when they were far from New York they usually carried a letter and gave it to him when they saw him again.

Actually such souvenirs are not "air-mail" letters, for while they were carried aboard a plane, the pilots were not authorized by any postal administration to carry mail. The postage stamps and the postmarks were applied by favor of a postmaster and substantiate the fact that they were carried. These are in fact vivid souvenirs of a pioneer period when aviation was being weaned; of a period when but a handful of optimists realized that an airplane was something more than a sportsman's toy and transcontinental and transoceanic flights were more than stunts to make the headlines of the press.

One factor in particular takes Mr. Heinmuller out of the class of financially wealthy collectors who have obtained their vast treasure hoards through fortunate circumstance and puts him high in the roster of the world's great philatelists. Instead of simply accumulating valuable specimens for the sake of the selfish pleasure of ownership,

Mr. Heinmuller is another advocate of using a stamp collection to enhance one's knowledge of philately in particular and information in general. He has used his collection to establish facts concerning dates, names, and places in connection with stamp issues and flights. His covers are reckoned in terms of historical progress and not so many dollars. They formed the basis of a book published in 1944 and called *Man's Fight to Fly*, which already has been placed in reference libraries as the foremost handbook on aviation records and aerophilatelic information.

Mr. Heinmuller will not hesitate to loan his collection or parts of it to a serious student to uncover facts that he himself may not have discovered. Like every other prominent philatelist, Mr. Heinmuller forgets his social and professional prestige when he talks stamps. His swank Fifth Avenue office is always open to fellow stamp collectors, and his visits to some of the metropolitan stamp clubs are frequent. Whenever he can further the cause of philately he does so, and when he can financially assist a fellow stamp collector he goes out of his way to effect his benefaction.

A number of years ago an acquaintance met with an unfortunate accident which hampered his ability to earn a living at his former work. Mr. Heinmuller knew that the man was too proud to seek charity, so he suggested that the man act as his buying agent, and for years made his purchases only through him. On numerous occasions a dealer would get in touch with Mr. Heinmuller directly and offer him a rare cover, and always Mr. Heinmuller would refer the matter to his buying agent, saying that he was too busy to look at the offered material himself, just so that he might pay his agent a commission. On one occasion a Nassau Street dealer phoned to say that he had a cover for which he wanted $60. Mr. Heinmuller wanted that item and said he would send his agent down to pick it up provided the dealer would not disclose that he had already contacted him. That afternoon he called his agent and said he had been informed that somebody downtown had the cover and would he make the rounds until he found it. He gave the fellow $125 and said he could consider as profit anything between the purchase price and that amount.

Another time, when the fellow was especially hard pressed, Mr. Heinmuller purchased a lot only to "discover" that it was a duplicate. The following day he gave the material back and paid his man a commission to re-sell it.

Francis Cardinal Spellman

Of all the famous, internationally known personalities who have marched through the pages of history during the last century, none is more universally recognized as an ardent collector than His Eminence, Francis Cardinal Spellman, Archbishop of New York.

Nor has any person—living or now deceased—ever done more to propagandize the avocation by word and deed. All who have seen his collections, at his residence, at Regis College, where they are permanently housed,[1] or at exhibitions where they have been displayed, agree that he is a discriminating collector by nature and a serious philatelist at heart.

Like most of his philatelic brethren, he has more than a single interest. His collections may be divided into three major categories: (1) United States issues; (2) topical collections, such as "Religion on Stamps," "America, the Beautiful," "Poets and Poetry on Stamps," "The Madonna on Stamps," and (3) Presentation collections or single stamps.

It was the collection of United States stamps which first enkindled his philatelic interests years ago, when he witnessed the relaxation, pleasure, and satisfaction it provided for his close friend and schoolmate, Laurence Killian, now a Monsignor and pastor of the Sacred Heart Parish in East Boston. Since then, that collection has always remained his favorite and the one upon which he lavishes his more serious *philatelic* endeavors. In it, His Eminence has superb single copies of all issues, from the Postmaster Provisionals of 1845–47 right through the very latest issues.

Of course there are a few blank spaces—as there are in all collections whose owners are more interested in quality and perfection than in mere quantity—but even with those gaps, the Cardinal's albums are exceedingly important.

The topical collections are most widely known, for they have been displayed at exhibitions all over the United States and in foreign lands on five continents. These are exceptional collections and ones which demonstrate how exciting can be the popular

[1] When he was appointed archbishop of New York, Cardinal Spellman immediately had to write a will in which all his possessions automatically were left to his successor. Considering the collection a personal item he had started in Boston, he legally bequeathed it to Regis College, in Weston, in memory of an aunt who had been a nun there during her lifetime. But though it technically belongs to Regis, where it is housed in a specially built wing of the Library, His Eminence still works on it with no less enthusiasm than when it was his own.

fashion of collecting by subject instead of the traditional "by country" manner.

His Eminence expresses in these collections his ecclesiastical vocation, his profound love of America, and his interest in the literary arts. One of these includes all Vatican City issues; another such stamps as have designs related to religious subjects; another stamps which portray poets and authors or have poetry as their inscriptions; yet another consists of United States issues whose designs portray the natural, scenic, or historical wonders within our land and our territorial possessions.

These topical collections are of interest not only because of the stamps they include, but also because of the striking attractiveness with which they are mounted.

As His Eminence acquires new specimens for any of these collections, he studies their design and roughly outlines a page as he wants it. Because he is a poet he either will quote an appropriate verse or write an original one of his own to describe more dramatically the stamp or its design.

Once a page has been outlined he will send it to Rev. Sister M. Fidelma, at Regis, who serves as the curator of the Cardinal Spellman collection. She then will proceed to make arrangements for the actual mounting. Sometimes she will do the lettering and painting to satisfy His Eminence's suggestions. More often she will send the page to another person—a nun, priest, brother, or layman—who has artistic talents. His Eminence invariably invites new friends and members of the clergy whom he knows to be qualified amateur or professional artists, to mount pages. As a consequence, these topical collections represent a wide variety of artistic samples. The only thing they have in common is their style, for each must be on parchment and colorfully illuminated to resemble medieval monastic manuscripts. In many cases genuine gold leaf and silver are used for initial letters or fancy floral patterns.

Special pages are mounted and lettered by Sister Mary Andrew, one of the country's leading illuminating artists and on the staff of Mount St. Vincent College, in Riverdale, New York.

Not infrequently stodgy philatelic veterans wonder why a person who is such a serious collector will devote so much time and interest to topical collections.

The answer to that explains Cardinal Spellman's tremendous value as a "philatelic promoter." His Eminence knows stamps and people. No one knows better than he that displays of gold-medal and grand prix collections are much too serious, too deep, and too complicated for any but a philatelic scholar to appreciate.

Cardinal Spellman long has been an advocate of the principle that if stamp exhibitions are to serve their purpose of attracting more interest in stamps among noncollectors, such exhibitions must show material that will have some appeal for the persons who have never collected stamps before.

The noncollectors know nothing about the technical characteristics that make a collection important from a philatelic point of view, and care less. They want something they can understand at first glance.

Cardinal Spellman believes that if you show a neophite a collection that is eye-catching, colorful, and attractive he will at once be compelled to admit, "Say, I never knew stamps could be so exciting!" And once they have admitted that much, it is only a matter of time before they buy their first packet and album and begin a collection of their own.

Stamp exhibitions, therefore, accordiung to Cardinal Spellman, ought to be as dramatic as they possibly can be made. He thinks there ought to be two kinds of exhibits: the kind that satisfy advanced, serious scholars and those which will appeal chiefly to beginners and noncollectors.

The topical collections which he loans to exhibitions upon request include such stamps as are readily available at almost any stamp shop and which are within the financial means of even a youngster's restricted budget. It is not the price tag on a stamp that makes it interesting; it is the design. And, as every veteran knows, most of the most exciting designs are on the least expensive stamps of the world!

The accuracy of His Eminence's reasoning has been demonstrated many times. The writer, who has been privileged to take the Cardinal's collection to a dozen international shows abroad since 1948, has frequently witnessed the popular interest it provoked.

In Utrecht, for instance, where the Dutch staged their centennial exhibition in 1952, the Cardinal's collection was placed in the Court of Honor with several other notable collections including that from Buckingham Palace.

The gems in this section were widely publicized by press, radio, and television. Thousands of men, women, and youngsters came to the display from all parts of the tiny country and from many foreign lands. You could identify the noncollectors immediately. They would take a quick glance at the great philatelic rarities with an air of confusion. Then they would see the Cardinal's collection. Here they would stand transfixed as they closely examined frame by frame, page by page with frequent Ohs! and Ahs!.

Even Bernhard, Prince of the Netherlands, halted his entourage to examine more completely His Eminence's pages, for here was something he, a noncollector could appreciate and comprehend.

It mattered little that *all* the stamps in the Cardinal's frames were worth less than any single stamp in the other displays. What did matter to the visitors and to philately was the fact that His Eminence has a collection which attracts attention and gives many people their first insight into how interesting the avocation of stamp collecting can be.

The continual desire on the part of His Eminence to introduce more and more people to our avocation was demonstrated in 1953, when the Society of the Propagation of the Faith marked the centennial of its existence in America with a huge exposition of missionary activities at the Rainbow Division's Armory in New York.

Several days before the exhibition opened His Eminence realized that the show would attract thousands of visitors. This, then, was a wonderful chance to expose some of them to stamps. He procured the Colonel's Room, an exquisitely panelled salon into which we set frames and display cabinets to house some of his philatelic possessions. During the week the exhibit was open several hundred thousand men, women, and youngsters filed from the main hall to this room to examine the stamps. It was a huge success.

Late in 1953, Mr. Bernard Davis, head of the National Philatelic Museum, in Philadelphia, thought it would be nice to have a special exhibit during the Marian Year. He asked me to discuss the possibilities of such a show with His Eminence. Only a mention was necessary to excite Cardinal Spellman's interest and elicit his support. The personal interest he took in this project was phenomenal. When His Eminence went to Rome for the canonization of St. Pius X, he personally presented the plan to Vatican officials and got from them a promise to support it by sending precious postal and philatelic treasures which had never before left the archives.

Cardinal Spellman also made possible the publication of a 220-page book devoted exclusively to Vatican stamps, history, and related topics—a book which has since been universally acclaimed as the finest of its kind ever published.[2]

When the show opened in September, 1954, it created the most sensational interest in the history of American stampdom. Celebrities came from far and wide, and for six long weeks thousands of visitors crowded the museum to see the Cardinal Spellman collection and other displays. The attendance set an all-time record: more people saw that single show than had seen all previous museum exhibits in the previous seven years of its existence.

Cardinal Spellman never misses an opportunity to further interest in postage stamps. When we carried on a three-year campaign to have the United States inscribe "In God We Trust" on regular stamps, it was the Cardinal who most strongly supported it and eventually got President Eisenhower to approve it after minor officials of the previous administration had rejected the proposal time and again.

Other Collectors

Another prominent world figure who has a serious interest in stamps is Lauritz Melchior, tenor of opera, radio, and screen. Mr. Melchior's interest dates back to his school days, when he amassed a rather large general collection which he subsequently sold for 1500 kroner to help finance his early musical training in Denmark. Although stamp collecting had to lay dormant in his life during the ensuing years, the issuance by Germany of a set of nine stamps honoring the works of Richard Wagner revived his enthusiasm in 1934. Since that time he has been quite active in filling new albums with material he hopes to leave his grandchildren, that they, too, may enjoy our universal hobby.

The highlight of his collection, which also was displayed at Grand Central Palace in 1947, is a complete assortment of deluxe presentation brochures especially prepared by Adolf Hitler for his ministers and containing specimens of various Nazi issues made for the occupation of Poland. Exceedingly rare and valuable, these stamps were obtained by Mr. Melchior's son who was an intelligence officer with the United States Army assigned to take war

[2] Copies of the Vatican-Marian Year Book are available from Rev. Sister M. Fidelma, Regis College, Weston 93, Massachusetts, at $3 a copy.

criminal Dr. Frank into custody for the Nuremburg trials. In searching through Frank's residence, young Melchior came upon the stamps and, knowing of his father's interest in matters philatelic, sent them to him. As far as can be ascertained, this is the only such set in existence in the United States.

Among the great American students of today we must mention a number of collectors who have accomplished much and are continuing to contribute to our knowledge of stamps and our philatelic and postal history. Among these was the late Dr. Clarence W. Hennan, Chicago surgeon, who specialized in such Latin-American lands as Brazil, Costa Rica, El Salvador, and the Dominican Republic. His collections of these stamps are so completely annotated and studied out that they are recognized as "the finest in existence" even by the governments of the lands by which they were issued. When Brazil recently staged a national exhibition in Rio de Janeiro, the government paid all of Dr. Hennan's expenses to bring his albums to the show and honor him officially for his contribution "to better understanding between Brazil and the United States through the universal hobby of stamp collecting."

One of the famous figures to emerge from World War II, who has found considerable relaxation through the collection of postage stamps is General Mark W. Clark. All during the Italian campaign and the occupation of Austria, General Clark arranged to have his collection of United States stamps kept up to date. Even when the pressure of his work had him occupied in Europe, General Clark managed to find time for correspondence with friends here in connection with his stamps. After his transfer to San Francisco he informed me that "one of the first things I did upon returning to the United States after five years of absence was to gather up my old stamp collection and look it over. I now have it here with me at the Presidio and find many pleasant opportunities to work on it."

Carter Glass, of Lynchburg, Virginia, too, had been a stamp collector for many years and even was president of the American Philatelic Society for the maximum term. Although he was interested in stamps generally, he had made a specialty of air-mail issues and flown covers. Admiral Jesse G. Johnson, one of the Navy's great heroes of World War II (among other intrepid exploits, he captured the first Nazi U-Boat), has not only built an impressive collection but has co-authored the standard reference work on Alaskan air-mail history. C. Brinkley Turner, Philadelphia broker, accumulated what was known as the finest collection of the stamps of Jamaica that has ever been assembled, while Arthur D. Pierce, editorial writer for the *Philadelphia Inquirer*, is our foremost student of the stamps of Bermuda.

To compile a complete list of all the great American philatelists alive today would be impossible. But to give the reader some idea of how many we have, and how diversified are their professional lives, we shall tabulate a few of the more prominent ones.

General E. A. Aisenstadt	United States Army
Roger Babcock	Economist
Erwin Balluder	Airlines vice-president
Leon Bamberger	Sales Manager, R.K.O. Pictures
L. H. Barkhausen	President, Ducks, Unlimited
Julian Blanchard	Research engineer
Harold C. Brooks	Business executive
Harry M. Buten	Paints manufacturer
Dr. George Camnitzer	Dentist
Mrs. Frieda Bulger	Attorney
E. O. Cocke	Vice-President, T.W.A.
George P. Collier	Latin American Manager, Singer Sewing Machines
Beach Conger	Travel Editor, New York *Herald Tribune*
Dr. J. M. Coopersmith	Music director, radio-TV
Mrs. Caroline P. Cromwell	Socialite
Philip H. Cummings	World news commentator
Bernard Davis	Textile manufacturer
Albert Deane	Executive, Paramount International Pictures
Vincent Domanski, Jr.	Insurance executive
George R. M. Ewing	Retired financier
Joseph Furey	Executive, Metropolitan Life Insurance Company
Walter Fuller	President, Curtis Publishing Company
L. B. Gatchell	Executive, Standard Oil Company
Edward Gottlieb	Managing Editor, Newhouse Newspapers
Dr. John Freehafer	Professor, Temple University
Norman Haac	Textile manufacturer
Jasha Heifetz	Concert violinist
Bernard Heineman	Financier
Fernald Hutchins	Massachusetts state official
H. C. Honegger	President, Pestalozzi Foundation
Morton D. Joyce	Stock broker
Rt. Rev. Laurence Killian	Catholic prelate
Harry M. Konwiser	Historian
Arthur Linz	Chemical engineer
H. E. Lobdel	Dean, Massachusetts Institute of Technology

[17] Franklin Delano Roosevelt

The name of Franklin Delano Roosevelt will blaze as brightly in the annals of stampdom as in the pages of world history, for never before has a single person given the hobby the impetus which justified his being universally known as "America's number one stamp collector."

Men and women in all walks of life have enjoyed the avocation for decades, and while even such figures as King George V of England, King Fouad of Egypt, and the Earl of Crawford were known as avid philatelists, it was not until Franklin D. Roosevelt came to the White House, and so frequently referred to the relaxation and pleasure his stamps gave him, that the hobby gained the prestige it so richly deserved.

With the President of the United States as a devoted advocate of stamp collecting, shy adults no longer hid their interest under a bushel; no longer did anyone among the uninitiated dare think that stamp collecting was the simple pastime of children and eccentrics.

Mr. Roosevelt was a stamp enthusiast all his life. He began his interest in postal adhesives at the age of seven, when his mother gave him an accumulation of stamps that had franked mail sent from Hongkong by his grandfather. His album accompanied him throughout school and college; it grew from a single book to many volumes as he advanced in government service. In the words of Mrs. Eleanor Roosevelt, "everything that my husband did, everywhere he went and every position he held, served the purpose of increasing his collection, since he never forgot this hobby of his which filled a great many leisure hours."

Mr. Roosevelt never referred to himself as a *philatelist;* in his own eyes and to his friends he was simply a *stamp collector.* And to those of us who were given the good fortune of knowing him and his hobby personally, he was a dyed-in-the-wool collector—the type of hobbyist who turns to a stamp collection purely and solely for the fun, education, and pleasure an album can provide. If it was a postage stamp, Mr. Roosevelt was interested in it; and if one would fill a blank space in any of his albums, he was not content until he owned it, whether it catalogued two cents or had a market value of several hundred dollars. Dealers like J. J. Klemann, Jr., Max Ohlman, and the late J. Murray Bartels, who supplied stamps on his want list, could tell numerous stories about his determined philatelic hunts in those days when the name Roosevelt was more closely associated with "Big Stick Teddy" than it was with "F.D.R."

The stamps that he personally accumulated are of the type which philatelists might regard as "junk." He had a callous disregard for *condition*. Many a juvenile hobbyist of today who has become a victim of "conditionitis" would not tolerate in their albums stamps that failed to reach the perfection standards with which Mr. Roosevelt was satisfied. Yet this statement cannot be regarded as deprecating his collection interests: it was obvious that he saw in each stamp something that many persons who insist on superb condition in their specimens cannot find. He regarded every stamp in his albums as a source of information about the country or the peoples by which it had been issued. He studied stamp designs and learned geography, history, and culture.

That what he learned stood him in good stead when he needed finger-tip knowledge is manifested by a report about a meeting of the Allied Pacific War Council, which consisted of Mr. Roosevelt and the leading representatives in Washington of the nations that were at war with Japan. At this meeting, which was held about a year after Pearl Harbor, Mr. Walter Nash, the New Zealand deputy prime minister, proposed that our forces occupy a certain Pacific island as a steppingstone in our drive toward Tokyo. President Roosevelt thought for a moment. "That would be all right," he said. "But Mangareva would be better." Nash said he was embarassed to admit that he wasn't acquainted with that island, which is in the Tuamotu Achipelago, under the postal administration of Tahiti. "Oh, it's a few thousand miles from New Zealand," the president told him. "I know the place because I'm a stamp collector." It wasn't long after that our forces moved into Mangareva.

To recount all the reports concerning the wealth of information Mr. Roosevelt gleaned from the stamps in his personal collection is unnecessary. They have appeared in newspapers and magazines; have been broadcast on the radio. I have had numerous occasions to verify this knowledge. On one occasion, at the request of Colonel Hans Lagerloef, I brought to the White House a sheet of the 20-kroner Swedish air-mail stamps which the Colonel had just received from Postmaster General Anders Oerne of Stockholm, and which he wished to present to Mr. Roosevelt. The President took one look at these beautiful stamps and without a moment's hesitation remarked at the similarity between their design and those of the flamingo stamps which the Bahamas had issued seven years before to pay air-mail rates between Nassau and Miami. When we remember that there have been many thousands of distinct designs reproduced on postage stamps, it is evident that only a collector who is thoroughly conversant with the entire world's postal paper could possibly have made such a comment.

"Roosevelt, Franklin D." appeared on the roster of the American Philatelic Society and the Collectors Club long before it loomed on the horizon as a potential presidential nominee. When he moved to the White House in 1932, not only his albums but also his enthusiastic interest in our grand hobby accompanied him. To collectors, the presence of a collector in the White House was an endorsement for which they must be eternally grateful; to him it was an opportunity to get ever more stamps for his collection. Almost as soon as he got settled in the executive mansion clerks in the State and other departments, which received large quantities of mail franked with high denominations of stamps from other lands, began saving them and sending parcels to the White House at regular intervals.

But stamps, many of them rarities—came to President Roosevelt from other quarters, too. Because of his many public statements, there was scarcely a person alive who did not know that Mr. Roosevelt was a stamp collector. Many of them exploited this interest to obtain political favors or simply an acknowledgment that stamps which they had donated were accepted by the President of the United States. From every corner of the world came stamps. They were gifts from governments, public officials, prominent figures, stamp dealers, and just ordinary fellow collectors. One New York auctioneer is said to have forwarded to Mr. Roosevelt every stamp upon which he had bid, without a bill, simply in return for the publicity value attached to the fact that F.D.R. was one of his customers. At one time, Sam Rosoff, the contractor, purchased a philatelic item at a public auction for $250, and sent it to Mr. Roosevelt as a gift. It was only after his personal collection was sold at auction in 1946 that the philatelic world could see how vast was the amount of material that had been sent to Mr. Roosevelt.

Before the outbreak of the war in Europe, Mr. Roosevelt often entertained stamp-collector friends and philatelic writers. The arrival at the White House of a person with whom he could "talk stamps" often kept other visitors waiting and played havoc with his prepared schedule. I remember one of the first times I dropped into the White House. John L. Lewis lingered in a waiting room for nearly half an hour while the President discussed the difference between postmarks on Palestine's first issue!

After Hitler's rape of Poland Mr. Roosevelt restricted his activities but never surrendered them. He devoted a definite period of time to stamps as regularly as to his meals—usually a half hour at night before he switched off his light. It was a tranquil period. The counterpane was dotted with stamps, and the president, propped up on his pillows, lost himself in the peculiar bliss of the hobbyist as he fixed the bright pieces of paper in his albums. Mrs. Roosevelt explained that "he got a relaxation absolutely unknown, I believe, to most people. It refreshed him like nothing else for his next day's work." In Mr. Roosevelt's case, the stamp-collecting habit was without a doubt mental therapy of the highest order.

Mr. Roosevelt's presidency was crammed with vital matters of national and international concern. Yet, busy though these kept him, there were few philatelic activities which did not attract his personal attention. He admitted that he not only read the magazines of the societies of which he was a member, but always followed the stamp columns of his favorite newspapers on Sunday mornings before breakfast was served to him.

And when he went on his epochal global tours, at least one album was always in his personal effects. For instance, when he flew to the Casablanca Conference, he carried with him a large assortment of stamps. The President's stamps always were among the heaviest items in his luggage, whether he was going on a fishing trip or a Big Three Conference. For this particular journey, he told his valet to pack several albums, even if they displaced a few extra changes of clothes that might be needed in the warm climate. At the conference, as everybody must recall, Roosevelt and Churchill found themselves waiting for several days because of the antagonism that developed between de Gaulle and Giraud. During the deadlock, a member of the official party went to his room and found Mr. Roosevelt riding his hobby with more than usual intensity. He was studying a large upright stamp of the Argentine whose vignette includes a pair of clasped hands holding a staff surmounted by a cap of Liberty such as the French revolutionists wore in 1789. He showed his visitor the stamp and said, "I suspect that here we have the operation for Giraud and de Gaulle." The rest of the story is well known. The next day the two Frenchmen literally, and perhaps even figuratively, shook hands, and plans for the peaceful administration of North Africa were under way.

Late in 1942 I had a letter from the late General Edwin M. Watson, asking whether I could find it convenient to be at the White House at a certain time. When I got there Mr. Roosevelt devoted very little time to preliminary conversation but got to his problem almost immediately. It seems that a group of professional artists in New York had formed a committee under Paul Berdanier, then art director of the J. Walter Thompson Company, to advocate better designs for United States postage stamps. One of the members was so indignant that he urged the destruction of the plant which made them and the ousting of the official under whose direction our designs were made. These men, all of them artists who charged—and got—four- and five-figure amounts for a single drawing used for advertisements, volunteered to submit designs which would reflect the true artistic advancements of our country and went so far as to create several dozen suggestions for a "war issue." These, patterned after the then recently issued Canadian and South African "war effort" stamps, reflected our military might. They depicted cannons and tanks; destroyers and flying fortresses; soldiers, sailors, and marines.

"They're mighty fine designs," Mr. Roosevelt admitted. "But would such pictures reflect what we're trying to do? Wouldn't they convey to the minds of the peoples for whom we're fighting this war the idea that we are a militaristic and imperialistic nation?"

A secretary interrupted to announce the arrival of Admiral Leahy with "important news." The President asked that he be kept waiting while he continued to discuss an appropriate design for the stamps.

He advanced the idea of using the flags of each of the overrun nations of Europe, printed in their correct colors and set in a frame that included the picture of a phoenix to symbolize regeneration. "I know the phoenix has been used on Japanese stamps, and folks might get the idea that we're using an enemy's allegory, but the ancients mentioned this mythological bird long before we heard of the Nipponese, and I'm thinking of its true meaning. It might tell those suffering victims in Europe that we are struggling for their own regeneration."

A few months later, the Post Office Department announced that the flag stamps would be issued in honor of the overrun nations of Europe.

This was not the first time that Mr. Roosevelt had used his influence to aid in the selection of postage stamps. The designs of all 225 new stamps issued by the Post Office Department during his administration were approved by Mr. Roosevelt. The sketches, die proofs, and color trials all went to his desk for a final O.K. He suggested many revisions. One of them was to add a moustache to the face of the businessman in the N.R.A. stamp, because the engraver had created too close a resemblance to F.D.R. He also took off the silk hat the man wore in the original sketch because he thought it was bad psychology to show any symbol of wealth at a time when citizens were peddling apples on nearly every street corner. At the time the Graf Zeppelin was to make the flight from Germany to Chicago's Century of Progress Exposition, Mr. Roosevelt objected to the issuance of a special 50-cent stamp, on the grounds that our government had three years before paid postal tribute to the giant airship. It was only after Roy M. North, Deputy Third Assistant Postmaster General, revealed that the cancellation of the stamp might embarrass the government, that Mr. Roosevelt said, "Well, O.K., but I'm not in favor of it." It seems that an official had prematurely promised a Zeppelin official that the stamp would be issued.

When he saw the last proof of the Byrd Antarctic commemorative, which depicts a global map with the various routes Byrd previously made, he pointed to a line indicating the New York to Ver Sur Mer hop aboard the "America." "He landed farther north than that," Mr. Roosevelt said. They checked, found him to be correct, and made the alteration. James A. Farley once told me that the whole design for the Byrd stamp was of Mr. Roosevelt's personal creation and that the finished drawing was made by an artist who followed a rough sketch the President had made when the subject was first broached. The only one for which Mr. Roosevelt personally took credit was the 16-cent stamp issued to prepay simultaneously postal charges on a letter dispatched by air mail and special delivery. When his collection was sold, a full sheet of that stamp was found and, in a marginal note, inscribed in Mr. Roosevelt's own hand, "This stamp

[263]

was from my own design, Franklin D. Roosevelt." The sheet has since been broken up, but the block with the inscription was bought by L. W. Charlat, a dealer in air-mail stamps who has a tremendously important personal collection. This piece is unquestionably the finest single United States specimen in existence, by virtue of its many philatelic references, which make it unique.

At another time, when he was shown designs for the 25-cent stamp issued for the first transpacific air-mail service, he noticed that the Yankee clipper ship in the lower part of the design had only two masts instead of three. The mistake was corrected.

The many stamps issued during Mr. Farley's tenure as Postmaster General caused no uncertain complaints from certain quarters, and many of them were reported in the press, and so when, in 1940, Frank C. Walker took his place, the new head of the Post Office adopted a policy of "the fewer stamps the better." This came at a time when Mr. Roosevelt was preoccupied with other more important matters than the production of stamps. On one occasion I asked Mr. Roosevelt why no new stamps had been issued in several months.

"When Jim Farley was in office he used to come to me with ideas, if I didn't have any of my own. If I didn't agree with him on the selection of a design he'd sell me a bill of goods until I said yes. I don't know what's the matter with Frank. He comes in here with a stamp that some senator or civic group proposed, and if I don't give him an O.K. right off the bat he walks out and considers the matter closed. I often wish he'd give me an argument."

Farley gave him plenty of arguments on many occasions and frequently won out. For instance, in selecting the various persons who were to be placed on the different denominations of the thirty-five Famous Americans stamps, Farley suggested a portrait of Cyrus Hall McCormick for the two-cent denomination. Roosevelt insisted that no ancestor of the people who owned the *Chicago Tribune* would ever get on a stamp which he had to O.K.

"But Boss," Farley argued at one point, "you can't leave out the inventor of the harvesting machine, the greatest boon to agriculture, just because his descendents run lousy editorials about you." Roosevelt and Farley argued about it for about a week, and finally the president yielded, but not until he had switched the McCormick portrait to the three-cent denomination instead of the two. The two-cent stamp at that time was valid for local postage, while the three was good on letters going beyond city limits, and therefore were less frequently used.

Mr. Roosevelt enjoyed the hobby and advocated its pursuit to numerous friends on every occasion. Perhaps his greatest disappointment was that he never could get Henry Morgenthau to adopt it. "I send him a full sheet of stamps every time a new one is issued with a note that it's for his collection," he told me. "But that fellow just takes the stamps, says thank you, and puts them aside. Someday I'll make a stamp collector out of him yet."

When the national stamp societies met in annual convention, or when an outstanding exhibition was presented, a letter of congratulation was always written by Franklin D. Roosevelt. Mr. Roosevelt was on his way back from a tour of Alaska in 1944, when the Society of Philatelic Americans met in Chicago; yet, before the first business session was opened, a telegram wishing the officers and delegates continued success arrived at the LaSalle. That was typical of him; not even his absence from the country deterred his interest in matters pertaining to the hobby.

As a stamp collector, Mr. Roosevelt had no peer. Unlike most philatelists who can afford the services of a philatelic secretary, he never allowed anyone to touch the albums upon which he worked or to mount new stamps therein. About 1937 or 1938, he made a remark about my pages of Egyptian stamps. "I wish I had the time to mount my stuff like that. Some day, though, I'll get around to it." I ventured to offer my services. "Thanks, but working on the stamps myself provides all the fun of the hobby, so why should I let anyone enjoy it for me?"

Of course Mr. Roosevelt had many albums whose mounting represented the finest in artistic arrangement and elaborate lettering, but these were portions of his hoard which he hardly ever even examined. They were the ones that were relegated to his Hyde Park home or the trophy room at the White House. His own albums were characterized by the simplicity of their mountings. The number of penciled notations on each page was astonishing and betrayed the thoroughness with which each specimen was studied. A canceled stamp on which a postmark was incomplete, for instance, would be so mounted that Mr. Roosevelt could write the missing letters of the town name or date on the album page. If there was something unusual about a specimen, mention of that peculiarity also was annotated.

And like every other sincere collector, Mr. Roosevelt often said he was looking forward to his retirement when he could completely remount his collection as he ultimately wanted it. His collecting habits were so rabid that he grasped everything that came his way. If a stamp was already on a page and he got a second one which had a different postmark or was slightly different in shade, the extra copy was hinged underneath the first. Some items were represented by as many as fifty specimens.

Mr. Roosevelt collected *everything*. Of course, like all other collectors the world over, he had certain preferences, and even these preferences were broadened to include additional fields as they presented themselves. Hongkong, however, remained his prime pet throughout the years. He was interested in the Argentine, in Haiti, in Venezuela, and in certain British colonials, but the fact that he took and studied all stamps that came his way was perhaps the keynote of his full enjoyment of the hobby.

Just a few months before he died he confided that he had become enthusiastic about the field markings and censorship cachets applied by military postal authorities in various parts of the world. He got a big thrill from the identification of a postmark which was so designed as to protect the secrecy of the outfit which used it. Most of these markings included only the date and an "A.P.O." (Army Post Office) or "F.P.O." (Fleet Post Office) marking. Numerous collectors have endeavored to trace the geographical location of each of these various post offices, but by their very nature, they remained a mystery until long after the war was over, and even yet, all of them have not been identified. Mr. Roosevelt might have called upon officials and asked them to list the location of every service postmark. But he worked out his own problem. Every time he got a military letter whose envelope was no different from that which the correspondents of the ordinary G.I. used, he usually made a penciled notation on the cover to show whence it had come. Most of these, of course, came from high officials whom he personally knew; and so, while the postmark provided solely a number designated by the military and postal administration, he could tell where that marking was used because he knew where that particular correspondent was stationed.

At the time Mr. Roosevelt told me about this latest specialty interest he was as thrilled as though he had obtained a Post Office Mauritius. He had just received a Field Post Office marking from a remote

Libyan camp from one of his sons. "That marking puzzled me for a couple of weeks. I received a couple of them before but didn't know where they were from until I got this one."

In 1936, Basil O'Connor, his former law partner and one of the executors of his estate, told Mr. Roosevelt that his daughter was thinking of collecting stamps and asked the President for advice. In reply Mr. Roosevelt sent him the following memorandum from the White House:

I think it a grand idea that Sheelagh wants to become a philatelist. First of all, you should know how to pronounce this.

Second, as one of the earliest stamp collectors in the world's history,[1] I suggest to her that she start in by specializing. In the old days so few stamps had been issued in all the world that one could collect generally. Specializing means choosing anything from one country up to a dozen, or a continent. It is my thought that:

(*a*) Europe is very dull.

(*b*) Too many people collect United States stamps.

(*c*) The British colonies offer a rather high-priced field.

Therefore, if I were starting over again I think I would choose either South America or something like French colonies, or Dutch colonies. Or Sheelagh could take some one country like Cuba, Haiti, or Santo Domingo.

Mr. Roosevelt's greatest contribution to American philately was the enactment of the illustrations law which had so long hampered philatelic study and the production of more useful catalogues and albums.

For decades, while the Secret Service branch of the Treasury Department was headed by W. H. Moran, it was illegal to print the pictures of any United States postage stamp, and only reproductions of foreign issues might be made if the plates were defaced. Philatelists pleaded on many occasions for permission to circumvent the law, but each time they were given a flat denial, no matter how much it meant in the interests of the hobby. While that law was in effect, illustrations which included any United States stamp had to be so retouched that the design of the stamp could not be identified.

Of course the Secret Service had its reasons for such a law and could not well make an exception to benefit a hobby. The honest

---

[1] A slight exaggeration, for by 1889, when Roosevelt first began his hobby, some of the world's truly great collections had already been formed.

reproduction of a stamp would have no significance; it was the manufacture of a printing surface, and its possession for possible counterfeiting that they wished to forestall by law, backed with severe punishment.

The Secret Service is in business to protect the government from forgery attempts, and knowing that a prosecution required tangible evidence, Mr. Moran refused to back down on any law which might give a shrewd operator the smallest loophole that might lead to fraudulent abuse.

The Secret Service, in explaining its stand when it was asked to allow philatelic publishers to print stamp reproductions, envisioned a hypothetical manner in which such permission might give a counterfeiter a chance to defraud the government—and get away with his exploit.

Joe Doe is a criminal who'd like to try his luck in faking United States postage stamps. Under the present law, which makes the production and possession of plates a criminal offense, we've got an iron-clad defense against anyone we discover making or using such plates.

But suppose Joe discovers that, as a philatelic publisher, he can have such plates. Joe can set up a philatelic magazine as a "front," make plates so closely resembling actual stamps that his product might even escape detection before the Government has been defrauded out of thousands of dollars worth of postal revenue. His main object is counterfeiting, and even though we know it, apprehend him for this criminal act, and confront him with the plates from which he made his fakes, he can plead in court that he made the plates, not for counterfeiting, but simply to illustrate his stamp magazine. What chance will we have in prosecuting him—especially if he has a good lawyer?

So strong was this argument that while he was in office Mr. Moran was successful in blocking every philatelic move to have it modified. When he was slated for retirement, philatelic circles got together with both Mr. Farley and Mr. Roosevelt to have the law changed. And since Mr. Roosevelt, as a collector, could see the advantages of philatelic reproductions of our stamps, he immediately backed the proposals.

A bill was formulated, and in 1938 the current illustrations law was

presented to him for signature. The new law gave established philatelic publishers permission to reproduce any foreign stamp in any
size without a defacement; any United States postage stamp might
be reproduced, but only if it is either larger or smaller than the
size of the original. Reproductions, moreover, might be made in
black and white only; the use of color—even a color different from
the original stamp—still is strictly prohibited. When Mr. Roosevelt
signed the bill, he gave the pen with which he inscribed his name to
William M. Stuart, stamp-news editor of the *Washington Post*, "in
recognition of that veteran newspaperman's efforts in behalf of
amending the law."

That gesture of friendliness toward his philatelic friends, too, was
characteristic of the man. On one of my first visits to the White
House I asked the President to inscribe his autograph on a page of
my album.

He picked up his pen, looked at me for a moment, and put it
back on his desk. "I'll make a deal. I'll sign your album but only if
you'll autograph your booklet about Egyptian stamps which you
just brought me."

At another time, late in 1943, after we had finished a rather long
discussion of matters philatelic, the President leaned back in his chair
and asked if there was anything he could do for me. I expressed a
desire to have an inscribed photograph, for while I had a number of
personally written letters, and his autograph on several United States
stamps, I did not own a signed portrait.

"Sorry, but that's impossible. I haven't given any of those away
for a long time," he said.

"Well, if sometime you happen to come across an old photograph,
I'd certainly appreciate it," I answered and let it go at that.

In less than three weeks I had a letter from Major General Watson.
"The President recalled your request and he thought you'd enjoy
the inclosed substitute for a real photograph."

Attached to the letter was a White House card with a copy of
the Guatemala stamp pasted to it. The four-centavo stamp had been
issued as part of a souvenir sheet to honor the sesquicentennial of the
United States Constitution and portrayed Mr. Roosevelt in a favorite
pose. Across it was written, "To my friend, Ernest Kehr, Franklin D. Roosevelt."

President Roosevelt maintained his interest in stamp collecting
almost to the very moment of his death, as is revealed in a release

distributed by then Postmaster General Frank C. Walker on April 17, 1945.

In the release Mr. Walker stated that Mr. Roosevelt suggested the drawing and wording for the stamp which was to commemorate the first meeting of the United Nations Organization Conference in San Francisco on April 25, 1945. Mr. Walker wrote:

Like all the American people, President Roosevelt was deeply concerned with the conference. He wanted to be sure that nothing was neglected in marshalling the sentiment of the world toward making the conference a success. We had discussed the possibility of having a commemorative stamp for the conference. Late one night, the President called me from Warm Springs, Ga., and told me that he had been giving much thought to the proposed stamp, and he felt sure that we should have one. The design, he said, was to be as simple as possible. He then suggested the wording "Toward United Nations." The border, he thought, should be plain. He approved having a small branch of laurel at the bottom as the sole decorative detail.

The Bureau of Engraving and Printing promptly drew up several alternative sketches. I sent them on to Warm Springs, and history's most famous philatelist initialled the one he thought might be most inspirational to the conference destined to have such a profound influence upon the people of the world. Even the decision regarding the denomination of the stamp was based upon what might be most helpful in the cause of world peace because a five-cent value would be used on foreign first class mail.

Looking forward to the opening of the conference, and realizing fully the extraordinary demands that would be made on his time, President Roosevelt discussed with Secretary William D. Hassett the details of the first-day sale of the stamp. Ever mindful of focusing world thought on peace, he accepted my proposal that he himself should buy the first stamp from the Postmaster at San Francisco. This was his last official directive. A half hour later he was stricken.

Although the die for the stamp had been produced at the bureau in Washington, his death just thirteen days before the stamp was to have been issued led Mr. Walker to modify the design by the addition of Mr. Roosevelt's portrait and the signature below the inscription he had authored.

But appreciative though philatelists as a whole were of Mr. Roosevelt's stamp-collecting proclivities, antagonistic columnists and newspaper publishers grasped the opportunity of using his hobby to sling a bit of political mud. They often mentioned his "violation of the United States Constitution" which includes a paragraph, "No person holding any office of profit or trust under them, shall, without the consent of Congress, accept any gift, emolument, office or title of any kind whatever from any king, prince or foreign state."

The acceptance of stamp collections made up especially for Mr. Roosevelt because of his hobby, they charged, was a direct violation of this prohibition. And every time such a gift was made while Mr. Roosevelt was on a tour, or when a collection was presented to him by a visiting dignitary, the same editorial comment was dug out of the morgue and repeated.

While Mr. Roosevelt was alive, I had occasion to broach this subject. He told me that he had divided his collection into two distinct portions. His personal one and the one comprising gifts. The latter, he intimated, would be given, sometime after his retirement, to a public institution: after he had conceived the Hyde Park Library he thought this would be the proper place for the donated material. In fact, a number of collections had been earmarked for placement there and now are in the library's possession.

No provision had been made in his will, and obviously none of the executors were aware of his intentions, for it was *their* decision to sell the collection, privately accumulated and gifts to the President alike, at public auction.

The howl of protest that found expression in the press when H. R. Harmer, Inc., of New York, was announced as the auctioneer of this famous collection has never before been equaled. And by the same token, never before has any auction been so widely attended. The most vitriolic comments were directed at the sale of the twelve albums containing die proofs of every United States postage stamp manufactured at the Bureau of Engraving and Printing from 1894 through 1933.

Proofs are exactly what their name implies. They are prints made from original dies or plates which engravers and printers examine to check their work before actual production of stamps begins. The distribution of such proofs is new in neither postal nor philatelic history. Throughout the last century, and up to the administration of President Theodore Roosevelt, complete sets of them were given to interested parties in varying degrees of promiscuity. And because collectors with even the slightest influence could obtain them from officials for the asking, they commanded comparatively low cash prices. Even today, some of the nineteenth-century proofs are worth less than the actual stamps. In 1903, however, the general distribution of proofs was abolished because the practice led to "abuses."

After this prohibitive ruling, and because of the increased interest in them by specialists, market values began to be established for them. And in spite of the prohibition, a number of later officials obtained proofs of some issues and not infrequently these leaked into the market after the death of the persons to whom they had been given as "souvenirs." By virtue of their rarity, proofs of any stamps issued since 1903 are exceedingly valuable.

Those persons connected with the sale of the Roosevelt collection pointed to the precedent set by his predecessors, but avoided mention of the circumstantial difference surrounding the gifts which Mr. Roosevelt had accepted.

When his predecessors received proofs there was no market value for them. The value was set by dealers and collectors only afterward as an inducement to persuade heirs to part with the "souvenirs" which could be obtained in no ordinary way.

Clarence W. Brazer, an architect-turned-dealer in proofs and essays has publicly intimated that the gift of the proofs was a political expedient by an official of the Bureau of Engraving and Printing.

According to Mr. Brazer this official wished to enjoy the same favor of Mr. Roosevelt as he had during the administration of other presidents. Soon after the election of 1932, and before the inauguration, the dies of all stamps issued since 1894, and at least one which had not been issued, were brought out of the vaults, cleaned, and printed. And while there was no intrinsic value to such impressions—proofs have no postal value—the gifts had a collector's value of over $10,000. In fact, that figure was offered by Mr. Brazer to the official who showed him the set. When Mr. Roosevelt was in the White House, the twelve albums were given to him.

In a philatelic magazine, Cyril F. Dos Passos, an executive of the American Museum of Natural History in New York, wrote, ". . . Did Mr. Roosevelt have the authority to receive $40,000 [2] worth of government property? If so, there is no limit to the property

---

[2] The proofs were appraised at $40,000, but they brought in excess of $53,000 when they were sold.

of the government that may be given away. . . . People under a democracy rightly insist on being treated equally. They do not relish the enjoyment of special privileges by their elected officials."

The *Chicago Tribune* editorialized, ". . . the question isn't whether they (the proofs) were gifts, but whether the givers had any right to make free with government property." And Philip H. Ward, a Philadelphia dealer, vainly tried to have the executors restrained from selling these items.

The same public denunciations were aimed at the other portions of the offered material. They were aimed at collections which were made to order by the Soviet Union, the Postal administrations of France, Sweden, Costa Rica, Haiti, China, Poland, Nicaragua, Norway, Monaco, the Dominican Republic, and other countries.

But vehement as the complaints of these several persons and opposition newspapers were, the sale was staged and an entirely new field of philatelic endeavor was initiated. The fact that the ordinary collector might obtain for his albums at least one item which formerly belonged to "America's number one stamp collector," coupled with the attendant publicity given the sale, flooded the auctioneer with tens of thousands of mail bids and crowded the vast hall of the Parke-Bernet Galleries which had been rented for the occasion.

Never before had so many persons attended a stamp auction. The first session alone attracted nearly 1000 potential bidders, whereas even the Hind sale—which had offered many more philatelic rarities—had attracted only fewer than 250! Not all of the bidders were stamp collectors. Some of the material was sold to persons who wanted simply something that could be considered Rooseveltiana.

George B. Sloane, a Nassau Street dealer who had been retained by the Roosevelt estate within a month after the President's death, appraised the collection at $80,000. The auctioneers added $20,000 to that figure only on the basis of advanced prices between the months of the original estimate and the time of the sale.

So spirited was the bidding and so anxious were persons to obtain Roosevelt items—especially those which were initialed or signed by Mr. Roosevelt—that catalogue values and market worths were entirely forgotten. The entire collection—which had to be split into four sale sessions (February 4 and 5; April 1 and 2; July 16, and December 17 and 18, 1946)—brought a total of $221,000.

The dealers who purchased large lots of envelopes and covers, and even loose postage stamps, rubber-stamped the single pieces to authenticate them as having been part of the F.D.R. collection and offered them individually.

Overnight collectors began building separate collections in which were contained only stamps and items from the Roosevelt accumulation, and for several months prices for them boomed. One man, a realty dealer of Brooklyn, came to a sale and paid an average of thirty cents apiece for some three thousand letters that had been addressed to Mr. Roosevelt by correspondents all over the world. He knew little or nothing about postage stamps, but he offered them to other collectors at $3 apiece (and more, if he could get it) and sold enough of them to pay for the entire lot within two weeks.

Now that Mr. Roosevelt has been dead for some time and many foreign countries have memorialized him through the production and use of "Roosevelt Commemorative" stamps, the field is wide open. Men of means, former friends of the late president, and the veriest youngsters started collections of Roosevelt stamps. Jacques Minkus of Gimbel's Stamp Center, in New York, published a special "memorial" stamp album which contained articles about the philatelic activities of the late President, spaces for stamps that portray him, and blank pages in which material from his accumulation may be mounted. Recently several scores of persons united and organized a "Roosevelt Stamp Society" to which all hobbyists who collect this material are invited.

Today the Roosevelt collection is dispersed. Items from it repose in cities from Brooklyn to Brisbane; from Canarsie to Capetown and Calgary. The Franklin D. Roosevelt Library in Hyde Park, New York, does have a few lots which were consigned to it before the president died. It contains the following:

1. AMERICAN REPUBLICS. A portfolio of pages on which are mounted the stamps issued by eleven different countries in commemoration of the fiftieth anniversary of the founding of the Pan American Union. In addition to the stamps, each of the pages bears the signature of the ranking diplomat assigned to Washington by the country which issued the stamps, and the official seal of the nation. This was the gift of Ambassadors and Ministers of the American Republics, and is dated June 26, 1940.

2. AMERICAN REPUBLICS. A collection of twenty-three stamps all commemorating various acts of American Friendship. Autographed by the ministers of issuing countries during the Rio De Janeiro

Conference in April, 1942. Gift of President Getulio Vargas of Brazil.

3. AUSTRALIA. A block of half-penny stamps in a small frame. Presented by C. R. Sparks of Armcliff, New South Wales, 1941.

4. BRAZIL. An album containing ten Brazilian stamps issued in commemoration of the Pan American Union, at various times between 1890 and 1940. Gift of President Vargas.

5. CHINA. A set of four stamps issued in connection with the sesquicentennial of our Constitution, with a small buckram album.

6. CHINA. A similar lot, but the stamps have been mounted in the album.

7. DOMINICAN REPUBLIC. An album of stamps containing various issues of stamps from this country, given to Mr. Roosevelt by President Trujillo Molina in December, 1935.

8. FINLAND. A sheet of 3½-marrka stamps issued by this country to commemorate the settlement of Finnish immigrants in the Delaware River Valley 300 years ago. Gift of President Kallio of Finland, June 1, 1938.

9. FRANCE. An album containing a dozen die proofs and three pages of commemorative stamps for regular and air-mail service. Gift of the French Embassy.

10. GUATEMALA. Four sheets of four stamps each, issued by the country in commemoration of the Constitution Sesquicentennial. Gift of the President of Guatemala.

11. HAITI. An album of native stamps made up by Leon Montes and given to Mr. Roosevelt by President Stenio Vincent in April, 1934.

12. MEXICO. Six stamps in a leather album with photographs from which the stamps were made and issued in connection with the opening of the Mexico-City-Nuevo Laredo Highway in 1936. Gift of President Cardenas.

13. NICARAGUA. An album containing a complete set of the Will Rogers stamps and photographs from which the designs were made. Gift of President Somoza.

14. SARAWAK. A small album containing a complete set of the then-current stamps from that territory and inscribed, "From Their Highnesses, the Rajah and Ranee of Sarawak to Franklin D. Roosevelt, President of the United States of America."

15. UNION OF SOVIET SOCIALIST REPUBLICS. An album presented to the President in commemoration of the participation of the U.S.S.R. at the New York World's Fair, 1939, and containing unused and

canceled-to-order singles and blocks of all Soviet stamps issued. Gift of the Commissioner General of the U.S.S.R. to the fair.

16. UNITED STATES. A rather poor first-day cover of the Emancipation Proclamation. Gift of D. Fabian of Portland, Oregon.

17. UNITED STATES. A single Printing Press stamp mounted in a gold frame as a gift from J. A. Farley, February 17, 1940.

18. UNITED STATES. A framed picture of the White House and the President, surrounded by stamps of the presidential and several commemorative sets.

19. HAMBURG. Two sheets of various local stamps in varying degrees of imperfection, issued between 1858 and 1860. Gift of Peter Gunter, 1218 High Street, Little Rock, Arkansas.

Following the example of many other nations of the world, the United States issued this simple, yet striking design in 1942, to proclaim the Allies' intention of winning the war.

[18] Philatelettes

From its very beginnings, the hobby of collecting postage stamps attracted feminine followers, and today the ranks of stampdom's roster are generously accented by the names of women whose reputations are known and respected wherever the avocation is pursued. Some women—the daughters, sisters, and wives of philatelists—were converted to the hobby by exposure to the activities of their menfolk; others became collectors through their own initiative. Some of them have become members of the important general philatelic organizations of the world: the Royal Philatelic Society of London, The Collectors Club, the American Air Mail Society, the American Philatelic Society, and the Society of Philatelic Americans. Some others have formed clubs exclusively for women, and these groups have become prominent in their own right.

Perhaps the greatest collection ever assembled and owned by a philatelette is that of *Mrs. John D. Dale* of New Canaan, Connecticut, and of New York City. Mrs. Dale had the accidental advantage of being the daughter of Alfred F. Lichtenstein, and some folks are likely to belittle her activities as merely "playing with the albums built by her illustrious father." But this is far from true. What she knows and most of what she now owns is the exclusive handiwork of Mrs. Dale herself and the result of her personal individual effort. I recall a meeting of the Collectors Club not a few years ago to which Louise Lichtenstein came to give a talk on early French issues. That display of stamps and her intimate familiarity with postal history held veterans spellbound for over an hour. The facility with which she discussed the Bordeaux and Paris prints, and the thoroughness with which this teen-age girl answered questions posed by the regular members, provided ample evidence of her full knowledge of stamps and stamp collecting.

From that time until May, 1936, the activities of Louise Lichtenstein were known only to her close associates and friends; but when the Third International Philatelic Exhibition opened its doors at Grand

Central Palace, the philatelic world literally gasped at the collections she entered. Her display of Gambia and British colonies of Africa, America, and Europe captured top awards by a generous margin. She had assembled not only stamps, covers, and correlative material with a discrimination for perfection, but had worked out numerous problems concerning the issues she owns, and which had formerly perplexed many a student.

Early in the 'thirties, *Mrs. Mike C. Hoffman,* wife of a prominent textile manufacturer and collector, developed an interest in postage stamps issued for air-mail service. At first she plodded through the field as modestly as most folks, but with both the necessary time and financial means at her disposal, Mrs. Hoffman soon built a collection that was far above average. Upon the advice of friends, she entered some of her pages at a metropolitan stamp exhibition, and probably no one was more surprised than Mrs. Hoffman when it was selected by the judges as the best of its kind in the whole show.

Since then the name of Mrs. Mike C. Hoffman has never been absent from the catalogues of national and international stamp exhibitions. And because she has so consistently improved her albums by the addition of new material and more knowledge, she always has been able to hold her lead. It is said that she has won more trophies and grand awards for a collection of postage stamps than has any other person in the United States, philatelist and philatelette alike.

Mrs. Hoffman has taken an active part in philatelic circles, too. She is a member of the leading societies of the United States; has served as a vice-president and director of the American Air Mail Society, and as chairman of women's activities at the International Philatelic Exhibitions in New York in 1947 and 1956,

In the same class is *Mrs. W. R. M'Coy* of New York. Shortly after the death of her husband, Mr. Stewart, she became interested in postage stamps and for about five years devoted a major portion of her time filling regular printed stamp albums. Although she has kept adding to these books, Mrs. Stewart branched out to a specialized collection of United States issues, concentrating on such issues as the Columbian, Trans-Mississippi, and first air-mail sets of the United States. At one time she purchased a block of four of the famous 24-cent air-mail invert of 1918, and until the remainder of blocks retained by Colonel Green were auctioned, this piece was generally recognized as the foremost philatelic gem in the country and was eagerly sought as the highlight of numerous local and national exhibitions.

Mrs. Stewart was so active in the programs of the Collectors Club in New York that she became acquainted with and eventually married W. R. M'Coy, librarian of the club and editor of its quarterly periodical. Since her marriage Mrs. M'Coy has more or less given up her own specialized interest in order to work more closely with her husband and his study of United States plate-number singles, strips, and blocks, in which field he is one of the recognized experts.

Dr. Louise D. Larrimore, until her death on the staff of the Greenwich, Connecticut, Hospital, formerly practiced in New York and, during her stay in that city, was almost as eminent in philatelic as in medical circles. Besides enjoying herself, Dr. Larrimore did much missionary work among her friends and was instrumental in organizing the Women's Philatelic Society of New York, which was the first group in the country exclusively composed of philatelettes. She might be likened to the late Charles Lathrop Pack in that, although she had the means to purchase any rarity she desired, she instead concentrated on stamps which cost her little or nothing except a fortune in time, initiative, and energy.

In the United States and many foreign lands large firms regularly use so many postage stamps that huge stocks of them must be kept on hand in the outgoing mail rooms. And because unused stamps have a monetary value, not a few clerks of such firms have been tempted to purloin, for their personal use or sale, many dollars' worth of the boss's postage stamps. As a measure to prevent such potential losses, firms are given permission by the Post Office Department to punch initials through the stamps. By identifying a firm's stamps by "branding" them in this manner, postal inspectors may more easily track down a culprit should the firm's stamps be stolen and used by someone other than the "brand's" owner. Until Dr. Larrimore began her interest in these stamps, they were spurned by advanced collectors as being "damaged." But in them Dr. Larrimore found an unusually interesting and exciting avocational pursuit.

She became annoyed at fellow collectors' consignment of initialed stamps to the waste-paper basket and decided that perhaps a little study might reveal some useful fact concerning these philatelic outcasts. Friends were willing and anxious to supply her with material; she purchased cheap United States mixture lots from dealers and got all the incoming mail from several firms which received nothing but ordinary domestic letters. Hunting through stamps from these sources, Dr. Larrimore soon found several thousand different initialed stamps.

Whenever possible she obtained an entire envelope, so that the printed firm name in the corner might identify the initials punched through the face of the stamp. When she obtained a specimen whose initials she could not recognize, or which offered no other clew than the postmark, her hunting days really began. With all the diligence and perseverance of a super-sleuth, Dr. Larrimore tracked down every lead. Most of the time a portion of a postmark revealed either the name of the town or state in which the stamp was used. A check of telephone or business directories of that city usually provided a productive lead, but, failing that, she communicated with the postmaster and obtained the desired answer from him.

Quite often, though, this answer was a pitfall, for she found innumerable instances of an initialed stamp having been used in a town other than that in which the authorized company was located. Most of the time this happens when a mail clerk pilfers a single stamp or two to use on personal letters which he mails from his home community. Sometimes it happens because, although a firm may be located in one town, it may dispatch its mail from an adjacent town, and that post office may happen to be closer in distance but across a boundary line. One large firm in Newark, New Jersey, for example, dispatches its mail from the Irvington post office.

The information which Dr. Larrimore accumulated during the years of specializing in this "waste-paper basket" type of postage stamp is even more amazing than the number of specimens crammed between the binders of her twenty albums.

She classified initialed stamps according to the types of firms which used them—factories, public utilities, publishers, supply houses, drug companies, and so on. Cross references reveal geographical locations and alphabetical listings. She could look at the initials of a stamp used by a firm which has many branches around the country and tell you not only the name of the firm, but also which of its branches use that particular stamp.

Western Union, for example, punches all of its stamps with a large "W.U." But each of its largest branches has a "key punch." Dr. Larrimore discovered this through individual study; and when she checked to confirm her deductions, she found that not even the office managers of the various offices knew that such a key existed. The initials are composed of tiny holes punched through the face of the stamp, and while the size of the initials and the holes themselves are generally uniform, a single hole in the initial is slightly larger or smaller in the design used for the different cities. In one city the first hole of the "W" is of a different gauge; in another, the second varies; and so on. By hunting for the off-size hole it is possible to identify the branch office which used that particular stamp.

At first Dr. Larrimore concerned herself only with United States stamps, but later she covered the earth and was as familiar with the initials on stamps from New Zealand as those from New Salem or Newfoundland. So comprehensive was her collection and so complete her file of identification records that she was called upon to assist postal inspectors, the Secret Service, and the Federal Bureau of Investigation in cases where initialed stamps were involved as possible clews to crime detection.

The casual chit-chat at a cocktail party was responsible for the fame of another feminine philatelist, and the accumulation of one of the more important stamp collections in the United States, if not the whole world.

Ferrars H. Tows, who has already been mentioned, was giving a party in honor of Giovanni Martinelli while the Italian tenor still was in his prime, and as will inevitably happen wherever a stamp collector is present, the conversation turned to the hobby. Among the guests was *Mrs. Fay Jordan*, widowed cousin of Mr. Tows, and she became the butt of a frivolous joke.

"It's a wonder that you, with plenty of time on your hands, wouldn't help Ferrars with his stamp collection," Martinelli ventured.

"Oh, bah!" Mr. Tows scoffed. "She's much too busy with social obligations. Mah Jong and teas are more important to Fay. Besides, she wouldn't have the patience to treat and study stamps as she should."

That remark was just about all the auburn-haired socialite from Birmingham, Alabama, needed as a challenge. The next day she made a secret trip to the Scott Stamp and Coin Company, looked through the counter albums, and then and there decided that she would start clandestinely a collection of her own.

But her collection would be as individual as her nature. She was going to demonstrate that she not only had the ability to collect stamps, but also the originality to do something different. And that is how Fay Jordan's "Bunch of Violets" was conceived.

Instead of collecting in the orthodox manner of completing sets, she would collect stamps according to *color*. She selected violet and shades thereof. The beginning was quite simple. There are thousands of stamps printed in this color and its hues, and the matter of filling the first two albums was child's play.

It was only after she had made more than a substantial start that Mr. Tows learned of her hobby, and the progress she made astounded even him. For violet stamps were being issued almost as often as red, blue, or green ones, and so her job was never quite finished. She found that many of the older classics were printed in this color, and the hunt for them—some of these specimens are as elusive and rare as the Post Office Mauritius—was a challenge indeed. But today Mrs. Jordan has a steel cabinet in her Riverside Drive apartment that is filled with about forty albums containing only stamps of a single color. They are mounted on blank, loose-leaf pages. Every inscription, every title, every date is hand-lettered, also in violet ink, with a pen wielded by the lady who had been told that she had not the patience to be a stamp collector.

At the National Stamp Exhibition, held at Newark, New Jersey, in August, 1945, the *Bunch of Violets* filled seventy-two large frames and occupied a separate room decorated in violet. The buzz of philatelic chatter which that display started has not yet subsided.

Among the highlights included were the famous Department of Justice stamps overprinted, "Sepcimen" instead of the correct, "Specimen"; the Port Fouad stamp of Egypt; the rare Afghanistan tigerheads, and hundreds of similarly scarce and valuable gems.

Notable among the philatelettes is *Mrs. Catherine L. Manning*, the curator of the famous Smithsonian Institution's stamp collection in Washington. Beginning her business career in the late nineteen hundreds as a clerk with the J. M. Bartels Company, Mrs. Manning soon accepted a "temporary job" of mounting the few stamps which had been sent to the United States government by the Universal Postal Union. Now, nearly fifty years later, Mrs. Manning still is with the institution and has complete charge of the wing of the museum in which huge cabinets of stamps, all in specially constructed display frames, are kept. At one time Mrs. Manning has been vice-president of the American Philatelic Society and has appeared as guest speaker at innumerable conclaves of philatelic students from coast to coast.

Perhaps the oldest philatelette is *Mrs. Mary Garretson Cook*, of Philadelphia. This venerable stamp enthusiast is well over eighty years of age, and always, when she is complimented on her seemingly endless source of vitality, she attributes her health to the hobby of collecting postage stamps. Mrs. Cook has built several important collections which have won major exhibition prizes, and she invariably attends the shows, whether they are held in Philadelphia, New York, New Orleans, or San Francisco.

Two other philatelettes of the city of brotherly love have made an international name for themselves. They are the *Kleins*, *Mrs. Sarah* and *Miss Dolores*, the widow and daughter of the late Eugene Klein, who was one of the peers of the trade for several decades. They used to accompany him on business trips and convention assignments around this country and the capitals of Europe. Even while Eugene was alive they were as familiar in stamp circles as his black four-in-hand, so it was no wonder that, when he suddenly died a few years ago, the feminine members of his family should carry on his counter trade and auction service. Instead of selling the tremendous stock and living comfortably in retirement, both widow and daughter continued to fill orders to the Eugene Klein Company from collectors all over the world. In 1947 they sold their stock to Billig and Rich of New York, and continue now only as an auction firm.

Among the other philatelettes of note are *Mrs. Henry Diamant*, whose collection of Cape of Good Hope, early United States stamps, and Civil War and rare Valentine covers are internationally famous; *Miss Penn-Gaskell*, whose air-mail issues are the best in Europe; *Mrs. Caroline Prentice Cromwell*, who owns what is said to be one of the most important collections of Newfoundland in existence; *Miss Eleana Wheeler*, who has built the great collection of stamps from Crete and British colonies; *Mrs. Dorothy McEntee*, a general collector; *Mrs. Edwin E. Elkins*, who specializes in semi-postal stamps of the world.

Not a few women collectors have made prominent places for themselves as professional philatelettes. Like ever so many men, these ladies found that the knowledge acquired during avocational pursuits could be turned commercial in time of need or inclination.

For years C. E. Severn published *Mekeel's Weekly Stamp News*, and although his wife assisted him in the many thankless chores which beset the producer of stamp collectors' journals, it was not until after he died that *Mrs. Evelyn Severn* took over the complete editorial assignment. Mrs. Severn kept that magazine going and so continually improved its policies and contents that many students cannot decide whether it was better before or after Mrs. Severn became its editor.

Mrs. D. E. Dworak, owner and publisher of *Weekly Philatelic Gossip*, is much in the same situation. Upon the death of her husband, who had founded and built the magazine into one of the best in the country, she grasped the rein and steered it right up to the ranks of the "top three" of philatelic periodicals. In addition to the magazine, Mrs. Dworak (who signs herself simply "D. E. Dworak," and thus confounds many readers who do not know that the publisher is a woman) has produced a number of permanent philatelic reference works, including reprint editions of *Album Weeds*, a copious work on the detection of counterfeits; *The Postage Stamps of the United States*, by John N. Luff, a wholesaler's guide, and several smaller handbooks.

Perhaps the best-known editor of stamp catalogues was a woman, *Mrs. Hugh M. Clark*, wife of the former president of Scott Publications, Inc. A philatelette of no small fame, especially for her collection of Civil War Patriotic envelopes, Mrs. Theresa, as she is more widely known, had complete control over the listing and descriptions of every postage stamp that was chronicled in the standard catalogues and albums published by the firm. To her desk came communications from every corner of the world—from famous student, from postmasters general, from dealers, and from individuals who had discovered new varieties and believed that they should be given catalogue recognition.

Mr. Clark's own personal secretary, *Jean Koor*, is another philatelette who is widely known in professional circles, although she represents the reversal of the normal procedure. When she began work with the publisher she was not a collector; but through her personal contact with the hobby, and with the man who handled hundreds of thousands of stamp problems every year, Miss Koor was exposed to and bitten by the stamp collecting bug. Her personal collection consists of envelopes mailed by members of the Armed Forces all over the world during the war. Through them she has classified virtually every A.P.O., Fleet P.O., and Field P.O. marking used between 1939 and 1946, a philatelic work which soon will be published.

Mrs. Edith M. Fisher, of Montvale, New Jersey, is another woman whose name by-lines many articles of lasting interest in the philatelic press. A collector for several years, she knew how much the stories stamps tell aided her own children in better understanding their schoolroom lessons, so she began contributing such articles to the several philatelic magazines of the country. The response to these contributions, and the ever-growing interest in stamps among her friends and neighbors of northern New Jersey, inspired her to convince the editor of the *Bergen Evening Record* that it should have a regular stamp column. When she finished, she had sold him not only the idea but was hired to write it. As a result, the *Bergen Evening Record* carries a stamp-news department three times a week—a more frequent appearance than that of any other exclusive stamp column in the country. Since 1947, she has, in addition, been writing a weekly stamp news column for the *Newark Sunday News*.

When the war called a number of men philatelists into uniform, some of their wives strode right into the office and kept the business going; now that manpower shortages have imposed difficulties on the stamp trade, the wives of others are behind counters; in some instances, dealers have engaged philatelettes who previously had been only collectors. There are Miss Reddy, who manages the retail department of the H. E. Harris Company; Mrs. Nathan Deutsch of the Radio City Stamp Shop; Mrs. Ed Buser, Jr., who has partnered her husband's firm since it began fifteen years ago; Miss Emily Cruz, who for many years has managed the office of the Nicolas Sanabria Company, and dozens of others.

In addition to the real stamp collectors among figures in the public eye, there are a number who have been called "philatelists" by their press agents simply for the sake of getting a little more publicity. There are any number of celebrities who have at one time or another been publicized as collectors, or who have made statements concerning their interest in the hobby.

I recall the build-up that was planned around Deanna Durbin when she first started her motion-picture career. At the time I was writing the stamp column of the *New York World-Telegram* and often mentioned famous persons who were collectors, and their collections. Every week for a few months I received, from the New York press agent of the young singing star, short paragraphs telling about her "stamps" and "albums." The "exclusive" releases always were short and rather vague, so I paid little attention to them until one day came word that Deanna Durbin had just acquired an envelope which had been salvaged from the wreck of the *Hindenburg* after it had exploded and burned at Lakehurst. I phoned the press agent and asked her to make an appointment for me with Miss Durbin the next time the star came to New York, for a celebrity who had such material was worth a feature story, not simply a paragraph mention now and then.

Within a month Deanna Durbin came to New York and the desired appointment had been set up. I was to meet the press agent in the lobby of the Essex House on Central Park South, and we would go to the apartment together. Half an hour after the prearranged time the agent had not arrived, and thinking I had misunderstood the meeting place, I phoned to Deanna Durbin's apartment. The star's mother answered that the agent had not arrived but asked me to come up anyhow. A few minutes later I met Deanna Durbin in her apartment overlooking Central Park.

Somewhat contrary to her screen characterization, this delightful exponent of adolescent pulchritude was reticent and quiet, answering only direct questions, and then only after her mother had supplied a suggestive lead.

She spoke of Hollywood and its studios, of Philadelphia and recordings, of Radio City and broadcasts, but when the subject turned to hobbies she admitted that her training and actual work before the Klieg lights and cameras allowed little time for avocations.

"I haven't much time for any hobby in particular," she smiled, "so I enjoy several hobbies as they strike my fancy from time to time." Collecting match folders appealed to Deanna for a while, and she acquired several hundred of them, ranging from tiny ones to large gaudy ones.

"They were the only souvenirs I could honestly take from cafes, restaurants, and hotels I visited."

When conversation turned to philately, Deanna admitted that she hadn't done anything with stamps, but her mother explained that her Pacific Coast press agent had given her an album and a packet of stamps six months before and that since that time she had got many additional ones from fan-mail envelopes from the same source. Perhaps some day Deanna might have time to do something with them. I asked her about the *Hindenburg* crash cover which she was supposed to have received.

"Why I don't know of any such envelope," she stated quite frankly.

Deanna preferred to talk of other subjects and almost lost her stoic poise as she exhibited a few relics Dr. Roy Chapman Andrews had given her earlier in the afternoon and which might form the nucleus of a new hobby.

On a visit to the American Museum of Natural History she had met Dr. Andrews, who is known for his work on pre-historic monsters. As souvenirs he gave her a chip of a dinosaur bone, a bit of petrified wood, and a million-year-old stone.

That was the last time I heard from the press agent, though from time to time the name of Deanna Durbin still is linked with philately.

Lily Pons is another celebrity who has been listed as a stamp collector, but whose collection once consisted of but a single cover. In 1936, when work started on the international stamp exhibition, a representative of the Constance Hope Associates, who was engaged in publicizing various operatic stars, came to our committee and sought means of linking her clients with the exhibition, that they might share the publicity that filled the newspapers.

Among the ideas was that of exhibiting a "rare cover" which Lily Pons owned, and as this could be arranged without disrupting the display plans, the cover was accepted as the entry of Lily Pons of the Metropolitan Opera Company.

It seems that some months before Lily Pons had been singing in Europe when she received a request to do a benefit performance in Rio de Janeiro. Anxious to oblige, she found that by boarding the *Graf Zeppelin* at Friederichshafen and flying to Rio she could fill the engagement and be back in France to continue the operatic season there. On the return voyage, Miss Pons noted that several fellow passengers were mailing to their friends letters and cards which were neatly postmarked with a special obliteration which identified the mail as having been posted aboard the giant airship during flight.

Miss Pons thought this was a "fascinating idea," and proceeded to make one for herself. The clerk asked her what kind of stamps she desired, and knowing nothing about such matters, took one of each variety on board. She then addressed an extra-large envelope to herself, affixed all of the stamps to it, and had it postmarked "Graf Zeppelin—An Bord."

About a year later, when I was chatting with Miss Pons at a party which she was giving in the Ritz Towers Hotel to introduce a protégé, I mentioned the cover. In her usual graceful manner she said I might have it and instructed her secretary to see that it was sent to me. I mounted it in an album containing material of human-interest value and there it remains.

About a year or so after she had given it to me, the National Broadcasting Company began a series of radio programs devoted to interviews with prominent philatelists, and one day Robert L. Graham discussed stamp collecting with Lily Pons. She told about Lilly Ponds, Maryland, a small town which changed its name to Lily Pons in honor of the coloratura, and how she usually mails all her Christmas cards from that post office each year, and about famous women who have been honored by American postage stamps. In conclusion, Miss Pons told the story about the cover mailed on board the *Graf Zeppelin*. Apparently to heighten the effect of the broadcast, the script was presented as though she actually was showing the cover to Mr. Graham, who then told the radio audience how attractive it was.

I smiled to myself as I heard that dialogue, for at the moment the cover, together with the rest of the album in which it had been mounted, was on display in Sydney, Australia, where I had sent it to the special stamp exhibition held in honor of the centenary of the founding of New South Wales.

Fortunately only a few press agents have exploited their clients as philatelists to get their names into the stamp columns of newspapers and into the philatelic magazines, so that the celebrities who are genuinely interested in our mutual hobby have not suffered. Herbert Hoover, ex-president of the United States, often is referred to as a stamp collector, as is Jean Hersholt, the Dr. Christian of radio and character actor of the screen. I have had several occasions to meet both these gentlemen, and while they had a modest collection in years gone by, neither has a collection today. Jerome Kern, the composer, on the other hand, was one of the keenest philatelists and had a collection of superb United States issues—old and modern—that would have won a medal at any important exhibition; but he was so secretive about his activities as a collector that only his closest friends and the dealers with whom he placed orders knew about it. Clara Bow, the "It" girl of the 'twenties, and Penny Singleton are other motion-picture stars who collect.

[19] The Fabulous Fortunate

Philatelic history has been punctuated by any number of figures who have made tremendous collections that have been marked rather by bulk than by their ability to add to knowledge. They are men who have been attracted to stamps for one reason or another, and then have pursued the accumulation of items modified by monetary value with an insatiable ardor. By the time they completed their endeavor they left their heirs or estates fabulous fortunes, they left stampdom lavish legends, but they added not one iota to philatelic knowledge.

Head and shoulders above all these fabled fortunates stands Philipp la Renotiere von Ferrary. Ferrary was the son of the Duchess de Galliera, who was one of the richest of ancient Italian nobility and landlord of a great portion of the city of Genoa. According to the late Fred Melville, the founder of the family was a Genoese banker named Ferrary who amassed great wealth and who left a son who increased it and finally became the Duc de Galliera and Prince of Lucedio. Melville records an eccentricity of this fellow, who maintained a private library to which not even his wife was admitted. Shortly after his death, the widow entered the room for the first time and found there some 300 volumes, each of which was fastened with a gold clasp lock. Every page of every volume consisted of a 1000-franc government bond! In all there were over 3,000,000 francs in this part of the treasure!

Ferrary, the collector, was born in 1848. During his lifetime his mother domiciled him at the famous mansion which stood at 17 Rue de Varenne in the heart of fashionable Paris, which had been built originally by the Marechal de Montmorency in 1721.

On the death of his mother, Ferrary learned that she had left the mansion to the Austrian government as its Parisian Embassy with the provision that Philipp have the use of one wing for as long as he should live. Philipp, then a minor, became the adopted son of Ritter (Sir) Emanuel la Renotiere von Kriegsfeld, a distinguished officer of the

Austrian army. So it was that he accepted his name as a combination of the names of his real and adopted parents.

For most of his life, Ferrary set aside three rooms of his home for his philatelic proclivities. One of them was a sort of reception hall; another was for his collection of stamps, in charge of Pierre Mahe, the son of another French philatelist; the third, in charge of Smithe de Wilde, was devoted to collections of envelopes, post cards, money cards, and other *entires*.

In those days at the turn of the century, there were relatively few men to whom stamps of great price could be sold. And so when it became known that Ferrary had the acquisitiveness and the means to pay for such things, dealers all over the world beat the proverbial path to his door. The fact that he was a hoarder made it even easier for them, for rarely did he return a high-priced item.

Some of the old-timers who remember Ferrary personally always talk about his budget scheme. In the anteroom was a spiked board in front of Mr. Mahe's desk, and every Monday morning M. Progin, the treasurer of the Ferrary fortune, would fill the series of sharp nails with French banknotes in denominations of 50, 100, 500, and 1000 francs until about 50,000 francs worth hung there, ready to be used for incidental purchases. If, during the week, an unusually large purchase was to be made, Ferrary would write a check.

The second room, the one in which Ferrary kept his stamps, was covered with cupboards, each containing shelves about six inches apart. The stamps were arranged on these shelves in alphabetical order, mounted on loose sheets of stout paper about 12 by 5 inches.

Although he purchased thousands of single items, Ferrary built the bulk of his collection by purchasing entire collections which came on the market at the death of earlier philatelists. Among the huge collections he purchased intact were those of Baron Rothschild of Paris, Judge Philbrick of London, Sir Daniel Cooper, the governor of New South Wales, and many others.

When World War I broke out in August, 1914, Ferrary was in the Netherlands. He returned to Paris in 1916, but the French refused to grant him refuge because of his Austrian parentage, and accordingly he moved to Switzerland, where he had been naturalized in Lugano in 1908. His stamps were left in Paris, and when he died on May 20, 1916, probate disclosed that the entire lot had been left to the Imperial Postal Museum in Berlin, which until then was matched only by the Tapling collection as the outstanding public stamp collection in the world.

The French government not only refused to give the collection to the Germans but sequestered it as well, stating that receipts from its sale would be applied to reparations charged against the defeated nation.

The government retained Gerard Gilbert, a well-known dealer and philatelic student of Paris, to break the hoard into lots and manage the auctions, which were staged at the Hotel Drouot in Paris between June, 1921 and November, 1925, in a series of some fourteen sales of several sessions each.

News of the sales spread around the world, and when the descriptive catalogues were published collectors in even the remotest sections of the earth were attracted to it like camels to an oasis. Items which Ferrary had acquired quietly came to light; rarities which were not generally known to exist were suddenly offered for sale, and the specialists descended upon the Hotel Drouot en masse, either in person or through agents.

Allowing for the varying exchange of the French franc at the time of the sales, when French economy was not as stable as it might have been, the total amount realized, according to Mr. Phillips, who kept a record of it, was $1,632,524.

Today, well-known collections are studded with single items, each of which is "ex-Ferrary." In a way, it was fortunate indeed that the world had such a hoarder as Ferrary, for although he did not knowingly aid the hobby, he did indirectly help philatelic students.

Because of his insatiable desire to accumulate stamps, whenever large blocks or extraordinary pieces were offered he bought them intact and so saved them for posterity. Had he not been so enthusiastic, many a dealer would have broken up sheets and blocks and sold them individually at the time they were found. The fact that they were saved intact gave students an opportunity of having study pieces of inestimable value at their disposal.

In our own country we have had Ferrary's counterpart in Colonel Edward H. R. Green, fabulous son of fabulous Hetty Green, the female financial wizard of Wall Street. How or when this man ever became interested in postage stamps is uncertain, for it was not until he was well on his way that stampdom realized an American Ferrary had stepped upon the stage. Hugh M. Clark, then head of the Scott Stamp and Publishing Company, vaguely recalls that one day a strong, stocky man limped into his store and asked for an album and some stamps "for a young friend." Some weeks later the man returned, again called on Mr. Clark, and asked if he had any complete collections for sale. One collection after another was brought out from the stock room and shown to the stranger. The man glanced through the pages, asked the price, and without comment pushed it aside on the counter and asked to see another. Finally, after showing him everything available and pretty much disgusted that he had not made a definite sale, Mr. Clark abruptly told his customer that he had no more to show. To his surprise, the stranger told him to wrap up the entire lot, handed him payment for the material, and stalked out as heavily burdened with albums as Mr. Clark was with amazement.

All during the early 1920's Colonel Green made the rounds of stamp dealers, buying virtually everything that was offered without questioning the price. Many of the old-time dealers admitted that the presence of such an "angel" turned their business into a lucrative heydey. When the imperforate sheets of the five-cent error were discovered, Colonel Green bought the bulk of the find; when the 24-cent air-mail invert was turned up, every dealer to whom Mr. Robey, the man who bought it at the post office in Washington for $24, tried to reach Colonel Green who was traveling in Texas at the time, but failed to do so. Uncertain as to whether he might buy a sheet of stamps at the five-figure price which Mr. Robey asked, and unable to reach the colonel, they turned it down. Only by chance was the late Eugene Klein able to track Green down and get a commitment of $20,000 from him, to enable Klein to give Robey $15,000 and make a $5,000 profit on the transaction.

Green was so determined to accumulate stamps that he sometimes spurned well-intentioned advice. At one time he came to Mr. Clark and showed him a sheet of stamps which someone else had offered. Clark suggested that he refrain from paying the price asked. Colonel Green stalked out of the office and never again purchased a single thing from the Scott Stamp and Coin Company.

Stories about this man were as plentiful as taxicabs in New York on a sunny day. And while most of them may have been exaggerated, I am personally inclined to believe them, for I had an opportunity to meet him and experience his idiosyncrasies late in 1934. By that time Colonel Green had withdrawn from philatelic activities and devoted most of his time to the acquisition of American gold coins. Although I had never met Colonel Green before, or had any contact with him, I was invited to his Round Hill, Massachusetts, home for the Labor

Day week end for a reason I was never to learn. I simply had a communication from Mr. Marshall, his secretary, inviting me up.

I arrived at New Bedford and was met by a station wagon which drove across the strip that connected the city with the Green Estate. It was late in the evening, and after supper I was shown to a gorgeous room. In the morning I met the colonel for the first time. The old gentleman came down to the sumptuous dining room in a private elevator, had breakfast, and seemed to enjoy his own meal not quite as much as he did seeing his small Boston bull terrier eat from a gold plate which had been set by the side of the colonel's chair. A collar, generously trimmed with gold, silver, and diamonds, sparkled in the light which filtered in from the massive windows. From that breakfast until I left four days later, I had a chance of witnessing many of this man's eccentricities. He told me he had heard of some of my broadcasts about stamps, but while he no longer had any interest in the hobby, he thought that he would like to see me.

"I don't let everybody come up here, y'know," he drawled in a voice that had a Southern flavor. "A couple of weeks ago Floyd Gibbons wanted to come up here. Had to have him shown off the property three times before he got the idea I didn't want him around."

Before I went up I had spoken to Prescott H. Thorp, who then was editor of *Scott's Monthly Journal*, and he had asked me to see what I could learn of the inverted air-mail sheet. There were rumors that three other sheets had been found and secretly sold to Colonel Green, but no one had been able to discover whether they were true or false. I asked my host about this, but all I got was, "Don't remember. All my stamps are down in New York, locked up in the vaults of the Chase National Bank and in safes of my office at Trinity Place." That was the only conversation about postage stamps.

For the next several days I did little except explore his vast estate and generally enjoy a moment of luxurious living. The home was a vast fifty-six room mansion set far back on the knoll after which the estate was named. To one side was the huge greenhouse and servant's quarters, a long meticulously cared for garden, and a large windmill. It seems that some years before the colonel had come across this relic of colonial days and had had it moved to his estate not only for decoration and the preservation of a historical structure, but also to grind every bit of flour that was used by the household.

The many driveways that webbed the three-thousand-acre estate were curbed, not with stones in the usual manner, but with the links of anchor chains. For many years the colonel placed a standing order for all anchors and chains from ships that were scrapped by some of the larger yards around the country. The chains were used for curbs, the anchors were heaped in a special square especially arranged for the purpose.

There were scores of them—of every size, shape and kind. There were small ones made entirely of metal; other large ones had come from ancient windjammers and had broad flukes and wooden spars. Just off to the left of the home was a completely equipped radio station which he had once had built so that he might broadcast his own programs, but which at the time had been turned over to the National Broadcasting Company as its New Bedford outlet. Beyond that was a modern airport with three hangars. The colonel had planes of his own but scarcely used them. He did have a full staff of meteorologists and mechanics to service any itinerant planes that might happen to drop in. The colonel was known to airmen of the country, and any of them could land and be serviced and refueled with his compliments. One day while I was there a flight of Marine planes en route to Washington dropped in, had their motors checked, their tanks loaded with gasoline and oil, and then left again without having to pay a dime.

The airport also included a blimp hangar which had been used by a dirigible that once had caught the colonel's fancy. He no longer owned it, but when experiments in atomic energy were inaugurated at the Massachusetts Institute of Technology, Colonel Green gave the institution the use of its hangar to construct the atom-smasher device. When he found that professors and students were inconvenienced by having to travel a considerable distance between his estate and New Bedford where they were domiciled, he had a sort of barracks built for thirty persons so they might be nearer their work.

Down by the waterfront were more evidences of his interests. A lover of whaling ships and the tradition which accompanied them, Colonel Green owned the finest ship of its kind and had it on his estate. Extending out from the grounds was a large pier alongside which the old *Charles W. Morgan* was moored—not alone with hawsers, but permanently. The whole hull of the ship was encased in a block of concrete so that the sea would not destroy the ancient timbers. The colonel maintained a complete crew aboard to polish the brass, scrub the decks, and keep the fittings in trim. The assortment of harpoons were polished to mirror brightness; the ropes were coiled on decks; the blubber vats were brilliant and the woodwork gleamed. The captain, an old-time whaler himself, and the crew lived and worked aboard the ship as though it were ready to sail on the afternoon tides. A short way up the beach was a small rigger's shop, complete with every tool and fitting just as it was in the days when men went down to the sea in ships.

All but the grounds immediately surrounding the mansion were open at all times to the public. Folks used to come in from neighboring communities and take advantage of it. There was a splendid bathing beach and bath houses where they might don their swim suits. A fellow with hot-dog and ice-cream wagon mingled with the fun-seekers and supplied them with beach snacks—all free of charge. At the very corner of the estate was a huge bandstand where nightly concerts were given to entertain young couples who could listen as they parked in their cars amidst the tall trees, or older folks who came simply to enjoy good music beneath the stars.

When he felt like it, Colonel Green would ride along his roadways in an ancient electric car whose entire body consisted chiefly of glass so that he could look out in every direction. While I was there Colonel Green was not particularly well and spent most of his time in his private bedroom. Except for a few meals, he ate in bed, propped up by pillows and in the company of his secretary. One wall of the room was lined with seventeen different radio sets, each tuned to a different station. Twirling dials and setting volume controls were too much bother, so when he wanted a program he need only switch on the radio which was tuned to the particular station. Beneath his bed he had several boxes of sweets, sent to him each week by Dean's in New York.

At the moment his secretary did little except polish and arrange his gold American coin collection. Specimens came to him from all numismatic dealers in the country and even from some foreign ones. It appeared that he was buying gold coins with the same enthusiasm that he had bought stamp collections.

The evening before I left, his secretary mentioned the need of a new dress. He thought a moment and agreed with her. He ordered the car, allowed the valet to help him dress, and together they went into town. They went to a small shop just south of New Bedford, and as he sat there his secretary selected a dress.

When she had picked one that satisfied her the colonel asked the price. "Twenty dollars," the clerk said.

"How much do they cost wholesale?" the colonel asked.

"About sixteen dollars in dozen lots."

"Sounds fair enough. Give her a dozen of them," the colonel replied. He peeled some bills from his roll and when they had boxed a dozen dresses, he limped out of the shop and drove back to his home.

When the 1936 international exhibition was planned, the committee named Colonel E. H. R. Green an honorary vice-president, and attempted to get him to exhibit portions of his hoard, hoping that through such participation he might be influenced to renew his interest in the stamp hobby. Indeed, some of the dealers missed his profitable trade and sought all sorts of means to restore it.

But before the show opened Colonel Green died. His death started a nation-wide legal battle, for several states sought to establish his legal residence in order to profit by the taxes that could be levied against the fabulous estate. Meanwhile, dealers who eagerly sought to obtain his stamps entered into negotiations with the executors.

Finally, after several years of negotiations, the stamp world was surprised to hear that Walter S. Scott and the late Percy Doane had been retained to appraise the hoard and arrange for its sale through a series of auctions.

Speculation was rampant; dealers and even the appraisers could not be sure what would happen when this hoard, which had been appraised at $1,298,444, would be offered for sale. Some said the dumping of these stamps would break the market; others thought that perhaps it would enhance interest by reason of the fact that so many great rarities would again get into the hobby.

Scott, who was really the guiding force behind the sale, decided to offer a section of the hoard at a series of seven auction sales and assigned quantities of material to seven dealers who had previously engaged him as their auctioneer as a sort of reward for past business. The dealers assigned to sell this trial section were: Hugh C. Barr, Percy C. Doane, Harmer, Rooke & Co., Laurence and Stryker, J. C. Morgenthau, Irwin Heiman, all of New York, and Daniel Kelleher, of Boston.

The first of these sales, staged on September 23, 1942, was enough to indicate what would happen. Almost every lot went at or above the appraised value. By the time the rest of the sales were held in succession for the remainder of the season, it was clear that even the optimists had not been optimistic enough. The results encouraged the estate to offer the rest of the material, and by the time the whole hoard had been sold nearly $3,000,000 was paid for it, setting an all-time record for the sale of a single person's stamp holdings. Instead of breaking the market, the disposal of the supplies actually spurred it. Nearly everyone wanted at least one item from the famous collection, and mail bids poured in from all corners of the world with which communications still were open during the war.

So many dealers and collectors wanted some of the stamps on which Colonel Green had a corner that prices for them soared beyond all reasonable limits. Several wealthy operators got together and set out to buy certain items, such as the blocks of the inverted air mails and the imperforate errors of the United States. Regardless of what competitive bidding compelled them to pay, these operators usually topped the bids and again got most of them into one place.

The Green hoard—we must call it a hoard and not a collection because the colonel himself never knew what he owned and probably cared less—has been sold. The colonel is dead. But as long as there is a stamp collector alive, the name of Colonel Edward H. R. Green will always stand bright in the annals of our hobby.

George H. Worthington, Cleveland businessman, was another of the fabulous fortunates who collected more for the pleasure and pride of building a valuable collection than one from which he could learn the many things a stamp album can teach. He was a colorful man, but pale in comparison to Colonel Green. Alvin Good, now living in Orrville, Ohio, was for several decades Worthington's philatelic secretary, and probably knew more of this man than anyone else alive. Mr. Good recently published a booklet called *The Life and Aventures of a Philatelist,* in which he recounts the many experiences he had in connection with the acquisition of stamps for Mr. Worthington. Since nothing could be said here without plagiarizing Mr. Good's accounts, readers are referred to the book, if they would have a comprehensive picture of this man who accumulated stamps until he had one of the most outstanding lots ever got together in the United States.

Stamp collecting has been referred to many times as the "king of hobbies and the hobby of kids and kings." And rightly so, for while millions of youngsters have pursued this fascinating avocation, we have had any number of kings to whom the collection of postage stamps meant as much as the intrigues of international politics.

The greatest of them all was the late King George V, a man who was an enthusiastic collector for his entire life and who did much to advance the principles of the Royal Philatelic Society. In 1890, when the British Empire was commemorating the golden jubilee of the first postage stamps of the world, the Duke of Edinburgh was guest of honor at a luncheon in London, at which time he announced: "Today Prince George of Wales starts from Chatham in *H.M.S.*

Thrush to the command which he has been appointed. He is a stamp collector, and I hope he will return with a goodly number of additions from North America and the West Indies."

Three years later, when he was again in London, the Prince of Wales joined the Royal Philatelic Society, and from that time on persistently admitted his interest in the hobby and did everything he could to advance the hobby and his knowledge of it.

In a sense, King George was a counterpart of President Roosevelt, but unlike F.D.R., His Majesty was a keen philatelist who devoted many hours to the study of his specimens and the accumulation of perfect specimens without using his royal position to help him along.

Offers of stamps by his subjects were invariably returned to the sender with a note from a secretary that His Majesty could not accept the gift. During his lifetime he often visited the Royal Philatelic Society and contributed several articles to the society's monthly publication, *The London Philatelist,* on different philatelic subjects of lasting reference value.

King George concentrated on the stamps of the British Commonwealth of nations and built up collections of them that surpassed any others in existence. Although he was able to obtain such unique items as original drawings and die proofs of British and British colonial issues from the archives of the government and printing firms, many of the great rarities which his collection housed were obtained in the open market, albeit through agents who bid in His Majesty's behalf.

When World War I broke across Europe, King George publicly announced that he was forsaking his stamp-collecting activities and devoting all his waking hours to the prosecution of a victorious conflict.

But not long afterward the monarch reversed his decision. According to his own admission, playing with his postage stamps, delving into the problems they posed, so absorbed his mind that he was more relaxed and could better undertake his serious obligations. And so he scheduled three to four periods of time every week for a visit to the philatelic room in Buckingham Palace. Although he worked at the stamps himself, he engaged the services of Sir Edward Denny Bacon, the man who had worked on the Tapling collection, as philatelic curator of "The King's Collection."

For as long as King George was alive, he remained the king of philatelic kings. But after he died, shortly after his Silver Jubilee, stampdom was alarmed at the possible disposition of the more than three hundred red Morocco-bound volumes in which this magnificent lot was housed. Of course it was said that the then-Prince of Wales had been a collector but that he never could achieve the stature of his late father.

The late Charles J. Phillips, who often boasted of his personal acquaintance with famous collectors, published an article in which he told how he encouraged the young prince to begin a collection with the stamps of Prince Edward Islands and that the young man "jumped at the idea and said he would start at once." Reports of the Prince of Wales' interest in stamps could not be found elsewhere, and so collectors generally were not sure whether he would take up where his father left off. In 1941, after the prince had been King Edward VIII and resigned the throne, and while he was governor of the Bahamas, the Duke of Windsor came to New York and through the courtesy of a mutual friend who was his host for a day, I was invited to a luncheon at the American Museum of Natural History. During the three hours that the fourteen luncheon guests were together for a tour of the Roosevelt Hall and the Planetarium, I had occasion to talk to His Royal Highness several times. When an opportunity afforded itself I mentioned the Phillips reference to his collection.

"All wrong," he said. "I never owned a collection of my own in all my life. It is true that I passed many hours looking at Father's albums, and I do have a complete set of sheets of the stamps issued when I was king."

After the abdication, philatelic concern again arose. King George VI was definitely not a collector and it was feared that the collection might be consigned to the royal vaults. Just at about that time Sir Edward Bacon died, leaving the royal household without anyone to care for the precious stamps. Out of a clear sky, Buckingham Palace announced that Sir John Wilson, Bart., former president of the Royal Philatelic Society, and one of the great of the younger scholars alive had been appointed to take over where Sir Edward left off.

Sir John kept the collection up to date, and not many years after the new monarch's accession, London newspapers carried a picture-story showing His Majesty examining the royal collection with a note stating that the king had developed an interest in it and personally was beginning to learn the intricacies of an advanced philatelic nature. During the International Stamp Exhibition staged at the British Pavilion of the New York World's Fair, I prevailed upon the commission to persuade the king to submit twenty pages from the royal collection for the show and these arrived in June, 1940. For the 1947 show, Alfred F. Lichtenstein went to London and after several meetings at Buckingham Palace, announced that His Majesty had agreed to loan enough material to fill twenty frames in the Court of Honor. This material consisted of stamps and documents, essays and proofs relating to the first postage stamp of the world.

Second to King George V of England, as a royal philatelist, was King Fouad I of Egypt. The King of Egypt was as enthusiastic a collector as could be found anywhere. He built up a collection of stamps and covers dealing with the postal history of his country that was second to none. Until then the collection of Mackenzie-Lowe of England was one of the finest, and when it was offered for auction by H. R. Harmer, the king purchased it intact. This lot, augmented by the material which his majesty had procured elsewhere, was amalgamated into one astounding collection of Egyptian stamps. Later, and shortly before he died in 1936, King Fouad turned his attention to the stamps of the Confederacy and made an amazing start in this difficult specialty, but he never could complete it before he died.

King Farouk I, his son, was a young man and his sudden ascendance to the throne of Egypt imposed more problems than he could handle immediately. Meanwhile, however, upon the encouragement of several philatelists in the court, he gradually turned to stamps, and in February, 1946, when the Egyptian Philatelic Society in conjunction with the Department of Posts staged an international exhibition to commemorate the eightieth anniversary of the first Egyptian stamps, His Majesty accepted the patronship and scheduled a fifteen-minute visit to the Royal Agricultural Hall, where the stamps were on view. He was so impressed with the many collections that had been submitted from various parts of the world that he stayed for three hours and at the end of his tour asked that Ibrahim Chaftar, president of the society and chairman of the display, be brought to him that he might confer upon him the title of Bey in recognition of his services. Reports of the royal visit included many tributes to the king and his comments, which unmistakably indicated that he knew much about the hobby.

Among other members of royalty to whom stamps meant fun and relaxation were King Alphonse XIII, of Spain; King Carol, of Romania; Czar Nicholas, of Russia; Manoel, of Portugal; Otto, of Hapsburg, exiled ruler of Hungary; the Queen of Italy; Baron Takahara Mitsui of Japan, and several lesser wearers of the purple.

Part V
Glossary

Philatelic Definitions

ACCESSORIES—Articles used by collectors in the study and mounting of stamps, such as hinges, magnifying glasses, perforation gauges, water marks detectors, etc.

ADHESIVES—Stamps printed separately and usually gummed on the back to be affixed to letters or packages as distinguished from stamps printed or embossed directly on envelopes or wrappers.

A.E.F. BOOKLETS—Stamp books prepared for the A.E.F. in France in 1918 of one-cent and two-cent denominations in pages of thirty stamps.

AIR-MAIL OR AIR-POST STAMPS —Stamps issued specifically for air mail.

ALBINO—A colorless embossed envelope stamp accidentally impressed without the ink. These are frequently found mixed with stocks of stamped envelopes and are good for postage. They are interesting varieties but are not rare.

ALBUMS—Books to hold stamp collections. These are made in bound volumes or in loose-leaf form with or without printed spaces for the stamps. Collectors who like to arrange their own pages and write in stories or data regarding their stamps prefer the blank loose-leaf albums.

ANILINE DYES—Colors derived from coal tar. However, collectors usually understand the term to mean a brilliant color which is spoiled by immersion in water. See Pink Back.

APPROVALS—Selections of stamps arranged on sheets or cards and sent out by dealers or collector-dealers for sale or exchange. See page 116.

ARROWS—Small V-shaped markers in the margins of sheets of stamps usually at the ends of guide lines and placed there to aid in the registering, where several colors are used in the printing, or as an aid in feeding the sheets into the perforating machines. Arrow blocks of stamps are blocks of four or more showing the arrow in the sheet-margin attached. In some of the United States commemorative stamps and in all of the imperforates it is possible to get blocks which show the arrows intact, but in most of the ordinary varieties, since the panes sold in the post offices are cut from large sheets, the arrows are divided in two by the cutting knife. Thus arrow blocks of this last type show half arrows at the corners only. See Guide Lines.

AS IS—A term used to describe stamps about which there is a question of identification, genuineness, or condition. Stamps sold with this designation are bought at the risk of the buyer and are not returnable.

AVERAGE COPIES—Stamps in the usual run of condition and centering but otherwise sound copies.

BACK STAMP—A postmark usually found on the back of a cover indicating date of receipt at destination.

BANK MIXTURE—A mixture of current stamps supposedly from the mail of banks.

BATONNE—See Laid Paper.

BENZINE—See Watermarks.

BILINGUAL—Stamps with legends in two languages, such as those current in Canada and New Hebrides. Sheets of Union of South Africa stamps show alternate varieties printed in English and Afrikaans.

BISECT—A half of a stamp used to pay half the rate of the original stamp. This variety is only recognized if on the original cover with the postmark covering the cut, and then only on the early issues when postmasters were unofficially allowed to resort to this expedient when shortages existed in the required denominations. The practice is no longer customary. A bisect may be a diagonal half, horizontal half, or vertical half.

BLOCK—An unseparated group of stamps at least two wide by two deep.

BLUED OR BLUISH PAPER—A paper which has turned partially or wholly blue through the chemical action of the ink. It is found in certain early varieties of Great Britain and Colonies, printed by Perkins Bacon & Co., of London. Bluish paper also refers to those stocks which were tinted by the paper mills.

BOGUS STAMPS—Labels made privately to deceive collectors. These sometimes are in the form of fictitious denominations or colors of regular government issues, or stamps of non-existing governments, or purport to be from governments that never issued stamps of their own.

BOND PAPER—Strong tough paper made from linen.

BOOKLET PANES—Small sheets of stamps bound in booklet form for convenience in carrying. For collecting purposes these should have the binding margin attached. See *A.E.F.*

BUREAU PRE-CANCELS—Sometimes called Bureau Prints. Stamps precanceled during the process of manufacture of the stamps themselves at the Bureau of Engraving and Printing at Washington, as distinguished from stamps precanceled by handstamp or local printing ordered by the postmaster.

BURELE OR BURELAGE—A network pattern of fine lines or dots usually in a different color printed on the back or face of a stamp to prevent counterfeiting. See *Moire*.

CACHET—A special handstamp or printed device indicating mailing on an anniversary, the inauguration of some particular postal service, or the first-day use of a new stamp. Cachets are official when authorized by the postal authorities and unofficial when sponsored by private individuals. See *First Day*.

CAMPAIGN COVER—An envelope bearing the picture or publicity of a candidate for political office.

CANCELLATION—A mark applied to a stamp by a postal authority to prevent its further use.

CANCELED-TO-ORDER — Stamps canceled by postal authorities while still in unused condition. The practice is indulged in by some foreign governments to dispose of obsolete or surplus stocks at prices below face value. Such stamps are less valuable than genuinely used copies.

CARRIER POSTMARK—Postmarks indicating delivery of mail by government carriers.

CARRIER STAMPS—Stamps issued to pay local charge for delivery from post office on a regular delivery. They were no longer required in the United States when free city delivery was instituted in 1863.

CATALOGUE VALUE—The value placed on a stamp by standard or dealers' catalogues, usually above the market value but indicating the scarcity of the stamp.

CENTERING—A term used to describe the position of a stamp with regard to its location within the lines of perforations or imperforate margins. A centered stamp is one with even margins all around—the condition desired by discriminating collectors.

CENTER LINE—See *Guide Line.*

CHALKY PAPER—A surface applied to stamp papers before printing and intended to do away with cleaning. Chalky surface stamps are usually ruined by soaking.

CHANGELING—A stamp the color of which has been chemically changed either by accident or intent.

CHARITY STAMPS—Also called Semi-postals. Stamps sold at an advance over their value, the surplus to be devoted to some charitable purpose. See pages 76–80.

CHROME STEEL—It has been found that by adding a chrome steel wearing surface to an ordinary steel plate the life of the plate is materially lengthened. This surfacing can be renewed several times, and these renewals often result in variable minor varieties such as appearing and disappearing hair-cracks, dots, etc.

CLEANED STAMPS—Stamps from which the cancellations have been removed. These are sometimes offered as unused specimens, especially where there is a great difference in value between the unused and the used.

CLICHÉ—A single stereo or electrotype for printing a stamp, a number of which may be clamped together to form a printing form or surface.

COIL STAMPS—Stamps issued in rolls for use in affixing or vending machines. These stamps are usually perforated one way only, but in some countries, England, for instance, the rolls are made from the regular perforated sheets. See *Join.*

COLOR TRIALS—Proof printings in various colors to determine the most suitable one for the issued stamp.

COMMEMORATIVE STAMPS—Stamps issued for a special occasion and usually on sale for a limited time.

COMPOUND PERFORATION—A stamp with perforations of different gauges on different sides. These usually have uniform perforations on opposite sides. In designating perforations the first number is the top and bottom gauge and the second that of the sides. Thus, "Perf. 10 x 12" means 10 at top and bottom and 12 on the sides of the stamp.

CONDITION—The state of a stamp regarding centering, cancellation, etc. Collectors look upon stamps as superb, fine, good, and poor—with varying grades between—but without any uniformly accepted scale of comparison. See *Repaired.* Also see Chapter 11.

CONTROLS—A term used by English collectors for the numbers on the margins of sheets of British stamps. The term is also applied to numbers printed on stamps, such as those on the backs of some Spanish stamps, to prevent counterfeiting.

CORK CANCELLATION—A cancellation from a home-made design cut in cork or wood.

CORNER—In stamped envelopes, the full corner of the envelope including both front and back. See *Cut Square.*

CORNER BLOCK—A block showing marginal or other evidence that it is from the corner of a sheet of stamps.

COUNTERFEIT—See *Forgery.*

COVER—The entire wrapping or envelope which has carried a letter through the mail.

CRACKED PLATE—A stamp showing the irregular jagged impression from a crack in a plate. Cracks in the earlier issues where the plate was actually split are not to be confused with the curvature or shrinkage hairline cracks in the chrome-steel surfacing of modern plates.

CREASE—A paper defect objectionable to many collectors. Creases, particularly in mint stamps, are likely to grow worse with age. They are caused by careless handling of stamps.

CROWN CA—A watermark in British Colonial stamps. The "CA" indicates *Crown Agents.*

CROWN CC—Same as above, the "CC" indicating *Crown Colonies.*

CUT CANCELLATION—A cancellation cutting through the stamp and intentionally made by knife-like cancelling dies.

CUT SQUARE—An envelope stamp cut out with a square margin. Envelope stamps are collected as "entires," "corners," or "cut square." Envelope or other stamps cut to shape, except the great rarities, are usually valueless.

CUT TO SHAPE—See *Cut Square.*

DEMONETIZED—Stamps rendered invalid for postage by official decree of the issuing government.

DEPARTMENT STAMPS—See *Official Stamps.*

DIAGONAL HALF—Description of a bisect, which see.

DIE—The original steel engraving from which the plates for printing stamps are made. A die proof is a printing from the die and can usually be told by its clear impression and large margins.

DIE PROOF—See *Die.*

DOCUMENTARY—A type of fiscal or revenue stamp.

DOUBLE GRILL—A grill accidentally impressed twice, showing overlapping of the design.

DOUBLE IMPRESSION—A sheet of stamps that has gone to press twice, showing the second impression distinctly overlapping the first.

DOUBLE PAPER—Stamps printed on an experimental "safety" paper made by pasting two sheets together, or printed on the "pasteup" joining two sheets of the regular paper.

DOUBLE SURCHARGE—See *Double Impression.*

DOUBLE TRANSFER—The terms *double transfer, shift,* and *re-entry* are used indiscriminately by many collectors to describe extra lines found in certain stamps made while transferring the design to the plate. According to King and Johl, a shift shows extra lines displaced outward at one end or one side of the design. Double transfers occur when the first impression of the transfer is misplaced, the incorrect impression only partially eradicated, and a new impression superimposed in the correct location, some of the original impression appearing in the printed stamp. Double shifts are lines misplaced in opposite directions at the sides and ends of a stamp. Triple transfers are the result of a third impression of the transfer roller. Re-entries are sometimes made to freshen up positions which show wear after a plate has been in use. These frequently but not necessarily show double transfers which did not appear in the early state of the plate.

EL—An imprint found on recent United States stamp plates indicating that they were made by an electrolytic deposit process instead of by pressure transfer. See *Transfer Roll.*

EMBOSSED—Designs raised in relief, See *Albino.*

ENCASED POSTAGE STAMPS—During a shortage of small coins during the Civil War, postage stamps encased in metal containers were used for money. These are of more interest to coin collectors than to philatelists.

ENGRAVED—Stamps printed from engraved plates made either by hand engraving each position, in which case each stamp will vary slightly from the others, or by transfer from an original die, in which case variations will be accidental only.

ENTIRE—A complete envelope bearing an envelope stamp. See *Cut Square.*

ERRORS—Stamps with accidental mistakes in color, paper, inscriptions, watermarks, etc., or bicolored stamps with centers inverted. See pages 169-185.

ESSAY—A suggested design printed in stamp form but not approved for issuance. See *Color Trials.*

EXHIBITION PANES—See *Souvenir Sheets.*

EXPRESS STAMPS—Stamps issued privately by express companies or, in some countries, special delivery stamps. See *Locals.*

FACE—The front face of a cover with stamps and postmarks intact. Collectors prefer the entire cover; hence, a "face" is not a particularly desirable item.

FACSIMILE—An imitation of a stamp represented as such.

FAKES—Stamps altered to resemble more valuable varieties by adding or cutting away perforations, adding counterfeit overprints, altering colors, cleaning off or adding cancellations, etc.

FIRST-DAY COVER—A cover bearing a new stamp and canceled on the day of issue at a post office officially designated for first-day sale. See *Cachet.*

FIRST FLIGHT—The inauguration of a new air-mail route. Covers carried usually bear special postmarks or cachets.

FISCAL—A revenue stamp or a postage stamp with a revenue cancellation.

FLAT PLATE—Stamps printed in sheets from flat-bed as distinguished from rotary presses, where the plates are curved around a cylinder and the stamps printed on "endless" rolls of paper. When both flat and rotary plates are made for the same stamp, they are transferred from the same original die, but the curving of the rotary plate afterward causes the design to lengthen slightly around the circumference, thus making the latter stamps longer in one direction than those made by flat-plate printing.

FORGERY—A fraudulent imitation of a stamp. See *Fake.*

FRANK—A mark or label indicating postage paid or the right of free postage enjoyed by Congressmen, etc.

FREAK—A stamp, not an error, having some conspicuous difference from normal, caused by the paper being folded before printing, or some similar accident.

FUGITIVE COLOR—One which may fade or run when wet. Sometimes used purposely to prevent washing off postmarks for fraudulent re-use of stamps. Soluble inks are used for many of the current foreign stamps printed by the photogravure process.

GENERAL COLLECTION—A collection containing a wide variety of stamps without limitation to any special group. See *Specialized Collection.*

GRANITE PAPER—One containing visible silk fibers, also called *Silurian.* See *Silk Paper.*

GRILL—An embossed design of a number of small pyramids impressed in the paper to break the surface and thus render it so absorptive of canceling ink that cleaning is impossible. The grills found on United States 1867 to 1870 issues are rectangular in pattern and are listed in millimeters and also by the number of points in the horizontal and vertical rows, this latter being the best identification. Since the pyramids measure four to ⅛ inch, they can easily be counted and counterfeits quickly detected. The collection and study of grilled issues is one of the most fascinating specialties for United States philatelists.

GUIDE DOTS—Small dots placed on stamp plates to aid the plate maker in aligning the rows of stamps.

GUIDE LINES—Also called Center Lines. These are lines printed on the sheets of stamps to aid registering them in printing or in the perforating machines. Guide-line or center-line blocks are blocks of stamps containing the horizontal or vertical lines, and crossed-guide-line or crossed-center-line blocks are those from the center of the sheet showing the crossing of the lines. Center-line and crossed-center-line blocks are usually obtain-

[307]

able only from imperforate sheets. See *Arrows* and *Position Sets.* The center lines found on rotary press coil stamps are not guide lines but are lines made by the joints between the halves of the cylindrical plates.

GUM—The adhesive material on the back of the stamp. Mint designates stamps in post-office state that have never been hinged; *O.G.,* stamps with original gum. See *Regummed.*

GUM BREAKER BARS—Colorless marks across the backs of some rotary press stamps placed there during manufacture to prevent the stamps from curling.

HABILITADO—An overprint on Spanish and Latin-American stamps indicating "made valid."

HANDSTAMP—A stamp design, postmark, or overprint struck from a single metal, wood, or rubber die attached to a handle.

HINGE—A small piece of gummed paper folded with the adhesive side out and used for attaching stamps to album pages. The hinge should be placed at the top of the stamp to allow examination of the back without bending the stamp. Peelable hinges are the best, as these can be removed without injury to the stamp or album page.

HYPHEN-HOLE—A type of roulette perforation consisting of small rectangular holes resembling hyphens.

HORIZONTAL HALF—See *Bisect.*

IMPERFORATE OR UNPERFORATED—Stamps without perforations. Where stamps exist both with and without perforations, it is usually necessary to have the latter in a pair or block to insure identification.

IMPRINT—An inscription printed on the margin of a sheet of stamps, or sometimes under each stamp, giving the name of the manufacturer and other data.

INDIA PAPER—A soft thin wove paper used for proof impressions.

INTAGLIO—Recess or line engraving. See pages 156-157.

INVERT—A bicolored stamp with one portion of design printed upside down in relation to rest of printed subject. The term also applies to an overprint erroneously applied.

JOIN—Before the adaptation of the rotary press to the printing of long sheets of stamps for coils, these were made by pasting ordinary sheets together, then cutting them into long ribbons, which were rolled into coils. Pairs at the junction of two sheets are known as join, joint, or paste-up.

KILLER—A heavy cancellation consisting usually of bars, circles or other figures but without inscription to identify place or date of application.

KING'S HEADS—Stamps with portraits of Edward VII or George V as distinguished from those picturing Queen Victoria.

KNIFE—The size and shape of the die-cut papers from which envelopes are folded.

LAID PAPER—A paper showing alternate light and dark parallel lines when held to the light or immersed in benzine. *Laid batonne* has additional lines at right angles to the closer laid lines.

LAST DAY—A cover canceled on the last day of the stamp's legal use or a post office's existence.

LETTER SHEET—A sheet of paper bearing a stamp which can be folded to enclose the written message.

LETTER TAX STAMPS—Stamps issued by some countries to raise funds for specific purposes such as unemployed relief, etc. They are not good for postage, but must be used with regular postage stamps.

LINE—See *Guide Lines.*

LINE ENGRAVED—See *Engraved.*

LINE PAIR—A pair showing the guide line or rotary plate division line between the stamps.

LITHOGRAPHED STAMPS—Stamps printed by the lithographed process. These usually have a dull appearance in contrast to the sharp raised lines of engraved stamps. See page 158.

LOCALS—Stamps issued for use in restricted areas either by governments or private carriers. Many varieties of the latter were used in this country from 1842 to 1862, but, although always illegal, their use could not be stopped until the government adopted free city delivery.

LOZENGE PERFORATION—A term describing the shape of perforation holes.

MANILA PAPER—A coarse, brownish paper used for envelopes and wrappers.

MANUSCRIPT CANCELLATION—A pen cancellation giving the name of the post office, date, or postmaster's initials. See Pen Cancellation.

MARGIN—The paper surrounding a sheet of stamps or, in imperforate stamps, the paper surrounding a single copy.

MATCH & MEDICINE STAMPS—See Private Proprietary Stamps.

METER—A post-paid device printed by a machine after the envelope is sealed. Usually used by large firms to save time in mailing large quantities of letters.

MINIATURE SHEET—If stamps are produced in sheets of two sizes, the smaller is called a miniature sheet. Where stamps are issued only in small sheets for the convenience of the printer or otherwise, they are not considered miniature. See Souvenir Sheets.

MINT—See Gum.

MISSION MIXTURE—Mixtures of common stamps gathered in large quantities by religious organizations. See page 114.

MIXTURES—Aggregations of the cheapest current stamps generally sold by weights. They are known as bank, mission, post office, etc.

MOIRE—A pattern of wavy lines resembling watered silk printed on the face or back of stamps to prevent cleaning. See Burele.

MOUNT—Another term for hinge. Also, stamps placed in an album are said to be mounted.

MULREADY—The letter sheets and stamped envelopes designed by William Mulready and issued in England May 6, 1840. Sometimes erroneously called the first stamps.

MULTIPLE WATERMARK—A watermark repeated so frequently in a sheet that parts of it appear several times on a single stamp.

NEWSPAPER STAMPS—Stamps issued exclusively to pay postage on newspapers. In the United States the stamps were not attached to the newspapers but given as receipts for postage paid on bulk shipments.

NEWSPAPER TAX STAMPS—issued by several foreign countries to collect a tax on newspapers. They are fiscal rather than postage stamps.

NUMBERING—Collectors number the stamps in a pane or sheet from left to right, beginning in the upper left corner and ending in the lower right corner. These numbers facilitate the identification of any stamp's position in a full sheet.

OBLITERATION—The same as Cancellation.

OBSOLETE—Issues which have been demonetized by a government.

OCCUPATION STAMPS—Stamps issued in foreign territory by another nation during military occupation such as the stamps issued by Germany during the occupation of Belgium or Finnish stamps issued by Russia.

OFFICIAL SEALS—Special labels used by the Post Office Department officially to seal mail which has been opened by mistake, damaged in transit, or opened at the Dead Letter Office. These seals are not good for postage.

OFFICIAL STAMPS—Special stamps prepared for government use, sometimes issued for each department. They are not sold for private use.

OFF-CENTER—A stamp not centered within the perforations. See *Centered*.

OFF-SET—An impression from the face of a wet sheet of stamps on the back of another sheet. The designs always appear reversed and are not to be confused with stamps actually printed on the back.

OFFSET PRINTING—A process whereby the inked impression from a metal surface is transferred first to a rubber roll and then to the paper. Stamps so made have a blurred appearance.

OLIVE BACK—Certain British Colonial stamps are printed on paper bright green on the face and olive green on the back.

ON COVER—A stamp still on the envelope or wrapper as it was used in the mail. See *Face*.

ORIGINAL GUM—Generally called O.G. See *Gum*.

OVERPRINT—Any printed inscription added to a stamp after it was otherwise finished and ready for use. See *Surcharge*.

OXIDIZED—Incorrectly but commonly the name applied to a change in color of a stamp due to contact with sulphur fumes. When thus exposed, vermilion, orange, and yellow colors assume shades varying from brown to black. A better term would be *sulphuretted*.

PACKET—A selection of stamps in a sealed envelope. See page 114.

PACKET CANCELLATION—A special cancellation used for letters mailed on shipboard.

PAIR—Two unsevered stamps in either vertical or horizontal relation to each other.

PANE—A portion of a full printed sheet and thus cut to facilitate handling and sale at post offices.

PARCEL-POST STAMPS—Stamps specifically issued for use on parcel-post matter.

PART-PERFORATE—Stamps with perforations on two opposite sides, the other two sides remaining imperforate.

PASTE-UP—See *Join*.

PATRIOTIC COVER—Any of the envelopes bearing special designs or verses used throughout the North and South during the Civil War and later during the Spanish War. Some 11,000 varieties are known, many of which are common in unused condition. Collectors prefer postally used specimens.

PELURE PAPER—A hard, tough, thin semitransparent paper.

PEN CANCELLATION—A cancellation made by penstrokes. Generally the least desirable of cancellation varieties. See *Manuscript*.

PENCE ISSUES—Stamps of Canada and Ceylon, issued when currencies of these territories were still reckoned in pence as opposed to the later stamps that are inscribed cents, dollars, and rupees.

PERCE-EN-ARC—A roulette perforation consisting of small semicircles turned alternately in opposite directions. See pages 161–162.

PERCE-EN-SCIE—Saw-tooth perforations, which see.

PERFORATED INITIALS—Initials punched in stamps by business houses to prevent unauthorized use or resale. The addition of these private initials makes these stamps practically valueless for collecting purposes.

PERFORATIONS—Line of small cuts or holes placed between rows of stamps to allow easy separation. These are found in many forms, their names in general being descriptive of the type used. Unless otherwise noted in the catalogues, round holes are understood.

PERFORATED HORIZONTALLY —Stamps with perforations top and bottom only.

PERFORATED VERTICALLY— Stamps with perforations at the sides only.

PERFORATION GAUGE—A small cardboard, celluloid, or metal gauge for measuring perforations. Perforations are gauged by the number of holes occurring in two centimeters of length. Thus a stamp perforated 10 would have 10 holes in two centimeters measured along the side or end. Handy gauges priced from 10 cents and up can be secured from stamp dealers.

PHILATELY—The collection and study of stamps.

PHILATELIST—One who by study adds to the knowledge of stamps.

PHOTOGRAVURE PRINTINGS— Stamps printed by the photogravure process are the handsomest yet produced and show the designs in all the detail of photographs with soft color effects that cannot be obtained by any other method. Unfortunately many of the colors are fugitive and some of them even are soluble in benzine.

PINK BACK—In some United States stamps printed with aniline inks a pink tinge permeates the paper and shows on the back.

PLATE NUMBER—The number of a plate usually found in several positions in the margin of a sheet of stamps.

PLATE NUMBER BLOCK—A block of four or more stamps with the plate number attached. Where the plate number is at the corner of the sheet, as in the rotary press printings, a block of four is taken, and where the numbers are near the center of the sheet, top, bottom, or sides, as in the flat plate printings, blocks of six make a balanced piece. Some collectors, however, prefer blocks of eight, which can afterward be divided into two blocks of four if desired. In the recent printings for the electric eye perforating machine blocks of ten show the plate number and the corner of the sheet which identifies them as stamps from these special plates.

PLATE PROOFS—See *Proofs.*

PLATING—Reconstructing an original sheet from single stamps, pairs, strips, and blocks where the stamps have individual characteristics which fix their positions on the original plate.

PLEBISCITE STAMPS—Stamps issued under international commissions, such as that in the Saar, pending an election to determine the political status of the territory.

PNEUMATIC POST—Mail carried between stations in cylinders propelled through tubes by compressed air.

POSITION SETS—Sets of blocks from the identifiable positions on the plate such as corners, arrows, center line, plate numbers, etc. In imperforate stamps the crossed center line and four arrow blocks are considered a set, although some collectors add the corner and plate number blocks.

POSTAGE CURRENCY—A series of fractional notes of 5-, 10-, 25-, and 50-cent denominations picturing the then current 5- and 10-cent stamps issued during a shortage of coin money at the time of the Civil War.

POSTAGE DUE—Stamps placed on mail at the post office to indicate a deficiency in postage. See *Surcharge;* also *Unpaid.*

POSTAL FISCALS—Revenue stamps officially used for postage during a shortage of regular issues.

POSTMARK—A mark used to indicate the name of the post office, date of mailing, etc. It is generally used with a "killer" which cancels the stamp but may itself be used for canceling.

PRECANCELED—Stamps canceled in quantity before attaching to mail matter and used under permit by large mailers. The precanceling is done by printing the town name on each stamp in a sheet. See *Bureau Pre-cancels.*

[311]

PRINTED ON BOTH SIDES—A stamp with printed impressions both front and back as a result of feeding a sheet through the press twice. Not an *offset*, which see. Stamps printed on the back are very rare.

PRINTERS' WASTE—Portions of sheets left over or spoiled in printing. Many oddities in stamps in the past were the result of this waste accidentally getting into collectors' hands. The rare rotary press compound perforation varieties of 1919 and 1922 were the result of an attempt to use the waste from the ends of long sheets printed for coils.

PRISONERS' LETTERS—Letters from Civil War prisoners which went through the lines under flag of truce as attested by the double stamps and postmarks.

PRIVATE PERFORATIONS—Coil stamps made from imperforate sheets of stamps with the addition of special types of perforations for use in the mailing and vending machines of the Brinkerhoff, Schermack, and other companies.

PRIVATE PROPRIETARY ADHESIVES—Stamps issued under government sanction by manufacturing companies to pay taxes on medicines, matches, playing cards, etc.

PROOFS—Trial printings of a stamp either from the original die or finished plate. These are in various colors and on various papers. Although generally made before a stamp is issued, proofs of some of the earlier varieties were made subsequently for various reasons.

PROPRIETARY STAMPS—Revenue stamps to pay taxes on medicine, matches, photographs, playing cards, and other proprietary articles.

PROVISIONALS—Stamps prepared locally for use during shortages of regular issues.

QUADRILLE PAPER—A paper with a watermark design of crossed lines at right angles to each other.

RAILWAY MAIL—Mail showing various railway cancellations indicating that the mail was posted in the train mail box or handed to the railway mail clerk. These vary from the common modern *RMS* to older and rarer cancellations which included the name of the railroad.

RECONSTRUCTED PLATE—See *Plating*, pages 166–169.

RECUTTING—The re-engraving of various lines on a plate which have become worn through use. The recut lines are usually readily distinguishable after the plate has again gone to press. It is sometimes necessary to recut lines by hand which have been defectively transferred on new plates. Such retouching makes a stamp differ slightly from adjoining specimens. Recuts and retouches are varieties much sought for by advanced collectors.

RE-ENGRAVED—Stamps from any plates made from a second die differing slightly from the original, an expedient often to strengthen a design or correct a slight defect in the original engraved or transferred design.

RE-ENTRY—See *Double Transfer.*

REGISTRATION STAMPS—Special stamps for prepaying extra fees on registered letters.

REGUMMED—A stamp on which gum has been added to simulate the original gum and thus fraudulently add to the value of the stamp, since unused stamps having original gum are more desired by collectors.

REISSUE—An official reprinting of a stamp after it has once been discontinued. See *Reprint.*

REMAINDERS—Stocks of stamps on hand after the issue has been discontinued. In some foreign countries these are demonetized and sold much below face value, thus accounting for many of the oldest stamps which are commoner unused than used.

REPAIRED STAMP—One that has been mended by having tears closed, thin spots strengthened, margins added, etc., in an attempt to make valuable something which otherwise was practically worthless.

REPERFORATED—Stamps which originally had one or more natural straight edges to which perforations have been privately applied. Attempts are also made to change the gauge from a common to a rare variety. Reperforated stamps are considered fakes.

REPRINTS—Stamps reissued officially are sometimes called reprints and as such are valuable, but when reprinted in quantity by private parties who have somehow secured the old plates they are considered little better than counterfeits.

REVALUED—See *Surcharge*.

REVENUE STAMPS—Stamps issued for use in collecting special taxes on documents, proprietary articles, etc. Stamps for taxes on tobacco, beer, etc., are called Tax Paid. These last are collected only by specialists.

RIBBED PAPER—Paper with fine parallel ridges on one side only.

ROTARY PRINT—Stamps printed on the rotary press. See *Flat Plate*.

ROULETTE—A type of perforation consisting of short knife cuts.

SAFETY PAPER—A tinted paper specially made to prevent cleaning. Used principally for bank checks but occasionally for stamps.

SAMPLE—A term sometimes applied to a trial printing. See *Proofs, specimen*.

SANS-SERIF—Block or Gothic letters of the alphabet.

SAW-TOOTH—A type of roulette giving the perforation a saw-tooth appearance.

SECRET MARKS—Small marks placed on the original dies for identification purposes.

SEMI-POSTALS—Stamps issued for the dual purpose of paying postage and raising revenue for some outside activity not always confined to charity, which see.

SERIFS—The thin projecting ornaments on letters of the Roman alphabet.

SERPENTINE ROULETTE—A roulette of wavy lines.

SERRATE ROULETTE—One made by cuts producing notched teeth similar to saw teeth but with blunted points.

SE-TENANT—Refers to stamps of different values or stamps with or without overprint joined together in a pair.

SHIFT—See *Double Transfer*.

SILK PAPER—Paper with silk threads similar to United States note paper. It differs from granite paper in that the threads are larger and not so thoroughly mixed with the pulp.

SILK THREAD—Paper with continuous silk threads running through the sheet in parallel lines, one or more appearing on each stamp.

SILURIAN PAPER—The same as granite paper.

SKINNED—A stamp that has had part of the paper stripped away making it thin and therefore defective.

SLEEPER—A rare stamp accidentally or ignorantly priced as a commoner variety.

SLOGANS—Advertisements or propaganda included in postmarks, such as, "Air Mail Saves Time," etc.

SOFT WOVE PAPER—See *Wove Paper*. See also pages 151–155.

SOLDIERS MAIL—Mail of soldiers marked for free carriage in wartime.

SOUVENIR SHEETS—Sheets of a small number of stamps in the same or different designs generally with marginal inscriptions relative to national anniversaries, philatelic exhibitions, etc. The stamps may or may not have been issued regularly in full sheets for ordinary postal use.

SPACE FILLER—A defective copy of a rare stamp used temporarily to fill an album space until a perfect specimen can be secured.

[313]

SPANDREL—The decorative design between the border and circular or oval center of a stamp.

SPECIAL DELIVERY STAMPS—A stamp of special design indicating an extra fee charged for immediate delivery on arrival at the addressee's nearest post office. Also called Express Stamps.

SPECIAL HANDLING STAMPS—Stamps issued by the United States to be used in addition to parcel postage to secure delivery of the parcel with first-class mail.

SPECIALIZED COLLECTION—A collection confined to a single stamp or small group, but including all possible varieties of printing and postal use.

SPECIAL PRINT—Stamps of current designs or re-issues printed usually on a better grade of paper and in brilliant colors. They are available for postage but seldom do postal duty. During the Centennial in Philadelphia in 1876 the government made special printings of all current and earlier issues, which were sold to the public at the exhibition grounds post office. The Farley stamps of 1935 are a recent example.

SPECIMEN—(1) An individual stamp. (2) A stamp overprinted "Specimen" to be distributed through the Universal Postal Union as samples. This device is now seldom used. (3) An overprint found on the special prints of United States Department stamps sold to the public at the Philadelphia Centennial in 1876.

SPECULATIVE ISSUES—Stamps not necessary for postal needs and often issued for the purpose of raising revenue from sales to collectors. There are various grades, from the Central American Seebecks to, technically speaking, our current commemoratives. A hard and fast line cannot be drawn.

SPLIT GRILL—A stamp showing parts of two grills.

STAMPLESS COVERS—Envelopes or folded letters without stamps which bear evidence of having passed through the mail. These are of two kinds, those used in the days before stamps and those used afterward, but before the prepayment of postage by stamps was required. Modern government-franked envelopes are classed by themselves and are not considered stampless covers.

STAR PLATES—In 1908 and again in 1925 the Bureau of Engraving and Printing experimented with the spacing between stamps to make the perforations more uniform. To distinguish them from the ordinary, stars were added to the imprint in the margins of the experimental plates.

STITCH WATERMARK—An accidental watermark made in the paper during the manufacturing process. It consists of a series of short parallel lines crossing the stamp from top to bottom or from side to side, thus:)))).

STRAIGHT EDGE—The plain edge of a stamp which is otherwise perforated. Although scarcer than fully perforated specimens, collectors prefer the latter; consequently, straight-edged stamps have to be sold at a discount.

STRIP—Three or more unsevered stamps in a vertical or horizontal row.

SULPHURETTED—See *Oxidized*.

SUPPLEMENTARY MAIL—Mail dispatched to a carrier such as a steamship after the regular mail has closed and for which an extra fee is charged. Mail so handled bears postmarks or additional stamps attesting to that fact.

SURCHARGE—(1) An overprint changing the value of a stamp, sometimes erroneously understood to be any overprint, which see. (2) Another term for postage due on stamps of Grenada.

SURFACE COLORED—A tinted paper with color only on the face.

SURFACE PRINTED—Same as off-set printing, which see.

TAILLE-DOUCE—French for Line Engraving.

TEETH—The projections between perforation holes.

TELEGRAPH STAMPS—Stamps issued to prepay or frank telegraph tolls. They are not postage stamps.

TÊTE-BECHE—A French term denoting a pair of stamps, one upside down in relation to the other.

THINNED—See Skinned.

TIED ON—A stamp on a cover or part of a cover on which a postmark properly ties the stamp to the cover, thus insuring that the combination passed through the mail and that the stamp was not added afterward. For instance, a 10-cent stamp of 1861 off cover is worth possibly 50 cents, but properly tied on a Pony Express cover is worth several hundred dollars.

TINTED PAPER—Paper colored at time of manufacture.

TOO-LATE STAMP—A special stamp issued in Victoria to show the extra fee paid to insure forwarding after the regular mails had closed. See Supplementary Mail.

TRANSFER ROLL—In engraved plate manufacture, the roller used to transfer the design from the original die to the finished plate.

TRIAL PRINTINGS—Experimental printing similar to proofs, which see.

TRIPLE TRANSFER—See Double Transfer.

TYPESET—Stamps printed from movable type designs made up in a printer's shop usually to fill an emergency. Also applies to overprints.

TYPOGRAPHED—Stamps printed by a process similar to the offset method.

UNPAID—A letter for which postal charges have not been prepaid by the sender.

UNPERFORATED—Same as Imperforate.

UNUSED—A stamp with or without original gum which has not done postal duty. See Cleaned Stamps.

USED—Ordinarily a stamp which has done postal duty as evidenced by the cancellation. See Canceled-to-Order.

VERTICAL HALF—Description of a bisect, which see.

VALE—An overprint on Spanish-American stamps indicating change in value.

WAR TAX STAMPS—Stamps issued in wartime to collect a tax on letters. While in themselves not good for postage, they were required to be used with postage stamps.

WATERMARK—A design worked into the paper by thinning at the time of manufacture. These designs are in the form of letters, numerals, crowns, and other patterns and can be seen by holding the stamp before a bright light or by placing it face down on a black surface and moistening it with benzine. For this purpose many collectors use a shallow black glass dish with an air-tight cover to prevent evaporation while the dish is not in use. The benzine should be of the best quality, free from other oils which might stain the stamps. Pure benzine will not injure the stamps * or dissolve the gum. Since benzine is highly inflammable, it should be kept away from fire. Other liquids have been tried from time to time for detecting watermarks, and are reasonably satisfactory.

WOVE PAPER—Paper of plain, even texture. Soft wove paper usually has the appearance of a fine mesh when held to a bright light.

ZEPPELIN STAMPS—Stamps issued for use on mail carried by the German dirigible Graf Zeppelin.

* This is true only for the older varieties. Some of the brilliant colors on late European issues printed by the photogravure process are soluble in benzine.

Philatelic Abbreviations

A—On various South American or Spanish stamps. *ANOTACION*. To designate registration service.

A.A.M.S.—American Air Mail Society (A national organization for collectors of air-mail stamps. Headquarters at Albion, Pa.

A D—On playing card stamps of the United States. Abbreviation for Andrew Doherty, the card manufacturer.

A.E.F.—On the Postage Due stamps of France. *Afrique Equatoriale Francaise.* For use in Chad, under which colony the stamps are listed.

Afft.—On the stamps of Syria. *Affranchisement.* "Good for Postage."

A.M.—On the stamps of Greece. *Axia Metaliki* (value in coin).

A.M.S.—Air Mail Service.

AMvJ—On the stamps of Dutch Indies. *Amsterdamische My voor Jongemannen.* To designate semi-postals issued for young men's societies.

ANZAC—On the stamps of New Zealand, Australia, or as a cancellation on Egyptian issues. Australia-New Zealand Army Corps.

A.O.—On stamps of Congo. Allemand Occupation (German Occupation). Listed under German East Africa.

A.P.S.—American Philatelic Society. One of the large national stamp clubs with headquarters at State College, Pa.,

A.R.—On various South American stamps. *Aviso (de) Recepcion.* To designate acknowledgment of receipt which is almost like our own "return receipt requested" service.

A.S.—On the stamps of Sudan. Army Service.

A.S.D.A.—American Stamp Dealers' Association, a national organization for dealers with headquarters in New York.

A.S.I.B.—On stamps of the Dutch Indies. *Allgemeen Steunfonds (voor) Inheenische Behoftegen.* To designate semi-postal issues of 1937.

A & T—On the stamps of French Colonies, Annam and Tonkin, under which country they are listed.

A.Z.—On the stamps of Albania. Ahmed Zogu, the first president, who later became king under the name Zog I.

B—On the stamps of Nicaragua. Bluefields, a town on the seacoast and in the province of Zelaya, under which such stamps are listed.

B—On the stamps of Straits Settlements. Bangkok, under which country they are listed.

Baj.—On stamps of Roman States. *Bajocchi,* a unit of currency.

B.C.—On the stamps of Charkhari. Bundelkhand Central, to designate one of the Native Feudatory States of Central India.

B.C.A.—On the stamps of Rhodesia. For use in British Central Africa, under which country they are listed.

B.C.M.—On the stamps of Madagascar. British Consular Mail.

B.G.—On stamps of Modena. Bollo Gazette, to designate newspaper stamps.

B.I.T.—On the stamps of Belgium and Czechoslovakia. *Bureau International (du) Travail.* International Labor Bureau.

B.L.C.I.—On the stamps of Bhopal. Bhopal Central India.

B.L.P.—On the stamps of Italy. *Bute Lettere Postali*, to designate stamps sold at a discount to the national federation for the assistance of war invalids.

B.N.F.—On the stamps of Castellorizo. *Base Navale Francaise.*

Brapex—On the stamps of Brazil. Brazil Philatelic Exhibition.

C—On the stamps of Nicaragua. *Cabo (Gracias a Dios)*, under which country they are listed.

C—On the stamps of Paraguay. Campana (country). To validate stamps on hand at post offices thereby rendering useless for postage a quantity of stolen ones.

C.A.—Central America.

CA—As a watermark on the stamps of various British Colonies. Crown Agent.

C.A.M.—As a cancellation or cachet on United States stamps and covers. Contract Air Mail (route).

C.C.—Collectors Club, the foremost American philatelists' organization, with its clubhouse at 22 East Thirty-fifth Street, N.Y.

CC—As a watermark on various British Colonial stamps. Crown Colony.

C. Ch—On stamps of French Colonies. Cochin China, under which country they are listed.

C.C.C.P.—On Russian stamps. Union of Soviet Socialist Republics.

C.E.F.—On the stamps of India. Chinese Expeditionary Forces.

C.E.F.—On stamps of Cameroons. *Corps Expeditionaire Francais.*

C G H S—On stamps of Upper Silesia. *Commission (du) Gouvernement Haute Silesie.*

C I H S—On the stamps of Upper Silesia. *Commission Interalliee Haute Silesie.*

C.M.T.—On various issues. *Compana*

Militare Timbru, to designate stamps for military service.

C.P.—On the stamps of Belgium. *Colis Postaux*, to designate stamps for parcel-post service.

C.R.—On stamps of Fiji. Cakambau Rex, King Cakambau.

C.S.—On various United States issues.

C.X.C.—On stamps of Bosnia. See *S.H.S.*

Cytra—On stamps of Argentine Republic. *Corres y Telegraphos. Republica Argentina*, on stamps and souvenir sheets issued in honor of the Buenos Aires Philatelic Exhibition in 1939.

D—On stamps of Dutch Indies. *Dienst*, to designate stamps for official service.

D.F.U.—On stamps of Denmark. *Dansk Filatelisten Udistilling.* Danish Philatelic Exhibition.

D.M.—On stamps of Danzig. *Dienst Marke* (Official Stamp).

Dpto.—On the stamps of Nicaragua. *Departmento* (Official).

D.Y.—On stamps of Turkey. *Devlet Demi Yollari*, to designate "Railway of the State" stamps.

E—On stamps of Bavaria. *Eisenbahn* (Railroad)

E.C. de M.—On stamps of Mexico. *Ejercito Constitucionalista de Mexico* (Constitutional army of Mexico).

EΔ—On stamps of Greece. *Elleniki Dioikesis* (Greek Administration).

E.E.F.—On stamps of Palestine. Egyptian Expeditionary Forces.

E.F.—On stamps of Bolivia. *Estado Federal.*

E.F.O.—On stamps of French Oceanica. *Etablissments Français (deL') Oceanie.*

E.R.I.—On various British Colonial issues. Edward, Rex (et) Imperator (Edward, King and Emperor).

E.S.—On various South American issues. *Estado Soberano* (Sovereign Government).

ET.—On stamps of Greece. *Ellenikon Takudromeion* (Greek Postal Service).

EU do—On various South-American issues. *Estados Unidos do* . . . (United States of . . .).

F A M—As a cancellation or cachet on stamps or covers of the United States. Foreign Air Mail.

F.I.S.—On stamps of Austria. Federation International Ski.

F.M.—On French issues. *Franchise Militaire,* to designate military postal service.

F.R.—On German stamps, *Fredericus Rex* (King Frederick Wilhelm IV) of Prussia.

G—On stamps of the Cape of Good Hope. Griqualand, under which country they are listed.

Gab.—On stamps of French Colonies. Gabon, under which country they are listed.

G.C.M.—In the form of a monogram on the stamps of Mexico. *Gobierno Constitucionalista Mexicano* (Constitutional Government).

G & D—On stamps of Guadeloupe. *Guadeloupe et Dependences.*

GD—On stamps of Luxemburg. Grand Duchy.

G.E.A.—On stamps of East Africa and Uganda. To designate use in German East Africa, under which country they are listed.

GFB—On various. *Gane Faka Buleaga* (On government service).

Gl. O.Z.—On stamps of Haiti. General Oreste Zamor.

Gobno—On various Spanish issues. *Gobierno* (Official).

G. P. de M.—On stamps of Mexico. Gobierno Provisorio de Mexico (Provisional Government of Mexico).

Gpe.—On stamps of French Colonies. Guadeloupe, under which country they are listed.

G.R.I.—On various British Colonials. George Rex (et) Imperator. George, King and Emperor.

Gt. Pre.—On stamps of Haiti. *Government Provisoire* (Provisional government).

H.P.—On stamps of Russia. *Hagagan Post* (Armenian post), under which country they are listed.

Hrv.—On stamps of Bosnia and Herzegovina. Hrvatska (Croatia). Listed under Jugoslavia.

I.A.A.—On various European issues. *Internationales Arbeits Amst* (International Labor Bureau).

I.E.F.—On stamps of India. Indian Expeditionary Forces.

Imperf.—Imperforate. See "Philatelic Definitions."

I.R.—On stamps of United States. Internal Revenue.

I.R.—On stamps of Great Britain. Inland Revenue.

IPOSTA—As a watermark on the stamps of Germany. *Internationale Postwertzeichen Ausstellung* (International Philatelic Exhibition).

J.H.S.—On stamps of Italy. *Jesus Hominum Salvator* (Jesus Savior of Mankind).

J.P.S.—Junior Philatelic Society, one of the world's greatest organizations, founded in London in 1899 by Fred. J. Melville. Has headquarters in London, England.

K.K.K.—On the Aguinaldo stamps of the Philippine Islands. *Kataas-tassan, Kagalang-galang Katipunan* (Most High and most revered society of the sons of the country).

K.G.C.A.—On stamps of Jugoslavia. *Karuska Glasoona Cona A* (Carinthian Governmental Commission for Zone A). Listed under *Carinthia.*

K. Π.—On stamps of Greece. *Koinoniki Pronia* (Money of the realm).

K.P.K.—On stamps of Denmark. *Kopenhaganer Philatelisten Klubs.*

Kr.—On stamps of Austria. *Kreutzer* (A unit of currency).

K u K—On stamps of Austria or Bosnia. *Kaiserliche und Konigliche* (Royal and Imperial).

L.E.—On stamps of Egypt. *Livre Egyptienne* (Egyptian pound, to distinguish it from the English pound which is worth four piastres less).

L.F.F.—On stamps of Liberia. Liberian Frontier Forces.

L.H.P.A.—On German States issues. Lübeck-Hamburg Post. Amt.

L.K.I.S.—On the stamps of Latvia. *Latwijas Kars Invalidu Savienib* (Latvian Society of War Invalids).

L.O.F.—On the stamps of the Philippine Islands. London-Orient Flight.

M.A.—On the stamps of Argentine. *Ministerio Agricultura* (Department of Agriculture).

M.C.—On stamps of Corrientes. *Moneda Corrientes.*

M.G.—On stamps of Argentine. *Min. Guerra* (Department of War).

M.H.—On stamps of Argentine. *Min. Hacienda* (Treasury Department).

M.I.—On stamps of Argentine. *Min. Interior.*

M.J.I.—On stamps of Argentine. *Min. Justicia-Instruccion* (Department of Justice and Education).

M.M.—On stamps of Argentine. *Min. Marina* (Navy Department).

M.O.P.—On stamps of Argentine. *Min. Orbas Publicas* (Department of Public Works).

MQE.—On stamps of French Colonies. Martinique, under which country they are listed.

M.R.C.—On stamps of Argentine. *Min. Relaciones Exteriores y Cultos* (Department of Foreign Affairs).

M. vi R.—On stamps of Rumania. Military Administration of Rumania.

M.V.S.N.—On various issues. *Militia Voluntaria (par la) Sicurezza Nationale* (Volunteer Militia for National Defense).

NABA—On stamps of Switzerland. *Nationale Briefmarken Ausstellung* (National Stamp Exhibition).

NCE—On stamps of French Colonies. New Caledonia, under which country they are listed.

N.F.—On stamps of Nyassaland. Nyassaland Forces, listed under German East Africa.

NRA—On stamps of the United States. National Recovery Act.

N.S.B.—On stamps of French Colonies. Nossi Be, under which country they are listed.

N.S.W.—New South Wales.

N.W.P.I.—On Australian stamps. North West Pacific Islands, under which country they are listed.

N.Z.—New Zealand.

Ob. Ost.—On stamps of Germany. *Ober Ostgebiet* (Northeastern district). Listed under Lithuania.

O.B.—On stamps of the Philippine Islands. Official Business.

O.F.—On stamps of France. *Occupation Francais.* Listed under Castellorizo.

O.H.E.M.S.—On stamps of Egypt. On His Egyptian Majesty's Service.

O.H.H.S.—On stamps of Egypt. On His Highness's Service.

O.M.F.—On stamps of France. *Occupation Militaire Francaise.* Listed under Cilicia or Syria.

O.N.F.—On stamps of French Levant. *Occupation Navale Francaise.* Listed under Castellorizo.

On C.G.S.—On stamps of Cochin. Cochin Government Service.

On H.M.S.—On stamps of India. His Majesty's Service.

On K.D.S.—On stamps of Kisengarh. Kisengarh Durbar Service.

On L.F.S.—On various British stamps. Local Funds Service.

On S.S.—On stamps of Travancore. State Service.

On S.S.S.—On stamps of Sirmoor. Sirmoor State Service.

O.S.—On various issues. Official Service.

O.S.G.S.—On stamps of Sudan. On Sudan Government Service.

Ostropa—On stamps of Germany, in the form of a watermark. *Osteuropaische Postwertzeichen Ausstellung* (International Philatelic Exhibition of Eastern Europe).

O.W.—On stamps of Great Britain. Office Works.

P.A.A.—On various South-American stamps and also in some foreign postmarks. Pan American Airways.

PD—On stamps of St. Pierre and Miquelon: Paid. When used as a postal marking: Paid to Destination.

P.E.—On stamps of Egypt. *Poste Egiziane* to 1879. *Postes Egyptienne*, after that. Also, Piastre Egiziane and Piastre Egyptienne, a unit of currency.

Perf.—Perforated. See "Philatelic Definitions."

Pexip—On stamps of France. Paris— *Exhibition International Philatelique.*

P.G.S.—On stamps of Straits Settlements. Perak Government Service, under which country they are listed.

PI–US—On stamps of the Philippine Islands. Philippine Islands—United States, to designate stamps for Clipper air-mail service.

P.L.—On stamps of Persia. *Poste Locale.*

P.M.—On stamps of United States. Postmaster.

Pmk.—Postmark.

P.P.—On various issues. Post Payee or Post Paid.

P.S.—In the form of a monogram on stamps of Cauca are the initials of the postal administrator.

P.T.—On stamps of Egypt. *Piastre Tariff.*

P.T.T.—On many foreign issues. Posts, Telephone, and Telegraph.

R—On various South-American issues.

Recomendada to designate registry stamps.

R de C—On stamps of Nicaragua. *Recargo de Construccion* (Building Tax).

R.B.D.—On stamps of Denmark. *Rigsbank Daler* (A unit of currency).

R.F.—On various French issues. *Republique Francaise.*

R.H.—On stamps of Great Britain. Royal Household.

Rl. Pta.—On stamps of Cuba. *Real Plata.* Silver Money.

R.O.—On stamps of Turkey. *Roumelia Oriental* (Eastern Roumelia, under which country they are listed).

S—On stamps of Straits Settlements. Selangor, under which country they are listed.

S.A.—South Australia.

SCADTA—On Semi-officials of Colombian Republic. *Sociedad Colombo Alemana de Transportes Aéreos* (Colombo-German Company for aerial transportation).

S de N—On stamps of Switzerland. *Societe de Nations* (League of Nations).

S.F.—On stamps of Denmark. *Soldater Frimaerke* (Military stamps).

S.H.S.—On stamps of Bosnia. *Srbija Hrvatska Slovenija* (Serbia, Croatia and Slovenia, for use in Jugoslavia).

Sld.—On stamps of Austrian Levant. Soldi, a unit of currency.

S.O.—On stamps of Czechoslovakia. *Silesia Orientale* (Eastern Silesia, under which country they are listed).

S.P.—On stamps of Luxemburg. *Service Publique* (Official Service).

SPM—On stamps of French colonies. St. Pierre and Miquelon, under which country they are listed.

S.U.—On stamps of Straits Settlements. Sungei Ujong, under which country they are listed.

S.W.A.—On stamps of the Union of South Africa. South West Africa, under which country they are listed.

T.—On various issues. Taxe, designating stamp postage due.

T.E.O.—On stamps of France or Turkey. *Territoire Ennemis Occupes* (Occupation of enemy territory). Listed under Cilicia or Syria.

T.L.—On stamps of Tonga. Tonga-Lavinca. The name of the king and queen.

T.M.—On various issues. *Timbre Ministerial* (Official stamps).

U.P.U.—On various stamps. Universal Postal Union.

U.S.P.S.—United States Postal Service.

V.R. or V.R.I.—Various British Colonials. Victoria, Regina (et) Imperatrix (Victoria, queen and empress).

W. or Wmk.—Watermark.

W.I.P.A.—On Austrian issues. *Wien-Internationale Postwertzeichen Ausstellung* (Vienna-International Philatelic Exhibition).

Z.—On stamps of Bolivia. Zeppelin, to designate use on mail carried by the Zeppelin.

Z.A.—On stamps of Armenia. *Zapadnya Armia* (Western army).

Z.A.R.—On stamps of South Africa. Zuid Afrikaan Republic.

A "bi-lingual" issued for South West Africa, where both English and Afrikaans are official languages, and therefore used for inscriptions on all stamps.

Philatelic Nicknames

ARABESQUE ISSUE—A name applied to the first set of Egyptian stamps, issued in January, 1866, because the entire design is made up of only Mohammedan arabesques.

BASEL DOVE—A stamp issued by the Canton of Switzerland in 1845, so called because its central vignette depicts a dove with a letter in its beak.

BLACK HONDURAS—A stamp of Honduras, provisionally overprinted *Aero Correo* in 1925, and one of the rarest of all air-mail stamps.

BLACK JACK—A 2-cent stamp issued by the United States in 1862, which has a large portrait of Andrew Jackson as a central vignette printed in black ink.

BLUE PAPERS—A term used to describe stamps of the United States 1908 regular issue and Lincoln commemorative printed on an experimental paper containing a large percentage of rag, giving it a dark color which, however, is gray rather than blue.

BOMBA HEADS—The 1859 set of Sicily, which portrays King Ferdinand II. So that his face would not be marred by postmarks, he had special cancelers made which would obliterate the frame of these stamps but would leave the vignette untouched.

BRINKERHOFF—One of a series of United States stamps sold by the government in imperforate condition to the Brinkerhoff Vending Machine Company, which added private perforations to fit its machines.

BROKEN CIRCLE—A name given to the 6-kreutzer stamps of Bavaria's 1849 series in which the inner circle of the design is interrupted by the lateral panels. It also applies to the one-half-cent United States Bicentennial set of 1932, in which the circle inclosing the figure of value is broken due to a plate flaw.

BROKEN HAT—A minor variety of the 2-cent stamps of the United States Columbian issue of 1893, in which the hat of Christopher Columbus has a gash, caused by a plate defect.

BULL'S EYE—The first stamps of Brazil (1843), which comprise only a large oval of lathe work and a figure of value, so arranged that they look like large eyes.

BUREAU ISSUES—All United States stamps made by the Bureau of Engraving and Printing in Washington since 1894, when private engravers were no longer given the contracts for this work. The Overrun Nations stamps of 1943-1944 are the only exception.

CANTONALS—Between 1843 and 1850 the various cantons of Switzerland produced their own stamps, which are now known by this name.

CIPEX—A term used to refer to the Centenary International Philatelic Exhibition, held in Grand Central Palace, New York, from May 17 to 25, 1947.

CIRCULARS—The first issues of British Guiana, crudely designed and printed in Georgetown, B. G. in 1850 and 1851. The vignette comprises only a rough circle enclosing the words *British Guiana* and the figure of value. They are extremely rare.

COAMO—The name given to a scarce provisional stamp issued at Coamo, Puerto Rico, in 1898.

CONTINENTALS—Stamps of the United States, produced by the Continental Banknote Company and issued in 1873. These are similar to the designs of the National Bank Note Company, except that a "secret mark" has been added to each value.

CORONATIONS—Various stamps issued by the different colonies and dominions of the British Empire in honor of the coronation of King George and Queen Elizabeth in 1937.

CUBIERTAS—The large stamps issued by the Colombian Republic as Insured Letter Receipts.

DILIGENCIAS—The stamps issued in Uruguay in 1856 whose design includes only a brilliant sun, the word "Diligencia," and the figure of value. The diligencia was a stage coach by means of which mail was carried in Uruguay.

DOM PEDROS—The early stamps of Brazil, issued in 1866, and portraying Emperor Dom Pedro II.

DOUBE GENEVA—The first stamp of Geneva, Switzerland, issued in 1843 and comprising two sections, each of which had a franking value of 5 centimes when severed and 10 centimes when in one piece.

ELECTRIC EYES—To insure more perfect centering of United States stamps, the Bureau of Engraving and Printing experimented with a photoelectric mechanism that would guide rotary press stamps through the perforating machines. These stamps have slugs or dashes of color in the marginal selvage, which is the only means of distinguishing them from the regularly perforated types.

EMBOSSED ISSUE—A series of stamps issued by Great Britain in 1847 in which the portrait of Queen Victoria was embossed instead of printed.

EPAULETTES—The stamps of the first issue of Belgium, in which King Leopold I is portrayed in a military uniform with the shoulder ornaments visible in the design.

EYE OF THE OX ISSUE—See *Bull's Eye*.

FARLEY ISSUES—The special printings issued in 1935 to stop the uproar of collectors caused by Postmaster General James A. Farley's presenting imperforate sheets of new issues to government officials and others.

FARWELLS—Another type of private perforations applied to United States stamps by the Farwell Vending Machine Company to imperforate sheets supplied them by the Post Office Department.

FIVE-CENT ERROR—A United States stamp of 1917 with a 5-cent design, but printed in red, the color of the 2-cent stamp, by mistake.

FLAGS—A set of thirteen stamps issued by the United States in 1943 and 1944, to pay tribute to those nations overrun by the Axis powers. They are so named because the flag of each honored nation appears as the central design. These were printed in the actual colors of the flags, by the American Bank Note Company, and are the only stamps of our country to have been produced outside of the Bureau of Engraving and Printing since 1894.

FOOCHOW PROVISIONAL—The special overprint applied to half of a 2-cent stamp of China on October 22, 1903. Though this is not a very valuable item, it has been counterfeited so widely that collectors are admonished to buy copies from only reputable dealers.

FULL-LENGTH VICTORIAS—The second issue of Victoria in which the queen is pictured on her throne.

HOWE ISLAND PROVISIONAL— When the stock of twopence stamps on Lord Howe Island became exhausted in 1930, the local postmaster took a few of the Sturt Commemoratives (of Australia and wrote "2d Paid P.M.L.H.I." in black ink. These are extremely rare and valuable despite the fact that the American catalogue does not list them.

ILE DE FRANCE PROVISIONALS
—In order to frank mail carried on an experimental ship-to-shore flight from the French liner *Ile de France* in 1928, the ship's purser surcharged several sheets of the 90-cent and 1 Fr. 50 Pasteur stamps with a new value of 10 Fr.

IMPRIMATURS—Each time a new stamp is issued in England the first sheet from the plate is filed at the Somerset House for reference. Stamps are sometimes cut from these sheets, which get into the hands of collectors who prize them highly. They are, in a manner of speaking, first plate proofs.

JUBILEES—Various stamps issued by some British colonies and dominions in honor of the diamond Jubilee of Queen Victoria, celebrated in 1897 (see also *Silver Jubilee*).

KANGAROOS—The first issue of stamps for the Australian Commonwealth, upon which the picture of a kangaroo is montaged on a map of the continent.

LARGE CENTS ISSUE—Canadian stamps of the 1868 series which are similar to the following set except in size.

LAUREATED NAPOLEONS—The French stamps of 1868-1870, which depict Louis Napoleon with a laurel wreath after he became emperor of France.

LAUREATED VICTORIAS—The second issue of New South Wales upon which the queen is portrayed with a laurel wreath.

LINE-ENGRAVED ISSUE—A series of stamps issued in England between 1840 and 1857 as distinguished from subsequent issues that were surface printed.

MAFEKINGS—Stamps issued in the Cape of Good Hope in 1900, during the Boer War when Mafeking was beseiged, and on account of which General Baden-Powell fell into disfavor with Queen Victoria.

MAIL-O-METERS—Another type of privately perforated stamps of the

United States which were used by the Mail-o-Meter vending machines.

MERRY WIDOWS—A nickname given to the special delivery stamp of the United States issued in 1908, which depicts the helmet of Mercury.

NATIONALS—The stamps of the United States printed by the National Bank Note Company and issued in 1870 and 1871.

NESBITTS—A type of embossed envelope stamp made by the Nesbitt Company and issued in the United States between 1853 and 1870.

OFFSETS—A series of stamps printed by the Bureau of Engraving and Printing and issued during 1918 and 1920. They may be distinguished from regular stamps in that they are less clear, since they were made from rubber "offset rollers" and not directly from engraved plates.

OMAHAS—Another name given to the Trans-Mississippi series of 1898, because they were issued in Omaha, Neb.

OVERRUN NATIONS SET—See Flags.

PEACE AND COMMERCE TYPES
—Stamps of France and French Colonies, issued between 1876 and 1892, upon which the allegorical figures of Peace and Commerce are depicted in the central vignette.

PEACE ISSUE—Another name for the Victories, which see.

PLIMPTONS—Envelope stamps embossed and printed by the Plimpton Company and issued by the United States in 1874.

PONCE ISSUE—A provisional stamp printed and issued in Ponce, a town of Puerto Rico, in 1898 under American dominion.

PORT FOUADS—A provisional issue of Egypt sold in conjunction with the dedication of Port Fouad, a modern city built opposite Port Said. On account of the limited number of copies available, the rush for them on December 21, 1926, was so great that several people were killed and many more were injured.

PORT HOOD PROVISIONAL—When he ran out of stamps of the 2-cent denominations, the postmaster at Port Hood, Canada, took a few sheets of the 3-cent stamps, portraying Queen Victoria, and overprinted them with either a 1 or 2, then cut them into thirds and sold them to the natives of the town in January and July of 1899.

POSTMASTER PROVISIONAL—Before the United States Post Office Department had federal stamps, the postmasters of several towns produced their own stamps and authorized their use on local mail. Copies exist for such towns as: Alexandria, Va., Annapolis, Md., Baltimore, Md., Boscawen, N. H., Brattleboro, Vt., Lockport, N. Y., Millbury, Mass., New Haven, Conn., New York, N. Y., Providence, R. I., St. Louis, Mo., and Tuscumbia, Ala., They are the rarest of U. S. stamps.

PUERTO PRINCIPES—A series of stamps provisionally issued in Cuba during the United States administration in 1898. They are the old Spanish designs overprinted with the word *Habilitado* and a new figure of value expressed in "cents" instead of "millesimas."

QUEEN'S HEADS—A popular designation for stamps picturing Queen Victoria.

REAYS—The envelope stamps embossed and printed by the Reay Company and issued by the United States Post Office between 1870 and 1873.

RED HONDURAS—A 5-centavo blue stamp of Honduras on which *AERO CORREO* was overprinted in red ink in 1925 when air-mail service was established in Central America. Only nine copies are known to exist, though a tenth has been reported. It is one of the rarest of air-mail stamps.

RIVIDAVIAS—The first portrait stamps of the Argentine Republic, issued in 1864 and portraying Bernardino Rividavia.

ROOSEVELTS—A series of stamps or sets of stamps issued by many foreign countries to "memorialize" the life and works of Franklin D. Roosevelt, after his death in 1945. Many of these were especially produced at the behest of unscrupulous operators who hoped to control the supply for subsequent sale to collectors at huge profits because of the enthusiastic interest in stamps associated with our late president.

SCHERMACKS—A type of privately perforated U. S. stamps for use in the Schermack Vending and affixing machines. These are listed in the Specialized U. S. Stamp Catalogue.

SEEBECKS—Between 1891 and 1898 N. F. Seebeck of the Hamilton Bank Note Company of New York secured contracts from Ecuador, Honduras, Nicaragua, and Salvador to furnish each a new issue of stamps each year. These stamps were furnished free of charge with the understanding that Seebeck would get all remainders and would be permitted to reprint obsolete issues. Reprints of some issues were made on heavy, coarse paper. Originals are known canceled to order and with fake cancellations on cover. Unfortunately, these stamps reacted unfavorably on all Central American issues at the time.

SILVER JUBILEES—A series of stamps issued by the colonies and dominions of the British Empire in commemoration of the twenty-fifth anniversary of the reign of King George V and Queen Mary in 1935.

SLANTING NUMERALS—The second issue of Brazil, issued in 1844 and similar in design to the Bull's Eyes, except that they are smaller and the numerals of value are slanting instead of upright.

SMALL CENTS ISSUES—Canadian stamps of 1870-1872, which are identical in design to the previous set (1868) in everything except size.

SMALL NUMERALS—Stamps of Brazil's 1850 issue which are quite similar to the previous set except that the numerals are placed upright.

SOUTH GEORGIA PROVISIONAL—A twopence stamp of the Falkland Islands surcharged 2½ for use in South Georgia in 1928 when the existing stock of this denomination was exhausted. They are very rare.

SOWER TYPE—A series of French stamps depicting "Liberty" sowing the seeds of Freedom, Equality, and Fraternity.

SYDNEY VIEWS—The first stamps of New South Wales, upon which were depicted scenes of Sydney, the first city of Australia.

TIN HATS—The Belgian stamps of 1919-1920, on which King Albert is portrayed in a trench helmet, familiarly called a Tin Hat.

TIPEX—Familiarly used by collectors for Third International Philatelic Exhibition (held in Grand Central Palace, New York, in 1936).

TREATY PORT ISSUES—Stamps locally issued by various ports in China opened to foreign trade by international treaties. These interesting adhesives are favorites with collectors but are not listed in the American catalogue.

VICTORIES—A set of stamps issued for each British possession early in 1947 to mark the end of World War II.

WOODBLOCKS—A set of Cape of Good Hope triangles which were locally produced in 1861. They are so called because the electros from which they were printed were mounted on small wooden blocks to bring them up to the proper printing height.

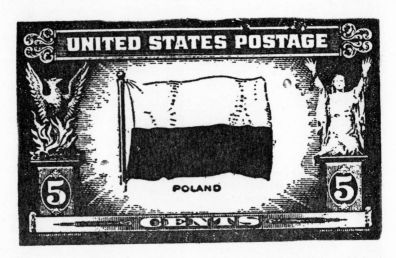

Because the stamps issued in honor of the Overrun Nations which the Allies were striving to liberate, depict their national banners, they are familiarly known as the "Flags."

Stamp Identification Tables

Stamps of some countries are without the country name or show names other than the countries to which they are assigned in the standard catalogues and albums. Words on the stamps by which such may be identified are printed first in the following list, followed by the country name.

A—Printed Inscriptions or Denomination Units

ANTANANARIVO—Madagascar.

ARABIE—Nejd.

AVIAPORTO—Denmark.

BASEL—Switzerland.

BENADIR—Italian Somaliland.

BRITISH NEW GUINEA—Papua.

BRITISH SOUTH AFRICA COM-PANY—Rhodesia.

CATALUNA—Spain (Carlist).

CHIFFRE TAXE—France (postage due).

COLOMBIA—(Isthmus map—Panama).

COLONIES POSTES—French Colonies.

CORDOBA—Argentina.

CORREIO—Portugal and Colonies, Brazil.

CORREOS—Spain and Colonies.

CORRIENTES—Argentina.

DEUTSCHES REICH—Germany.

DIENSTMARKE—Germany (officials).

DILIGENCIA—Uruguay.

DIOS PATRIA LIBERTAD—Dominican Republic.

DJIBOUTI—Somali Coast.

DRZVA—S.H.S.—Yugoslavia.

EIRE—Ireland.

EMP. OTTOMAN—Turkey.

ESCUELAS—Venezuela.

ETHIOPIE—Abyssinia.

FEN—Manchukuo.

FRANCO BOLLO—Italy and colonies, Roman States, Sardinia, Two Sicilies.

FREI DURCH ABLOSUNG—Prussia (official).

FREIMARKE—Prussia.

FRIMAERKE—Denmark and Norway.

FRM—Denmark.

GENEVE—Switzerland.

GRANA—Two Sicilies.

GRAND LIBAN—Lebanon.

HELVETIA—Switzerland.

HOLSTEIN—Schleswig-Holstein.

H.R.Z.C.L.—Schleswig-Holstein.

IMPUESTO DE GUERRA—Spain (war tax).

INKERI—North Ingermanland.

INSTRUCCION—Venezuela.

KARAJALA—Karelia.

KORCA—Albania.

KPHTH—Crete.

KRALJEVSTVO—Jugoslavia.

[327]

KREUZER, KR.—Austria, Hungary.
K. WURTT POST—Wurtemburg.
LAND POST—Baden.
LATVIJA, LATWIJA—Latvia.
LIETUVA—Lithuania.
LITWA (SRODKOWA)—Central Lithuania.
LOSEN—Sweden (postage due).
MAGYAR—Hungary.
NORD DEUTSCHER—Germany.
OSTERR(EICH)—Austria.
OFFENTLIG SAK—Norway (official).
O.K.C.A.—Russia.
ORTS POST—Switzerland.
PACCHI POSTALI—Italy.
P.C.C.P.—Russia.
PERCEVOIR—France and Colonies (postage due).
POLSKA—Poland.
PORT CANTONAL—Switzerland.
PORTE DE CONDUCCION—Peru (parcel post).
PORTE ESTENSI—Modena.
PORTE FRANCO—Peru.
PORTO GAZETEI—Rumania.
POST ZEGEL—Netherlands.
POSTAGE OR POSTAGE AND REVENUE—Great Britain and Colonies.
POSTA NAPOLETANA—Two Sicilies.
POSTE LOCALE—Switzerland.
P.S.N.C. (in corners)—Peru.
RAPPEN—Switzerland.

RAROTONGA—Cook Islands.
RAYON—Switzerland.
REPUBLICA ORIENTAL—Uruguay.
RUANDA URUNDI—Belgian East Africa.
SAUDI ARABIE—Nejd.
SEGNATASSE—Italy and Colonies (postage due).
S.H.—Schleswig-Holstein.
SHQIPENIA, SHQIPTARE—Albania.
SICILIA—Two Sicilies.
SIG. NOV. CAMB. AUST.—New South Wales.
SOLDI—Austria.
STATI PARM (ENSI)—Parma.
SUOMI—Finland.
SVERIGE—Sweden.
TCHAD—Chad.
TE BETALEN PORT—Netherlands and Colonies.
THURN AND TAXIS—Germany.
TJENESTE—Denmark, Norway.
TOGA—Tonga.
U.G. (typewritten)—Uganda.
ULTRAMAR—Spain and Colonies.
VANCOUVER ISLAND—British Columbia.
VAN DIEMAN'S LAND—Tasmania.
VOM EMPFANGER—Danzig (postage due).
Z. AFR. REPUBLIEK—Transvaal.
ZURICH—Switzerland.

B—Overprints

AUNUS (on Finland)—Russia (occupation).
BAGHDAD (on Turkey)—Mesopotamia.
BENGASI (on Italy)—Tripoli.
BRITISH SOUTH AFRICA COMPANY—(on Cape of Good Hope)—Rhodesia.

CORONA (on Italy—Dalmatia.
D.J. or DJIBOUTI (on Obock)—Somali Coast.
DRAVA (on Bosnia)—Yugoslavia.
EST AFRICAINE ALLEMAND (on Congo)—Belgian East Africa.
EUPEN (on Belgium)—Germany (occupation).

[328]

RIALCAR (on Great Britain)—Ireland.

R.O. or ROUMELIE ORIENTALE (on Turkey)—Eastern Roumelia.

RUANDA (on Congo)—Belgian East Africa.

SAORSTAT (on Great Britain)—Ireland.

IRAQ (on Turkey)—Mesopotamia.

KARNTEN (on Austria)—Carinthia.

KRALJEVSTVO (on Bosnia)—Yugoslavia.

LIBAU (on Germany)—Latvia (occupation).

LIETUVA (on Russia)—Lithuania.

LITWA (on Lithuania)—Central Lithuania.

OIL RIVERS (on Great Britain)—Niger Coast.

RARATONGA (on New Zealand)—Cook Islands.

VENEZIA GIULIA (on Italy)—Austria.

Y. Kp. H. P. (on Austria)—Western Ukrania.

C—Countries Some of Whose Stamps Are Inscribed in the Cyrillic (Russian) Alphabet

Azerbaijan — Batum — Bulgaria — Far Eastern Republic — Finland — Jugoslavia — Montenegro — Poland — Rumania — Russia — Serbia — Siberia — South Russia — Transcaucasian Federated Republic — Ukrania — Western Ukrania — White Russia.

D—Countries Some or All of Whose Stamps Are Inscribed in Native Script

Abyssinia — Afghanistan — Arabia (Hejaz) — Armenia — Cilicia — Eastern Roumelia — Egypt — Georgia — Hejaz (Arabia) — India, Native States — Japan — Mongolia — Nejd (Saudi Arabia) — Nepal — Persia — Siam — South Bulgaria — Syria — Tannou Touva — Thrace — Transjordania — Turkey — Turkey in Asia — Yemen.

Eire, which is listed as the Irish Free State in philatelic catalogues, is one of many countries which uses a non-Latin alphabet for its stamp inscriptions.

Technical Terms and Translations in Foreign Languages

Collectors will find these useful terms in corresponding with persons abroad.

English	German	French	Italian
average condition	Verschiedene erhaltung	condition moyenne	stato diverso
average copy	durchschnitts-druck	pièce moyen	esemplare mediocre
bisected	halbiert	coupé en deux	tagliato in due
block	block	bloc	blocco, ceppo
cancellation	abstemplung	obliterátion	obliterazione
cancelled	entwertet	obliteré	usato, obliterato
chalk paper	kreidenpapier	papier couché	carta incredata
collection	Sammlung	collection	collezione, raccolta
condition	erhaltung	condition	stato di conservazione
copy	stuck, exemplar	piéce	pezzo, esemplare
crease	bruch, spur	pli, trace de pli	rottura
defect	mangel	defaut	difetto
defective	fehlerhaft	defecteux	difettoso
double impression	doppeldruck	double impression	impressione doppia
corner of sheet	bogenecke	coin de feuille	angolo di foglio
error	fehldruck	erreur	error di stampa
error, plate	plattenfehler	erreur de gravure	errore di stampa
expertized	geprüft	expertisé	esaminato
face value	nennwert	valeur facial	valore faciale
fine	fein	fin	fino, squisito
full margins	vollrandig	merge de tous cotes	margine pieno
gum	gummi	gomme	gomma
hinge	falz	charnière	cerniera
imperforate	ungezahnt	non dentelé	non dentallato
insignificant	belanglos	insignifiant	insignificante
inverted	kopfstehend	renversé	inversem caovolto
large	breit, gross	large, grand	largo
letter, cover	brief	lettre, couvert-	lettera

English	German	French	Italian
margin	rand	bord, marge	margine
margin, sheet	bogenrand	bord de feuille	margine di foglio
mint	postfrisch	neuf	stato reginale
off-center	decentriert	mal centré	mal centrato
on piece of cover	briefstück	fragment	su pezzo de lettera
overprint	aufdruck	surcharge	sovrastampa
pair	paar	paire	pajo
pen cancelled	federzug, tin-	obliteré a la plume	obliterato con
	tenwertung		tratto di penna
perforated	gezahnt	dentelé	dentellato
perforation	Zahnung	dentelature	dentellatura
perforation,	Zahnungfehler	dentelure de-	dentellature diffet-
damaged		fecteuse	tosa
pinhole	nadelstich	trou d'epingle	puntura di ago
postage due	porto	taxe	segnatassa
repaired	repariert	réparé	reiparto
reprint	neudruck	reimpression	reimpressione
rouletted	durchstochen	percé	traforato a linee
scarce	selten	rare	raro
short, cut close	knapp	court	stretto
spot, stain	flecken	tache	macchia
set	satz	serie	seria
strip	streifen	band	striscia
superb copy	prachtsstück	pièce hors ligne	pezzo superbo
tear	riss	fente	crepatura
thin	dünn	mince	sottile
touched	angeschnitten	touché, coupé	intaccato
unused	ungebraucht	neuf	nuovo, non usato
used	gebraucht	usé	usato
variety	abart	variété	varieta
very fine copy	luxusstück	pièce de luxe	pezzo di lusso
very small margin	lupenrand	marge tres ètroite	margine scarso
watermark	wasserzeichen	filigrane	filigrane
without gum	ohne gummi	sans gomme	senz gomma

Stamp-Issuing Governments

A—by Dates of First Stamps

1840 Great Britain.
1842 New York (the City Despatch Post stamp).
1843 Brazil, Geneva and Zurich.
1845 Basel.
1847 Mauritius, United States.
1848 Bermuda.
1849 Bavaria, Belgium, France.
1850 Austria, British Guiana, Hanover, New South Wales, Prussia, Schleswig-Holstein, Spain, Switzerland, Victoria.
1851 Baden, Canada, Denmark, Hawaii, New Brunswick, Nova Scotia, Sardinia, Saxony, Trinidad, Tuscany, Württemberg.
1852 Barbados, Brunswick, Luxembourg, Modena, Netherlands, Oldenburg, Parma, Réunion, Roman States, Scinde, Thurn and Taxis.
1853 Cape of Good Hope, Chile, Portugal, Tasmania (Van Diemen's Land).
1854 India, Norway, Philippines, Western Australia.
1855 Bremen, Cuba, Danish West Indies, New Zealand, South Australia, Sweden.
1856 Corrientes, Finland, Mecklenburg-Schwerin, Mexico, St. Helena, Uruguay.
1857 Ceylon, Natal, Newfoundland, Peru, Russia.
1858 Argentina, Buenos Aires, Romania, Two Sicilies.
1859 Bahamas, Colombia, Cordova, French Colonies (general issue), Hamburg, Ionian Islands, Lübeck, Romagna, Venezuela.
1860 Jamaica, Liberia, Malta, Poland, Queensland, St. Lucia, Sierra Leone.
1861 Bergedorf, British Columbia–Vancouver, Greece, Grenada, Nevis, Prince Edward Island, St. Vincent.
1862 Antigua, Costa Rica, Hong Kong, Italy, Nicaragua, Wenden.
1863 Bolívar, Turkey.
1864 Dutch East Indies, Mecklenburg-Strelitz, Soruth.
1865 British Honduras, Dominican Republic, Ecuador, Honduras, Shanghai.
1866 Bolivia, Egypt, Jammu-Kashmir, Hyderabad, Serbia, Virgin Islands.
1867 Heligoland, Salvador, Straits Settlements, Turks Islands.
1868 Antioquia, Azores, Madeira, North German Confederation, Orange River Colony.
1869 Gambia, St. Thomas and Prince, Sarawak, Transvaal.
1870 Angola, Cundinamarca, Fiji, Paraguay, Persia (Iran), St. Christopher, Tolima.
1871 Afghanistan, Guatemala, Hungary, Japan, Portuguese India.
1872 Germany.
1873 Curaçao, Iceland, Puerto Rico, Surinam, Turkey.
1874 Dominica, Griqualand West, Lagos, Montenegro.
1875 Gold Coast, Jhind (state).

1876 Johore, Montserrat, Poonch.
1877 Alwar, Bhopal, Cape Verde, Mozambique, Nowanuggur, Samoa, San Marino.
1878 China, Falkland Islands, Panama, Perak, Selangor, Sungei Ujong.
1879 Bhor, Bosnia, Bulgaria, Cauca, Faridkot, Fernando Po, Labuan, Sirmoor, Tobago.
1880 Cyprus, Rajpeepla, South Bulgaria.
1881 Arequipa, Ayacucho, Cuzco, Eastern Rumelia, Guinea, Haiti, Moquegua, Nepal, New Caledonia.
1882 Bangkok, Puno, Tahiti.
1883 North Borneo, Siam (Thailand).
1884 Ancachs, Chachapoyas, Chala, Guadeloupe, Huacho, Macao, Madagascar, Paita, Pasco, Patiala, Pisco, Piura, Santander, Stellaland, Yca.
1885 Apurimac, Guanacaste, Gwalior, Jhind (province), Korea, Monaco, Nabha, St. Pierre and Miquelon, Timor.
1886 Bechuanaland, Chamba, Cochin China, Congo, French Guiana, Gabon, Gibraltar, Indore, Martinique, New Republic, Tonga.
1887 Jhalawar, Senegal.
1888 Annam and Tonkin, Bechuanaland Protectorate, Travancore, Tunisia, Wadhwan, Zululand.
1889 Indochina, Nossi-Bé, Swaziland.
1890 Bamra, British East Africa, Diégo-Suarez, Leeward Islands, Pahang, Rhodesia, Seychelles.
1891 British Central Africa, French Congo, Morocco, Nanogaon, Negri Sembilan.
1892 Angra, Anjouan, Benin, Cochin, Cook Islands, Eritrea, French Guinea, French India, French Oceania, Funchal, Horta, Ivory Coast, Mayotte, Mozambique Company, Niger Coast, Obock, Ponta Delgada.
1893 Duttia, German East Africa.
1894 Abyssinia, Bundi, Charkhari, French Sudan, Lourenço Marques, Portuguese Congo, Ste. Marie de Madagascar, Somali Coast, Zambesia.
1895 Bussahir, Inhambane, Uganda, Zanzibar.
1896 —
1897 Cameroons, Dhar, German New Guinea, German South West Africa, Grande Comorre, Las Bela, Marshalls, Nyassa, Sudan, Togo.
1898 Crete, Marianas, Portuguese Africa.
1899 Cuban Republic, Dahomey, German Morocco, Guam, Kishengarh, Philippines (U.S. Administration), Puerto Rico (U.S. Administration).
1900 Carolines, Cayman Islands, Kiaochow, Mafeking, Federated Malay States, Northern Nigeria, Turks and Caicos Islands.
1901 Magdalena, Papua, Southern Nigeria.
1902 Boyaca, Niue, Penrhyn, Somaliland Protectorate, Spanish Guinea.
1903 Aitutaki, East Africa–Uganda, Elobey, Annabon, and Corisco, Italian Somaliland, St. Kitts–Nevis, Senegambia.
1904 Cabo, Canal Zone, Jaipur, Zelaya.
1905 Rio de Oro.
1906 Brunei, Maldives, Mauritania, Mohéli, Upper Senegal–Niger.
1907 British Solomon Islands, Middle Congo.
1908 New Hebrides, Nyasaland Protectorate.
1910 Trengganu, Union of South Africa.
1911 Gilbert and Ellice Islands, Kelantan.
1912 Kedah, Lybia, Liechtenstein, Samos.
1913 Albania, Australia, Quelimane, Tete, Thrace, Tibet.

1914 Epirus, French Morocco, New Britain, Nigeria, Orchha, Togo.
1915 Bushire, British Cameroons, North West Pacific Islands, Ubangi.
1916 Cape Juby, German East Africa, Hejaz, Ile Rouad, Kionga, Nauru.
1918 Czechoslovakia, Estonia, Fiume, Latvia, Lithuania, Mesopotamia, Palestine, South Russia, Ukraine, Western Ukraine, Yugoslavia.
1919 Azerbaijan, Batum, Cilicia, Georgia, Siberia, Syria.
1920 Allenstein, Armenia, Carinthia, Castellorizo, Central Lithuania, Danzig, Eastern Silesia, Far Eastern Republic, La Agüera, Marienwerder, Memel, North Ingermanland, Saar, Schleswig, Transjordan, Turkey-in-Asia, Upper Silesia, Upper Volta, Wallis and Futuna Islands.
1921 Barwani, Dalmatia, Kenya and Uganda, Tanganyika.
1922 Ascension, Barbuda, Bel. East Africa, British East Africa, Chad (Tchad), Ireland, Karelia.
1923 Corfu, Cyrenaica, Iraq, Kuwait, Southwest Africa, Transcaucasian Republic, Tripolitania.
1924 Algeria, Mongolia, New Guinea, Southern Rhodesia, Spanish West Sahara.
1925 Alaouites, New Guinea, Northern Rhodesia, Oltre Giuba, Saudi Arabia.
1926 Tannu Tuva, Yemen.
1927 Lebanon.
1928 Andorra, South Georgia.
1929 Vatican City State.
1931 Latakia, Morvi.
1932 Inini, Iraq, Manchukuo.
1933 Bahrain, Basutoland.
1935 Bijawar.
1936 French Equatorial Africa.
1937 Aden, Burma.
1938 Alexandretta, Greenland, Italian East Africa.
1939 Bohemia-Moravia, Carpo-Ukraine, Hatay, Slovakia.
1940 Pitcairn Island.
1941 Croatia, Idar, Ifni.
1942 Jasdan.
1943 French West Africa, Inner Mongolia.
1944 Campione d'Italia Grahamland, Muscat, South Orkneys, South Shetlands.
1946 Philippine Republic.
1947 Norfolk Island, Pakistan, Trieste.
1948 Bahawalpur, Israel, Penang, Perlis, Ryukyu Islands, Singapore, Tokelau.
1949 Dutch Antilles, Jordan, Malacca, Rajasthan, Spanish West Africa.
1950 Dutch New Guinea, Indonesia, Somalia.
1951 Laos, United Nations, Vietnam.
1952 Cambodia, Tristan da Cunha.
1955 Cocos (Keeling) Islands.

B—The Independent Americas

Ancachs	1884	Bolivia	1866
Antioquia	1868	Boyacá	1902
Apurímac	1885	Brazil	1843
Arequipa	1881	Buenos Aires	1858
Argentina	1858	Cabo Gracias a Dios	1904
Ayacucho	1881	Canal Zone	1904
Bolívar	1863	Cauca	1879

Chachapoyas	1884	New York	1842
Chala	1884	Nicaragua	1862
Chile	1853	Paita	1884
Colombia	1859	Panama	1878
Cordoba	1859	Paraguay	1870
Corrientes	1856	Pasco	1884
Costa Rica	1862	Peru	1857
Cuban Republic	1855	Pisco	1884
Cundinamarca	1870	Piura	1884
Cuzco	1881	Puno	1882
Dominican Rep.	1865	Salvador	1867
Ecuador	1865	Santandar	1884
Guanacaste	1885	Tolima	1870
Guatemala	1871	United Nations	1951
Haiti	1881	United States	1847
Honduras	1865	Uruguay	1856
Huacho	1884	Venezuela	1859
Magdalena	1901	Yca	1884
Mexico	1856	Zelaya	1904
Moquegua	1881		

C—Africa

Bel. East Africa	1922	Liberia	1860
Congo	1886	Somalia	1950
Egypt	1866	(See also under various empires)	
Ethiopia	1894		

D—Asia-Pacific

Afghanistan	1871	Laos	1951
Armenia	1920	Lebanon	1927
Azerbaijan	1919	Manchukuo	1932
Batum	1919	Mongolia	1924
Bushire	1915	Persia (Iran)	1870
China	1878	Philippine Republic	1946
Far Eastern Republic	1920	Ryukyu Islands	1948
Guam	1899	Samoa	1877
Hatay	1939	Saudi Arabia	1925
Hawaii	1851	Shanghai	1865
Hejaz	1916	Siam (Thailand)	1883
Indonesia	1950	Siberia	1919
Inner Mongolia	1943	Syria	1919
Israel	1948	Tannu Tuva	1926
Iraq	1923	Tibet	1913
Japan	1871	Transcaucasian Republic	1923
Jordan	1949	Turkey-in-Asia	1920
Korea	1885	Yemen	1926

E—Europe

Albania	1913	Bavaria	1849
Allenstein	1920	Belgium	1849
Andorra	1928	Bohemia-Moravia	1939
Austria	1850	Bosnia	1879
Basel	1845	Bulgaria	1879

Campione d'Italia	1944	Luxembourg	1852
Carinthia	1920	Marienwerder	1920
Carpo-Ukraine	1939	Memel	1920
Central Lithuania	1920	Monaco	1885
Corfu	1923	Montenegro	1874
Crete	1898	North Ingermanland	1920
Croatia	1941	Norway	1854
Czechoslovakia	1918	Poland	1860
Dalmatia	1921	Prussia	1850
Danzig	1920	Romania	1858
Denmark	1851	Russia	1857
Eastern Rumelia	1881	Saar	1920
East Silesia	1920	Samos	1912
Epirus	1914	San Marino	1877
Estonia	1918	Serbia	1866
Finland	1856	Slovakia	1939
Fiume	1918	South Bulgaria	1880
France	1849	South Russia	1918
Geneva	1843	Spain	1850
Georgia	1919	Switzerland	1843
Great Britain	1840	Thrace	1913
Greece	1861	Trieste	1947
Greenland	1938	Turkey	1873
Hungary	1871	Ukraine	1918
Iceland	1873	Upper Silesia	1920
Ireland	1922	Vatican City State	1929
Karelia	1922	Western Ukraine	1918
Latvia	1918	Yugoslavia	1918
Liechtenstein	1912	Zurich	1843
Lithuania	1918		

F—British Commonwealth of Nations

Aden	1937	Brit. Solomon Islands	1907
Aitutaki	1903	Brunei	1906
Antigua	1862	Burma	1937
Ascension	1922	Cameroons	1915
Australia	1913	Canada	1851
Bahamas	1859	Cape of Good Hope	1853
Bahawalpur	1948	Cayman Islands	1900
Bahrain	1933	Ceylon	1857
Bangkok	1882	Cocos (Keeling) Islands	1955
Barbados	1852	Cook Islands	1892
Barbuda	1922	Crete	1898
Basutoland	1933	Cyprus	1880
Batum	1919	Dominica	1874
Bechuanaland	1886	East Africa–Uganda	1903
Bechuanaland Protect.	1888	Falkland Islands	1878
Bermuda	1848	Fiji	1870
Brit. Central Africa	1891	Gambia	1869
Brit. Columbia–Vancouver	1861	Gibraltar	1886
Brit. East Africa	1890	Gilbert and Ellice Islands	1911
Brit. Guiana	1850	Gold Coast	1875
Brit. Honduras	1865	Graham Land	1944

Great Britain	1840	Leeward Islands	1890
Grenada	1861	Madagascar	1884
Griqualand West	1874	Maldives	1906
Heligoland	1867	Malta	1860
Hong Kong	1862	Mauritius	1847
India	1854	Mesopotamia	1918
Alwar	1877	Montserrat	1876
Bamra	1890	Muscat	1944
Barwani	1921	Natal	1857
Bhopal	1877	Nauru	1916
Bhor	1879	Nepal	1881
Bijawar	1935	Nevis	1861
Bundi	1894	New Britain	1914
Bussahir	1895	New Brunswick	1851
Chamba	1886	Newfoundland	1857
Charkhari	1894	New Guinea	1925
Cochin	1892	New Hebrides	1908
Dhar	1897	New Republic	1886
Duttia	1893	New South Wales	1850
Faridkot	1879	New Zealand	1855
Gwalior	1885	Niger Coast	1892
Hyderabad	1866	Nigeria	1914
Idar	1941	Niue	1902
Indore	1886	Norfolk Island	1947
Jaipur	1904	North Borneo	1883
Jammu-Kashmir	1866	Northern Nigeria	1900
Jasdan	1942	Northern Rhodesia	1925
Jhalawar	1887	North West Pacific Islands	1915
Jhind	1875	Nova Scotia	1851
Kishengarh	1899	Nyasaland Protectorate	1908
Las Bela	1897	Orange River Colony	1868
Morvi	1931	Pakistan	1947
Nabha	1885	Palestine	1918
Nandgaon	1891	Papua	1901
Nowanuggur	1877	Penrhyn	1902
Orchha	1914	Pitcairn Island	1940
Patiala	1884	Prince Edward Island	1861
Poonch	1876	Queensland	1860
Rajasthan	1949	Rhodesia	1890
Rajpeepla	1880	St. Christopher	1870
Scinde	1852	St. Helena	1856
Sirmoor	1879	St. Kitts–Nevis	1903
Soruth	1864	St. Lucia	1860
Travancore	1888	St. Vincent	1861
Wadhwan	1888	Samoa	1877
Ionian Islands	1859	Sarawak	1869
Iraq	1923	Seychelles	1890
Ireland	1922	Sierra Leone	1860
Jamaica	1860	Somaliland Protectorate	1902
Kenya and Uganda	1921	South Australia	1855
Kuwait	1923	South Georgia	1928
Labuan	1879	South Orkneys	1944
Lagos	1874	South Shetlands	1944

Southern Nigeria	1901
Southern Rhodesia	1924
Southwest Africa	1923
Stellaland	1884
Straits Settlements	1867
Federated Malay States	1900
Johore	1876
Kedah	1912
Kelantan	1911
Malacca	1949
Negri Sembilan	1891
Pahang	1890
Penang	1948
Perak	1878
Perlis	1948
Selangor	1878
Singapore	1948
Sungei Ujong	1878
Trengganu	1910
Sudan	1897
Swaziland	1889

Tanganyika	1921
Tasmania (Van Diemen's Land)	1853
Tobago	1879
Togo	1914
Tokelau	1948
Tonga	1886
Transjordan	1920
Transvaal	1869
Trinidad	1851
Tristan da Cunha	1952
Turks Islands	1867
Turks and Caicos Islands	1900
Uganda	1895
Union of South Africa	1910
Victoria	1850
Virgin Islands	1866
Western Australia	1854
Zanzibar	1895
Zululand	1888

G—French Empire and Union

Alaouites	1925
Alexandretta	1938
Algeria	1924
Anjouan	1892
Annam and Tonkin	1888
Benin	1892
Cambodia	1952
Cameroons	1915
Chad (Tchad)	1922
Cilicia	1919
Cochin China	1886
Dahomey	1899
Diégo-Suarez	1890
France	1849
Fr. Colonies (general issue)	1859
Fr. Congo	1891
Fr. Equatorial Africa	1936
Fr. Guiana	1886
Fr. Guinea	1892
Fr. India	1892
Fr. Morocco	1914
Fr. Oceania	1892
Fr. Sudan	1894
Fr. West Africa	1943
Gabon	1886
Grande Comorre	1897
Guadeloupe	1884
Ile Rouad	1916
Indochina	1889

Inini	1932
Ivory Coast	1892
Latakia	1931
Madagascar	1889
Martinique	1886
Mauritania	1906
Mayotte	1892
Middle Congo	1907
Mohéli	1906
Morocco	1891
New Caledonia	1881
New Hebrides	1908
Nossi-Bé	1889
Obock	1892
Réunion	1852
Ste. Marie de Madagascar	1894
St. Pierre and Miquelon	1885
Senegal	1887
Senegambia	1903
Somali Coast	1894
Tahiti	1882
Togo	1914
Tunisia	1888
Ubangi	1915
Upper Senegal-Niger	1906
Upper Volta	1920
Vietnam	1951
Wallis and Futuna	1920

H—German Empire

Baden	1851	Marianas	1900
Bavaria	1849	Marshalls	1897
Bergedorf	1861	Mecklenburg-Schwerin	1856
Bremen	1855	Mecklenburg-Strelitz	1864
Brunswick	1852	Memel	1920
Cameroons	1897	Morocco (German)	1899
Carolines	1900	North German Confederation	1868
Germ. East Africa	1893	Oldenburg	1852
Germ. New Guinea	1897	Prussia	1850
Germ. S.W. Africa	1897	Saxony	1851
Germany	1872	Schleswig	1920
Hamburg	1859	Schleswig-Holstein	1850
Hanover	1850	Thurn and Taxis	1852
Kiaochow	1900	Württemberg	1851
Lübeck	1859		

I—Italy, Italian States and Colonies

Castellorizo	1920	Oltre Guiba	1925
Cyrenaica	1923	Parma	1852
Eritrea	1892	Romagna	1859
It. East Africa	1938	Roman States	1852
It. Somaliland	1903	Sardinia	1851
Italy	1862	Tripolitania	1923
Lybia	1912	Tuscany	1851
Modena	1852	Two Sicilies	1858

J—Dutch Empire

Curaçao	1873	Dutch New Guinea	1950
Dutch Antilles	1949	Netherlands	1852
Dutch East Indies	1864	Surinam	1873

K—Portuguese Empire

Angola	1870	Mozambique Company	1892
Angra	1892	Nyassa	1897
Azores	1868	Ponta Delgada	1892
Cape Verde	1877	Portugal	1853
Funchal	1892	Portuguese Africa	1898
Guinea	1881	Portuguese Congo	1894
Horta	1892	Portuguese India	1871
Inhambane	1895	Quelimane	1913
Kionga	1916	St. Thomas and Prince	1869
Lourenço Marques	1894	Tete	1913
Macao	1884	Timor	1885
Madeira	1868	Zambesia	1894
Mozambique	1877		

L—Spanish Empire

Cape Juby	1916	Elobey, Annonbón, and	
Cuba	1855	Corisco	1903

Fernando Po	1879	Rio de Oro	1905
Ifni	1941	Spain	1850
La Agüera	1920	Spanish Guinea	1902
Marianas	1898	Spanish West Africa	1949
Philippines	1854	Spanish West Sahara	1924
Puerto Rico	1873		

Bibliography

SCOTT PUBLICATIONS, INC., New York.
  Standard Postage Stamp Catalogue. Published annually.
  United States Stamp Catalogue. Published annually.
  Standard Catalogue of Airpost Stamps. Published annually.
AMERICAN AIR MAIL SOCIETY, Albion, Pa.
  American Air Mail Catalogue. Published every five years.
SANABRIA, INC., Nicolas, New York.
  Sanabria's Airpost Catalogue. Published annually.
STANLEY-GIBBONS, INC., New York.
  Price List of United States Stamps. Published every few months. Free.
HARRIS COMPANY, H. E., Boston, Mass.
  United States Stamp Price List. Published twice a year. Free.
  British Colonial Price List. Published twice a year. Free.
  Air Mail Stamp Price List. Published three times a year. Free.
BILLIG, FRITZ, Jamaica, N.Y.
  Billig's Philatelic Handbooks.
DORCHESTER, BARCLAY.
  They Dreamed and They Dared. The Steck Company, Austin, Texas.
GREGORY, JOHN.
  Heroes on Your Stamps. Alfred A. Knopf, New York.
FLOHERTY, JOHN J.
  Make Way for the Mail. J. B. Lippincott Company, Philadelphia.
HAHN, MANNEL.
  So You're Collecting Stamps. Dodd Mead and Company, New York.
HARLOW, ALVIN.
  Old Postbags, also *Old Waybills.* Appleton-Century Company, New York.
  Paper Chase. Henry Holt and Company, New York.
HALLGREN, MAURITZ.
  All About Stamps. Alfred A. Knopf, New York.
HUNTER, DARD.
  Paper Making. Alfred A. Knopf, New York.
HEINMULLER, JOHN V. P.
  Man's Fight to Fly. Funk and Wagnalls Company, New York.
KIMBLE, RALPH A.
  Commemorative Postage Stamps of the United States. Grossett and Dunlap, New York.
LOWE, ROBSON.
  Regent Empire Stamp Encyclopaedia. London, England.
LOSO, FOSTER W.
  Stamp Collectors' Round Table. Frederick A. Stokes Company, New York.
NICKLIN, JOHN
  Fabulous Stamps. Hastings House, New York.

PETERSHAM, MAUD AND MISKA.
America's Stamps. The Macmillan Company, New York.
SMITH, HENRY LADD.
Airways. Alfred A. Knopf, New York.
THORP, PRESCOTT HOLDEN.
Commemorative Stamps of the World. Scott Publications, New York.
UNITED STATES GOVERNMENT PRINTING OFFICE.
A Description of United States Postage Stamps.
WARREN, F. B.
Pageant of Civilization. D. Appleton-Century Company, Inc., New York.

Some of the unusual stamps of recent years. The diamond-shaped one
from Brazil honors an agrarian exposition. At left is one from the Gold
Coast issued for air-mail service. This depicts Christiansborg Castle at
Accra and cocoa pods. The one at right is from New Guinea and depicts
native huts in a palm grove.

Index

Bavaria, 7, 22, 46
Bear Stamps, 29
Bechuanaland, 81
Becton, W. D., 231
Belgian East Africa, 59, 66
Belgium, 22, 77, 79
Bell, James, 84
Berdanier, Paul, 262
Bergamo, 6
Berger-Levrault, George O. F., 40, 91
Bermuda, 22, 213, 254
Bern Conference of 1874, 34
Bernhard, Prince, vi, 107, 253
Better stamp design campaign, 89, 262
Bible, reference to posts mentioned in, 3
Billig and Rich, 283
Birchin Lane, 41
Bisects, *see* Splits
Bismarck, 8
Blood and Company, D. O., 27
Boccaccio, 71
Boer War, 77
Bogert and Durbin, 97
Boggs, Winthrop S., 229, 236
Bogus labels, 92
Bohnsack, Christie, 49
Bomba Heads, 148
Bond, Dr., 93
Boscawen Provisional, *29-31*
Boston, Mass., 23, 28, 29, 92
Boulac Printing Office, 175
Bounty, H.M.S., 66
Bow, Clara, 288
Boy Scouts of America, 78
Boyd's City Express, 27
Bradbury-Wilkinson, 82, 143, 183
Brattleboro Provisional, 29
Brazer, Clarence, 272
Brazil, 21, 26, 64, 155, 187, 216
Breitfuss, Frederic, 227
Bremen, 7
British Colonials, 101, 225, 278
British Guiana, 159, 227, 232; one-cent error, *121-126,* 129; two-cent rose, 134-135
British Museum, 230
British North America, 47
Brooklyn Stamp Club, 113-114
Brown, Arthur W., 140
Brown, Edith Adams, Mrs., 60
Brown, Mount, 91
Brown, William P., *92-95,* 134

Bruechig, Emil, 124
Brundige, J. Merritt, 100
Bruns, Franklin R., 48
Brunswick, 7
Brussels, 7
Bryan, Daniel, 29
Buccleuch, Duke of, 195-196
Buchanan, James M., 29
Bull's Eyes, 21
Bureau of Engraving and Printing, 32, 50, 52, 83, 89, 163, 170, 174, 176, 196, 256, 270, 271
Burger Brothers, 96
Burgundy, 7
Burrus, M., 123, 129, 130
Buser, Ed, Mr. and Mrs., 98, 285
Byrd, Richard E., Admiral, 114, 141. 248; stamp honoring, 263

Caesar Augustus, 4, 71
Calman, Henry, 97
Camel posts, 6
Cameroons, 65
Canada, 47, 85, 89, 153, 171, 187, 232, 236, 262
Canal Zone, 97
Cancellations, 266; made-to-order, 69; pigeongram, 139; removal of, 20; special, 148
Cancer Fund, 107
Cape of Good Hope, 91, 159, 175, 232, 234-235
Cape Verde, 174-175
Carinthia, 46
Carol, King, v, 107, 301
Carrier service, 20, 24
Caspary, Alfred, 102
Catalogues, 41, 43, 45, 65, 74, 117, 142, 200, 210-216
Cech, Monsignor Ferdinand, 58
Censorship, mails used for, 8-9, 11
Century of Progress, Chicago, 50
Ceylon, 65
Chaftar Bey, Ibrahim, 301
Chalmers, Patrick, 16
Chamberlain, Herbert, 83
Champion, Theodore, 135
Changelings, *177-178*
Charity stamps, *see* Semi-postals
Charlat, L. W., 264
Charlemagne, 4
Charleston, S.C., 29
Charnley and Whelan, 194

Magazines, stamp, 41, 76, 95, 185, 188, 193, *217-220*, 268, 283-284
Mahe, Pierre, 290
Mails, dependability of the, 3, 6, 34
Manley, John, 10
Manning, Catherine L., Mrs., 98, 282
Manufacture of stamps, 17-18, 25, 31-32, 44, 72, 74-75, 79, 82, 122, 127, 132, 134, 183, 228, 271-272
Map stamps, 59, 171-172, 263
Marian Year, 253
Marie, Queen, 112-113
Market values, 30, 45, 54, 93, 183, 198, 200, 216, 227
Marquis, Frank, 30-31
Marshall Field, 102
Martin, Alexander, 195-196
Martinelli, Giovanni, 281
Maryland issue, 50
Mason, Laurence B., 238
Masonic Home, 194
Masonic Order, 104, 253
Mauritius, 21, *127-131*, 230, 232, 243
McCormick, Cyrus Hall, 264
McEntee, Dorothy, Mrs., 283
McKenner, Neil, 122
M'Coy, W. R., Mr. and Mrs., *278-279*
Measor, Paul, 15
Mecklenburg-Schwerin, 7, 239
Meghrig and Sons, 100
Mekeel's Weekly Stamp News, 220, 283
Melchior, Lauritz, *254*
Melville, Fred, 289, 318
Merchant, Atlas Sky, 106-107
Mermoz, Jean, 141
Meters, postage, 61
Michel, Eugene, 74
Michel's Catalogue, 215
Microphotography, *144-145*
Millbury Postmaster's Stamp, 29
Minkus, Jacques, *101-102*, 274
Mirabaud, Paul, *225-226*
Mixed franking, 33
Mixtures, 114
Moens, Jean B., 39, *91*, 93, 129
Mohrmann, Edgar, 130
Montgolfier, Joseph M., 3
Moran, W. H., 267
Morgenthau, Henry, 265
Morgenthau, J. C., 130, 234, 296
Morris, Robert H., 21, 27
Mother's Day issue, 51
Mount St. Vincent School, 251

Mozambique, 65, *175*
Muestra, 36
Müller, Edwin, 98
Müller, Ernst, 215
Mulready, William, 19
Murray, Philip, *59*
Museum stamp collections, 131, 190, 230, 243, 290
Mythological stamps, 58

Naguib, Mohammed, vi
Nash, Walter, 259
Nassau Stamp Company, 48, 98, 234
Nassau Street, 30, 41, 47, 93, 96, 214, 249
Nasser, Gamal A., vi
National Bank Note Company, 32
National Broadcasting Company, 49, 288, 294
National Parks issue, 52, 53
National Philatelic Museum, 190
National War Fund, 78, 106
Needham, Henry C., 25-26, 238
Netherlands, 7, 9, 47, 77
Neuropes, 46
New Brunswick, 147, 237
New Guinea, 54, 66, 81
New Haven Postmaster's Stamp, 29
New South Wales, 22, 77, 239
New York Postmaster's Stamp, 21
New Zealand, 16, 54, 66, 85, 89, 145, 150, 165, 216
New Zealand Herald, 138
Newburgh peace issue, 50
Newfoundland, 54, 65, *139-140*, 180, 195, 232, 236
Newspaper stamp columns, 47, 61, 76, 246, 261, 285
Nicaragua, 79, 172
Nicholas, Czar, 301
Nicholas, Madame, 91
Niuafoo, 145-146
North, Roy Moses, 263
North Borneo, 67
North German Postal Confederation, 34
North Pole, v
N.R.A. issue, 50, 263

O'Connor, Basil, 106, 267
Oerne, Anders, Postmaster General, 260
Official stamps, 199
Offset printing, 32, 158, 177